# CATALOGUING
## THEORY AND PRACTICE

# CATALOGUING
## THEORY AND PRACTICE

*SIXTH EDITION*
Revised and Enlarged after the
Anglo-American Cataloguing Rules 2, 1988 revision

**C. G. VISWANATHAN** Hony. Fellow I.L.A.
*Formerly* Professor of Library and Information Science :
Lucknow University,
Banaras University
&
Andhra University

**1990**

**Ess Ess Publications**

New Delhi

Caduveti Gurusubrahmanya Viswanathan (1907)
ISBN 81-7000-110-2



| | |
|---|---|
| **First Edition** | **1954** |
| **Second Edition** | **1959** |
| **Third Edition** | **1965** |
| **Fourth Edition** | **1970** |
| **Fifth Edition** | **1983** |
| **Sixth Edition** | **1990** |
| **First Reprint** | **2002** |
| **Second Reprint** | **2007** |

Cataloguing In Production (C.I.P.) Data

025.32 Viswanathan, C.G.
Cataloguing theory and practice; 6th edition, New Delhi
Ess Ess Publications, 1990

xxvii, 450 p.illus., Pt., 23cm
1. Cataloguing. II. Title.

**ISBN 81-7000-110-2**

**Price:Rs. 1050/-**

Published by Sheel Sethi (Mrs.) For Ess Ess Publications,24, Ansari Road, Darya Ganj, New Delhi and printed at Printline, New Delhi-110 002

To my wife

**SAVITRI**

OTHER BOOKS OF THE AUTHOR

1. University Libraries of India.
2. Public Library Organization
3. High School Library
4. Public Library Operations and Services
5. Prouda Shala Grandhalaya (Kanarese)
6. सार्वजनिक पुस्तकालय संगठन की रूपरेखा
7. Elements of Information Science and Technology
8. A Book on Books

# PREFACE TO THE SIXTH EDITION

The necessity and validity of the sixth edition of this work arose as the previous fifth edition was declared out of print in 1985. But the demand for the book has not only been continuous but also compulsive, because most of the university centres providing courses in library and information science had adopted it as a textbook for study and teaching. Perhaps it is the one of its kind to have run into six editions during the last thirty years, and secured a permanent place among other such text books. The comments of the late Mr. Henry A. Sharp stimulated its value and usefulness.

Another significant reason is that there has been important developments in the area of cataloguing during this short interval. The COM catalogue exerted its thrust in library operations so forcefully, that it could not be overlooked. Gradually the traditional card catalogue, which was manually operated lost its ground to an appreciable extent in the advanced Western libraries. The MARC techniques, and the on line interactive services like the BLAISE proved valuable and quick in the retrieval and delivery of information to the users of libraries. Further, the AACR 2 1988 revision had also contributed towards this revision.

The work projects an analysis of the *pros* and *cons* of continuing the cataloguing procedures, and techniques evolved during the last eighty years, and of maintaining the card catalogue or to computerise the entire cataloguing system. The users' reaction to the automation of cataloguing activity, and the cost effectiveness for the administration has been studied.

Two new chapters, *Computerised Catalogue* (ch. 8) and *Headings for Name Entries* (ch. 27) according to AACR 2 1988 revision have been newly added. The data and procedures wherever warranted have been brought to date. A brief account of the British Library's *Cataloguing Conversion Project* of the British Museum's General Catalogue to Machine Readable Form presents an exciting experience. The Library of Congress MARC System has also been given due consideration. The working bibliography for cataloguers has been revised. The order of the chapters has been as in the previous edition, retained. Reference/citation from AACR 2 1988 revision has rendered the text more authoritative, and the author is grateful to the editors and the publishers of this valuable source of reference.

The author records with grateful pleasure of the help and cooperation rendered by the British Library's Bibliographic Services Division and the Library of Congress Cataloguing Management and Services Division in providing the reference sources of information. The humble expectation of the writer of the sixth edition of *CATALOGUING THEORY AND PRACTICE* is that the work would continue to command the same respect of his colleagues as has been given to his other works, and justify its value as an Unfailing Companion in all Cataloguing Assignments.

It would be a valuable assistance to the writer, if the users of the book communicate their suggestions for improving the presentation. Finally, the publisher Ess Ess Publications, has tried to produce the book in a short period, without compromising on the maintenance of standards. The author thanks him for his sincere cooperation.

C. G. Viswanathan

" SAVITRI "
C-2444, Indiranagar,
Lucknow.-226016. India
26th September, 1989

# PREFACE TO THE FIRST EDITION

"Librarianship is too old a craft for anything in it to be new." Therefore it will be too much to expect any newness in this work. There has still been an imperative need for such a work, from the viewpoint of the background and attainments of the students, pursuing a course of study in Cataloguing, as a vital part of the education for Librarianship, in India. Established text books, manuals and outlines of Cataloguing by H.A. Sharp, Margaret Mann, Susan Akers and others do exist. But they have not been easily available to the students in this country. Continued and repeated representation to provide them a simple guide to cataloguing theory and practice, from batch after batch of students of Library Science, whom I had the opportunity to teach Cataloguing, for the past fifteen years in the School of Librarianship, Andhra University, Waltair and the Banaras Hindu University Faculty of Library Science, stimulated the writing of this book.

There is a Persian saying that "Who so desireth a faultless friend, remains friendless", and "it is no less true that he who intends to write a faultless book, writes nothing". I am conscious of my limitations and the magnitude of the task of presenting a guide book to the student of Library Science, as well as to the working Cataloguer.

I have brought to bear on this study, the variety of my experience, as a Lecturer in Cataloguing and Bibliography for a considerable length of time. It envisages an analysis of the purpose, function, methods and processes of Cataloguing as practised in several leading libraries. The aim has mainly been to initiate the student of Library Science to the realms of Cataloguing and to place a simple concise and handy guide book to enable him to understand the principles of cataloguing and apply them with ease and discretion in constructing a sound catalogue. With this end in view, typical examples of books have been worked out, as far as possible using familiar titles.

Any sound catalogue is compiled after an equally sound code of catalogue rules. The code of rules recommended for adoption is the A.A. Code, 1908, although, a second edition of it has been published in 1949. I am fully conscious of the defects of the Code of 1908, as well as its revision of 1949, which is not drastic. But in the absence of a better and more widely adopted code, it has been considered proper to follow the original code which still remains a prescribed book in Cataloguing in the curriculum of several library schools of professional centres of education for Librarianship.

Standard works on the subject, like H.A. Sharp : Text Book of Cataloguing; A.A. Code, 1908; A.L.A. Catalogue rules; 2nd ed., 1949; Norris : Cataloguing; M.S. Taylor : Fundamentals of Practical Cataloguing and periodicals like the Library Journal, Library Quarterly and Library Association Record and B. N. B. have been frequently referred to and used in the preparation of the text. I acknowledge my indebtedness and thank the authors and publishers of these works.

I am deeply obliged to my colleagues Mr. Anand Prakash Agrawal, M.A., LL.B., Dip. Lib. Sc., Dr. Aditya Kumar Ohdedar, M.A., Ph.D., Dip. Lib. Sc., and Mr. B.N. Ghatak, B.Sc., Dip. Lib. Sc., who were my students also, for going through the manuscript and furnishing necessary material for illustration and other valuable suggestions. My sincere thanks are nonetheless due to Mr. Ram Naresh Singh, Cataloguing Typist of this University, who converted the manuscript into the typed script, thereby accelerating the progress of composition. I should be failing in my duty, if I do not acknowledge my gratefulness to Mr. Rama Krishna Das, Manager of the Banaras Hindu University Press for printing the book, within a limited time. Finally I express my respectful thanks to Pt. D. Subrahmanyam, M.A., Librarian, Banaras Hindu University Library for the continued encouragement I have received from him in the completion of this book.

It is my earnest desire that the guide book will contribute to a better understanding of the objectives and processes of cataloguing and render it a more imaginative, fruitful and creative pursuit in the field of librarianship. I shall be happy to receive any suggestions, for its improvement from all concerned so that I may incorporate them in a subsequent edition.

*Banaras Hindu University,*
*Department of Library Science,* C.G. Viswanathan
*February 20, 1954.*

## CONTENTS


*Preface to the Sixth Edition* *v*
*Preface to the First Edition* *vii*
*Explanation of Abbreviations and Symbols* *ix*

1. Library Catalogue : Its Nature, Functions, and Importance in a Library System 1
2. History of Modern Library Catalogues 12
3. Catalogue Codes : Origin, Growth and Development 19
4. Principles of Planning and Provision of the Library Catalogue 45
5. Catalogue Entries and their Functions in Achieving the Objectives of the Library Catalogue 59
6. Descriptive Cataloguing 72
7. Physical Forms of the Catalogue-I Manual Catalogues 83
8. Physical Forms of the Catalogues-II Computerised Catalogue 105
9. Varieties of Catalogues, their Scope and Functions 113
10. Subject Cataloguing 125
11. Cataloguing Department: Organization and Administration 132
12. Cost Analysis of Cataloguing Procedures and Suggested Economies 140
13. Co-operation and Centralization in Cataloguing 145
14. Union Catalogues and Subject Specialisation 153
15. Cataloguing of Special Material 161
16. Arrangement, Filing, Guiding of Catalogue and Instructions for its Use 184
17. Education and Training of Cataloguers 190
18. Documentation: An Extension of Cataloguing and Classification Applied to Isolates 196
19. Catalogue Cards, Their Style and Reproduction Methods 201
20. Work of Personal Authors 210

| | |
|---|---|
| 21. Choice and Entry of Personal Names | 228 |
| 22. Works of Corporate Authors | 250 |
| 23. Legal Publications | 258 |
| 24. Choice of Headings for Corporate Bodies | 276 |
| 25. Works of Unknown Authorship : Entry under Uniform Titles | 299 |
| 26. Access Points to Books and Meta-Books by A-ACR2 | 315 |
| 27. AACR 2 1988 revision : Choice of Access Points to Name Headings and Uniform Titles | 368 |
| 28. Added Entries Other Than Subject Entries | 382 |
| 29. Subject Entries | 392 |
| 30. Analytical Entries | 395 |
| 31. Series Note and Series Entry | 400 |
| 32. Contents, Notes and Annotation | 405 |
| 33. References | 409 |
| 34. Display of Entries | 414 |
| *Appendix I* Select Aids and Guides for the Cataloguer | 419 |
| *Appendix II* Definitions of Terms Commonly used in Cataloguing | 426 |
| *Appendix III* Cataloguing Examination: Select Questions | 437 |
| *Appendix IV* Implications of the adoption of A-ACR2 | 442 |
| *Index* | 447 |

## *Explanation of Abbreviations and Symbols*

| | |
|---|---|
| A.L.A. | : American Library Association |
| A.A.Code | : Anglo-American Code, 1908 : Cataloguing Rules, Author and Title Entries |
| A.L.A. Rules | : American Library Association Cataloguing Rules for Author and Title Entries, 1949. |
| A-ACR | : Anglo -American Cataloguing Rules, 1967. |
| ASLIB | : Association of Special Libraries and Information Bureau, London. |
| B.M. | : British Museum |
| CCR | : Catalogue Code Revision Committee |
| CCC | : Classified Catalogue Code by S.R. Ranganathan |
| Comm. | : Commentator ; Commentary |
| Comp. | : Compiler ; Compiled |
| Ed. | : Editor ; Edited |
| Front. | : Frontispiece |
| Gt. | : Great |
| Illus. | : Illustrator ; Illustrated |
| I.C.C.P. | : International Conference on Cataloguing Principles, Paris, 1961. |
| I.F.LA. | : International Federation of Library Associations |
| Intro. | : Introduction |
| Jt. auth. | : Joint Author |
| L.C. | : Library of Congress |
| n.d. | : No date |
| N.C.L. | : National Central Library, London |
| O.p. | : Out of print |
| p | : Page |
| Pin | : Prussian Instructions, 1886 by K. Dziatzko |
| RDC | : Rules for a Dictionary Catalogue, 1904 by C.A. Cutter |
| tr. | : Translator, Translated |
| U.D.C. | : Universal Decimal Classification |
| v. | : Volume(s) |
| x. | : 'See' reference from |
| xx | : 'See also' reference from |

# OPERATIONAL CHART

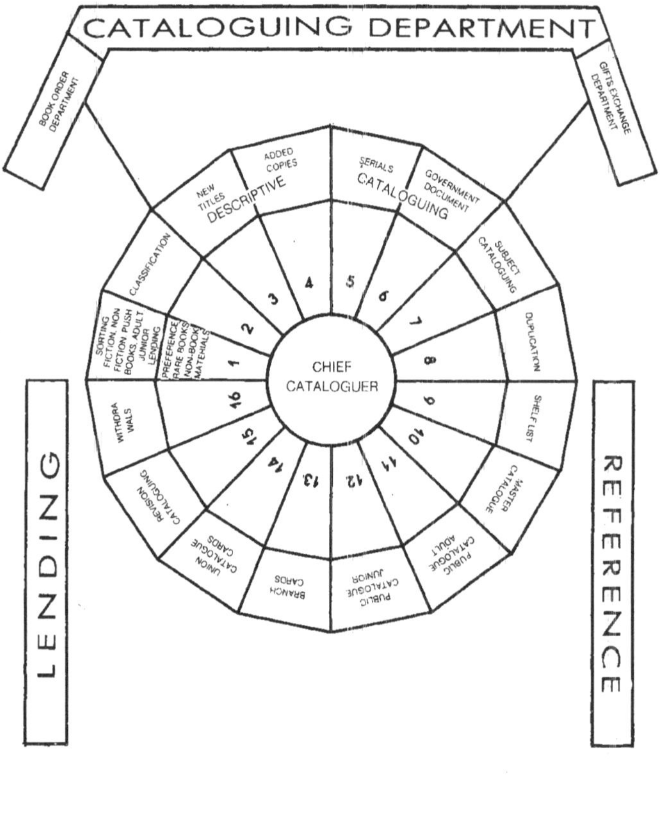

# LIBRARY CATALOGUE : ITS NATURE, FUNCTIONS, AND IMPORTANCE IN A LIBRARY SYSTEM

The Library *Catalogue* is a list of books and other reading material in the holdings of a library or a group of libraries. The list contains entries of books, arranged according to some definite plan. As distinguished from a *bibliography*, it is a list which records, describes and indexes the resources of a collection, a library or group of libraries in a locality or country.

This definition of a library catalogue was appropriate till 1960. In view of the automation's impact on library functions, and the sophisticated technological advance in electronics during the last two decades, i.e. from 1960, this definition of a library catalogue calls for re-examination and change, if necessary. The new definition of a library catalogue should be coextensive with the present form of library catalogues. The change in its form and functions have been gradual, but perceptible.

In the early modern period, the library catalogue contained entries of books on paper, either hand written/type written. Subsequently, it was printed in book form; and lastly it was on cards of standard size 7.3 × 5.3 cm, and filed in trays, which were kept in cabinets, placed on a stand at a convenient height, usually 3 ft. 6 inches, in order that persons of average height could reach the topmost trays and refer them. Perhaps the British Museum catalogue, consisting of handwritten slips of paper pasted on the appropriate page guard books of an unusual size, (and not available to the public, only the staff of the British Museum, on request by a reader for a book or information would refer, and locate the given author/book) had to be converted into machine readable catalogue.

Since 1980, all these manual methods adopted for the physical forms of library catalogues have given way to automated systems: specially the MARC system, and computer storage of information and its retrieval, and on-line interactive catalogues are found in their places. These forms of catalogues are subsequently treated in detail.

*Cataloguing* denotes the various processes adopted in preparing the entries of the reading material in a catalogue and its maintenance.

*Cataloguing and classification* are the twin processes adopted in modern *library administration* to help readers in locating the desired books and other reading material quickly and conveniently. They are intended "to relate and display together the editions which a library has of a given work and the works which it has of a given author." In view of the importance of the catalogue in providing access to the resources of a library, large sums of money are spent and competent persons are employed as cataloguers.

"The library catalogue does not—or should not—exist as an end itself. It is one part of the total bibliographic system and must be responsive to changes that take place in other parts of the system".[1] *Studies of catalogues and cataloguing* carried out indicate the gradual changes in the form, style and techniques of catalogues. The reader's approach to books and reading, the physical features of the book, and the advances made in the field of classification have all had their impact on the library catalogue. "The modification, however, have been unnecessarily slow, and sometimes inadequate, because of incomplete understanding of the nature and *functions of the catalogue* and its place in the system as a whole."[2] *Cataloguing practice* from the beginning is determined by the set of rules followed by a library, *e.g., the British Museum* has its "Rules for compiling the catalogues of Printed Books, Maps and Music in the British Museum" revised edition, 1936; and the *Library of Congress* has its own Rules, "Despite the fact that cataloguing has been referred to as an art, these rules as *Seymour Lubetzky points out, have shaped our catalogues and determined their usefulness.*"[3]

A *Sumerian clay tablet* (2000 B.C.)? inscribed with 62 titles is one of the earliest artifacts, that can be considered a catalogue. The earliest known form of library catalogue indicates that it was compiled to serve as a simple inventory or list of the library resources. "The lists 'pi ivakes' which Callimachus drew up at Alexandria probably contained the names of those authors only which he found in the library with which he was connected there, and they may, therefore, be regarded as class-catalogues for that particular subject."[4] It is that analytical and critical mind of Callimachus, as a classifier and cataloguer, which is evidenced in his 'piivakes' that is of far-reaching importance to the modern cataloguer. Callimachus gave the name of the author, place of birth, name of his father, his teachers and education, his nickname or pseudonym, a short biography, the title of his work or works; if the work lacked a title he provided one, a comment on its authenticity, and finally a stichiometric note giving the first words of the work (often the ancient title) and the exact number of lines of the manuscript (of each work and of all the author's writings). The last was an important bibliographical detail, used to control the size of the manuscript and determine the compensation to the scribe as well as for general reference.

"There is no doubt that our whole concept of author entry first came with the Greeks; it never once appeared in any work which has survived from the earlier civilizations of the East. Even today in the Orient, the traditional entry for a book is its title."5 Most of the oriental writings of well known authors have been better known under their titles than under their names, e.g. Raghuvamsa of Kalidasa; Kadambari of Bana; Leelavati of Bhaskaracharya; perhaps the approach of the readers was towards the title or subject covered by it rather than the person who wrote it. It signifies the impersonal and objective bent of mind of oriental readers which seems to be better than the subjective approach. Will not people read and appreciate the dramas of Shakespeare, had they been written by some person other than Shakespeare as superbly as was done by him? It cannot be said that the title approach to the work of an author signifies unnaturalness or an undemocratic attitude.

*Callimachus* seems to have adopted the following Main Divisions of knowledge for classifying the manuscripts:

I. Epic and other Non-Dramatic Poetry
II. The Drama
III. Laws
IV. Philosophy
V. History
VI. Oratory
VII. Medicine
VIII. Mathematical Science
IX. Natural Science
X. Miscellanea

The authors were arranged in the alphabetical order of their names, under the appropriate class of knowledge to which their works related. The 'pi ivakes' (the word means tablets) were kept with the wall book cases.

"Thus the *Pinakes* was the first great library catalogues of western civilization, just as the *Bible of Gutenberg* was the first great printed book. Thus, as in all intellectual efforts, the Greeks fixed the *canons of cataloguing, which have been incorporated, more or less, in our Library of Congress*, European and other system. However, the Pinakes was more than a catalogue. It was the work of the foremost man of letters of his age.... That the original Pinakes (120) is lost is a major disaster to learning. We repeat we would rather have the priceless 120 volumes of Callimachus even than 'Livy whole'."[6]

The catalogue of the library at the *Convent of St. Francis of Assisi*, dated 1 January 1381 indicates that the library was in two divisions : (1) for the use of the brethren; (2) for loans to outsiders. This catalogue has a brief preface stating that it includes "all the books belonging to the library of the Holy *Convent of St. Francis* at Assisi whether they be chained, or whether they be not chained." [7]

"The compiler of the catalogue goes through the library case by case, noting (at least in the Latin Library) the position of the case, the subjects of the books contained in it, and their titles. This is succeeded by an enumeration of the number of volumes, so as to show in a couple of pages, how many the whole library contained."[8]

The foregoing examples of *catalogues* of the early and medieval libraries tend to indicate that the catalogue was more a record for the keeper or custodian of the books than one for the public.

It also discloses that the number of books 'or manuscripts' in those libraries was small and did not create problems which great national, university, and public libraries of today with millions of volumes have to face. The use of the library was also restricted to certain classes of people.

Many *medieval libraries* had such small collections that lists of any kind were found unnecessary. In several cases it was only a rough inventory. Books were valuable property and so had to be protected and enumerated among, the treasures of a house. The emphasis on the material values of books continued in many library records until the sixteenth century. Secular corporations followed the example set by the church and lent their manuscripts, but only on security. A remarkable example of a loan transaction of a work on medicine at the *Ecole de*

*Medecine, Paris*, astonishingly illustrates the property value attached to library books and manuscripts. When Lous XI, the King of France, wanted a work on medicine from this library, he was asked to deposit a security of 12 marks' worth of plate and 100 gold crowns before he could borrow it. The king deposited the security, borrowed the work, and after use returned it on 24 January 1472, when the money was returned to him.

There were some monastic libraries which listed books not to catalogue them but to commemorate the donations received. Some other medieval libraries maintained lists of works as a check against loss or theft. "Still, again, there were *'catalogues'* written in metrical form, which suggests that the young monks were required to commit the lists to memory. Only in the larger monasteries do we find real catalogues., i.e. guides to the content and location of books available for use. Thus, the earlier *medieval catalogues* were primarily shelf lists. True author and subject records were a later development."[9]

With the advent of the printing press and its product – printed books – the volume of literature has been growing steadily. Books became not only cheap to suit the means of ordinary people but also grew in variety. Booksellers established standards for the description of titles in their lists or catalogues by giving the size, number of pages, quality of binding, price and also a brief annotation of the book or its contents. Library catalogues soon adopted this practice more or less fully in describing the books in catalogue entries, in order to help the readers to identify the books from the catalogue. With the growth in the number of serial publications, specially in the field of science and technology, newer techniques and standards of description became necessary.

What scholars expect of *cataloguing* now can be gauged from the views expressed by a Professor of History (*William B. Hamilton* of Duke University), and a Professor of Biochemistry (*Joseph S. Fruton* of Yale University):

> Here are some of the expectations about the catalogue that I have gathered from my colleagues :
>
> In some cases, governed by local opportunities and responsibilities, it ought to constitute an exhaustive bibliography on a subject.
>
> It ought to open up most subjects to the uninitiated.
>
> It ought to point the scholar to the works and keys that will lead to a thorough exploration of the subject.
>
> It ought to list the holdings of the library under the headings obvious to anyone with

both a little ingenuity and a little knowledge of the conventions of subject headings.

The catalogue ought to have headings for subjects or titles that are on everyone's tongue.

The catalogue ought not, in the opinion of a heretic, to be carved into parts and distributed throughout the library. A single dictionary catalogue would not defeat or fool the students as easily as one split up into subjects, author-title, serials, documents, special collections, etc.

In regard to the part of the cataloguing process that is called descriptive cataloguing, I need only reiterate that the card catalogue is of secondary importance to most scientists. It is consulted as a finding list to help in locating items which cannot readily be found on the shelves: because they are in use, because their classification is not clear, or for some other reason. Obviously too, the catalogue must be checked for official purposes, particularly in connection with the ordering of books.

It is clear that a card catalogue is necessary as a finding list. Beyond that it is simply a question of how detailed the entries in the card catalogue need to be. The scientist would like all details on catalogue cards to be accurate and reliable, but, once that has been stipulated, he will be content with sufficient information to identify the items. It should be added that he would like a cataloguing system that gets books and journals into use with the smallest possible delay.[10]

A *library catalogue* is expected to satisfy every kind of bibliographic demand made on it, if possible without reference to other types of services in a library. But this is an untenable proposition, because a library catalogue is largely dependent on ordering, *acquisition*, *classification*, *stock control* verification, revision, discarding and other operations in a library.

*A modern library catalogue* of a satisfactory type, in general, displays the record of a library's resources with a view to making them easily accessible for study and reference; serves as a dependable tool of communication of ideas and subjects dealt with in the books to the readers who use the library; provides basic bibliographic information to systematic study and research; functions as a select author and subject bibliography.

The above characteristics of a modern library catalogue distinguish it from the early and medieval catalogues, which were little more than inventories of the collections in libraries. The shelf list and the accession records maintained in libraries today perform the functions of an inventory of the stock, thereby relieving the load on the catalogue of the library. It is but natural that as the reader became more important than the books, the objectives of the library catalogue changed from inventory to retrieval or location of particular items or groups of items in a library collection, which has become the most important function of the library catalogue. *The catalogue entry* may provide a wide variety of information on or about the *author*, his *collaborators*, *subjects* and *titles*, forms and aspects, etc.

It will be in order to consider here if readymade, standard and comprehensive *bibliographies* of authors and subjects, which contain a full description and evaluation of the titles included in them, can supplement *library catalogues*; or if any they render them valueless duplicate records of such works as are in the holdings of a library, as well as included in the bibliography.

Bibliographies, obviously, are not limited to a specific collection; every compiler of a bibliography though swearing by selectivity, ends in partial universality. But the cataloguer's field is limited to the works which every library finds it suitable to acquire and maintain in its stock. Several small libraries do not find it worthwhile and possible to acquire the *bibliographies*. In such circumstances, a library catalogue must be maintained fairly fully in order to perform the function of both a finding list as well as a bibliography. But in large library systems, titles in the library catalogue may represent a high percentage of titles included in bibliographies; *e.g.* The Catalogue of Printed Books in the *British Museum*, or the *London Library Catalogue*. "At the Columbia Institute Mr. Frarey reported that studies of subject coverage in catalogues and bibliographies show duplication ranging from 75 to 90 per cent."[11] Here the library catalogue certainly becomes a secondary tool. If libraries follow the order for arrangement of books, identical to the order adopted for arrangement of titles in bibliographies and check-mark the holdings, the need for a separate library catalogue seems superfluous.

The current trend towards open access to shelves in libraries and adoption of satisfactory systems of *classification* for arrangement and display of books has gradually lessened the reader's dependence on the catalogue. Is it not then time to consider the extent of the importance and indispensable character of a library catalogue, when mounting *costs of cataloguing* and arrearage in the work have become a universally chronic feature of the working of libraries both big and small?

It seems to me that the process of revaluation of library administration may equally be well initiated by cataloguers as by chief administrators. If we examine what we do in the cataloguing department, ask ourselves why we do it, if these reasons are really valid, or if they merely rationalize an activity which is no longer so admirable or necessary as it was, we may indeed be able to suggest a revision of policy which benefits not only the cataloguing service but also other procedures in the library. If we ask, is cataloguing for eternity really necessary ? We discover, it is done thus because all books are assumed to have potential research value in the future and are not discarded but relegated to a store.[12]

Aims and *methods of cataloguing* will best be chalked out, not in drab uniformity, but according to the individual library's needs and circumstances. But the basic *functions of a catalogue* "(1) accurate and speedy determination of whether or not an item known by author or title is in the collection, and if so, where it may be found; and (2) what materials the library contains upon a given subject and where they may be found,"[13] will remain unaltered.

There are thousands of libraries in our country. They are administered by private, public, school, college and university institutions. Some of them have large and rich collections of books. A few of them have been functioning for nearly a century. All these libraries have been acquiring and storing books, according to their ability and resources. A survey into the working of these libraries will readily reveal that the time, labour, and money spent on books have not produced results commensurate with their endeavours. Books wanted by the readers are not in the holdings. Books in their stock are not readily available for use, as their location could not easily be found. The value and prestige of a library, be it large or small, depends upon its usefulness in time. The public wanting a fact or information from the printed page has a right to demand the appropriate book which may contain it. If the library fails to locate the book at the time of demand, it ceases to be a library and becomes a hoarding house of books.

Every kind of library will agree to perform this basic function, as it is fundamental to the existence and future of libraries. If libraries aim to achieve this object fairly completely, there is no short cut, except to provide a workable catalogue of their contents. Some may ask what have these libraries been doing all the time? Have they no *catalogues* of their book collections? The answer is 'yes' to the enquirer. Then, why cannot these catalogues be summoned to yield the type of information required? Our reply would be that these existing catalogues were neither designed nor compiled for performing this function. The enquirer continues "why then were they at all made and who made them?" The answer would be "they were no doubt made with all earnestness but by those who did not know the art of compiling library catalogues. Therefore, the catalogues assumed a different turn." Instead of leading and guiding the user they often misled, confused, and left the readers disappointed. Consequently, a dissatisfied reader concludes that the library is no good, and it is a wasteful effort to maintain it at public expense. Surely such a feeling on the part of the public is fatal to the existence and future of libraries and librarians.

If this undesirable feature is to be totally eliminated, there is one drastic remedy. It is to provide a satisfactory, simple, workable, and useful catalogue of the books in a library. Before adding new books, it is imperative on the part of any library to compile such a reliable *catalogue* for the existing collection of books. Once the catalogue of a library is compiled on proper principles, its further maintenance as a serviceable tool can be guaranteed. There is ample truth in the statement that a good catalogue will serve as a key to unlock the contents of a library. It will multiply the number of readers. It will economise time and expenditure of the public and the library staff. It will conserve the library's resources. It will build and increase the reputation of a library, for the true measure of the value of a library is not the number of its books, nor its large and magnificent building, nor its vast financial resoruces, but its usefulness to the reader in time. A good catalogue is, therefore, a necessity to every library and proper attention should be paid to its planning and provision.

Besides this pragmatic value, a library catalogue possesses a historical value, because it is one of the basic documents on the history of a library. "It may often be the only document that has survived the accidents of time, and it is ordinarily the one that is most easily available for study. Although we cannot always interpret it fully, it records gifts and acquisitions and enables us to perceive the growth of the library and the ideas that determined the purchase and the arrangement of books. A history of a library can be a valuable bit of cultural history and becomes even more valuable when it is set in a large background."[14]

*The Bodleian catalogues* of 1605 and 1620, the catalogues of the *British Museum, the Leyden University catalogues* from 1595-1741 and the catalogue of the *Bibliotheque Nationale de Paris* are excellent examples which reveal the cultural trends of the time.

The catalogues of private libraries appear to be more valuable sources of information for writers of intellectual history than catalogues of institutional libraries. While institutions usually acquire standard books related to the objectives for which they are established, private libraries may contain unusual books of a specialised nature and on unexplored fields of great value to the study of academic discipline. These catalogues are usually found to employ a classified arrangement and are capable of disclosing information on "what men once wrote, bought, read, and thought," in addition to indicating the tastes and interests of the book collector.

Apart from their historical and reference value, these catalogues can be put to diverse uses—to identify authours and titles, to assess the material value of books, to select books on a subject, to study the book industry and trade, and the growth and development of those libraries. In short these catalogues deputise for the books in those libraries, which have become things of the past and can answer a variety of questions in a silent and unassuming manner.

Perhaps the futuer historian of our civilization may well consider the catalogues of our libraries as sources of information reflecting the intellectual ideals and aspirations of our generation. Cataloguers should, therefore, realise that they are not only serving the present community of readers but they are providing for the future needs of the intellectual community.

Some fundamental questions on the compilation and care of library catalogues have been raised time and again, and repeated by Grose and Line,[15] without providing any precise, direct, or relevant answer or solution to them. Cataloguers normally are aware of these problems, and as no better or simple substitute to a library catalogue has been possible to produce, in spite of mechanization, computerization, etc., cataloguing as was conceived by Panizzi, or even the Greeks is bound to continue as long as books and other library materials represent human knowlege and libraries acquire and organize them for use. There is simple truth in the statement of Gorman, "yet it is hard to imagine a library without a catalogue, and hard to imagine what might replace it."[16] Perhaps this may well be an answer to the credo of cataloguing research.

## REFERENCES

1. **J.H. Shera** and **M.E. Egan**. The **Classified Catalog**. Chicago, American Library Association, 1956, p. 1.
2. **Ibid.**
3. Maurice F. Tauber, ed. "**Current Trends in Cataloguing and Classification,**" **Library Trends**, v. 2 : 2, Oct. 1953, p. 174.
4. John Wills Clark. **The Care of Books,** Cambridge University Press, 1909, p. 21.
5. Ruth F. Strout. "**The Development of the Catalog and Cataloging Codes,**" Library Quarterly, XXVI, 4, Oct. 1956, p. 257.
6. **Edward Alexander Parsons. The Alexandrian Library,** London, Cleaver-Hume Press, 1952, p. 217-218.
7. John Wills Clark. **The care of Books**, Cambridge University Press, 1909, p. 200.
8. **Ibid.**, p. 214.

9. **James Westfall Thomoson. The Medieval Library,** N.Y. Hafner Pub. Co., 1957, p. 613.
10. Edwin E. Williams, ed. **Problems and Prospects of the Research Library,** N.Y., the Scarecrow Press, 1956, pp. 67-74.
11. **Paul S. Dunkin. "Criticism of Current Cataloguing Practice,"** Library Quarterly, XXVI, 4, Oct. 1956, p. 295.
12. **Mary Piggot. Cataloguing Principles and Practice : an Inquiry,** Lond., Library Association, 1954, pp. 6-7.
13. J.H. Shera and M.F. Egan. **The Classified Catalog.** American Library Association, 1956, p. 9.
14. **Archer Taylor. Book Catalogues : their Varieties and Uses.** Chicago, the Newberry Library, 1957, p. 149.
15. M.W. Grose and M.B. Line : **On the construction and care of white elephants.** Library Association Record, v. 70 No.1, January 1968, pp. 2-5.
16. **Michael Gorman:** A-A 1967 : **The new cataloguing rules,** Library Association Record, v. 70 No. 2, February, 1968, p. 27.

# 2

# HISTORY OF MODERN LIBRARY CATALOGUES

The subject of cataloguing seems to have received the most serious attention of librarians and trustees of libraries, as well as of the readers using them, almost a hundred years ago. It has been customary to fix 1850 as a convenient date to make a study of modren library catalogues, because some of the outstanding printed book catalogues of libraries were produced only after that year.

"Modern *library cataloguing* has been little influnced by ancient cataloguing. Whatever developments there may have been in the compilation of catalogues in antiquity, no remains of them survived. There was no carry-over into the Middle Ages, for during that period cataloguing as we conceive it did not even exist; neither did the Renaissance turn up anything about cataloguing from classical periods except the barest and most conjectural evidence. Therefore, with the exception of the fact that the Greeks taught us to refer to books by their authors, it is not far wrong to maintain that the art, the technique, of cataloguing is a completely modern development."[1]

Among the varieties of catalogues, the author catalogue seems to have been more commonly used in several libraries, although the classified and dictionary forms were occasionally found in some. The absence of a common code of cataloguing rules for adoption in the libraries is conspicuous, as each individual library produced a set of *cataloguing rules* for its own use in compiling the catalogue.

### Catalogues of the British Museum

The first general catalogue of the library was an author catalogue, without press marks, compiled by *P.M. Maty, S.S. Harper,* and *S. Ayscough* under the title *Librorum impressorum qui in Museo Brittanico, adservantur catalogues* in two volumes 1787. In order to serve the visitors to the Reading Room and the staff of the library, this printed catalogue was kept up to date by means of the addition of entries in manuscript in an interleaved copy.

It was revised during 1807 to 1810 and printed between 1813 to 1819 in 7 volumes. By 1834 this catalogue extented to 23 volumes. The Trustees of the British Museum ordered that a new author catalogue be compiled. *Panizzi* drew up his famous XCI Rules to be followed in compiling the catalogue, which are reproduced in the preface to the first volume of the catalogue printed in 1841. The imperfections in the first volumes were so glaring that it was considered futile to continue the printing of further volumes. It was then decided to continue the 1813-1819 catalogue by inserting manuscript additions for subsequent volumes acquired in the library.

In 1849, an important change in the technique of compilation was adopted by writing a separate slip for each book. The slips ware secured by pasting them on blank leaves in large folio volumes. In 1850, this catalogue was in 150 volumes. By 1880, the collection had increased so much as to extend the catalogue to nearly 2,500 volumes. Some volumes became so bulky that the binding gave way. In view of the enormous size of the catalogue in manuscript slips, it was again decided to print the catalogue from 1881. It was known as *Catalogue of the Printed Books in the Library of the British Museum*, Printed by order of the Trustees by William Cloves and Sons, Limited, 1881-1900. A supplement containing the additions of 1882-1899 was issued from 1900-1905.

A new edition of the General Catalogue was begun in 1930 with the title : *British Museum General Catalogue of Printed Books*. By 1953 volumes 1-50 covering only the alphabets A-Denz were published.

A new approach was made in order to speed up the printing of the catalogue in full within a short period of five or six years. The plan envisaged provisions of the whole of the material now included in the 'working' copies of the catalogue in the British Museum. To produce the new edition, one of these working copies was taken and the entries in it were photographed in one alphabetical sequence and from these photographs lithographic plates were made from which the new volumes were printed by offset lithography. The *British Museum-* General Catalogue of printed books, photo-lithographic edition to

1955, is in 263 volumes, 1959-66 (o.p.). Supplements covering additions to 1970 have been published.

### Current State of British Museum Catalogues

British Library Catalogue Conversion to Machine Readable form in 1987 is a historical decision, for the centuries old catalogue of printed books, both in manuscript and print, has been restructured to be in line with current trends and uses of this valuable record. The conversion to machine readable form of the General Catalogue of Printed Books was necessitated by the need to use staff and space effectively and economically.

In order to overcome the inherent disadvantages of a printed catalogue : (1) it is out of date, as soon as, if not before it is printed and published, because the library acquisition of books is a continuous process; (2) it is extremly difficult to correct and rectify errors noticed after printing; (3) the linear form in an A - Z sequence restricted and impaired its use. "The first two factors, particularly, signify the importance that the catalogue must represent a living collection (up to date) and in some sense a living entity by itself. Machine readable files, especially those, with a separately linked authority file, make global editing and rapid correction a reality. The increased search capabilities of a machine held file cut across the restrictions of the present printed form by offering such basic possibilities as search on title word or search on publisher which will open up the catalogue to clients accessing the database, but to those in the library concerned with more efficient collection and management. The structure of the British Library is ideal for a print based catalogue, but unsuited for producing functional records for a machine held database. The current concept of *unit record* as typified by a catalogue card or a MARC record is missing. One main entry, author heading is enough for several of his works and on the page it is not possible to see the secondary/added entries, and references mentioned in the tracing. The current conversion project, therefore, has not only to translate the British Library General catalogue from print to computer readable form, but to restructure the data in such a way as to create unit records compatible with those already in existence in the databases produced by the library.

The process is scheduled for completion in 1991, when the first moves into the new British Library building at St. Pancras are expected.

Primary access to the catalogue will be on-line, the British Library Catalogue database taking its place alongside the records for post 1975 accessions, which are already available in machine readable form. It is likely that the converted records will be available through the BLAISE LINE service.

The general catalogue of the British Museum Printed Books has been acknowledged as a valuable source of bibliographic information. When it was printed, it commanded a wide circle of its users, and now converted into machine readable form, its sphere of use has further broadened to remote centres of the world.

This scholarly and consistent catalogue will not only be catholic in the coverage of material but will prove the most comprehensive, largest single catalogue ever published.

In addition to the General Catalogue of Printed Books there are separate catalogues for Oriental Printed Books and Manusripts and Catalogues of the Manuscript Collections.

Cataloguing books and manuscripts is a process which must be continuously carried on in libraries, small and big, as long as reading material is added to the collections. The British Museum is no exception. Even with an appreciable staff of cataloguers, specialists, and administrators, the British Museum finds itself in arrears. Some of the catalogues in the Oriental languages have not yet been printed. Only manuscript catalogues are available in these departments.

## The Catalogues of the London Library

Thomas Carlyle's dissatisfaction with the British Museum's services led to the creation of the *London Library* in 1841. Eminent persons like Lord Clarendon, William Ewart Gladstone, Lord Houghton and others were associated with Carlyle on the first committee. The library functioned from 24 May 1841 as a subscription library and within one year its holdings reached the figure of 14,000 volumes.

"Mr. Gladstone prepared the first list of works dealing with ecclesiastical history, and Grote and Hallam devoted hours to drawing up short catalogues dealing with classical and medieval history and literature."

It is essentially an author alphabetical catalogue and under each author the titles of their books are again alphabetically arranged. When books are entered under the same name, they are arranged in the following order : (1) Anonymous Books and place names;

(2) Periodicals and Societies; (3) Christian names with distinctives titles, epithet or place name, and (4) Surnames.

The general plan and arrangement follows the pattern of the *British Museum Catalogue*. Today the main Catalogue of the London Library is in 2 volumes, v.1, A-K, 1913, 1395p., v. 2, L-Z 1914, 1339p., compiled by C.T. Hagbert Wright and C.J. Purnell, with the first supplement, 1913-1920 ; second supplement, 1920-1928, third supplement, 1928-1950, published in 1953.

Sir Leslie Stephen, President of the London Library, in 1893 decided to provide a subject-index, for he felt that "the Library can never be really useful, now that it has grown to its present size, until we have a subject index." The work was started in 1905 and has since been continued without interruption.

The books themselves suggested the subject headings which were noted regularly for future reference in the "Headings Book" corresponding to an authority list. *The A.L.A. list of Subject Headings*, 1901 was used as a basic source. The procedure did not compel the staff to suit the books to any readymade system of classification.

"The Subject-Index is a Supplement to the Author Catalogue, and is not intended to be used quite independently of it, though, generally speaking this is possible.

"The headings are arranged in alphabetical order, all compound words and phrases, such as Land Taxation ; Stone Implements, etc., being for this purpose reckoned, as if spelt in one word. Special attention must be given to this point."[2]

The Subject-Index is now in 4 volumes; v.I, 1909; v.2, (additions, 1909-22), 1923; v.3, (additions, 1923-28) 1938; and v.4, (1938-53), 1955.

In Europe, the first printed catalogue for a general collection at the university of Leyden was produced by Petrius Bertius in 1595; while the printed catalogue in America was brought out by the Harvard University in 1723.

### The Prussian State Library

This national library began the publication of a *Gesamtkatalog der Preussischen bibliotheken* in the year 1931. It is considered to be a fine example of cooperative cataloguing. This union catalogue is an author alphabetical catalogue of all the works in the *Prussian Libraries*, the Bavarian State Library at Munich, and the National Library at Vienna.

The number of cooperating libraries was increased and it was known as *Der Deutscher Gesamtkatalog* from 1936 until publication ceased in 1944, owing to the disruption caused by the war.

## United States

In the United States, there are outstanding examples of printed catalogues at the Boston Athenaeum, the Surgeon General's office, the Carnegie Library at Pittsburgh, and in the public libraries at Brooklyn and Detroit.

## The A.L.A. Catalog

In a true sense, the *A.L.A. Catalog* is not a catalogue of a collection in a library or group of libraries. It is really a select bibliography, which serves as a model for printed page catalogues of libraries. Students of Cataloguing and libraries will surely profit by a study of its methods, plan and arrangement. The American Library Association has been publishing these catalogues from 1893-1941, at varying intervals. The 1904 edition, which was prepared by the New York State Library and the Library of Congress under the authority of the A.L.A. Publishing Board and entitled *A.L.A. Catalog : 8,000 volumes for a popular library, with notes* is an outstanding example of a printed page catalogue containing the classified arrangement of titles in part I and the dictionary arrangement of titles in part II. An experimental study of the two forms, the classified and dictionary forms is possible with the aid of this edition. The 1926 edition is more exhaustive and the later supplements of 1941-1949 cover select titles published from time to time which are considered standard ones for inclusion in the stock of general libraries. The *A.L.A. Catalog* is considered as the first general book selection tool prepared on a cooperative basis for American public libraries.

The examples of these printed catalogues cited above lead us to the conclusion that a growing library and a printed catalogue can never pace together. A remedy was found by issuing periodically supplementary volumes to provide information on books added to the library after the publication of the original catalogue. Numerous supplements to the original edition naturally created a necessity for cumulation. The cumulative process involved no less time and money than the original compilation. It was, therefore, considered by several libraries towards the beginning of the 20th Century that printing catalogues was uneconomic and the best method to maintain the catalogues up-to- date was to adopt the cards of standard dimension for the purpose. But the bibliographic value possessed by a printed book catalogue still holds good and therefore, its possible revival and popularity with scholars cannot be discounted. A remarkable example of a successful printed catalogue can be found in the *'Library of Congress Author Catalog'* which is described in Chapter Seven. More recent book catalogues of America are discussed and described by *Richard H. Shoemaker* in his contribution. " Some American twentieth century book catalogs : their purposes, format, and production techniques."[3] Arecent publication, Gavien L. Higgens: Printed Reference Material; 2nd ed L.A, 1984. is a valuable source for printed catalogues and bibliographies.

REFERENCES

1. **Ruth French Strout. "The Development of the Catalog and the Cataloging Codes,"** Library Quarterly, XXVI, 4 Oct. 1956, p. 274.
2. **London Library**. Subject-Index,1909, p. xv.
3. **Lib. Resources**, 4 (3) 1960, 195-207.

# 3

# CATALOGUE CODES : ORIGIN, GROWTH AND DEVELOPMENT

"*Library Catalogue* is an Ancient Library tool. But catalogue code of a rigorous kind is of recent origin. It first attained rigour in stray local codes, i.e., individual libraries. Now it is attaining rigour in national codes. An international code is yet to be established."[1] Agreement on the principles to govern an international code of cataloguing at least for author and tittle entries, has been reached at the conference of the *International conference on Cataloguing Principles*, at Paris, in 1961.

It is very appropriate to designate the three men of genius, *Antonio Panizzi, Charles Ammi Cutter,* and *Seymour Lubetzky* as the forerunners in the task of producing a code of cataloguing for author/title entries.

"Panizzi came to cataloguing when it was an occupation for drudges and indigent clergymen; he left it a systematic and intellectually respected activity. Many of the ideas contained in his ninety-one rules are as valid today as when written, and all the strengths of the great British Museum author catalogue can fairly be said to result from his achievement."[2]

*Panizzi*. It was in the middle of the 19th century that organized effort seems to have been made to formulate catalogue codes. The earliest code of cataloguing which has exerted considerable influence over the subsequent codes is Panizzi's 91 rules printed as prefatory matter in the *British Museum* catalogue of 1841. These rules are for the entry of authors only. A keen controversy took place over these rules, specially on the degree of details to be included in the author headings, which, if lengthy, took a longer time and delayed the progress in cataloguing.

The Trustees of the *British Museum* finally approved the adoption of Panizzi's code of rules for cataloguing and even today it forms the basis on which the *British Museum Catalogue* is being compiled. Till 1887, the original 91 rules were faithfully adopted in the cataloguing processes of the British Museum. There have, subsequently, been many editions, the most recent being that of 1936 revised edition reprinted by offset lithography in 1948 and 1951 under the title "*Rules for Compiling the Catalogues of Printed Book, Maps and Music in the British Museum*," reduced to 41 rules, with directions for cataloguing maps and music at the end.

A reconsideration of the *British Museum Rules* is engaging the attention of the authorities of the British Museum with a view to satisfying the present readers in the fields of Science and Technology and to economize the expenditure by adopting a common set of rules for entries in the *British Museum Catalogue* and the *British National Bibliography*, which catalogues almost all copyright material received in the British Museum. The *British National Bibliography* entries are filed separately and displayed in the Reading Room of the British Museum as an experimental measure to test the reader's reaction to this card catalogue in relation to the printed volumes of the *British Museum Catalogue*. It is too soon to expect that a century old practice of maintaining the printed page catalogues in the British Museum will soon be given up in favour of the *British National Bibliography* cards, at least for current British publications.

These rules influenced the cataloguing practice considerably of the libraries in the English speaking areas. Perhaps Panizzi's rules pointed the direction in which the future practice governing the author and title entries was to be formulated. Esdaile says 'Panizzi's rules were the first thorough code ever drawn up."

"The objectives implicit in our rules for entry are two. The first objective is to enable the user of the catalogue to determine readily whether or not the library has the book he wants. The catalogue is constantly searched by many readers and members of the staff, and the quicker this information can be found the better the catalogue. The second objective is to reveal to the user of the catalogue, under one form of the author's name, what works the library has by a given author and what editions or translations of a given work.... The need for the second objective arises from the fact that the works of an author may be issued under different names as a result of a change, translation, transliteration, or even misprint of the author's name, and the editions of a work may be issued under different titles for similar reasons and could, therefore, otherwise be separated in the catalog. The cataloger is thus required, in recording a work, to establish the identity of the author and the relationship of the work.

"Both these objectives were staunchly defended by *Panizzi* before the Royal Commission in 1849 and have since been pursued in the *Anglo-American Cataloguing rules*."[3] These two objectives have more succinctly been enunciated by the CCR in 1960. This is an evidence of the remarkable farsightedness of Panizzi.

*Jewett.* At about 1850 the American libraries seriously considered the need to bring out a code of cataloguing rules. Professor *Charles C. Jewett*, librarian of the Smithsonian Institution prepared a code of 39 rules in 1852. These rules were modelled after Panizzi's rules and issued under the title "*On the construction of catalogues of libraries, and their publications by means of separate stereotyped titles, with rules and examples*." These rules were again limited to the author entries, but included a model subject index.

*Crestadoro.* In 1856 *Andrea Crestadoro* brought out a pamphlet entitled "*The art of making catalogues of libraries.*" When he was the librarian of the *Manchester Public Libraries*, these rules were adopted in compiling the catalogues of the library. These rules laid stress on the recording of the titles of books in full, leading off with the author's name, and the arrangement to follow no precise order, except the order of receipt of books. The entries were to be consecutively numbered and provided with an index of authors and subjects in a brief form with the number referring to the entry in the main part of the catalogue. The subject denoted by the title on the title page was to be the subject index entry. The other composite and related subjects dealt with in the book had no provision in the subject index.

*Cutter.* No systematic code of cataloguing rules were produced till 1876 when C.A. Cutter published his "*Rules for a dictionary catalog*" which forms a part of the "Special report of the United States Bureau of Education on the history, condition, and management of public libraries in the United States of America." In the first edition, there were 205 rules which were tested by applying them to the collection in the library of the Boston Athenaeum. The second edition, in 1889, the third in 1891 and the fourth, in 1904 were issued. (Cutter died in September, 1903.)

In the fourth edition the number of rules increased to 369. It still remains the most comprehensive code ever produced by a single mind. It soon became a national code, reflecting the versatile imagination and genius of the author. "Its limitation was only in the linguistic context.

The library profession has been fortunate in the author of this code. He was a genius. This is seen in the ring of certitude and the profoundness of penetration found in the rules and the commentaries of *Rdc*. They are like the external epigrams of a sage. *Rdc* is indeed a classic. It is immortal. Its influence has been overpowering."[4]

The growing desire of the public to use the library books and library catalogues with a view to obtaining material or information on specific subjects and related subjects, soon created a problem in cataloguing. Hitherto all the available codes provided rules for author and title entries. "Cutter strengthened the concept that catalogs not only should point the way to an individual publication but should also assemble and organise literary units. While this was not an entirely new principle, since Maunsel in 1595 had used the heading "Bible" to assemble its various versions and translations, *Panizzi* in 1841 had strengthened it as a concept by introducing corporate and government entries, and Jewett had given it still further support by his use of real names rather than pseudonyms, yet it was Cutter who actually stated it as a formal principle. "In regard to the author entry it must be remembered that the object is not merely to facilitate the finding of a given book by the author's name." "If this were all, it might have been better to make the entry under... the form of name mentioned in the title, but we have also... [that other object] to provide for [of showing what the library has under a given author"][5] and Cutter provided rules governing the choice of subject headings in his *Rules for a Dictionary*.

Catalog on pages 66-82, which have not yet been superseded by any better set of rules. The unsatisfactory nature of the classification systems produced, on which the classified forms of library catalogues depended for their compilation, has tended to the adoption and continuation of the alphabetic subject catalogues. *Cutter's rules* for *subject cataloguing* are bound to stay till the need for alphabetic subject catalogues is totally eliminated. Which in the opinion of experts is quite remote.

*Prussian Instructions.* A significant contribution to cataloguing rules, after Cutter, is found in Prussian Instructions. "*Pin* may be taken to be the second important code of a non-local nature."[6] It was designed originally for compiling a Union Catalogue of the then German State Libraries.

In 1886 *Professor K. Dziatzko*, a German Librarian published his "*Instruction fur die ordnung der Titel im alphabetischen Zettelkatalog der Koniglichen and Universitats Bibliothek zu Breslau*," which was translated into English by an American librarian, *K.A. Linderfelt* and published in 1890 under the title "*Eclectic card catalog rules* : author and title entries, based on *Dziatzko's "Instruction*", compared with the rules of the *British Museum*, Cutter, Dewey, Perkins, and other authorities". It is minute and extensive in details covering all possible forms of authors' names. The appendix includes a list of oriental titles and occupations with their significance. Its profound influence over the German libraries could be attributed to its excellent principles (1) of not being a theoretical and loose jumble of rules but being a pragmatic code, (2) of adopting simple, direct and appropriate language with clear definitions of all terms used, and (3) of not forsaking the basic features of cataloguing codes for practical exigencies.

An attempt made in 1931 to change the rule which called for grammatical arrangement of titles was turned down. The post-war period in Germany, whose libraries had been completely devastated by bombing during the war, witnessed reconstruction of libraries and with them their catalogues. Although the fine Union Catalogue of the *Prussian State Library* was devastated, the catalogue for new books, was made on cards, while maintaining the manuscript page catalogues for the older stock. Simplified cataloguing was adopted for less frequently used material. The State and University Library of Hamburg, with a view to providing a workable catalogue as early as possible, followed simplified cataloguing by omitting from the catalogue entry (1) subtitles of books when not essential, (2) the occasion or circumstances leading to the publication, (3) the imprint, except date, (4) pagination, (5) the supplying of forenames in place of initials unless the surname was common or unless a Humburg author was involved, and (6) added entries for editors, translators, etc.

A keen interest in the revision of the *Prussian Instructions* became marked in both zones of Germany, especially on the treatment of the so-called *anonymous works*, which according to the Anglo-American tradition and practice were not really anonymous, but works of corporate authorship. The German practice, which considered all works issued by corporate bodies as anonymous for purposes of entry, when they have no personal author, was not universally acceptable.

Use of (1) corporate entries as well as titles in mechanical order into the new public catalogue of the *Deutsche Staatbibliothek* (the former Prussian State Library), (2) natural word order instead of grammatical, (3) added entries for the so-called anonymous works under names of government departments, societies, institutions, whose names are mentioned in the title pages, are some of the items considered for revision of the Prussian Instructions up to 1956. Indications are there that the *German Cataloguing practice* will fall in line with the I.C.C.P., 1961.

*Anglo-American Code. The American Library Association* and *The British Library Association*, established in 1876 and 1877 respectively, issued independently a set of cataloguing rules in 1878 and 1883. The American version was almost a condensation of Cutter's rules, while the British rules incorporated the features of the *British Museum rules* and *The Bodleian rules*. With a view to establishing greater cooperation and uniformity, the two associations combined together for the purpose of issuing a joint code in 1908, under the title "*Cataloguing Rules, author and title entries, compiled by the Committees of the American Library Association and the Library Association*." L.S. Jast, Henry Guppy, the two eminent British librarians, and *Melvil Dewey* representing the American libraries, played a significant role in producing the joint code in 1908. Tolerance and accommodation pervades this code, as is evidenced by some alternative rules, *e.g.* noblemen, married women, etc., provided.

Time and again, the deficiencies, inconsistencies, and complexities of this joint code have been the subject of discussion among librarians in conferences and in day-to-day work in libraries. The need to replace it by a more satisfactory code was unanimously felt. A period of brisk activity in current criticism and revision of the 1908 code began in 1941, when the American Library Association issued the preliminary second edition of the code in two parts, (1) Entry and heading; and (2) Description. It was circulated widely among cataloguers inviting their views. One outstanding criticism was that of *A.D. Osborn* in his "*Crisis in Cataloguing*."[7] The views expressed by Dr. Osborn were no doubt sweeping generalisations on the cataloguing practice of the past but were quite catching. His target of attack was on the "legalistic" theory. He was convinced that cataloguing is an art and needed only a few basic rules, which are simple and delightful to practise.

In 1949, the *American Library Association* published the final second edition "*American Library Association, A.L.A. Cataloguing Rules for Author and Title Entries*," with the indication that it was "an expansion and revision of the rules of 1908." In his review of the 1949 code J.H. Shera[8] provided a clear analysis of the revision and of the basic principles implied on it. "The 40-some pages on entry in 1908 had blossomed into over 200 in 1949, an increase in bulk of some 500 per cent, while the 15 or more pages of descriptive cataloguing in 1908 were now over 100." "To the cry for greater simplification" he proclaimed "the answer of the profession has been to expand the code from a total of 88 pages in 1908 to a total of 406 pages in 1949."[9]

Observations made on the 1949 edition of the *A.L.A. Cataloguing Rules for Author and Title Entries*, called for serious consideration to be given in any revision to an analysis of the purpose and function of the rules with particular reference to the cataloguing of publications of corporate authors. Mr. Seymor Lubetzky, consultant on Bibliographic and Cataloguing Policy of the *Library of Congress*, was assigned the task of reviewing and analysing the A.L.A. rules in this respect. He carried out a thorough investigation and provided a penetrating analysis in his "*Cataloguing rules and Principles, a critique of the A.L.A. Rules for Entry and a proposed Design for their Revision*" which was published by the Library of Congress in 1953. The first chapter "Is this Rule Necessary" produced a logical "No" to every rule dealt with in it. Many of the rules were shown as unnecessary and unrelated to other rules. Each rule applied to an isolated case rather than the general condition which the case represented. Lack of purpose and unity in the rules was glaring.

All the effort and time given to produce a simple and practical code for over ten years left the problem unsolved. The favourable reaction to Lubetzky's critique and the clear necessity to produce a satisfactory cataloguing code led to the appointment of the Code Revision Committee of the A.L.A. This Committee was aided by several sub-committees. The outcome of their labours is the draft code: Code of Cataloguing Rules: Author and Title Entry, an Unfinished Draft, 1960.

"The editor, the committee, the institutes, the LC discussions, and published articles: all have contributed to the development of **CCR.**

"The editor and the Committee are responsible to the Cataloguing and Classification Section of the Resources and Technical Services Division of the **American Library Association**. The completed version will have to be approved by A.L.A.

"CCR approaches works in terms of their authorship, and the rules are arranged in four main groups relating to

(1) **Personal Authors**, (2) **Corporate Authors**, (3) **Governmental Authors**, and (4) Works of Unknown, Complex, or Changing Authorship."[10]

An evalution of the new code CCR is made by **Paul S. Dunkin** as commentator in his Epilogue to the unfinished draft of CCR. He states that "it is not really a new code. It has a central theme as old as catalog codes themselves : authorship and the title of books."

**The objectives are stated in the code as well as followed all through to the end.**

The new code is not a conglomeration of little rules to deal with special little questions. Rather it is a statement of broad rules resting on basic principles. This does not mean that the new code will not answer special little question....But anyone with any imagination at all will find that the rule answers more questions than a code maker could think of in a life time.

"The new code is the spirit of the law ; it is not the detail of the law. It demands that the catalogers have brains ; it demands that the catalogers have imagination. Cutter was not the first to say that cataloguing is an art, nor was Osborn the last."

It is due to these reasons that the new code is brief and contains only 72 rules, as compared to the *A.L.A. cataloguing Rules*, which are 158 in number, with several sections under each rule.

Epigrams and axioms are brief but imply a good amount of truth and philosophy. Commentaries and explanations are needed to bring out the full implications in such laconic statements. For example' the *Vedic Sutras* have given place to Vedangas, Upanishads, and Bhashyas. In a similar way, the new code will need all the support from commentators and cataloguers to make it fully understood and followed with confidence.

CCR is the work of many hands. First **Seymour Lubetzky**, the editor draws up a rule or block of rules. These are submitted for discussion and revision to the steering committee of **A.L.A's Catalog Code Revision Committee**. The resulting versions are then submitted to the full Committee, some thirty people drawn from all kinds of libraries. The Chairman of the Committee is **Wyllis E Wright**, librarian of Williams College, Williamstown, Massachusetts.

In addition, there have been two institutes on code revision, one at Stanford University in 1958 and the other at McGill University in 1960. Each was a week long, attended by some 200 people (anyone who wished could attend), and devoted to study and discussion of the draft code and a series of working papers on particularly difficult problems.

Perhaps even more important than this formal machinery within A.L.A. was an informal arangement with the **Library of Congress**, the result of John Cronin's kind suggestion. When Mr. Lubetzky submitted a draft to the A.L.A. Committee, he would also submit it to the section heads and specialists in the Descriptive Cataloguing Division ofLC. In a series of weekly meetings they would offer criticisms. The revision benefited not only from these meetings but also from the fact that LC officials were thus kept informed of what was going on.

Finally, **Library Resources and Technical Services** and occasionally other periodicals have published articles and notes on the theoretical and practical implications of the draft.

The two issues of the **Library Journal**, N.Y. v. 86 No. 9. May 1, 1961 and No. 15.

September 1, 1961 contain significant criticisms on the Draft Code and also the defence and reply of **Mr. Seymour Lubetzky**, **Mr. Summer Spalding** and also Professor **Paul S. Dunkin**.

In Great Britain the *Library Association's Cataloguing Rules Sub-Committee* was reconstituted in 1951, with *Mr. Henry A. Sharp* as its Honorary Secretary, with the aim of producing a simplified code to replace the 1949 American definitive second edition. The British sub-committee dealt with all the rules in which the two committees failed to reach agreement in 1908 noting the changes prevailing in the 1949 American edition, and for the most part have tentatively agreed to follow the American rules as they appear in 1949 edition. With a view to promoting international agreement and co-operation, the renewed collaboration of the British committee was sought in the hope of producing a current Anglo-American code. The British Sub- committee "resolved that, with a view to arriving at agreement with the United States of America on a joint code, examination of the A.L.A. Rules, 1949 be continued in the numerical order of the rules...and that throughout this examination the committee should have the production of a simplified code of cataloguing rules as their objectives."[11]

"The most promising development to date is an expression of willingness to go along with American practice in the case of those 1908 rules on which British and American librarians chose to disagree. Another promising sign is the warm welcome accorded to the ideas of Seymour Lubetzky."[12]

While the *American Code Revision Committee* failed to consider the proposed revision of the rules in relation to a printed catalogue, the *British Cataloguing Rules sub-Committee* was well aware of the need for taking printed book catalogues into account in developing a new code. There are indications that the card catalogue is gradually losing its hold on readers, who appear to be favourably reacting towards a printed book catalogue.

The British Sub-Committee examined in detail the draft rules formulated by Mr. Seymour Lubetzky, who took over as editor of New Code—the present Anglo-American cataloguing Rules, 1967. Mr. Lubetzky resigned from the office of editor in 1962, and was succeeded by *Mr. C. Summer Spalding*, of the Library of Congress. The new code based on the Paris principles adopted by the International Conference on cataloguing principles in 1961, is considered international in its scope and achievement. The revised draft of the rules, as recast by Mr.

Spalding has been scrutinised by the British Sub-Committee under the Chairmanship of Mr. N.F. Sharp. The departure from the Paris principles is in the non-adoption of rules 24, 98 and 99 of the North American text, in the British version of the *Anglo-American Cataloguing Rules, 1967.*

Another significant feature of the *A-ACR* is the inclusion of the rules for descriptive cataloguing, and for the cataloguing of non-book materials.

In 1962, a descriptive cataloguing Rules sub-Committee under the chairmanship of Miss Mary Piggot was set up. This sub-committee approved that the '*Rules for descriptive cataloguing in the Library of Congress*, 1949, which was officially adopted by the American Library Association, and the rules for non-book materials separately issued by the Library of Congress and amended in parts II and III of the North American Text of A-ACR, should form the basis for the descriptive cataloguing Rules in the British Text. These rules have been simplified and issued in a form, which can command wide usage in different catalogue systems. in respect of the rules for separately published monographs, serials, maps and music, the British Text differs from the American text. The *Anglo-American Cataloguing Rules*, 1967 is thus a valuable contribution and successful, example of international co-operation in librarianship. Wyllis E. Wright, Chairman, Catalog Code Revision Committe observes in his preface to the North American Text "Although agreement among the three groups has not been completed, it has been close enough so that the present work can reasonably be entitled *Anglo-American Cataloguing Rules*".

The application of a code of cataloguing rules for cataloguing the collection of a library should be preceded by a complete understanding of the nature, content, and structure of the rules. The *Anglo-American Cataloguing Rules*, 1967, "have been drawn up primarily to respond to the needs of general research libraries. This represents a continuation of the orientation that has characterised the rules of the American Library Association since the 1908 edition (*Catalog Rules : Author and Title Entries*)....Within the framework of this research-library orientation, however, an effort has been made to respond as much as possible to the needs of public libraries in which research considerations are not paramount. When the needs of research libraries and those of other libraries are irreconcilable, alternative rules have been provided for the use of the latter"[13] Provision for direct, less complex, and normally used heading has resulted in more practical adoption of the code by all types of libraries. The rules are not only comprehensive enough to cover cataloguing of almost all types of library materials, but are equally flexible to allow the intercalation and merging of the entries of book and non-book material in the same catalogue. The rules are designed to meet the requirements of multiple entry alphabetical catalogues in which all entries for particular persons or corporate bodies are presented under a uniform heading and are connected by reference entries. All possible manner of reader approach and use to the catalogue has been anticipated in prescribing the number and form of entries and references for different library materials. The line of distinction between main and added entries has been maintained under the rules, inspite of multiple entry character, and use of unit cards.

A close observation of the rules of 1908 and 1949 codes with the rules of 1967 code reveals that the latter one is based on a set of principles which have been consistently followed to a good extent, with least prejudice to existing practice. In short a case study approach has been replaced by a system approach in the evolution of a catalogue code. The rules on *choice of entry* enables to determine authorship responsibility. "The rules on *choice of heading*, for main and added entries, are usually adequate and often very useful; the rules on *form of heading* or reference are rarely less than comprehensive and brilliant both in their wording and results."[14]

As any code of cataloguing rules, if it is to sustain and be serviceable, has to be revised in accordance with the changing needs of reading circles and librarianship, it will be an error of judgement to consider that this code is perfect and will for ever remain the tool of cataloguing. Farsightedness demands that a standing agency or committee is set up to watch, the reception given to the new code, the reaction of the users of the catalogue compiled after the code rules, and to draft the revision, amendment, or supersession of the present rules, if warranted. The preparedness to improve upon the current code or to produce a new one is not to discount the merits of *A-ACR*, 1967. A generally accepted view among cataloguers is that the *A- ACR*, 1967 has enunciated "for the first time for many decades an acceptable standard of discipline and technique in cataloguing suitable to all levels – public and special, academic and bibliographic,"[15] Adoption of this code by libraries, as a matter of national policy for cataloguing may well establish national cataloguing policy, resulting in all-round benefits and economy in library organization.

The first edition of the *Anglo-American Cataloguing Rules*, 1967 is considered the best cataloguing code we have and the first we are likely to have for a long time was the considered prognostication of Michael Gorman, who is again one of the two editors of *A-ACR2* 1978. But the second edition of the Anglo-American Cataloguing Rules was brought out in 1978. The first edition of this title was certainly a land mark in the history of modern cataloguing of books, book like materials, and non-book materials in libraries and other collections as well. Eminent professional members in cataloguing and other disciplines involved in the management of library and information services, like Seymour Lubetzsky and C. Summer Spalding were charged with the production of the first edition. The second edition is conjointly prepared by the *American Library Association, The British Library, The Canadian Committee on Cataloguing, The Library Association* and *The Library of Congress*; edited by Michel Gorman and Paul Winkler.

"A-ACR1 (1967) may be seen as the final flowering of the old tradition of author and title book cataloguing ...Nevertheless a new edition was soon needed, partly because residual faults in A-ACR1, and partly because of world-wide developments in cataloguing which rendered much of it out of date. Looking at A-ACR1 in retrospect one can see :

(a) that despite a very large measure of agreement, there were still two texts British and North American ;
(b) that there were several amendments, some tending to bring the two texts into line and some working the other way ;
(c) that the code was still concieved as an author and title code for cataloguing *books*, with emphasis on choice on main entry, the cataloguing of *non-book materials* being treated as a modification of that for books ;
(d) that there were still areas of traditional author and title cataloguing which were unsatisfactory, notably the treatment of corporate authorship."[16]

Every one who has to do with the catalogue code has a right to ask the question, why after an interval of only twelve years a new edition of this code was found necessary and appropriate. The answer for this question is provided in a general way in the preface to the A-ACR second edition, 1978 by the chairman Peter R. Lewis, Joint Steering Committee for Revision of A-ACR. This does not supersede their work but continues it, for inspite of the changes in processes and conditions which it introduces, these are still the *Anglo-American Cataloguing Rules*, having the same principles and underlying objectives as the first edition, and being formerly based on the achievements of those who created the work first published in 1967".

The experiences and observations of the performance of 1967 edition in meeting the needs of a large number and kind of libraries across the world during a period of a decade, had encouraged and influenced the preparation of *A-ACR2*. Considerable growth in libraries and extensions of cataloguing processes, bibliographic services, and national library services throughout the world has been significant and called for a revised edition of *A-ACR1*, overcoming certain lapses, in order that A-ACR could meet the challenges posed by new developments in Cataloguing, Bibliography and Information Services. The critical test of application over a wide range and variety of professional practice throughout the world has been carefully adopted in the preparation and presentation of this new code. Further during this period, mechanisation, automation, the growth of centralised and cooperative services and networks, the developments and unification of services in the national libraries, specially in Canada and United Kingdom have their impact on the preparation and formulation of the text of this new edition. In view of the emerging pattern of the new media of communication provided for in highly developed libraries the processing and cataloguing in the traditional manner which obtained since 1908 has to be revised and integrated in order that the new code is able to come upto the expectation for the subsequent cataloguing practices at the turn of the 20th century and also in the beginning of the decades of 21st century.

The objectives and the policies of the new code, stated in the memorandum of agreement arrived at a tripartite meeting consisting of one representative each from the three "Anglo- American" countries, USA, Canada, Britain—representing both the library association and the national library, held in March 1974, are :

(1) to reconcile in a single text the North American and the British texts of 1967 ;
(2) to incorporate in the single text all amendments and changes already agreed and implemented under the previous mechanism ;
(3) to consider for inclusion in A-ACR all proposals for amend-

ment urgently under discussion among the participating organizations, the American Library Association, the Library Association (London), the Canadian Library Association, and the British Library and also any proposals of national committees of other countries in which A-ACR is in use, and

(4) to provide for international interest in A-ACR by facilitating its use in countries other than the United States, Canada, and the United Kingdom, which was held as a condition for the financial grants to be met by the *Council on Library Resources*.

The *Paris Principles* which was the origin and the guiding factor in the production of 1967 Code have been confirmed to and rendered it easily possible for the introduction of new proposals by the substitution of uniform titles for form sub- headings in relation to section 9.5. (Entry of Constitutions, Laws, and Treaties, and certain other works having similar characteristics).

The subsequent additions and deletions to be found in the present Code, as changes from the *A-ACR1* are : some of the contents of the *A-ACR1* are deleted. These relate to provision of options, also called alternative. This is because, one of the objectives of the second edition is to evolve a uniform procedure and display in principal cataloguing.

The absence of the details deleted, which were a feature of the A-ACR1 does not necessarily mean that certain libraries adopting them should give them up, because they are not found in *A-ACR2*.

The additions of details provided for in A-ACR2 chiefly relate to the newer categories of library materials, and are expected to guide the work of cataloguers, when processing such materials. Adoption of *ISBD* (G) (International Standard Bibliographic Description) (General) standards all through the chapters on descriptive cataloguing (Part 1) would meet the international requirements, and the claims of non-book materials have been met by generalising the rules for descriptive cataloguing, and providing supplementary rules for the various media, among which books come first among equals."[17] Another striking change is that the descriptive aspect of cataloguing process is conferred a privileged place preceding the author title cataloguing rules in Part II. The justification or the advantage in altering the sequence of these parts, whatever may be put forward, seems not very convincing for the reason that the author heading is the essential and most important access point in a catalogue, specially from the users' point of view. There seems to be a good amount of logic in giving the author heading as the most important aspect of cataloguing, because its faulty choice would nullify completely the labour and time expended on other groups of entries in descriptive cataloguing which by itself is mere physical exposition than intellectual effort which is required in a much greater degree in choosing the author heading.

In *A-ACR2* the treatment of description, corporate headings, uniform titles, and fullness of names are provided with a new set of directions which is different from those found in *A- ACR1*. No serials entry, limitations on main entry for corporate bodies resulting in more serials to be entered under their titles as main entries, replacement of form headings for certain legal and religious texts by *uniform titles* are significant alterations provided for in A-ACR2. But all the rules in this chapter are 'optional', thereby allowing the continued adoption of those entries according to A-ACR1 by cerain libraries, in their catalogues. These changes are expected to provide, with the increased flexibility of modern systems, for processing bibliographic data and of catalogue formats. The inertia of the retrospective file is much less than it has been in the past. There has been in general satisfaction in big research libraries with the introduction of these new guide lines. Students of the history of Catalogue Codes would be advised to refer to the bibliographic sources contained in the preface to A- ACR2. page X! of the preface.

Taking the publication of the AA Code, 1908 as the starting point in modern cataloguing, one could state that in the history of Catalogue Codes, after 70 years of the AA Code 1908, A-ACR2 has been brought out in December, 1978.

The time and effort involved in the preparation of all the three codes, by committees and individuals mentioned in the preface or introduction to each code reveals that it was voluntary, spontaneous, and activated by a sense of devoted service to scholars and to the ordinary reading community. An objective appraisal of A-ACR2 would disclose that it has satisfactory guidelines and specific rules for Cataloguing special items like, radio broadcasts, and scripts, television and other recordings of telecommunication and electronic system. In all fairness to the participating four professional bodies on both sides of the Atlantic, the far-sighted and wise decision to produce a single common code after the required reconciliation is of immense benefit to everyone concerned— the user, the publisher and the libraries. It is a remarkable achievement in the field of *library co-operarion* and perceptible gains out of a single text would save time, labour and cost. "A single code endorsed by the national libraries of Britain, Canada, Australia, and the United States is a great achievement".[18] There has been more or less an unfounded and vague fear that the on-line information of the computer and data systems would replace the traditonal catalogue systems and may even end in its requiem. Experience gained so far indicates that these newer systems, computerised and automated, would be supplementing or be supplemented by general traditional catalogues of libraries. At least in India and similar areas, in the East the traditional system of cataloguing library materials has to be continued for a long, long period of imprecise limit. This is because of the social, economic, and linguistic factors peculiar to these countries and the diversity of the approach to information by different communities with varying levels of literary skills, and a load stone of totally illiterate groups of people in rural areas.

The decision and action taken by the *British Library* in adopting the A-ACR2 fully, as stated by Richard Coward, Director General, Bibliographic Services Division of the British Library is cited in brief as an example for the benefit of other national and smaller libraries, which may opt for the adoption of A-ACR2 in cataloguing their library materials. The conclusion of his views, however, provides a note of caution for protagonists of mechanical and electronic devices in place of the traditional catalogue, to perform its functions in serving the library users.

Catalogue Codes are not produced once and for all. As books undergo change in their form and style of authorship and titles, catalogue codes need changes in their rules, according to the changing views and demands of users of catalogues. The changes may be very slight or total in their effect. This has been observed during the last 80 years from 1908 to 1988. This period covers the publication of A.L.A. Catalogue Code: Author and Title Entries through the revisions of 1949, 1967, 1978, and 1988 A- ACR2 revision. Five professional bodies, one national library—the Library of Congress, and four associations American, British, Canadian and Australian agreed to institute a Joint Steering Committee as set down in the 1977 agreement. The terms of reference of this Joint Steering committee are :

(1) to advise the editor Michael Gorman of the abridged edition (the Concise A-ACR2, 1981) prior to its publication;
(2) to assess the use and sale of A-ACR2 and assist the users of A-ACR2 on its application and adoption, and grant permission

to translate it into other languages;

(3) to keep under review the need for amendment and revision of the code ;

(4) to act as a form of discussion of fresh proposals on rule interpretation in order to ensure consistency of use and to promulgate agreed rules and interpretations;

(5) to define and approve grants for work on A-ACR2 from the Library Resources Council ; and

(6) maintain liaison with the IFLA and the UBC office, in order to facilitate the interests of A-ACR2 in any programme of international standardization in the cataloguing field.

The use of A-ACR2 by cataloguers revealed inconsistencies in different libraries and ambiguous wording. Such anomalies were eliminated. The committee issued three sets of revisions, in 1982, 1983, and 1985 in order to inform the users of the changes. All these revisions were codified in the 1985 edition, and care was taken to keep the 1978 edition as the guiding and determining source warranting changes. Additional revisions approved by the Joint Steering Committee for revision of A-ACR2 during 1986 seeks to rationalise the rules further in accordance with the principles of A-ACR2, making them easier to apply and remedying deficiencies brought to notice by users.

Areas of the code where the rules have been revised or reorganized relate to the treatment of computer files, cartographic materials, uniform titles for music, and materials for the visually impaired. More specific rule changes cover the selection of source for series titles, choice of main entry for revised texts, provision for subordinate entry for those subordinate corporate names that do not convey the idea of a corporate body; deletion of articles from uniform titles and headings for corporate bodies.

With all the care taken, it would be seen that CIP of the British and American forms differ and both forms and levels of CIP of A-ACR2, 1988 revision are printed on the verso of the title page of the code; edited by Michael Gorman and Paul C. Winkler published compositely by Canadian, British, and American Library Associations in 1988, xxv, 677 pages, $ 13.75. (paper back)

The code is in two parts: I. Description, and II. Headings Uniform Titles, and References. Part I contains rules 1-13, and part II. rules 21 to 26, and Appendices: A. Capitalization, B. Abbreviations, C. Numerals, and D. Glossary. The structure of the rules continue to be based on 1978 edition.

The effect of the application of these rules of the revised code by libraries both big and small should be observed with keen interest in overcoming anomalies and increasing consistency of application.

Seven agreed Rule Changes affecting Headings from 1988, in order that the uniformity in their adoption is possible in libraries following the A-ACR2 1988 revision are given in brief abstract. These may be seen with examples in the text of the A-ACR2 1988 revision.

## CHANGES IN TITLE PROPER

**21.2A.** [Delete and substitute:]

**21.2A Definition**

In general, consider a title proper to have changed if any word other than an article, preposition, or conjunction is added, deleted, or changed, or if the order of the first five words (the first six words if the title begins with an initial article) is changed.

However, in general do not consider a title proper to have changed when :

(1) the change is in the representation of a word or words (e.g., abbreviated word or symbol vs. spelled out form, singular vs. plural form, one spelling vs. another);

(2) the addition, deletion, or change comes after the first five words (the first six words if the title begins with an initial article) and does not change the meaning of the title or indicate a different subject matter;

(3) the only change is the addition or deletion of the name of the issuing body (and any grammatical connection) at the end of the title;

(4) the only change is in the addition, deletion, or change of punctuation.

In case of doubt, consider the title proper to have changed.

As appropriate, record in the note area (see 1.7B4) those changes not considered to constitute a change in the title proper. Make an added entry (see 21.30J) if necessary for access.

**21.30J.** [Delete second paragraph and substitute :]

If considered desirable for access, make an added entry for any version of title that (see 21.2A) does not constitute a change in the title proper.

**ENTRY FOR PERSONS USING MORE THAN ONE NAME**

**22.1A.** [Delete and replace with : ]

**21.1A.** In general, choose , as the basis of the heading for a person, the name by which he or she is commonly known. This may be the person's real name, pseudonym, title of nobility, nickname, initials, or other appellation. Treat a roman numeral associated with a given name (as, for example, in the case of some popes, royalty, and ecclesistics) as part of the name. For the treatment of certain authors using several pseudonyms, or a real name and one or more pseudonyms, see 22.2B. For the form of name used in headings, see 22.4-22.17.

[**22.1B.-22.1D.** as printed.]

**22.2.** [Delete and replace with :]
**22.2. CHOICE AMONG DIFFERENT NAMES**
**22.2A. Predominant name**

If a person (other than one using a pseudonym or pseudonyms, see 22.2B) is known by more than one name, choose the name by which that person is clearly most commonly known, if there is one. Otherwise, choose one name or form of name according to the following order of preference :

(1) the name that appears most frequently in the person's works;
(2) the name that appears most frequently in reference sources;
(3) the latest name.

**22.2B. Pseudonyms**

**22.2B1. One pseudonym.** If all the works of a person appear under one pseudonym, choose the pseudonym. If the real name is known; make a refernce from the real name to the pseudonym.
For the treatment of a pseudonym used jointly by two or more persons, see. 21.6D.

**22.2B2. Separate bibliographic identities.** If a person has two or more bibliographic identities, as indicated by the fact that works of one type appear under one pseudonym and works of other types appear under other pseudonyms or the person's real name, choose, as the basis for the heading for each group of works, the name with which it is identified. Make references to connect the names (see 26.2C and 26.2D). In case of doubt, do not consider a person to have separate bibliographic identities.

**22.2B3. Contemporary authors.** If a contemporary author uses more than one pseudonym or his or her real name and one or more pseudonyms, use, as the basis for the heading for each work, the name appearing in it. Make references to connect the names (see 26.2C and 26.2D).

If, in the works of contemporary authors, different names appear in different editions of the same work or two or more names appear in one edition, choose for all editions the name most often used in editions of the work. If that cannot be determined readily, choose the name appearing in the latest available edition of the work. Make name-title references from the other name or names (see 26.2B1)

**22.2B4.** If person using more than one pseudonym (or his or her real name and one or more pseudonyms) neither has established separate bibliographic identities (see B2, above) nor is a contemporary author (see B3, above), choose, as the basis for the heading, the name by which that person has come to be identified in later editions of his or her works, in critical works, or in other reference sources (in that order of preference). Make references from other names.

Disregard reference sources that always enter persons under their real names.

**22.2C. Change of name**

If a person (other than one using a pseudonym or pseudonyms) has changed his or her name.....[text and examples as printed in 22.2B].

## ENTRY UNDER PHRASE

**22.11A** [Delete and substitute:]

**22.11A.** Enter in direct order a name that consists of a phrase or appellation that does not contain a forename.

Also enter in direct order those phrases that consist of a forename or forenames preceded by words other than a term of address or a title of position or office. Make a reference from the forename(s) followed by the initial word(s).

**22.11B.** [Delete and substitute :]
**22.11B.** If a phrase consist of a forename preceded by a term of address (e.g., a word indicating relationship) or title of position or office (e.g., a professional appellation), enter under the forename. Treat other word(s) as additions to the forename(s). Refer from the name in direct order.

## ADDITIONS TO PERSONAL NAMES : FULLER FORMS

**22.16.** [Delete]
**22.17.** [Renumber as **22.16**]
**22.18.** [Renumber as **22.17**]
[Add new rule:]
**22.18. FULLER FORMS**

If a fuller form of a person's name is known and if the heading in accordance with the preceding rules does not include all of that fuller form, add the fuller form to distinguish between headings that are otherwise identical. Add all of the fuller form of the inverted part of the heading and/or the fuller form of the entry element, as appropriate. Enclose the addition in parentheses.

The most common instances of such additions occur when the heading as prescribed by the preceding rules contains initials and the spelled out form is known. Less common instances occur when known forenames, surnames, or initials are not part of the heading as prescribed.

Refer from the fuller form of the name when appropriate.

*Optionally*, make the additions specified above even if they are not needed to distinguish between headings. However, when following this option, do not add: unused forenames to headings that contain forenames; initials of names that are not part of the heading; unused parts of surnames to headings that contain surnames.

**22.19A.** [Delete and substitute:]
**22.19A Names in which the entry element is a given name, etc.**

If neither fuller form of the name nor dates are available to distinguish between identical headings of which the entry element is a given name, etc. devise a suitable brief term and add it in parentheses.

**22.19B.** [Delete text of Ist paragraph and substitute:]
If neither fuller form of the name nor dates are available to distinguish between indentical headings of which the entry element is a surname, add a term of address, title of position or office, initials of an academic degree, initials denoting membership in an organization, etc., that appear with the name in works by the person or in reference sources.

**22.20.** [Delete text and substitute:]
If no suitable addition (dates, fuller form of the name, or distinguishing term) is available, use the same heading for all persons with the same name.

## ADDITION OF LARGER PLACES TO PLACE NAMES

**23.1.** [Delete and substitute:]
The names of geographic entities (referred to throughout this chapter as "places") are used to distinguished between corporate bodies with the same name (see 24.4C); as additions to other corporate names (e.g., conference names (see 24.7B4)); and commonly, as the names of governments (see 24.3E) and of communities that are not governments.

**23.4B. General rule**
Add to the name of a place the name of a larger place as instructed in 23.4C-23.4F. For additional instructions on distinguishing between place names used as the headings for governments, sec. 24.6. For instructions on abbreviating place names used as additions, see Appendix B.14.

**23.4C Places in Australia, Canada, Malaysia, United States, U.S.S.R., or Yugoslavia**

**23.4C1. States, etc.** Do not make any addition to the name of a state, province, territory, etc., of Australia, Canada, Malaysia, the United States, the U.S.S.R., or Yugoslavia.

**23.4C2. Other places.** If a place is in a state, province, territory, etc., of one of the countries listed above, add the name of the state, etc., in which it is located.

**23.4D. Places in the British Isles**

**23.4D1**. Do not make any addition to the names of the following parts of the British Isles: England, the Republic of Ireland, Northern Ireland, Scotland, Wales, the Isle of Man, the Channel Islands.

**23.4D2** If place is located in England, the Republic of Ireland, Northern Ireland, Scotland, Wales, the Isle of Man or the Channel Island, add *England, Ireland, Northern Ireland, Scotland, Wales, Isle of Man, or Channel Island*, as appropriate.

**23.4E. Other places**

Add to the names of places not covered by 23.4C-23.4D the name of the country in which the place is located.

**23.4F. Further additions**

**23.4F1. Distinguishing between otherwise identical place names**. If the addition of a larger place as instructed in 23.4C-23.4E is insufficient to distinguish between two or more places with the same name, include a word or phrase commonly used to distinguish them.

If there is no such word or phrase, give the name of an appropriate smaller place before that of the larger place.

**23.4F2 Identifying places.** If considered necessary to identify the place as in the case of community within a city give the name of an appropriate smaller place before that of the larger place specified as an addition by the preceding rules.

## ADDITIONS TO CORPORATE NAMES

**24.4C1** [First sentence as printed,. Delete second sentence and option, and substitute:]
Add such a word or phrase to any other name if the addition assists in the understanding of the nature or purpose of the body.

**24.4C3.** [Delete second paragraph and example]
Footnote 11 to be deleted.

With every transformation in the communication methods, systems and techniques, it has been found necessary to suitably invent a new kind of tool for the organizer of information and its user, both for its outer format and its internal structure and display of the access points. This consequently created a demand for a suitable code of cataloguing, which could never reach the ultimate stage, as it has to deal with newer library materials, and also to satisfy the newer variety of approach and use arising from time to time. Whatever may be these forms and techniques, one thing remains a permanent feature in cataloguing discipline – that is the facility and satisfaction of the user, which should remain the first and foremost object ; and cataloguing by using any given code is but a means to this end.

*Vatican Rules.* Papal collections at the Vatican which are among the richest in Europe, had a catalogue which was more of an inventory type. In 1927 the *Vatican Library* was offered aid by the *Camlgie Endowment for International Peace* to compile a new catalogue of its collections. The American influence prevailed in this programme in which eminent American Librarians like William Warner Bishop, J.C.M. Hansen and a few others played a prominent part.

As the dictionary form of catalogue was decided upon, Cutter's Rules provided a basis, for this was the only code to contain rules on the choice of subject headings for a dictionary catalogue. Existing Italian Rules for the compilation of the Alphabetical Catalogue, 1911, and the *A.L.A. Rules* were taken together in evolving the Vatican rules, which was translated from the second Italian edition by W.E. Wright and published by the A.L.A. in 1948. It is described, by its editor, as "the most complete statement of American practice." It is one of the few modern codes to cover the whole field of cataloguing author entry, the description of the book, subject entry, and filing.[19]

*Rangnathan's Classified Catalogue Code.* The *Classified Catalogue Code* 1934 of *Dr. S.R. Rangnathan*, "was shaping unexpressed, below the conscious level, except while teaching cataloguing," till 1933, the year of publication of the *Colon Classification*. The CCC, in its third edition in 1951, aims at becoming a universal catalogue code. It takes into account '(1) the language of the library, and (2) the scale of language in which the language of the library comes first and the others come in the descending sequence of favouredness.' The author expects to issue an edition free from faulty wording of the rules. Unfortunately, the authors' death occurred before this was done.

### Conclusion

For the first time since 1908, basic re-thinking of cataloguing rules is going on in all parts of the world. "Be it noted that the whole history of cataloguing consists of one generation redoing the work of another. Our own day is no exception. The difficulties stem largely from the conventions that are adopted; so perhaps firmer ground can be reached by the adoption of practical and natural entries in place of conventional forms."[20]

All alive to the present cataloguing situation admit the prevalence of a general sense of discontent, frustration and purposelessness in cataloguing practice and procedures. It has become more significant since 1941. There have been seasoned and vigorous attacks, sometimes based on personal judgement and at some other times on objective analysis, on cataloguing and the codes. The criticism swung round (1) the basic principles (2) simplification of the rules (3) readers' use of the catalogue (4) subject approach, (5) cost of cataloguing and re-cataloguing (6) the vocabulary, and (7) unity leading to international or even universal acceptance. It is no doubt ideal to achieve a Bible of Cataloguing which will transcend national and international barriers and thereby render it possible to locate and use the book resoures of the world's libraries from any locality with considerable ease and quickness. One leading librarian went as far as to suggest piously that books should be published with title pages conforming to such specifications as the overworked cataloguers wish in order to mechanize their work of entry and heading. It seems to us that the volume of criticism on the present cataloguing procedures and catalogues has certainly shaken up the lethargic lingering traditions but has not led to the production, at least up till now, of a fresh and original design for a code and a catalogue. The old order changeth yielding place to new. But the new order is really the old order, with a new face. That is where the cataloguing situation remains.

REFERENCES

1. **S.R. Rangnathan. Heading and Canons**, Madras, S. Viswanathan 1955 p. 255.
2. **Michael Gorman. A-A** 1967 : **the new cataloguing rules**. Library Association

Record, v. 70. No. 2, February 1968, p. 27.

3. **Seymour Lubetzky. Cataloguing Rules and Principles**. Washington, Library of Congress, 1953, pp. 38-39
4. **S.R. Rangnathan. Heading and Canons**. Madras, S. Viswanathan 1955. p. 14.
5. **Ruth French Strout**, "Development of the Catalog, and Cataloging Codes" **Library Quarterly**, XXVI, 4. Oct. 1956, p. 272.
6. **S.R Rangnathan. Heading and Canons**. Madras, S. Viswananthan 1955. p. 15.
7. **A.D. Osborn**. "The Crisis in Cataloging." **Library Quarterly**, XI, 1941, p. 393-411
8. **J.H. Shera**. "Review of the 1949 Cade", **Library Quarterly**, XX, 1950. p. 147-50.
9. **Paul S. Dunkin**. "Criticism of Current Cataloging Practice," **Library Quarterly**, XXVI, 4 Oct., 1956 p. 288.
10. **Paul S. Dunkin**. "The Draft Code : An Outline," **Wilson Library Bulletin, V. 36, 6 February, 1962. p. 446.**
11. **Mary Piggott ed. Cataloguing Principles and Practice : an Inquiry**. Library Association. 1954. p. 16.
12. **A.D. Osborn. "Cataloguing and Cataloguing Codes in other countries today." Library Quarterly**, XXVI 4 October, 1956, p. 281.
13. **C. Sumner Spalding. Introduction to Anglo-American Cataloguing Rules**, 1967. p.1.
14. **Michael Gorman**. A-A 1967: The new cataloguing rules. Library Association Record. v. 70 No. 2, February 1968, p. 31.
15. **J.C. Downing**. A national cataloguing policy. Library Association Record, v. 71 No. 3,. March, 1969. p. 61.
16. **A.G. Curven**. Review of AACR; 2nd ed. 1978. in Jl. of Librarianship, v. 12, 1. jan. 1980 pp: 57-58.
17. **Ibid.**
18. **Ibid.**
19. **Mary Piggot. ed. Cataloguing Principle and Practice : an Inquiry** Library Association, 1954. p. 22.
20. **A.D. Osborn**. "Cataloging and Catalog codes in other countries today," **Library, quarterly XXVI, 4 Ocotber 1956. p. 277.**

# 4

# PRINCIPLES OF PLANNING AND PROVISION OF THE LIBRARY CATALOGUE

A study of the early *history of catalogues* and *cataloguing practice* reveals that the making of a library catalogue was considered a routine. It was felt that any one could compile a library catalogue and that any set of rules determined by individual cataloguers or libraries was sound enough for adoption. This was true of catalogues, at least till 1900. All that was required of the early cataloguer was the ability to transcribe correctly and mechanically the information contained on the title page of a book on to the catalogue entry. The cataloguer was seldom conscious of the principles underlying particular rules, nor did the codes express them explicitly. The result was the emergence of catalogues which lacked logic, unity, and simplicity of purpose and use.

The principles governing the various kinds of catalogue entries were unfortunately not adhered to, due to lack of facilities, specially in Asia up to 1930, in imparting instruction in this branch of library science to persons entrusted with cataloguing. As the books were acquired, they were entered in a list, which was usually a manuscript register, in the order in which they came into the library. It is a simple fact that not all books belong to one specific field of knowledge. Books are varied in their content, scope usefulness, authorship and imprint. Some of them are very closely related to one another and some others stand far apart. If a book on "History of India; and the other on "Electromagnetism" were received in the library together, the incompetent cataloguer entered them one after another in the catalogue. In this way the catalogue contained entries of books quite unrelated to one another. The larger and more varied the contents of a library, the greater is the need to provide a good catalogue, which is truly a '*finding list*'. The finding list must be capable of indicating a specific book at its location, the relative location among other books of its class, the author and collaborators and their works, etc.

After some experience, the early cataloguer realised that instead of entering the books in the order of their receipt, it was worthwhile to enter them in his catalogue in groups of subjects, close to one another. The catalogue assumed the form of a list of subjects in which the order of subjects in each group was based on the alphabet.

It can be better demonstrated by an example. Suppose there were 100 books in library on various subjects. The cataloguer sat in judgement over each book to decide on its subject. If the 100 volumes in question were to deal with 100 different specific subjects, there would be then 100 different groups under which books would be entered. The order of these groups of subjects would be purely alphabetical as in the following manner.

e.g. Anatomy, Human.
Bengal—History.
Charities.
Dynamics.
English Drama.
Farming.
Gold-mining.
Happiness.
India—Population.

This order of subjects no doubt helped in finding out what book or books were in the collection on a desired subject, while it did not bring together subjects related to one another. Such a catalogue is called the *Alphabetical Subject Catalogue*.

The next stage was to make a catalogue by grouping subjects related to one another in a logical manner. The logic involved was the logic of a system of *book classification* adopted for arranging the books on the shelves of the library. If the library adopted *Dewey's Decimal Classification* for the purpose of arranging the books, the catalogue for these books followed the same order in arranging entries for the books in it. The class number of the subject of a book determined the place of its entry in the catalogue. If there were 100 books on the shelves, arranged according to the progressive order of a system of classification, there were 100 entries for these books adopting an identical order in the catalogue. This kind of catalogue is called a classified catalogue. Entries for books in such a catalogue will be in the following manner, if *Dewey's Decimal Classification* is adopted.

000 GENERALIA

Beeton, Science, art, and literature; a dictionary of universal information.

100 PHILOSOPHY

Durant, Will. Mansions of Philosophy

200 RELIGION

James, William. Varieties of religious experience.

300 SOCIOLOGY

Barnes, H.E. An introduction to the history of sociology.

400 PHILOLOGY

Taraporewala, I.J.S. Elements of the science of language.

500 SCIENCE

Thompson, J.A. Outline of science.

600 APPLIED SCIENCE

Hiscox, G.D. ed. Henley's 20th century book of formulas, processes and trade secrets.

700 FINE ARTS

Read, Herbert. The meaning of art.

800 LITERATURE

Redman, B.R. What can literature do for me.

900 HISTORY

Child, Gordon. Dawn of history.

This order of grouping the subjects is expected to bring together books on the same subject as close as possible, within the limits of the system adopted. The order of entries in such a catalogue will be governed by the class number fixed for books. The cataloguer follows strictly, for good or bad, the order of the classification system. If the system of classification is sound and satisfactory, its adoption for compiling a catalogue produces an equally sound and satisfactory one. The cataloguer is, therefore, required to judge a system of classification, to find out if it is suitable for adoption. Unfortunately, the early cataloguers were all laymen, with little knowledge of the functions of a library catalogue. Any method of arrangement of the books adopted in a library was considered fit enough in making a library catalogue, with the result that the so-called 'systematic' catalogue also imbided all the undesirable features inherent in the system of classification. Ultimately this catalogue did not find much favour with the general public using the library. It was a tedious process to locate a desired book and if the *'classified' catalogue* was not provided with an accurate alphabetical index of authors, subjects and titles, a lay reader would not obtain much help from it.

To obviate these difficulties, the succeeding generation of cataloguers, early in the 20th century, changed the form and fullness of the catalogue. This kind of catalogue was to be a true index to the library collection. It assumed largely the form of a dictionary and aimed to function with all the ease and facility of a dictionary. Therefore, the name given to it, was the *Dictionary catalogue*. The dominant idea was and is to help the reader in getting his book or information from the library, by placing at his disposal, a simple, quick and dependable catalogue. It is not as easy to produce one such catalogue, as it is easy to aim at it.

"Good Cataloguing is part of the very essence of the librarian's job."[1] "Some kind of catalogue will do" is a dead slogan in the wrong direction, for it is only an apology for it. Good catalogues in libraries are rare, because of the paucity of efficient cataloguers. Therefore, if a library intends to provide a good catalogue of its contents to its readers for their use, the first and right step is to appoint a well qualified and efficient cataloguer, to take charge of the planning and provision of the catalogue.

To a layman, the work of a cataloguer is apt to appear simple and lengthy, and established codes of cataloguing a device of librarians to obscure the obvious.

Another important step in the planning of a library catalogue is the decision to follow a standard catalogue code. The cataloguer should be thoroughly familiar with the various rules in the code and apply them appropriately, in the case of each book that is catalogued. Unless such a code of catalogue rules is adopted in compiling the catalogue, its helpfulness to readers is doubtful. A catalogue not governed by a code will lack consistency, uniformity and simplicity, in style and fullness of its headings and entries, which are basic laws of cataloguing. The purpose of these rules is not to achieve mechanical uniformity but to assist the reader to find his way amongst thousands of entries, to the book wanted, as easily and quickly as possible. In order to attain this end there must be the "rules of the road."

A reader not finding a book in the catalogue, even though it is in the holdings of the library, will condemn the catalogue as undependable and sheer waste. So the rules of the catalogue should be comprehensive, yet simple and entirely based on commonsense. Such a code alone will result in the compilation of an efficient and useful catalogue. In other words, "cataloguing is organised commonsense, based on experience and applied to the description of printed matter."

"Like Chemistry, it is essentially a laboratory art. It cannot be learned by memorizing a code. It must be applied; one becomes a cataloguer by cataloguing. Every art is not merely a practice. It is a valuable discipline. Of no art is it truer than that of cataloguing. It is a discipline in accuracy. Without accuracy, it becomes an offence. It is a discipline in Consistency and a discipline in co-operation. People who cannot acquire and practise these rules of discipline can never be good at cataloguing." This view of *L.S. Jast*, is unchallengeable and should be faithfully followed.

The importance of the catalogue in a library is uniformly recognised. A good catalogue is an indispensable necessity to the functioning of a good library. If the starry Heavens reveal the glory of God, the catalogue reveals the glory of a library. If the catalogue is to play such an important role in the working of a library, careful planning, with vision and realism, is essential. There is a growing demand for the communication of research information, by the libraries, to those engaged in scientific investigation and research. None could overlook this important aspect of library service through its catalogues but it is doubtful, if the traditional card catalogue with its standard of description of titles, its broad subject headings, and limited number of entries of books, can fulfil this expectation of scientists and research workers by achieving the necessary bibliographic control. Ways and means should be thought out to render this library catalogue serviceable to both the general reader and the specialist.

## Reader Group

The first principle can be enunciated in a simple statement "Suit your catalogue to your immediate public."[2] The principle visualises that the catalogue is for the public for their use. It is not to be a mere symbol in the set up of a library. It should be a reality. If your library serves the children in the schools, the entries and headings in the catalogue of that library should confirm to the style and fullness suited to children, for whom it is intended. If for adults, it must be different in style, fullness, and terminology. Therefore, the catalogue of different classes of libraries, will vary in style, fullness of entries, but not in respect of the fundamental principles, *Accuracy, Consistency* and *Uniformity*, which are common to the catalogues of all libraries.

### Code of Cataloguing Rules

The second principle can be laid down in equally simple terms, "Build your catalogue on sound structure." The sound structure of a catalogue is obtained by making its various entries by following a *code of cataloguing rules,* tested by use and time. *Cutter's Rules for a dictionary catalogue* (1904) and *A.L.A. Cataloguing rules, author and title entries* (1908) have served the cataloguers in a helpful manner since their publication. The later code and its revisions up to 1978, more or less of international recognition and adoption, could profitably be studied and used, to build the catalogue on sound lines. But as its field is limited to the making of author and title entries only, adoption of rules for making subject entries, such as those given by Cutter in his Rules for a Dictionary Catalogue is necessary.

The various entries and headings in a catalogue are like the tested bricks and corner stones in the foundation of a building. If the bricks and corner stones that go to make the foundation of a building do not confirm to specification, the strength of the superstructure is not ensured. Similarly, every heading and entry in a catalogue should definitely follow a rule or rules in the code in order to produce a catalogue, which will be sound and satisfactory to the user.

### Up-to-date Record

The third principle is "Keep the catalogue up-to-date." This principle takes into cognizance the fact that a library's collection and its catalogue should grow together. The catalogue cannot afford to lie behind, for its function demands that it keeps pace with the growth of the collection. As long as knowledge advances and gets transformed into books, which libraries acquire for public use, it is incumbent that the catalogue of such collections should contain entries for all new books added. Otherwise readers will not obtain the information on books added to the library's stock from time to time. A wise cataloguer will, therefore, take care to provide entries for new additions of books with least delay in the catalogue. A book made ready for circulation implies that the corresponding entries for it have been made and filed in the library's catalogue in appropriate places. Some people, including scholars, professors and trustees of library boards, ask "When will the catalogue be completed:" We can as well tell them that a library's catalogues will never attain completion and finiteness. At best it can be kept up-to-date.

### Guidance in Its Use

The fourth principle is "Make the catalogue effectively usable." It is important that a catalogue, which is compiled at enormous cost, time, and labour, should be in a perfectly usable condition. The readers should be attracted to the catalogue which should tell them, "Here I am at your service to save your time in locating the desired information or book." The catalogue should contain in its front, instructions and guidance in its use. Otherwise, the best catalogues are likely to remain unused. Thousands of entries in it (on cards) will bewilder an unfamiliar person till he learns how to handle it. The perfect mechanism of an aeroplane, is confusing and complex to an air passenger while it looks simple to the pilot because he has learnt to apply his hands to it. Likewise every reader in a library should learn to use the catalogue. But the responsibility of making readers learn the art of using the catalogue rests with the cataloguer. Therefore, every library catalogue should be freely display simple, short but effective guidance to the readers. Then alone the catalogue becomes usable.

### Check Abnormal Growth

The fifth principle is "Keep the catalogue under control". The catalogue has an inherent tendency to grow at an alarming rate. For one book added to a library's collection, three to five entries (cards) for it are made and filed in the catalogue. If one is to five is the proportional rate of growth between the book and its catalogue entries, should not the cataloguer keep a watch over the growth of the catalogue? If he does not excercise his control over the catalogue entries, unwanted entries find their way into the catalogue and begin to well its size, to the detriment of wanted entries. They become bad neighbours. The cost of maintenance of the catalogue slowly increases. The usefulness and effectiveness of the catalogue gradually declines. In order to keep the catalogue from undesirable growth, necessary precautions and checks should be taken at the right time. When the various entries for a book are decided upon, careful scrutiny and vigilance over their need is called for. Every entry goes to increase the bulk, cost, and complexity of the catalogue. Question its propriety at the time making it. Is it essential to make the entry? If it is made, will it find ample favour with the public ? If it is not made, will it leave a serious gap? Such general tests are necessary to be carried over the making and provision of each catalogue entry. If such care and precaution are taken, unwanted entries get eliminated, thereby increasing the effectiveness of the catalogue.

### Reader Use

The sixth principle is "know the Reader's approach to books." This principle will demand of the cataloguers and more particularly from those engaged in the production of the cataloguing systems, codes, classification tables, lists of subject headings, appreciable knowledge and understanding of the way in which the users of the catalogue approach and search out their problems.

"If a catalogue is not used, or infrequently used, the reason may be that its general structure is unintelligible or that in forming the traces for particular books insufficient attention has been paid to the mental habits or limitations of the public to be served. We would of course train the public to familiarity with our frames of reference and our habits of designating characteristics, but this is only possibe within fairly narrow limits.

"One of the tasks of a theory of cataloguing will then be to discover by observation and experiment how our catalogues could be adopted to the peculiarities of our readers. This is not an undertaking that can be completed once and for all. People change and catalogues will have to change accordingly. Not the least of our obstacles will be the fact that many readers have only a vague idea of what they are in search of, and no conception of any frame of reference of any kind."[3]

Unless the cataloguer knows the various approaches to books by the public, he cannot provide for them. There are simple books and complex books. Usually a book may be asked for by mentioning the name of its writer, or its title or its subject. But books are not so simple as to be limited to these three characteristics, though they are common to a large number of books. Certain books have no specific subject through which they can be approached, *e.g.* Transley : *Brief facts.* Certain books fall into the form classes, have poetry, drama, essays, oratory, epistles and fiction in which the subject matter is of least attraction. *It is the manner or the form with which the reader is concerned, e.g. Scott : Ivanhoe*; Shakespeare : *Hamlet;* Kalidasa : *Sakuntala*; Milton : *Paradise Lost*; Goethe : *Faust*. Some books are published without an author's name, like Anonymous classics, Folk tales, Sacred books, and National epics and songs, *e.g., Nibelungenlied, Arabian Nights' Entertainments; Vedas; Ramayana; Mahabharata; Bhagvad Gita; Panchatantra; Hitopadesa*. Some other books are well known only by their titles, like the Anthologies, Puranas and Upanishads, e.g. *Pulitzer Prize plays, Garuda Purana, Agni Purana, Kena Upanishad, Brihadaranyaka Upnishad*. Some other books are well known by the name of the editor, translator, compiler, commentator, illustrator, e.g. Jowett, tr. Plato: *Republic*. P.V. Kane, Hindu Dharmasastra. We can go on multiplying other kinds of books which will have unusual approaches to them.

The cataloguer of a library collection has to visualise the readers' approaches to these different types of books. If the entries for all these categories are not consistently and uniformly made and under their best known form, the reader fails to get at them. All the labour spent on cataloguing them proves useless. Therefore, when every book is to be catalogued, it is essential for the cataloguer to understand and foresee how and in what possible ways the reader will ask for the books in the catalogue. Then he will be able to provide them in the catalogue. Here is a job which the cataloguer has to perform with all intelligence, logic, common sense, and adherence to catalogue rules. Even the very best catalogues have been found to fail on occasions by not yielding readily the appropriate information to the enquirer. This fact is enough to convince that compiling a good catalogue and maintaining it in sound condition is as complex as the manufacture of a spaceship and its proper upkeep, which can be done only by experts. It is becoming increasingly complex, with infinite variety of newer types of books and title coming out from the printing press.

Having considered the general principles in the planning of the library catalogue, it is necessary to arrive at decisions on (1) the external and internal form, (2) the *fullness of descriptive cataloguing*, and (3) *the subject cataloguing*, before the work commences on the provision of the catalogue.

1. The physical size, shape and material of the catalogue will be

considered under its external form. The traditional form of a library catalogue was the manuscript or printed book from the earliest times to the end of the 19th century. Transition from this conventional form to the card catalogue became significant in the 20th century, perhaps, influenced largely by the adoption and distribution of standard-sized catalogue cards by great libraries like the *Library of Congress*. Today, the card form of catalogue has generally been accepted as the normal physical form of catalogue in all kinds of libraries, although the return of the book form for static collections in big libraries and its continued use in big national libraries like the British Museum cannot be ruled out.

In a subsequent chapter on the display of catalogues further discussion on the advantages or otherwise of each form is provided. In between these forms, there is the *sheaf catalogue* which is supposed to combine the advantages of the book and the card forms. Every library should consider the adoption of one or more of these varieties before the cataloguing operations commence. There have been instances of libraries choosing one form and changing to another. The cost of such a change is tremendous and needs extra staff, material and money besides the temporary inconvenience caused to users during the period of transformation. It is therefore important that a definite decision on the form of catalogue to be maintained is arrived at in time.

In his remarks on the physical aspect of alternatives for the card catalogue, *Mr. C.D. Gull* states that "there does not appear to be a trend towards any devices which will replace the card catalogue in the near future as the basic record of each library."

"Since no library catalog is a complete record of the holdings of its library, and since few catalogs provide more than limited subject access to the cataloged material, librarians and scholars rely heavily on bibliographies, indexing services, and abstracting services, and on the published catalogs of large libraries for access to information in their own libraries, and for notice of information contained in other libraries. Collectively these published catalogs, bibliographies, indexes and abstracting journals are more than a substitute for the card catalog, as just noted, yet there is no evidence that any one or any combination of the current publications in this field can be used to replace the card catalog of any research library or of any large public library."[4]

A comprehensive survey of *Bibliographical Services, Their Present*

*State and Possibilities of Improvement* recorded by V.W. Clapp and K.O. Murra for the UNESCO/Library of Congress Bibliographical Survey covers the problem to 1950. This authoritative survey agrees with similar views already expressed that the possibility of replacing the card catalogue as a library's basic record by a better tools is very remote.

A comparative analysis of time and cost factors carried out by *Ralph R. Shaw* in his *Management, Machines, and the Bibliographic Problems of the Twentieth Century*[5] helps us in concluding that "the card catalog is not only far from obsolete but is in fact a remarkably efficient 'machine;. For most libraries, and certainly for small special libraries and libraries with relatively limited resources, the card catalogue is the practicable choice as to physical forms[6]

2. The patterns of arrangement of the entries in a catalogue will be considered under its internal form. There are only three chief types : (1) the alphabetic, by authors, titles, and subjects or combined in a single sequence, when it is called the dictionary catalogue; (2) the classed, in which arrangement of the entries is by the order of subjects as determined in a scheme of *book classification* which normally aims to bring together subjects related to each other; (3) the alphabetico-classed, a hybrid form of arrangement of entries, which aims to combine the advantages of the alphabetic and classed forms by arranging the major divisions alphabetically, with classified arrangement for subordinate subjects under each large group or arranging the major groups in classified order with the subordinate subjects in alphabetical sequence.

The third form has not been fully experimented in a large scale till now. It may, therefore, be assumed that the choice of the internal form of a library catalogue will fall on either the alphabetic or classified patterns. Volumes of material exist evaluating the relative merits of these two forms. Arguments in favour of the classed form, perhaps, outnumber those in favour of the alphabetic form. But it does not necessarily mean that the classed form is superior to the alphabetical form under all conditions. The individual needs of libraries will be the deciding factor. The anticipated reader use of the catalogue will determine in no small measure the choice of the internal form to be adopted. "But what values may be assigned to these weights, and what arguments take precedence over others in particular situations cannot here be specifically stated or even generalized. In actual practice, it may develop that the decision to adopt one form of catalogue in preference to another may not be too difficult if one knows what is to be expected of it. But what is to be expected of the catalogue? How does its use differ in varying libraries? Is alphabetic catalogue really "best" in the public library? Answers to such questions must of necessity wait upon the findings of an extensive programme of research."[7]

The commonly accepted view is that public libraries will find the alphabetical forms suited to their service; while scholarly, research, special, college, university libraries will prefer the classed forms. The classed forms too are gradually finding favour with the public libraries as the subject approach to reading material is becoming more popular than author and other approaches.

3. Descriptive cataloguing refers to the process of describing a book or other reading material on a catalogue entry, with a view to its quick identification by the user. It has attained a fairly uniform standard among libraries, since the adoption by the *American Library Association* of the Library of Congress Rules for *Descriptive Cataloguing*, 1949.

"The objectives of descriptive cataloguing are : (1) to state the significant features of an item with the purpose of distinguishing it from other items and describing its scope, contents, and bibliographic relations to other items; (2) to present these data in an entry which can be integrated with the entries for other items in the catalogue and which will respond best to the interests of most users of the catalogue."

In fulfilment of these aims, the book is described as, fully as necessary, bearing in mind that no superfluous item is incorporated in the entry. As this part of cataloguing work is largely responsible for its increasing cost, close scrutiny of its features, with a view to conserving funds, is advocated. The title page and other physical features of a book are the raw material of description in a catalogue entry. The cataloguer follows an accepted pattern in entering the class symbol, author, title, imprint, collation, notes, etc. on the entry. The minuteness with which these details are described on it, will depend on the need existing for them and the time and funds voted for this purpose. Small libraries with limited funds, a few hundred readers and one or two members on the library staff will necessarily give the most essential items, leaving out minute bibliographic details which large libraries will include. They may, for example, abbreviate titles, omit place and publisher in the imprint and omit the collation. The simplification of details on a catalogue entry is adopted in varying levels in the same library depending on the literary and material values of books. Recent studies conducted in this field indicate doubtful values attached to full and minute standards of description, because of the infrequent use made of such information by readers. It is, therefore, advisable to lay down a specification for descriptive cataloguing before the actual processing of books takes place. This decision will be of far-reaching significance for libraries which duplicate their catalogue cards by themselves by hand or machine, instead of using printed cards from a central distributing agency.

4. *Subject cataloguing*, which is no less important than author and title entries, has not been fully developed. It can perhaps be attributed to the lack of directives in its preparation, except the solitary instance in *Cutter's Rules* for a dictionary catalogue during the last 70 years. Perhaps the impression has erroneously continued to exist that it is unnecessary to provide subject entries in a catalogue arranged alphabetically, when the books themselves are classified by subjects and arranged on shelves in the order of class numbers by a given scheme of classification or that it is unnecessary to provide an alphabetical subject index to the classified catalogue. Some libraries, either with a view to economise cataloguing expenditure or because they attach only secondary importance to subject entries inalphabetical catalogues, do not prepare a subject catalogue. At best, they provide copies of the subject index to the classification scheme adopted in a library, for the use of such readers who may want to locate a subject in the *classified catalogue* or books on subject on the shelves.

Some libraries provide subject entries for books in specified departments of knowledge and some others provide only one subject entry for each book, although the book may deal with several subjects which require individual subject entries.

Subject cataloguing analyses the subject contents of the book which are indicated by suitable subject headings arranged in alphabetic sequence, with a view to providing accessibility to readers, when they approach the books from any subject aspect dealt with.

It is too hazardous to affirm that alphabetical subject cataloguing has been a failure and so it must be given up totally. Its total withdrawal from cataloguing operations will definitely leave a gap, which will remain unfilled for a long time to come. It can, therefore, be recommended that some kind of alphabetical subject cataloguing must find a place in the cataloguing services of libraries. It may be on the pattern of specific subject headings as in lists of subject headings or expressed in terms of class digits as is done in the *subject index* to the *British National Bibliography*, adopting the *'chain procedure'*. A fuller and detailed discussion on subject cataloguing can be found in the chpater on *Subject Cataloguing.*

REFERENCES

1. **L.S. Jast** in his introduction to *H.A. Sharp's Cataloguing*, p.XII.
2. *James Cranshaw, Library World*, V. 39. 1936-37, p. 179.
3. *P.C. Coetzee.* Syntactics and Semantics of the Subject Heading, an Essay in Catalogistics. University of Pretoria, 1957, *Mousaions Nr.* 21, pp. 4-5.
4. *C.D. Gull.* Substitutes for the Card Catalogue," *Library Trends,* V. 2 No. 2, Oct. 1953, pp. 318, 325-26.
5. Chicago University. Graduate Library School. *Bibliographic Organization.* Chicago, University of Chicago Press, 1951, pp. 200-25.
6. J.H. Shera and *M.E. Egan. The Classified Catalogue.* Chicago, American Library Association, 1956, p. 13.
7. *Ibid.* p. 21.

# 5

# CATALOGUE ENTRIES AND THEIR FUNCTIONS IN ACHIEVING THE OBJECTIVES OF THE LIBRARY CATALOGUE

Among the various technical operations involved in the preparation and production of a library catalogue, the decision on the number and kinds of entries to be provided for each book is of foremost significance. Be it a small or big library, the cataloguer has to examine book after book acquired for the library in order to provide its descriptive record in the entries in the catalogue. This may not fully be necessary in libraries using printed catalogue cards from supplying agencies like the Library of Congress or Wilson and Co., or the British National Bibliography. Even in such libraries, there will be some necessity for *indigenous cataloguing* of books for which the printed cards are not available. Libraries far away from agencies supplying printed catalogue cards will find it unsuitable to use them, because of the time and distance involved in obtaining them, and will, therefore, have to make their own catalogue cards.

Fortunately, the rules governing entries and the descriptions of books have been standardised. There is now a large measure of agreement on the form and fullness with regard to the entries for authors and titles. As much care and judgement is called for on the part of the cataloguer in deciding the number and varieties of entries for a book, as is expected of the classifier in assigning the class number to a book. Seymour Lubetzky attaches the utmost significance to the making of *catalogue entries* according to the revised standards. "If we shrink from the tasks which the revision presents, we shall forfeit not only the future of our catalogs, but also our national professional prestige."

Recent developments in *Catalogue Code Revision* that have been adopted in the United States and Great Britain and the efforts of the

*International Federation of Library Associations* at the *Paris Conference in October 1961* to formulate an International Cataloguing Code have very much influenced future cataloguing practice.

The objectives of the library catalogue, according to the authors of the *CCR* are two and almost similar to those of Cutter. They are:

(1) To facilitate the location of a particular publisher, *i.e.* of a particular edition of a work which is in the library, and

(2) To relate and display together the editions which a library has of a given work and the works which it has of a given author.

These objectives are "complimentary in function and both are essential to the effectiveness of the Catalogue."[1]

It must be noted that the *CCR* does not provide for the making of subject entries as that is considered a distinct function which must be provided for separately.

It considers that the concept of "*Main Entry*" as the chief or most important entry is unrealistic. (It, therefore, provides for *Entry* of a work and for *added Entries* avoiding the use of term "Main Entry").[2] Readers using the catalogue do not care to know the distinction between a main entry and an added entry, because the information required by them is available in almost all types of entries.

It seems to us that practical cataloguing will demand the maintenance of some distinguishing features between an entry for a work and the added entries for the same work. Further, economies in cataloguing suggest that the provision of the most essential and minimum particulars of a work in its secondary entries, in order to help the user to identify and locate the work, will be sufficient.

*CCR* enunciates the problems and principles governing the entries for a work in the catalogue by adoption of the Socratic method i.e., by stating 5 questions and eliciting the answers for these questions, which, for ready reference, are reproduced here.

(*i*) Who is to be regarded as the author of the work which a publication presents, particularly if it is prepared by more than one person?

*Answer*: A work produced by or issued in the name of a person or a corporate body is entered in the name of that person or corporate body; a work of multiple authorship is entered in the name of person or body represented as chiefly responsible for it; a work of complex, changing, doubtful or, unknown authorships entered under title.

(ii) By which name or form of the name is the author to be identified in the catalogue if he has used or has had more than one name or more than one form of the name?

*Answer*: An author is normally represented in the catalogue under the name and form of the name by which he is most commonly identified in his works, whether that is his real or assumed name, and in the vernacular, except when he has come to be best known in literary and reference sources by another name or designation; an author variously identified in his works is entered preferably under his real name; an author who has changed his name is normally represented under his latest name—except that in the case of a corporate body which is subject to constitutional changes, a change of name has to be treated as a change of identity.

(iii) Under which of its parts is the name to be entered in the catalogue, particularly if it includes a compound surname or a surname with a prefix?

*Answer*: A personal name with a surname is normally entered under the surname; in the case of a compound surname or one with a prefix, the author's own usage or the custom of his country is followed; a corporate name is entered directly in the form used.

(iv) How is that name to be distinguished from similar names of other persons in the catalogue?

*Answer*: The name of a person is distinguished from similar names of others by dates of birth and death or by the title or designation, by which he is commonly identified in his works or in reference sources; the name of a corporate body is distinguished by place of location, community represented or served, date of founding, or other appropriate qualification.

(v) By which title should a work be identified in the catalogue if issued under more than one title?

*Answer*: The work itself—which is the essence of a publication—whether entered under author or title, is normally represented in the catalogue under its original title, except when it has most frequently been issued or is commonly found in reference sources, under another title; a work whose original title is vague or unknown or one without an original title, is represented under the title by which it has come to be best known, or under a conventional designation.3

The *CCR* makes a further liberal provision for catalogues of libraries limited to materials in a particular language. The form of name or title by which an author or work is known in that language may be adopted for the entries of those works.

These principles had been implied and scattered in the previous two codes of 1908 and 1949 under scores of rules, *e.g.* rules nos. 23 to 57 of the *A.A. Code* governed the selection of form or part of the author's name to be adopted in the entry. The *CCR* rules provide norms for standard cataloguing and leave it open to the individual libraries to adopt these norms uniformly or with certain limitations to suit the convenience of the libraries.

*The International Conference on Cataloguing Principles, held in Paris in 1961*, reached an agreement on basic principles governing the choice and form of entry in the alphabetical catalogue of authors and titles. The official report on the statement of principles adopted at the conference is given below in order to provide a valuable basis of comparison with the identical principles and aims contained in the *CCR*.

1. *Scope of Statement*

The principles here stated apply only to the choice and form of headings and entry-words, i.e. to the principal elements determining the order of entries—in catalogues of printed books (books used to mean all reading materials in a library) in which entries under author's names and, where these are inappropriate or insufficient, under the titles of works, are combined, in one alphabetical sequence. They are framed with special reference to catalogues enumerating the contents of large general libraries; but their application to the catalogues of other libraries and other alphabetical lists of books is also recommended, with such modifications as may be required by the purpose of these catalogues and lists.

2. *Functions of the Catalogue*

The catalogue should be an efficient instrument for ascertaining,

2.1 Whether the library contains a particular book specified by:

(a) its author and title, or

(b) if the author is not named in the book, its title alone, or

(c) if author and title are inappropriate or insufficient for identification, a suitable substitute for the title;

2.2 (a) which works by a particular author and

(b) which editions of a particular work are in the library.

3. *Structure of the Catalogue*

To discharge these functions the catalogue should contain.

3.1 at least one entry for each book catalogued, and

3.2 more than one entry relating to any book, whenever this is necessary in the interests of the user or because of the characteristics of the book—for example;

3.21 when the author is known by more than one name or form of name, or

3.22 when the author's name has been ascertained but is not on the title page of the book, or

3.23 when several authors or collaborators have shared in the creation of the book, or

3.24 when the book is attributed to various authors, or

3.25 when the book contains a work known by various titles.

4. *Kind of Entry*

Entries may be of the following kinds : *main entries, added entries and references.*

4.1 One entry for each book—the main entry—must be a full entry, giving all the particulars necessary for identifying the book. Other entries may be either *added entries* (i.e. additional entries, based on the main entry and repeating under other headings information given in it) *or references* (which direct the reader to another place in the catalogue).

5. *Use of Multiple Entries*

The two functions of the catalogue (see 2.1 and 2.2) are most effectively discharged by

5.1 an entry for each book under a heading derived from the author's name or from the title as printed in the book, and

5.2 when variant forms of the author's name or of the title occur, an entry for each book under a *uniform heading*, consisting of one particular form of the author's name or one particular title, or, for books not identified by author or title, a uniform heading consisting of a suitable substitute for the title, and

5.3 appropriate added entries and/or references.

6. *Function of Different Kinds of Entry*

6.1 *The main entry* for works entered under author's names should normally be made under a *uniform heading*. The main entry for works entered under title may be either under the title as printed in the books, with an added entry under a uniform title, or under a uniform title, with added entries or references under the other titles. The latter practice is recommended for the cataloguing of well known works, specially those known by conventional titles.

6.2 Entries under other names or forms of names for the same author should normally take the form of *references,* but *added entries* may be used in special cases.

6.3 Entries under titles for the same work should normally take the form of *added entries*; but *references may be used when a reference can replace a number of added entries under one heading.*

6.4 *Added entries* (or in appropriate cases *references*) should also be made under the names of joint- authors, collaborators, etc. and under the titles of works having their main entry under an author's name, When the title is an important alternative means of identification.

7. *Choice of Uniform Heading*

The uniform heading should normally be the most frequently used name (or form of name) or title appearing in editions of the works catalogued or in references to them by accepted authorities.

7.1 When editions have appeared in several languages, preference should in general be given to a heading based on editions in the original language ; but if this language is not normally used in the catalogue, the heading may be derived from editions and references in one of the languages are normally used there.

8. *Single Personal Author*

8.1 The *main entry* for every edition of a work ascertained to be by a single personal author should be made under the author's name. An added entry or reference is made under the title of each edition in which the author's name is not stated on the title page.

8.2 The *uniform heading* should be the name by which the author is most frequently identified in editions of his works, in the fullest form commonly appearing there, *except that*

8.21 another name or form of name should be taken as the uniform heading if it has become established in general usage either in references to the author in biographical, historical and literary works, or in relation to his public activities other than authorship;

8.22 a further identifying characteristic should be added, if necessary, to distinguish the author from others of the same name.

9. *Entry under Corporate Bodies*

9.1 The main entry for a work should be made under the name of a *corporate body* (i.e. any institution, organised body or assembly of persons known by a corporate or collective name),

9.11 When the work is by its nature necessarily the expression of the collective thought or activity of the corporate body, even if signed by a person in the capacity of an officer or servant of the corporate body, or

9.12 when the wording of the title or title page, taken in conjunction with the nature of the work, clearly implies that the corporate body is collectively responsible for the content of the work.

9.2 In other cases, when a corporate body, has performed a function (such as that of an editor) subsidiary to the function of the author, an added entry should be made under the name of the corporate body.

9.3 In doubtful cases, the main entry may be made either under the name of the corporate body or under the title or the name of the personal author, with an added entry in either case under the alternative not chosen for the main entry.

9.4 The *uniform heading* for the works entered under the name of the corporate body should be the name by which the body is most frequently identified in its publications, *except that*

9.41 if variant forms of the name are frequently found in the publications, the uniform heading should be the official form of the name ;

9.42 if there are official names in several languages, the heading should be the name in whichever of these languages is best adapted to the needs of the users of the catalogue ;

9.43 if the corporate body is genrally known by a conventional name, this conventional name (in one of the languages normally is used in the catalogue) should be the uniform heading;

9.44 for states and other territorial authorities the uniform heading should be the currently used form of the name of the territory concerned in the language best adapted to the needs of the users of the catalogue ;

9.45 if the corporate body has used in successive periods different names which cannot be regarded as minor variations of one name, the heading for each work should be the name at the time of its publication, the different names being connected by references;

9.46 a further identifying characteristic should be added, if necessary, to distinguish the corporate body from others of the same name.

9.5 constitutions, laws and treaties, and certain other works having similar characteristics, should be entered under the name of the appropriate state or other territorial authority, with formal or conventional titles indicating the nature of the material. Added entries for the actual titles should be made as needed. Voting : For 47; Against 3; Abstention 11.).

9.6 A work of corporate body which is subordinate to a superior body should be entered under the name of subordinate body, *except that*

9.61 if this name itself implies subordination or subordinate function, or is insufficient to identify the subordinate body, the headings should be the name of the superior body with the name of the subordinate body as a subheading.

9.62 If the subordinate body is an administrative, judicial or legislative organ of a government, the heading should be the name of the appropriate state or other territorial authority with the name of the organ as a subheading.

10. *Multiple Authorship*

When two or more authors have shared in the creation of a work :

10.1 if one author is represented in the work as the *principal author*, the others playing a subordinate or auxiliary role, the *main entry* for the work should be made under the name of the *principal author*;

10.2 if no author is represented as the principal author, the *main entry* should be made under:

10.21 *the author named first on the title page*, if the number of authors is two or three, *added entries* being made under the name(s) of the other author(s).

10.22 the title of the work, if the number of authors is more than three, *added entries* be made under the author named first in the book and under as many other authors as may appear necessary. Voting : For 44; Against 14; Abstention 1.)

10.3 Collections

The *main entry* for a collection consisting of independent works or parts of works by different authors should be made.

10.31 under the *title of the collection*, if it has a collective title;

10.32 under the *name of the author*, or under *the title, of the first work in the collection*, if there is no collective title;

10.33 in both cases, an *added entry* should be made under the name of the compiler (*i.e.*, the person responsible for assembling from various sources the material in the collection) if known.

10.34 Exception: if the name of the *compiler* appears prominently on the title page, the main entry may be made under the name of the compiler, with an added entry under the title. (Voting: For 35; Against 22; Abstention 2.)

10.4 if successive parts of a work are attributed to different authors, the main entry should be made under the author of the first part.

11. *Works entered under Title*

11.1 Works having their *main entry under* the title are:

11.11 works whose authors have not been ascertained.

11.12 works by more than three authors, none of whom is principal author (see 10.22).

11.13 collections of independent works or parts of works by different authors, published with a collective title,

11.14 works (including serials and periodicals) known primarily or conventionally by title rather than by the name of the author.

11.2 An *added entry* or *reference* should be made under the title for:

11.21 anonymous editions of works whose authors have been ascertained,

11.22 works having their main entry under the name of the author, when the title is an important alternative means of identification,

11.23 works whose main entry is made under the name of a corporate body, but which have distinctive titles not including the name of the corporate body,

11.24 collections whose main entry is made exceptionally under the compiler.

11.3 *The uniform heading* (for main or added entries, see 6.1) for works entered under title should be the original title or the title most frequently used in editions of the work, *except that*

11.31 if the work is generally known by a conventional title, the conventional title should be the uniform heading.

11.4 The *uniform heading* for works of which successive parts or volumes bear different titles should be the title of the first part unless the majority of the parts of volumes bear another title.

11.5 When *a serial publication* is issued successively under different titles, a *main entry* should be made under each title for the series of issues bearing that title, with indication of at least the immediately preceding and succeeding titles. For each such series of issues, an added entry may be made under one selected title. If, however, the variations in title are only slight the most frequently used form may be adopted as a uniform heading for all issues.

11.6 multi-lateral international treaties and conventions and certain other categories of publications issued with non-distinctive titles may by entered under a uniform conventional heading, chosen to reflect the form of the work.

12. *Entry Word for Personal Names*

When the name of a personal author consists of several words, the choice of entry-word is determined so far as possible by agreed usage in the country of which the author is a citizen, or, if this is not possible, by agreed usage in the language which he generally uses.[4]

International agreement on the kinds and types of entries in alphabetical catalogues has rightly imbibed the cataloguing traditions of the past, whenever they had proved rational and helpful. The main entries and added entries will continue to be adopted in cataloguing.

Subsequent to the release of the official report of the Cataloguing Principles adopted by the International Conference, there has been an expression of their appreciation and critical evaluation.

"These Principles are not principles but a very broad draft code. They are in the tradition of the *British Museum Rules* and being even shorter lend themselves to even greater divergencies of interpretation. There is also probably a feeling that much talk of cataloguing principles cannot exist apart from cataloguing practice...The 'rules' of the conference are such that these undeclared assumptions could turn them in practice into hardly recognizable variants."[5]

The directions contained in 'rule' 5 Use of Multiple entries appear to be permissive, resulting in wide variety of choice of entries, depending on the kind of catalogue compiled and the standard of cataloguing adopted. This is likely to impede progress in international cooperation in the field of cataloguing, specially in union catalogues and lists.

'Principles 5 to 7 are essentially broad general rules whose [illegible]

tion is capable of considerable variation in many specific instances. Even the entry of well-known works, especially those known by conventional titles, under a uniform title is only recommended. Such moderation is hard to understand after Lubetzky had demonstrated with unanswerable force and clarity the disastrous results which follow from not entering works of this character under a uniform title."[6] In order to provide for all possible variation, desirable or expedient in the context of prevailing cataloguing practice in different libraries, the recommendatory character of the principles seems not only cautious but called for.

It is commendable that the conference has decided on the production of uniform lists of names for states, anonymous classics, and 'a restricted list of categories of publication which may be entered under a conventional heading reflecting the form of the work'. When such a list becomes available, appreciable uniformity in the author heading in the catalogues for works in these categories can be maintained.

The most outstanding achievement of the conference is the international agreement which produced the statement of the (Paris) Principles of Cataloguing. This will mean that all subsequent developments in cataloguing theory and practice should be decided at an international level.

The main entry will ordinarily be made under the author as heading, but in a few cases it may be made under the title, when the author is unkown or doubtful or the title is better known than the author, and occasionally under the editor, compiler and illustrator, etc. The added entries are made under the titles, subjects, and collaborators such as editors, translators, illustrators. The main entry generally contains fairly full information about a book while the added entry gives only the most essential items of information as called for by the heading. Let us examine a book for the types and number of entries.

'Mathematics and the imagination' by Edward Kasner and James Newman; with drawings and diagrams by Rufus Isaacs, London, Bell, 1949.

This book may be asked for under its authors, its title, its subjects and perhaps under its illustrator. When the decision is made about the need, kind and number of entries for a book in catalogue, the cataloguer has to make these entries under the appropriate headings. All headings for entries, except that for the author entry, are traced at the bottom of the main entry by using arabic numerals for subject headings and roman for others on the model of the L.C. printed catalogue cards. The function of the tracings is to direct the making of added entries under the appropriate headings.

Main entry:

| | |
|---|---|
| Author Heading, | Kasner, Edward. |
| Added entries: | |
| Jt. author Heading | Newman, James |
| Title ,, | Mathematics and the imagination, 1949 |
| Subject ,, | MATHEMATICS—PHILOSOPHY |
| ,, ,, | MATHEMATICAL RECREATIONS |
| ,, ,, | IMAGINATION |
| Illustrator | Issacs, Rufus |

*MAIN ENTRY*

Kasner, Edward,

Mathematics and the imagination by Edward Kasner and James Newman, illus. by Rufus Issacs. Lond., Bell, 1949.

xiv, 380 p., illus., diags., 20 cm.

Short biographical note about the authors at end.

1. Mathematics—Philosophy. 2. Mathematical recreations, 3. Imagination. I. Newman, James, Jt. auth. II Issacs, Rufus, illus, III. title

*Cross reference entries* are indicated on the reverse of the main entry and are made on separate cards which are filed in appropriate places in the catalogue.

(1) SCIENTIFIC RECREATIONS, *See also* MATHEMATICAL RECREATIONS.

(2) RECREATIONS, MATHEMATICAL, *See* MATHEMATICAL RECREATIONS.

*JT. AUTHOR ENTRY*

Newman, James, Jt. auth.

Kasner, Edward,

Mathematics and the imagination by Edward Kasner and James Newman. Lond., Bell, 1949.

*ILLUSTRATOR ENTRY*

Issacs, Rufus, illus.

Kasner, Edward,

Mathematics and the imagination by Edward Kasner and James Newman, Lond., Bell, 1949.

TITLE ENTRY

Mathematics and the imagination. 1949.

Kasner, Edward.

Mathematics and the imagination by Edward Kasner and James Newman. Lond., Bell, 1949.

*SUBJECT ENTRY*

(1)

MATHEMATICS—PHILOSOPHY

Kasner, Edward.

Mathematics and the imagination by Edward Kasner and James Newman; illus. by Rufus Issacs, Lond., Bell, 1949.

xiv, 380p., illus, diagrs, 20 cm.

(2)

MATHEMATICAL RECREATIONS

Kasner, Edward.

Mathematics and the imagination by Edward Kasner and James Newman; illus. by Rufus Issacs. Lond., Bell, 1949.

xiv, 380p., illus, diagrs, 20 cm.

(3)

IMAGINATION

Kasner, Edward.

Mathematics and the imagination by Edward Kasner and James Newman; illus. by Rufus Issacs. Lond., Bell, 1949.

xiv, 380p., illus, diagrs, 20 cm.

While the main entry for a book in an alphabetical catalogue is usually made under the name of its author or the best known form of the title when the authorship cannot be established with certainty, in a classified catalogue it is made under the subject indicated by the class number in which the book is placed. This entry under the class number is the only entry for the book in a classified catalogue, while index entries corresponding to the added entries of a dictionary catalogue are provided in the subsidiary files of the classified catalogue. These are called alphabetical indexes of authors, subjects and titles, which may either be kept separate or filed together in a single sequence. When a book contains more than one subject, the second or subsidiary subject is brought out by providing a subsidiary entry for the book under the class number of that subject with a reference to the class number where it is placed as determined by the first, primary subject. Similar to the tracing of the headings of added entries on the main entry in alphabetical/dictionary catalogues, class number of subsidiary subjects under which the book may be expected are given as tracings. The class number stands as substitute for the verbal subject heading traditionally adopted in dictionary catalogues.

e.g. *Main entry* in the *classified catalogue,* under class number

510.1

Kasner, Edward

Mathematics and the imagination by Edward Kasner and James Newman; illus by Rufus Issacs London, Bell, 1949.

xiv, 380p., illus, diagrs, 20 cm.

1. 155

Some libraries prefer to write the call number of the book on the top left corner and class number on the top right corner in a distinct manner. Giving class number in addition to call number is optional, because the call number consists of class number and the book number.

e.g. Entry for the subsidiary subject.

155

Kasner, Edward.

Mathematics and the imagination by Edward Kasner and James Newman, 1949, Book at 510.1

6

# DESCRIPTIVE CATALOGUING

In Chapter Four on 'Principles of Planning and Provision of Library Catalogues' a passing reference is made to the necessity of deciding the pattern of description of books on catalogue cards before the cataloguing operations begin.

In this chapter, a detailed discussion of the description of the various types of books and reading material in libraries is provided. Descriptive cataloguing has been defined as "that phase of the process of cataloguing which concerns itself with the identification and description of books"1 Studies of reader use of library catalogues disclose that several of them are already aware of the existence of a book or books on the subject of their interest. They refer to the catalogues primarily to find out (1) if such reading material is in the holdings of the library and (2) if so, where it is located. Identification precedes location. If any ambiguous characteristic were to be found in the verbal description of books, it would tend to its being overlooked or discarded by the reader. Descriptive cataloguing, therefore, helps in isolating book from book in the process of identification. This part of cataloguing is sometimes considered mechanical, but it is not so because the cataloguer has to use his judgement on the number and degree of minuteness of details to be adopted. They must be authentic and precise. The manner of presentation of details decided for inclusion in the order of priority will add to the artistic effect and ease of use. Irrespective of the alphabetical or classed form of catalogue, descriptive cataloguing has to be performed with same care and standard of performance.

Reading material in modern libraries is not only limited to printed books but also extends to maps, atlases, musical scores, braille books, sound records, etc. Each class of material poses its own problems of description. Even in books, the complexity transcends all imagination.

A simple analysis of books in modern libraries will result in the following main groups:

(1) Personal author publications, single and joint, with and without other collaborators like editors, translators compilers, etc;
(2) Corporate author publications (*a*) government (*b*) non-government, i.e. society, institution, other organizations;
(3) Publications of pseudonymous writers;
(4) Anonymous works;
(5) Serials and periodical publications;
(6) New editions and duplicates;
(7) Incunabula;
(8) Manuscripts;
(9) Issues and offprints;
(10) Motion pictures and filmstrips;
(11) Maps, globes, etc.;
(12) Music;
(13) Sound records;
(14) Pictures, designs, etc.

Items in each one of the above groups will need a distinct pattern of description. The Library of Congress Rules for Descriptive Cataloguing, (adopted by the American Library Association) 1949, provide the fullest directions for the descriptive cataloguing of such material. Most of these rules have been accepted by libraries as standard rules and followed in descriptive cataloguing. But as these rules are specially intended for use in the Library of Congress which is cataloguing its materials " to integrate them in a large general collection and in large special collections, other libraries, other libraries using the rules will have to decide for themselves at what point they wish to depart from them."[2]

Small libraries may decide to simplify these rules in accordance with their individual needs. It is still possible to maintain some standards of uniformity even in 'limited cataloguing' by following consistently the amended rules. It is obvious that the degree of fullness of descriptive cataloguing which is considered essential varies with the size of the library and the standards of cataloguing adopted. Wherever a catalogue is to be used as a simple finding list, as is the case in several large and small libraries providing open access to shelves, the value of the information contained in the descriptive cataloguing, except that which helps to distinguish edition from edition, seems to be doubtful. When books are available in open shelves placed in close proximity to the catalogue, a complete bibliographic description of the book, as given in the title page and elsewhere, adapted for its descriptive cataloguing, will be very infrequently used by the readers. "A cataloguing entry should contain no item which is not necessary."[3] The judgement on the necessity for inclusion of all or some bibliographic details of the book in the catalogue entry will rest on the principles and standards adopted in individual libraries and to some extent on the cataloguing personnel.

"To identify a work, author and title are usually sufficient. To identify a book* it is usually necessary to add the number of the edition and/or the place and date of publication. To enable comparison to be made with other appearances of the same work, it is necessary to add (where relevant) variations in the title, the name of the editor, translator, etc. the name of the publisher, the pagination, illustrative matter and size, the name of the series of which the book forms part. The nature and extent of further information will depend partly on the publishing history of the book, partly on the purpose of the catalogue.

With these priorities in mind and making adjustments in order to bring together items which together make up one part of the entry, the following sequence, of parts seems logical: title; edition; imprint; collation; series; other information."[4]

The description of library materials in a catalogue is covered in A-ACR 130-146, 152-156, for separately published monographs; 160-168 for serials; 180-185 for incunabula ; and 190- 191 for photographic and other reproductions. Part III of the A- ACR deals with the entry, heading and description of non-book materials. "The rules for description are a revision of the '*Rules for Descriptive Cataloguing in the Library of Congress* (1949)' including its separately issued supplementary rules: Manuscripts 1954, and *Pictures, Designs, and other Two- Dimensional Representations* 1959".[5]

130 : *Organization of the description:*

A. The objective of description of a bibliographic entity (a book in a catalogue entry is to enable the user of the catalogue to distinguish one work from another, and also one edition from another edition of the same work available in the library's collection. The details given in the description should be determined on this basis. If the informa-

* "A book is here distinguished as a single presentation of a work."

tion on the title page, and elsewhere in a book is inadequate to achieve this object, brief annotation, stating the credentials of the author, the scope and purpose of the work and its context among other related works is necessary.

A precise concept of descriptive cataloguing can be indicated by stating what a bibliographical description is and meant for. "A detailed description of a book, with an accurate transcription of the title-page and full collation of the contents, is likely to reveal unsuspected variations in other 'copies' when they are compared with it; some 'copies' may prove to be a different edition, a reprint from the same type with or without alterations, or they may contain insertions or cancellations. These are not only of interest in themselves, they also provide the material for the bibliographical analysis which tries to establish the order of these changes and their cause. Bibliographers now tend to describe an ideal copy which represents the book as the publisher intended it to be put on sale, without any variants with chance, negligence, or the publisher's afterthoughts may have produced. To establish the 'ideal copy' demands a close analysis of all variants and it has been suggested that ideally a description should be based on all extant copies. This aim can never be achieved with any certainty."[6]

It will be seen that the description of a book in a catalogue entry is to achieve a different purpose, and it should be designed accordingly.

B. The details of the book provided below the heading, i.e. in the 'body of the entry', consist of (1) title (including any sub-title or alternative title), (2) author statement, (3) edition statement, (4) imprint, (5) collation, and (6) series statement.

The author statement is liberally interpreted to include also the names of other collaborators, like compiler, editor, translator, illustrator, commentator, etc. The name of any or all of these collaborators can be given before the commencement of the imprint group. If additional information is required about the author or other items mentioned above, it is provided in a note or annotation as a separate paragraph, after the series statement, (vide specimen of catalogue cards in Chapter 18, for varieties of description).

In handwritten or typewritten catalogue cards, the name of the author used as heading is not repeated as a part of the title.

131 : *Source of the description*

By and large, the copy of a book for cataloguing provides most of the particulars required for descriptive cataloguing. Occasionally, a reference to outside bibliographical sources will be essential where the degree of precision needed, is not possible to attain from the book itself.

132 : *Relationship of the title page to the description of a book*

**A. General rules**

1. The title page of a work normally yields the information to be provided for in the body of the entry. When any of the details to be given in a standard description are obtained from reference sources, they are enclosed in square brackets to indicate that they have been furnished by the cataloguer from elsewhere.

The cataloguer must differentiate between (1) a title spread on two facing pages, and (2) two different titles or forms of title given on two pages facing each other. The first type is only concerned with space occupied by the title which is only one and should be treated just like any title on a normal title page. A work in more than one volume may be provided with a collective title covering all the volumes of the work, as well as an individual title for every volume comprising the work, *e.g.* the Second World War by Winston Churchill in five volumes has also an individual title for each of the volumes : I. The Gathering Storm, 1948; II. Their Finest Hour, 1949; III. The Grand Alliance, 1950; IV. The Hinge of Fate, 1950 ; V. Closing the Ring, 1951. A work in a single volume only may have two titles given on two pages facing each other, due to the text in original language and the translation in another, or the engraved title page and type set title page, and variety of other causes. The basis of description should be the appropriate title page in accordance with A-ACR 132C.

The information on edition, imprint, and series, even if obtained from elsewhere in the book, is not enclosed in square brackets. Punctuation is according to cataloguing conventions of separating itmes and groups by use of comma, semicolon, and full stop, at appropriate places. Abbreviations recognised and standardised for use in cataloguing and given in the codes are adopted.

**B. Publications without title pages**

The title page, with the data specified for descriptive entry of a book, as is found in the modern printed publications is an embelishment in the art of book production, which has passed through five centuries of gradual progress. The early specimens of books lacked title pages, as conceived now.

In certain very old books, due to wear and tear title pages are lost. The cataloguer has to supply the information for the body of the entry from anywhere in the book, if possible from cover title, half-title, caption title, colophon, running title, or even by reading the text. Failing all these methods appropriate reference sources may be of help in obtaining the information for description of the book. Whenever the title page is supplied the descriptive portion is enclosed in square brackets to indicate that it has been provided.

The fullness and exactness of the title on the body of the entry, additions to it when required are specified in A-ACR 133; the author statement as a part of title in 134; the edition statement in 135; editor, compiler, translator, illustrator, etc. in 136; the number of volumes in 137; illustration in 138; imprint in 139-42; collation in 143. The application of these rules in describing the copy of the book on the catalogue entry will result in uniformity in the presentation of the details. Reference to these rules would be more frequent when the student commences the practical cataloguing and in course of time, these become a routine application in daily work in libraries.

As serials (periodicals, continuations and other works published frequently and regularly, and for an indefinite length of time) form a sizeable collection in academic and research libraries, descriptive cataloguing of this library, descriptive cataloguing of this library material deserves special attention of cataloguers.

A-ACR 160-168 treat the description of serials, with these general aims:

(1) "to present an adequate account of the whole published set of each serial;

(2) to indicate and describe the library's holdings; and

(3) to construct entries which need the minimum of alteration because of changes during the course of publication of serials."

In cataloguing the periodicals in a library, it is convenient to group them into the following categories:

(1) current periodicals of which the library has complete sets up-to-date;

(2) finished periodicals of which the library has complete sets;

(3) current periodicals of which the library has (a) decidedly incomplete sets, (b) slightly incomplete sets; and

(4) finished periodicals of which the library sets are incomplete.

Adopt an open entry for dealing with groups 1, 3, and 4; a closed entryfor2 for 2.

A-ACR 160 *Source of description*

The information given in the body of the entry is preferably limited to a single source. If regular title page is not in the publication, the title on cover, caption, masthead, editorial pages or other place is adopted, and the fact stated.

As serials are entered under title, the title in the body of the entry may be used as heading. Change in title of a serial should be noted and the description should be based on the particulars from the latest volume or issue.

The subsequent rules 161-167 deal with physical aspects and the style and order of their entries, as well as notes on a library's holdings. The last rule 168 directs the making of analytical entries, when a part of serials is separately paged, and for other unusual types of issues.

The examples of entries for serials given on the next page are intended to serve as illustrations for easy comprehension by the student of cataloguing.

**Open entry for a current periodical of which the library has complete sets up-to-date**

*Endeavour*

Endeavour, a quarterly review designed to record the progress of the science in the service of mankind. London, Imperial Chemical Industries.

Library has:

v. 1—27     1942—1968
*in Pencil*     *in pencil*

1. Science,   Periodicals.

**Open entry for a current periodical of which the library has decidedly incomplete sets**

*The Indian Geographical Journal*

Madras, Indian Geographical
Society.
Qly.
Library has:
v. 22-26, 1947-1951
*in pencil*

see next card

2

Editors:
Kurian, George v. 22-26
Title varies
The Journal of the Madras Geographical Society. v. 1
1. Geographical, Periodicals.

**Open entry for a current periodical of which the library set is slightly incomplete**

*Journal of Genetics*

Journal of Genetics, London. Cambridge University Press.
Qly.
Library has:
v. 1—66 1910—1968
*in pencil* *in pencil*
Lacks: v. 20, 24, 47
*in pencil*

see next card

2

Editors;

| | |
|---|---|
| Bateson, W. and Punnett, R.C. | v. 1-16 |
| Punnett, R.C. | v. 17-26 |
| Punnett, R.C. and Haldane, J.B.S. | v. 27-33 |
| Punnett, R.C. | v. 34-46 |
| Haldane, J.B.S. | v. 47-62 |

1. Reproduction (Botany). Periodicals
I. Punnett, R.C. ed. II Haldane, J.B.S. ed.

**Open entry for a finished periodical of which the library set is incomplete**

*Life and Letters Today.*
London,
Monthly
Library has:
v. 14-63, 1936-1949
No more published
Lacks: v. 1-13, 20, 21, 34, 35, 37, 47—50
*in pencil*

see next card

2

Editors:
Herring, Robert. v. 14-59
Title varies
Life and Letters. v. 46-63

1. English literature. Periodicals.

**Closed entry for a periodical, of which the library set is complete**

*Journal of Geomoprphology. v. 1-5*
N.Y., Columbia Univ. Pr., 1938-42.
Qly.
No more published.

1. Geology, Strucutral. Periodicals
2. Physical geography. Periodicals.

**A periodical that has changed its title but has continued the sequence of volume numbers**

*The Journal of Pomology and Horticultural Science.*
London, Headly
Qly.
Library has:
v. 22-27, 1946-1952
*in pencil*

see next card

2

Editors:
Hatton, R.G. and Wallace, T. v. 22-27
*in pencil*
Title varies
The Journal of Horticultural Science.
v. 24—1948—

1. Fruitculture, Periodicals, 2. Gardening, Periodicals, I title: the Journal of Horticultural Science.

**A periodical that has changed its title and adopted a separate sequence of volume number**

*Quarterly Journal of Pharmacy and Pharmacology*

Incorporating the year book of pharmacy, London, Pharmaceutical Pr.

(Includes Proceedings of British Pharmaceutical Conference).
Title varies:

> Publication discontinued in 1948, and followed by Journal of Pharmacy and Pharmacology v. 1, 1949.

A separate entry as for a current serial is made, and the earlier title related to this is mentioned in a note.

*Journal of Pharmacy and Pharmacology.*

Lond. Pharmaceutical Society of Gt.
Britain.
Mly.
Library has:

| v. 1—4 | 1949—1952 |
|---|---|
| *in pencil* | *in pencil* |

Periodicals almost invariably provide indexes for each completed volume, and certain periodicals cumulate the indexes at regular intervals. *e.g.* The Decennial Index of the Chemical Abstracts.

A-ACR 167 B 14 provides directions for describing the indexes of a serial in the catalogue entry.

A combined index to consecutive volumes of a serial is mentioned in a note, if it is not entered separately. The note may also include information on a cumulative index within that set.

The information given for each index noted is recorded in the following order:

(1) kind of index, *i.e.* author, subject, etc.
(2) numbers and dates of volumes indexed.
(3) the number of volumes of the index, if separately published.
(4) the location of the index, in the set, if it is continuously paged with the serial's pagination, or numbered as a volume or part of the serial.
(5) the size of the index, if different from the serial.

> Institution of mining engineers, London
> Transactions
> Index (author and subject) to v. 76-108, 1928-1949 (in v. 108).

Mention may be made in notes of the inclusion of the serial in hand, in collective periodical indexes, *e.g.*,

Indexed in library literarture.
Indexed in British Technology Index.

## REFERENCES

1. A.L.A. **Glossary of Library Terms**. Chicago, American Library Association.
2. **Lucile M. Morsch.** Foreword to **Rules for Descriptive Cataloguing** in the Library of Congress. Washington, Library of Congress, 1949. p.vi,
3. **L. Jolley. The Principles of Cataloguing**. London, Lockwood, 1961. p. 135.
4. **Mary Piggott**. Uniformity in Descriptive Cataloguing. **Libri,** v.13, 1, 1963, p. 47.
5. **C. Sumner Spalding**. A-ACR (British Text). The Library Association, 1967, p. 5.
6. *David Foxon*. The Technique of Bibliography, London, National Book league, 1955. p. 5.

# 7

# PHYSICAL FORMS OF THE CATALOGUE

## ± Manually Operated

Books in all their forms have *influenced* the shape and structure of the catalogue. The ancient records of man's thought and achievement were preserved in clay tablets. Evidence from history reveals that the corresponding catalogues of books in clay tablets were also made of clay tablets. As the evolution in book production gradually changed the shape of books, resulting in modern printed books with all embellishments, their catalogues also kept pace with them. When there were manuscripts and block books, the catalogues conformed to that model. When the printing press established improved traditions for book production, the catalogues of such printed books adhered closely to those traditions resulting in printed page catalogues. Use and experience of the printed page catalogue lead to the modern form, the card catalogue in the present day. By 1900, the card form had displaced virtually all the previous forms of library catalogues. After decades of its popularity, the card form is being questioned and efforts are being made to find substitutes for the card catalogue.

Among the various *physical forms of catalogues in use today in libraries, importance should be given to the study of (1) Printed page catalogue,* (2) *Adjustable sheaf Catalogue and (3) Card catalogue cabinets.*

1. *Printed Page Catalogue*: It is also known as the book catalogue. This kind of catalogue has been a traditional form adopted in many large libraries, which used to publish a general printed catalogue of

their collections up to a date and then issue periodical supplements to keep the original volume up-to- date. Copies of these catalogues are placed in the public departments of the libraries and also sold to the public. The ease with which readers can use and carry them is unquestionable. Several entries on a page that a reader can see at a time, without the irksome necessity of turning over card by card in the card form is a decisive advantage and saves time and trouble. The compactness of the book catalogue enables its display in a minimum of floor space and with little equipment. No other form of catalogue can compete successfully with the *printed book catalogue as a bibliography* and information source to students and scholars in distant parts of the world. Because of the supreme value, several large libraries even now print thier catalogues, *e.g.* A catalogue of Books Represented by the library of Congress Printed Cards Issued to July 31, 1942 and later its Supplement, Cards Issued August 1, 1942 to December 31, 1947, altogether 209 volumes of about 600 pages each, has been published by Edwards. The Catalogue contains 2.500,000 entries and ranks among the great book catalogues of the world. "The success of the *Edwards Catalogue*, and the realization that its depository card catalogues represented a burden most depository libraries could not long afford to bear, led the *Library of Congress* to seek means of continuing the publication of its cards in book form as well as their sale for use in card catalogues....The cumulative catalogue method, adopted late in 1946, was carefully chosen compromise which took advantage of conditions peculiar to the Library of Congress to obtain the best results possible in printing a book catalogue from catalogue cards. Photo-offset lithography was considered the most effective printing method."[1] By careful planning of the process of alignment and adjustment a great deal of saving in space and size in the '*Library of Congress Author Catalogue*' is made possible. Instead of 18 entries to a page in Edwards Catalogue, the new Catalogue contains 38 entries to a page and is issued in 5 sections: (1) Authors, (2) Subjects, (3) Films, (4) Maps and Atlases and (5) Music and Phonorecords.

In 1950, the Library of Congress commenced the publication of the *Library of Congress Subject Catalog*, and the *Cumulative Catalog* was renamed the *Library of Congress Author Catalog*. With the publication of individual catalogues, in 1953 for maps, motion pictures, and film strips, music and phonograph records, the earlier catalogues became the *Library of Congress Catalog—Books:*

*Authors*, and the *Library of Congress Catalog—Books: Subjects.*

As a large number of entries in these catalogues were included in the *National Union Catalog*, it was considered appropriate that the *Library of Congress Catalog* should ultimately attain the status of a national catalogue of American library holdings. A.L.A's Board on resources of American Libraries appointed a sub-committee of the National Union Catalog under the Chairmanship of F.H. Wagman. This committee functioned from 1954 to 1956. The committee carefully considered the advantages of producing a National Union Catalog. "The inclusion of information about the location of the publications listed would make possible regional and national planning of acquisition programmes and should reduce the unnecessary duplicative purchases of expensive works; it should also lead to a more equitable distribution of the burden of inter-library loans. The ready availability of a great body of current bibliographical information should some what reduce cost of acquisition, cataloguing and reference work. Finally, it should give an impetus to editing and publishing the older section of the National Union Catalog and also to issue a current subject catalog of American library resources."[2]

The response to this proposal from libraries was enthusiastic and the new catalogue was issued under the title *The National Union Catalog: A Cummulative Author List,* 1956. This was a decisive and forward step towards the bibliographical control of library resources.

"The National Union Catalog in book form has shown an amazing growth over the last seven or eight years. The total number of its titles reported in 1956 was 103,000; and in 1962, 823,000. This growth may also be measured in terms of successive cumulations. The 1933 to 1967 cumulations appeared in 28 volumes, totalling 18,826 pages and it reproduced some 700,000 cards at a subscription price of $255.00. The 1958 to 1962 quinquennial runs to 54 volumes totalling about 35,000 pages. The latest cumulation contains 780,000 titles and 308,000 added entries and references and gives over 3,200,000 locations. In addition there are 239,000 entries for music and motion-picture film titles included."[3]

In 1974, the title of this publication was changed to the *National Union Catalog.*

The National Union Catalog, pre-1956 imprints published between 1968-1981 made accessible in book form the total information that had cumulated in the card file known as the National Union Catalog maintained at the Library of Congress since 1901. This retrospective portion of the National Union Catalog is now available in 754 volumes (published by Mansell) added about 20 million cards to the published record of the Union Catalog information collected at the Library of Congress.

*Library of Congress and National Union Catalog*

Author Lists, 1942-1962: a master cumulation, in 152 volumes, announced for publication in 1969, by Gale Research Company, includes the entries in the following four supplements:

(1) Catalog of Books Represented by Library of Congress Printed Cards-Supplement 1942-1947;

(2) The Library of Congress Author Catalogs 1948-1952;

(3) The National Union Catalog: A Cumulative Author List 1953-1957;

(4) The National Union Catalog: A Cumulative Author List 1958-1962.

*The NUC DATABASE. Growth*

The growth of the NUC Database has continued to accelerate at a record pace. The following table illustrates the growth of records in the file each year since its inception in November 1982.

*This figure includes records replaced by LC Cataloguing records and those that have some problem due to system failure and must be deleted and re-input. These also include later deleted by reveiwers as duplicates or excludes.

This *Printed Catalogue*, is bound to be a very valuable source book providing quick, easy reference to bibliographical and cataloguing data covering books, maps atlases, periodicals, and other serials catalogued by the *Library of Congress* during twenty-one years, 1942-1962, and by other North American Libraries, 1956-62. Over two million entries will be found in these 152 volumes—a bibliographical record resulting in saving the time and labour of scholars and library personnel.

"The *National Union Catalog: A Cumulative Author List,* has been described as a reference and research tool for a large part of the world's production of significant books, going far beyond the proportions usually considered national bibliography."[4]

The foregoing advantages possessed by a printed book catalogue can be offset with some disadvantages inherent to it.

| Fiscal Year | Records Added | Records Deleted | Net Total on File |
|---|---|---|---|
| 1983 | 4,753 | 28 | 4,725 |
| 1984 | 20,962 | 43 | 25,644 |
| 1985 | 66,924 | 225 | 92,343 |
| 1986 | 105,951 | 516 | 197,778 |
| 1987 | 123,055 | 3911* | 316,922 |
| 1988 | 144,035 | 2725* | 458,232 |

Libraries acquire books as the need arises for them. When open access to shelves gradually displaced closed shelves, more intensive use of the collection was no doubt made by readers, but one occassionally meets an irresponsible use also made of books. Books, sometimes, are stolen from libraries and are lost. Some books become obsolete and have to be withdrawn; otherwise unwanted reading material creates problems of congestion, by occupying the limited and valuable shelf-space.

Entries of books lost as well as withdrawn must be deleted from the catalogue, in order to keep it current just as new additions are entered in it. As the stock of modern libraries, particularly public libraries is constantly being revised, their catalogues also must be revised. The printed book catalogues do not yield, as spontaneously as other kinds of catalogues, to these changes. When entries are scored off or erased and when new entries are inserted in between two printed titles, the page looks confusing, and unattractive and after some time it has to be replaced by a new printed page or supplemented elsewhere.

Its production is laborious and disproportionately expensive. Before the catalogue entries of books can be printed on pages to be bound to give it the shape of a book, they have to be written legibly and accurately to be composed. The proofs of these sheets containing the entries have to be compared and errors in composition rectified before final printing is done. This process involves considerable time, before the catalogue is available for use. Even though the bookslk have been catalogued, their catalogue is not ready for public use. When the catalogue is completely printed and bound it will not admit incorporation of further entries of books added to the collection day by day with the result that the public have no information about new books, till a subsequent edition of the catalogue is printed. Remedies like periodical bulletins of new books and supplements for stated periods, have been tried but they have proved as laborious and costly as the making of the original catalogue. A growing collection of books in a library, a inherent feature of libraries and a printed catalogue do not keep good company. One is fast, the other is slow. There may be a few advantages with the page catalogue like convenient and familiar shape and size, portability and lightness, but they do not outweight the serious disadvantages of rigidity, inhospitability, obsoleteness and mounting costs. While the scholarly readers favour printed book catalogues, librarians will find card catalogues more convenient in administering their libraries. The American card catalogues appear to be affected by newer printing processes and book catalogues seem to be gaining popularity.

*The Sheaf Catalogue* Difficulties experienced in the maintenance of the page catalogue led to the adoption of an improved type known as sheaf catalogue which consists of individual sheets of tough paper cut to uniform size and notched at left edge and protected by boards on front and back and secured by mechanical clasp or metal fastener. One entry is made on each sheet and these entries can be arranged in any desired order or withdrawn from the sheaf holder with ease without affecting the preceding or following entries. Entries may be written or typed or printed on the standard sheets and operated like a loose leaf-holder. The spine of each volume of the sheaf catalogue contains a lable holder, in which the range of its contents can be displayed and these volumes can be arranged in a cabinet designed to house them.

SHEAF CATALOGUE

Front Section

Alphabetic Arrangement

| A-B | C | D-E | F | G-H | I | J-K | L | M | N | O |
|---|---|---|---|---|---|---|---|---|---|---|
| P | Q | R | S | T | U | V | W | X | Y | Z |

Classified Arrangement

| 100 | 200 | 300 | 400 | 500 |
|---|---|---|---|---|
| 600 | 700 | 800 | 900 | 000 |

The desired volume could be pulled out of its place in the stand and conveniently used on a table and replaced when done with. The sheaf catalogue combines advantages of the page catalogue,like portability and familiarity and certain good features of the card catalogue, like up-to-date quality, infinite expanding capacity and freedom of manipulation of the entries. With such advantages it could not attain the same popularity as that of the present card cataloge. Only a few libraries adopt this form. Splendid examples of sheaf catalogue are to be found in the United Kingdom at the Birmingham Reference Libraries, Liverpool Reference Libraries, Sheffield Central Library, and Westminister Reference Library. (Westminister Library is now printing its catalogues).

Although the sheaf catalogue provides a compromise between the printed catalogue and the card catalogue, it is not adaptable to *Library of Congress printed cards.* These is waste of blank space on the slips as the description of books seldom requires full area of the slips. But in regional library systems it is of immense value, because the location of a single volume may have have to be recorded in a number of branches in the region.A mobile library collection may be enterted in a sheaf catalogue and it may be carried in the vans provided the number of volumes of the catalogue does not exceed ten. Experience of filing newer entries in the sheaf catalogue indicate that the slips, being thinner and less tough than the cards, take a little more time than the cards.

LIBRACO SHEAF CATALOGUE
PLATE 2

Plate II *[Courtesy Libraco]*

*The Card Catalogue*: The card catalogue, which is familiar to all readers in modern libraries, is a creation of librarians after much

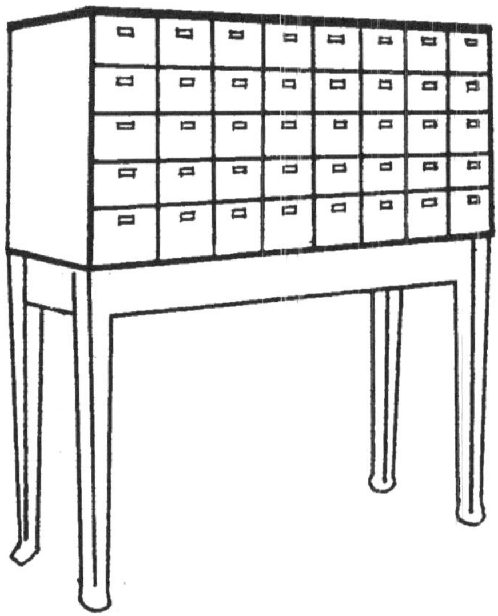

FORTY-TRAY CABINET ON STAND

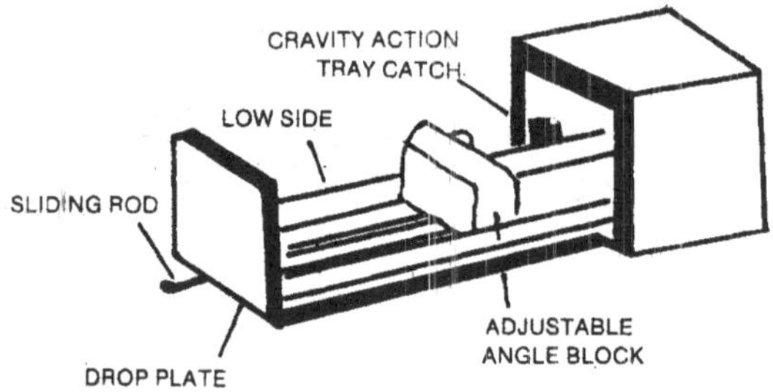


CATALOGUE CARD TRAY

Plate III

*[Courtesy Libraco]*

thought and experience. During the eighteenth Century, libraries in France had adopted cards for catalogues. In the nineteenth century, libraries and banks in England and the United States began using cards for their records. This form of catalogue took shape and attained immense popularity from the beginning of the twentieth century. It has been perfected in its internal structure and external shape. Each card of the standard dimension 7.5 cm × 12.5 cm (roughly 3 inches by 5 inches) contains a single entry. Copies of these cards can be duplicated in required quantity for the purpose of being filed in any desired location and sequence. These cards are arranged and filed in a drawer, designed to hold 1500 to 1800 cards in upright position. These trays or drawers are provided with a simple mechanism of self-locking metal rod with a groove in which a sliding metal plate falls of its own weight through the slit and catches the rod from being pulled out. The rod passes through the punched holes in the bottom of the cards and holds them securely and in order. The catalogue tray is secured in its cabinet by a gravity catch fixed to the side of tray hole in the cabinet, which falls into a groove cut on the side panel of the tray at the end. These trays are housed in a cabinet made of wood or steel. The cabinet is placed on a base, at a convenient height 3' or 3'6" above the floor. Cabinets could contain any number of trays according to design. Experience has shown that the expansion of the card catalogue cabinet is more convenient if it is in horizontal direction instead of in vertical direction. And a *card catalogue* with minimum number of vertical trays, will necessarily expand horizontally and will occupy ample floor space, affording a larger number of persons to use it than one which contains greater number of vertical trays.

The card catalogue has the fine quality of up-to-dateness, endless expansion and ease of withdrawal of entries, although it has no portability. The place of the card catalogue in library service appears to be secure, for library technology is yet to produce a finer and better variety of catlogue which can displace the existing card catalogue which can displace the existing card catalogue. The card catalogue is exquisitely suited for union catalogues and co-operative undertakings in cataloguing.

With all its advantages, the card catalogue, in so far as its size and growth is concerned, has been a matter of concern to librarians. The alarming growth and complexity tends to lesson its effective use and to increase the cost of maintenance. In order to reduce its bulk and keep it under control, remedies like divided catalogues, and selective cataloguing of more important material have been practised. The reliance on the card catalogue is expected to decrease gradually with the provision of adequate indexes, bibliographies and abstracts. Unless a special staff charged with its revision, maintenance, and control is employed, the card catalogue is likely to become administratively unmanageable and expensive.

Readers, even to-day, do not appear to be as kind to the card catalogue as they are to the *printed book catalogue*. It is the general view of readers in libraries, particularly in scholarly libraries, that card catalogues are difficult to consult. Only one title can be seen by them on a card at a time. *Guide cards* are never adequate and cross references drive them from one tray to another, which may be far removed from the one being consulted. There is every possibility of a user overlooking a desired entry in the card catalogue by oversight or hurried manipulation.

Preparation of additional copies of card catalogues is as labourious and costly as the original one. *Distribution of card catalogues* outside a library is not ordinarily possible. When once a careless or thoughtless reader removes a card from the tray of the card catalogue, its detection is only accidental. Imperfections are thus likely to occur in card catalogues.

American libraries have always been very active in finding out substitutes for a card catalogue. "Strangely enough the most modern and advanced substitutes for the card catalogue employ the earliest form of record used in libraries, a chronological list of receipts, better known to librarians as the accessions record, because they entail sequential scanning of the complete compliation to locate information... The new machines which accomplish sequential scanning of the complete record rapidly enough to be practical employ electronic devices to achieve their speed. They include two International Business Machine Sorters, which search 650 cards per minute: the Rapid Selector which scans 500 feet of microfilm or 12,000 choices a minute.

The new machines are commonly thought of as solving the problem of subject control, and while they could be employed in searching for author and title entries, they are not being used experimentally in that way now.

"The alternatives to a conventional card catalogue really are few: they are :

1. Sheets (Books)

A. Bound printed catalogues
   a. Successive editions
   b. Basic catalogue plus supplements
   c. Cumulative editions
B. Loose-Leaf manuscript and printed catalogues
2. Punched Cards (fully mechanized)
3. Continuous strips
   A. Microfilm
   B. Magnetic Tape and Wire
   C. Magnetic Disks

Table 1 details the value of these devices"[5] (plate 4).

At best, any or all of these substitutes can only supplement and not totally displace the card catalogue which seems fairly entrenched in library administration at least for small libraries.

Recent studies and discussions on the "Library Catalogue: Changing Dimensions" at the annual conference of the Graduate Library School, University of Chicago, August 5-7, 1963, forcast that Catalogues are undergoing a period of scrutiny and change of their format as well as their functions. Library automation is bound to have its rightful place in library administration.

"*The automation of Cataloges* , indexes, and other bibliographic tools offers the possibility of radically new and improved services to the library *user*"[6] "Eventual mechanization of many library operations is inevitable. The only present obstacles are economic ones, and the long-term trend is toward greater efficiency of machine processing compared to human processing. Unreasonable distrust of automation in libraries will lead to an abdication of human values to the machine of assuming that humans continue to perform machine-like-tasks. Librarians who accept systems analysis and mechanization as legitimate subjects to be studied and mastered will fall heir to the responsibility of planning future libraries, and to planning tasks that machines will perform. There will be no threat to, nor question of, their professional status"[7].

None can, at this stage of transition, predict the definite form of future catalogues. But one can be certain that there is bound to be a change, both in its form and functions. "Some of its functions will differ; its organizations will be altered; and it is quite thinkable that the entire system of entry may be revolutionized. But throughout all the planning

C.D. GULL
Table
Strengths and Weaknesses of Various Alternatives to Card Catalogs

| Name of Record | Physical Form | Arrangements Possible | Flexibility of Intercalating New Entries | Currency and Completeness | Ease of Consultation | Widespread Availability | Speed of Searches in Subject Arrangements |
|---|---|---|---|---|---|---|---|
| Card catalog 3x5 | Cards | 1. Numerical 2. Accessions 3. Alphabetic 4. Dictionary 5. Classified | Excellent | Excellent | Poor—only one entry visible at a time | Impractical—too expensive to distribute and maintain | Slow |
| Punched cards (fully mechanized-) | Cards | 1. Numerical 2. Accessions 3. Alphabetic 4. Dictionary 5. Classified | Excellent | Excellent | Poor—requiresemecanical searching for some types information | Impractical—too expensive to distribute and maintain cards; requires machine installation at each place of use | Medium |
| Manuscript book catalogs | Book | 1. Numerical 2. Accessions 3. Alphabetic 4. Dictionary 5. Classified | Poorer as entries become more crowded; | Excellent | Fair but eventually entries cannot be added in order | Impractical to make copies | |
| Printed book catalog | Book | 1. Numerical 2. Accessions 3. Alphabetic 4. Dictionary 5. Classified | None | Dependent on frequency of supplements, new | Very good for any one complete printing editions or cumulations | Excellent | Medium |
| Manuscript sheaf catalogs | Loose leaf book | 1. Numerical 2. Accessions 3. Alphabetic 4. Dictionary 5. Classified | Poorer as entries become more crowded; leaves must be rewritten or retyped | Excellent | Good, if leaves are rewritten or retyped to preserve order | Impractical to make copies | Medium |
| Printed loose-leaf catalog | Loose-leaf book | 1. Numerical 2. Accessions 3. Alphabetic 4. Dictionary 5. Classified | Excellent | Dependent on frequency of repla - cements sheets | Excellent | Poor—too expensive to hold type or cards for printing replaceent sheets; expensive to maintain loose-leaf volumes | Medium |
| Microfilm | Continuous strip | 1. Numerical 2. Accessions | None | Excellent | Poor—requires Rapid Selector plus photographic laboratory equipment | Poor—expensive to duplicate film; requires expensive machinerry forsearching | Very fast |

| | | | | | | | |
|---|---|---|---|---|---|---|---|
| Magnetic tape, wire, disks | Continuous strip | 1. Numerical 2. Accessions | None | Excellent | Very poor—requires costly searching equipment; provides slow printing of answer | Very poor—requires costly searching equipment | Undetermined, probably very fast |

Reprinted from the October 1953 Issue of LIBRARY TRENDS
a Publication of ILLIONOIS Library School.

for the future, one thing holds certain; the catalog, whatever metamorphosis it may have, becomes increasingly the central axis of the library. The organizers of the library of the future must also be the planners of the catalogs. The two functions cannot be separated. Thus far, at least prophecy can go."[8]

Librarians in 1970s have been experimenting with 'Library technology' with a view to apply it to Library processes, specially in the area of cataloguing procedures. A few such instances from the United States and a lesser number from the British Libraries have been reported in books and periodicals of the initial success and the encouraging results obtained by these libraries in finding alternatives to the card catalogue. The new media adopted for this purpose are:

1. *Machine Readable Catalogue (MARC)*
2. *Computer-Supported Catalogue (COM)* which will also include;

2.1 On-line Interactive Catalogues.

1. Machine Readable Cataloguing records have proved to be a viable alternative to unitary bibliographic records kept on standard cards of the dimension 7.5 cm × 12.5 cm, (appropriately 3"×5"). This has been estabilished by the successful experiements at *Ohio College Library Centre* (*ORCL*) and the *Library of Congress* (LC) The *MARC* distribution service making available machine readable bibliographic data at a very low cost, and the development of accepted formats for machine representation of bibliographic data, and also evolving standards to help their quick exchange were essential factors which led to its success.

*LC MARC I* began as an indoor laboratory experiment in 1961, when the council on Library Resources voted certain funds to the L.C. for applying computer technology to library activities. The L.C. engaged a private computer group to conduct a feasibility study to observe and report, if the L.C. library operations were appropriate for replacement by automated bibliographic systems. After two years of close study of L. C.s operations the report was presented in 1963, statng that conversion to automative system, would both be simple and feasible. Further, the consultant Gilbert King of the Computer agency also recommended the set up of a vast electronic system which would entirely transform the library operation and a national telecommunication network facilitating quick distribution and dissemination of information from the L.C. to libraries all over the U.S.

"During 1964, Inforonics was given a contract by CLR to study the recording of cataloguing data in machine readable form."[9] "The outcome of the recommendation was The MARCI format, and the *LC MARC Pilot Project*."[10] "Additional funds came forth from the CLR in 1966 enabling the LC to develope procedures and programmes for converting and distributing *MARC data.*[11]" The final format of MARCI and the libraries which would participate in the project were decided soon. Till June 1968, 50,000 records had been distributed and experience gained in the economics of the Scheme. *MARC formats* received international recognition and became an international standard (ISO-2709-1973). This was the beginning of *MARCII format.*

Another valuable and simultaneous development achieved by the LC was a standard character set for representing bibliographic data in all languages adopting Roman alphabets. This was a factor effectively contributing to the wide adoption and success of MARC distribution service. "By May, 1978 the LC scored one million MARC record."[12] In all *LC MARC records*, the AACR, LC subject headings, LC and Deway Decimal classification schemes are adopted as standards in determining the contents. However, automation experts consider that there is still room for standardisation for communication of bibliographic data in machine readable format.

For example, the overall dimension of the catalogue card 5" x 3" was approved standard, while the inner area for the transcription of the descriptive and identifying bibliographic data of the documents, the length of lines, the blank space in between etc. on cards and the type sizes were left unspecified, resulting in considerable variation of structural presentation of the format.

"Another complex issue faced is the wide range of languages following different scripts or characters, for bibliographic records. For convenience we may divide the world written scripts into (1) Roman, (2) Non-Roman. Non-Roman scripts need two further divisions: (a) Alphabatic scripts: Arabic, Cryllic, Greek, Hebrew Indic. etc. Even in this group, there is variation, because certain languages like Arabic, Persian, Urdu, read from right to left, and others from left to right. (b) Ideographic script- Chinese Japanese, Korean, the Chinese script is read from top to bottom (Inversely vertical order), which is being reformed to be read from left to right to keep pace with international developments in bibliographic standards.

*LC MARC* records have partially demonstrated that scholarship and libraries do not recognize linguistic barriers; hence an automated bibliographic system must be capable of accomodating a wide range of written languages; e.g. LC processes documents in over 70 languages using 20 different scripts or characters sets."[13]

"However, LC's unwillingness or inability to develop viable techniques for the transcription of the Non-Roman scripts in vernacular form is highly regrettable. This will doubtless complicate the problem of inplementing automated alternatives to card catalogue."[14]

MARC commenced its functioning in 1969 as a pilot project at the Library of Congress. Now two decades have gone by now. During this period, the project made rapid progress. Both developed and developing countries adopted its use in their libraries and for their data bases, and for exchanges of information, and other bibliographic records. The production of catalogue cards by MARC appears to be the most popular operation, although there are other applications of MARC as a time saver. In building up databases MARC will be effective. The online catalogue of MARC records has become the official catalogue of the Library of Congress, with the closing in 1980 of the manual catalogue.

MARC also paved its way to automation of library operations, and maintenance of standards for all activities. "Standard formats, character sets, codes, cataloguing rules, etc. have promoted the development of the systems that made possible the resource sharing, that is enjoyed today. What is now in place are the basic modules upon which the next generation of network implementation will be built. "*

*MARC uses in general*

A large number of uses of MARC data fall into the technical processing area. In order to serve the reference function, the item must be put under bibliographic control. Further the professional staff performing technical processing are involved in several repetietive functions. It is essential to relieve them of this routine job to save their

* Encyclopedia of Library and Information Science; ed. by Allen Kent. 1988. v. 443, supplement [illegible]

time, and utilise them to work, where their technical skill is essential, and appropriate. However, the reference function to a certain extent is fulfilled by SDI services, LC's MARC Retrieve, and the searching of index files of author, title, and subject.

*Selection and Ordering*

Current MARC tapes are used for selection purposes by printing out the records and routing them to persons responsible for selecting the materials for acquisition or for comparison of the tapes against stored data, and printing the records that match. Printed indexes are also prepared from the MARC files which help selection work.

*Searching in Catalogues and other files*

As MARC records are available for items to be ordered, manual bibliographic searching is eliminated.

*Catalogue Cards Production*

MARC records are used for making catalogue cards, and book form catalogue. The production forms include computer line printing, photo-composition, and micro forms; e.g. *Books in English* is printed and produced by merging B N B and MARC records with relevant MARC recors of the LC and it is an example of the Bibliography in microform.

Today MARC's impact on the majority of library functions nationally and internationally is obvious. A communication format designed to suit the transmission of data between systems, the content designation, and the data content essential for the identification and recording of the elements required for supporting the acquisitions, cataloguing, information retrieval, etc. was created and approved by all sharing resources libraries. Due to this uniformity prevailing in MARC uses, the LC distributes approximately 200,000 records annually. Many libraries have successfully implemented automated systems for one or more library operations. Card catalogue are being gradually replaced by on-line catalgoue for technical processing, and research functions. In these cases, where card or book catalogues are being used, the printed and microform products are computer produced.

"Although the *NATIONAL UNION CATALOG* and *NEW SERIES TITLES* are still major bibliographic tools, the shared cataloguing operations of the bibliographic utilities with member locations posted has resulted in machine readable union catalogues of great significance with the procedures for inter- library loan automated, and consequently much more effective," *

The mini-computer and Compact Disc-Read-Only Memory (CD-ROM) of the 1980s might replace individual processing and original cataloguing done locally.

*British Library's UK MARC Database*

The Bibliographic Service Division of the British Library announced that the British Library is firmly committed to the improvement of the currency of the UK MARC Database as it appears on-line *via* BLAISE LINE, in print as the British National Bibliography and in the other UK MARC record supply services.

Proposals for expanding the UK Cataloguing-in-Publication Programme have been widely circulated among libraries and publishers. A good number appear to have arrived at a broad concensus of approval. From January 1985, the British National Bibliography will print the style of CIP records. This is likely to result in sizeable economy in cost, time and labour in publishing British National Bibliography and ultimately benefit the library community. It may also serve the libraries as a ready and current reference source in answering varieties of readers' enquiries.

The Bibliographic Services Division of the British Library creates UK MARC records, distributes them in the British National Bibliography, in the UK MARC database available through BLAISE- LINE, and to other supply services.

These records enable the libraries to easily select and acquire books, serve as standard catalogue entries, and provide references to British Books and other publications for information retrieval.

The accelerated CIP Programme aims to provide advance information on forthcoming British books to meet the demands of libraries for book selection, cataloguing, and reference work. The willingness and cooperation of the publishers, who are asked to forward to the Bibliographic Services Division a complete data sheet with details of each of their forthcoming titles in a great facilities. Together with the data sheet, copies of the title page and verso, the preface, the introduction, the table of contents and any promotion material, if available, are also asked to be supplied.

The Bibliographic Services Division uses this information to create

* Encyclopedia of Library and Information Science; ed. by Allen Kent. 1988. v. 43, supplement 8, p. 159.

authoritative bibliographic records, adopting internationally agreed cataloguing rules, and subject classification, and indexing methods. With this voluntary cooperation of the publishers, the chief objectives-currency and completeness of the book resources are expected to be achieved. This CIP not only provides improved library service to readers, but also is likely to result in increasing sales, an advantage to publishers.

2. *Computer-Supported Catalogue (COM)*

The use of computer for catalogue cards production and maintenance is certainly an effective system. The OCLC production and distribution of catalogue cards among a number of U.S. Libraries since 1971 besides the L.C. cards, which were already in use, is an indication of its popularity, even though there are certain drawbacks inherent to the centralized catalogue cards production system whether manual or computerised.

The advantages of adopting the computer-produced cards has been stated that it "removes the need to consider divided catalogs, freezing existing catalogs or any other traumatic changes.....catalogs cards produced by computer can be just as easily integrated into an existing catalog as can overtyped LC cards. In fact OCLC cards can be more easily used, as they come already overtyped with headings and call numbers and are presorted for filing.

Nonetheless, there are certainly some disadvantages in the adoption of computer printed cards. They are almost similar to the adoption of LC printed catalogue cards, with only a small degree of difference.

"Far reaching administrative changes are usually effected along with the introduction of shared cataloguing systems into catalogs departments. Professional positions are often replaced with para professional staff for copy cataloguing; proof slip and depository card filing units as well as cards preparation units are disbanded. Administrators gain an opportunity to exercise professional creativity without the need to worry about technical consequences with which they are not in general very comfortable. *Computer-produced catalog cards* offer a relatively simple way to introduce automation with seemingly little risk".[15]

"*Computer output microform* is one of the means by which data manipulated by a computer can be rendered intelligible to a human being. A computer deals with information in the form of electrical signals. Thus the same computer data base that can produce line printer or photo-typeset output for a printed book catalog can be used to generate COM".[16]

Two basic types of microform (1) *Microfilm,* (2) *Microfiche.* The first kind is commonly found in libraries. The second kind is microfiche, which is used for source documents. Between these two forms, microfiche provides simpler and quicker access to a required group of frames, eliminating the irritating task of running through the microfilm roll. The user selects the appropriate fiche, which is inserted into the reader, and he can locate the frame containing the needed information. Both types consume the users' time before and after locating the page or information continuing the data desired, but the claim that it is less troublesome to the user than a traditional card catalogue is catching up with certain libraries in the western world, where telecommunication and electronics and applications have been vastly developed.

It seems, that in India, which is trying to catch up with the West in the field of electronic technology, is yet to attempt in a systematic way the production and use of COM catalogs. The funds at the disposal of the libraries in general including those of the Universities, Colleges, Research Organisations, which are a shade better provided for, are so limited that initial investment of capital for a computer to support a catalogue and produce catalogue cards or provide equipment for, MARC, appear to be distant feasibility. It is only with appreciable progress in overall literacy of the population and general living standard of people that library technology of the West for library processes and operations would be possible. Till then professional and semi-professional manpower available cheaply and plentily would perform the various operations in the libraries of large areas of the East. But a knowledge and familiarity of such developments by the students of library school and staff of libraries would be desirable and should be gained in order that they are in a state of preparedness to change over to automation as soon it is considered feasible. But a word of caution seems appropriate. The total familiarity with orginal source of information and an insight into the bibliographic description gained by the staff of libraries, when the traditional card catalogue is perpared to serve the users and staff will be denied, when machines take over most of the functions. To that extent libraries would be depleted with the strength of the informed personnel on the staff, because several of them would be lacking the rich experience gained in bibliographic documentation and information service.

*2.1 On-line Catalogue.*

"Automation has become entrenched in the Library and certainly in Processing Services. As a result we are very dependent on the Library's automated systems. Technical developments in the department revolve around the design and implementation of new applications and the refinement and expansion of existing bibliographic control systems. Some of these developments translate into new and enhanced products and services to our internal, local, national, and international constituencies.

"Beginning with the Books format, the MARC formats have been developed by LC staff for Serials, Maps, Films, manuscripts, Music and Sound Recordings, Visual Materials, and Machine-readable Data Files. The last format, MRDF for short, is nearly to be implemented at the Library so that online cataloguing can begin for this material.

"One of the prime uses for which library automation was expanded in the 1960s was to assist in the control of the Library's collections through automating its catalogs. To get an idea of what a monumental task it is to maintain control, a few statistics might be in order here. Currently, LC is the world's largest library. It contains over 500 miles of bookshelves, and its holdings amount to more than 84 million items.

"The on-line catalog of MARC records has become the Library's official catalog with the closing in 1980 of its manual catalog. The combined number of full cataloging records represented by the two catalogs is over 14 million. The MARC database totals over five million record. It includes records for Books Serials, Films, Maps, Music, and Name, Series, and Subject Authorities, in all languages cataloged at LC (over 450 languages at last count): the non-roman alphabet languages are represented in romanized form. The remaining cataloged records which are not in MARC have been converted to machine readable form by a commercial firm, and these records are being loaded into LC's data base in file which we call PREMARC. To date this file of converted records contains over 4.5 million records.

"ACQUIRE is the planned automation system which will make acquisitions status information in brief form available to users of LC's online catalog. For an institution that purchased over one million items in fiscal 1987, it is imperative that a such a system be in place. The system is expected to be operational in 1991 and will replace a system now over ten years old and which is so fragile that we sometimes lose control over important order information. In the future, it is planned that these two much needed systems will be ilinked with each other as well as with the files in the library's database." *

An on-line interactive catalogue is not only the latest development among the group of mechanical catalgues, but also highly flexible, as the on-line system is capable of providing instantaneous and sophisticated access to information, on account of direct interaction with the computer. It can also be smoothly integrated into a comprehensive library system. But it will be too much or even futile to expect that an on-line catalogue is a perfect tool capable of performing every function of an ideal catalogue, though it could save appreciably the users' time in the retrieval of information.

An on-line catalogue is made up of individual components, each of them requiring support and maintenance. Because of these multicomponents the investment and their proper upkeep ensuring flawless function requires large funds. Unless the economic burden is shared by participating libraries in the area, no single institution would find it possible to install this automation as an alternative to manual catalogue whether in card or book form.

"The foremost component of an inter catalogue system is a computer. There are two kinds: (1) *mainframe computers*, and (2) *minicomputers*. The chief difference between them relate to size, cost, and the availability of utility software (programmes). In order to further bring down the cost of minicomputers and that individual institutions might own one, computing devices known as microprocessors have been developed. It is estimated that a minicomputer may be available at not more than one fifth of the total cost of a mainframe computer, and also prove equally efficient in its performance.

The second important item of components in an on-line catalogue system is the "peripheral devices-" the input and output equipment in the form of key boards for input combined with *cathode ray tubes* (*CARTS*) and printers for output. The total cost for both items is estimated at $ 7000.00. A *CRT terminal* for bibliographic application is serviced at thirty dollars ($30.00) per month. Modems (Modulators demodultors) are required to provide the interface between system components and the telephone network for data transmission. The modems cost approximately $ 125.00 per month. In addition, main frame computer systems usually require a transmission control unit

---

* H.D. Avram: Library Technology in Processing Services, Library of Congress: in his address to the Seminar on Library Automation and Information Networks in Taiwan June 9, 1988.

(TCU) to control telecommunication. This may cost as much as $2000.00 monthly. Leased telephone lines have averaged about $ 100.00 monthly per mile." [18] All this estimation of cost is assesed as of 1978. It would be seen that in terms of rupees the total initial investments calculates to Rs. 56,000.00 and the total monthly maintenance comes to Rs. 1326.00. This is for a mini computer; while a mainframe computer would require an additional sum of Rs. 17,000.00 per month for maintaining (TCU) to control telecommunication. The large amount required for an on-line catalogue can not be measured against the benefits resulting out of its adoption as the library services have always been intangible benefits gained by the society. Perhaps the quick changing technological scene may render the quipments obsolete too soon.

The foregoing cost and the advantages and disadvantages of an on-line interactive catalogue system outlined above would enable libraries to opt for the system or to continue the traditional card catalogue.

REFERENCE

1. **C.D. Gull.** "Substitutes for the Card Catalogue." **Library Trends,** v. 2, 2, October 1953, p. 323.
2. **John W. Cronin.** The National Union and Library of Congress Catalogue; Problems and Prospects. **Library Quarterly,** v. 34, 1, January 1964, p. 81.
3. **Ibid.** p. 82.
4. **Ibid.** p. 86.
5. **C.D. Gull.** "Substitutes for the Card Catalogue." **Library Trends,** v. 2, 2, October 1953, p. 323.
6. **Don, R. Swanson.** Dialogues with Catalog. **Library Quarterly,** v. 33, 1, January, 1964, p. 113.
7. **Ibid.** p. 125.
8. **Ruth French Strout.** Introduction. **Library Quarterly,** v. 34, 1 January. 1964, p. 3.
9. **Hanriette D. Avram:** MARC: the First Two Years. L.R. and T.S., 12 (Summer 1968) : 245.
10. **MARCII Format,** Washington, D.C: LC Jan. 1968. p. 1
11. MARC: Its History and Implications. LC. 1975. pp. 5-7.
12. Library of Congress information Bulletin. 37 (July, 21, 1978) : 413.
13. **Lucia. J. Rather;** Special characters and Diacritical Marks used in Roman Alphabets. L.R. and T.S. 12, (Summer) 1968: 285.
14. **S. Michael Malinconico and Paul J. Fasana:** The Future of the Catalog. N.Y. Knowledge Industry Publications, 1979. p. 40.
15. **Ibid.** pp. 33-44.
16. **Ibid.** p. 59.
17. **Ibid.** p. 67.

# 8

# PHYSICAL FORMS OF CATALOGUES - II COMUPTERISED CATALOGUES

In the previous chapter 7, several physical forms of catalogues, which are chiefly operated manually have been described, their features and functions analysed, both in favour and against their continued use examined. Towards the end of the chapter, a brief account of the *COM*- Catalogues, and *ON LINE* Interactive catalogues is given. In order to enable the beginners to obtain an overall view of the catalogue in computerised form, a detailed study of the reasons for and against their adoption is provided.

During the last ten years, the comupterised catalogue has been gaining popularity, almost to the extent of blind faith, specially in libraries of the Western world, America, Europe and the United Kingdom. It has been vociferously expressed by certain industrial and commercial interests that the unlimited information available in books and periodicals, and other documents would readily be accessible, at fantastic speed, cheaper cost, and lesser time by a computerised catalogue than other forms of catalogues, hitherto adopted by libraries and information centres. But timely warning against total rapture with the computer to solve all human problems, of which library cataloguing is one, has been emphasised by another group of eminent individuals in a convincing and forthright manner, by stressing on the large capital for investment needed and recurring cost of maintenance, also quite high, in proportion to the results obtained.

Adoption of a computer for performing the functions of a card catalogue, which is manually operated should justify the decision. Objective assessment of the virtues of a computerised catalogue seems necessary to uphold its use. This can be done only, if one has knowledge of 1. what is a computer, 2. what validity is there for its use, 3. what is the user's reaction to the com-catalogue, in place of the traditional catalogues with which he is familiar, 4. what financial commitments are necessary for its installation, and maintenance, and 5. what standard of computer literacy is essential for programming, storing and retrieval of information. A brief inquiry and study of these issues are dealt with in the following pages.

1. What is a computer? An electronic machine, which performs complex calculations or clerical operations at unimaginable speed. It coprises of an arithmetic unit to work out the calculations, a store or memory-chamber to contain instruction and data, and a control unit to coordinate operations and carry out the instructions found in a programme. This is popularly know as the *heart of the computer*. This part contains the electronic circuits of the arithmetic and control units.

*Peripherals* cover input and output devices, and the secondary storage of magnetic tape/disc, which becomes necessary due to limited space in the original storage memory chamber.

*Sizes*. There are at present three or four sizes of computer: 1. a main-frame computer is the largest, and is intended to carry out simultaneously a number of different processing operations/tasks. 2. mini-computer is a small compact and low cost one. But it can function equally efficiently, and used for different purposes. 3. *micro- computer*: With a view to further bring down the cost of mini-computers, and also enable individual institutions to acquire it, a computing device known as *microprocessor* has been developed. This model is built around the *silicon chip* (an electronic circuit comprising many separate interconnected components manufactured as a single integrated unit) is a remarkable invention, which has revolutionised the computer production. When a basic computer is integrated on one sillicon chip, it is called a *microprocessor*. This performs the functions of a central processing unit, which is a vital part of the traditional computer both main frame and mini sizes. When it is used with other components, it is termed *a micro- computer*.

Irrespective of these three sizes of computer, the basic principle and techonology adopted is the same for all. Each one of them contains 1. a central processing unit, 2. a storage unit or memory chamber and 3. input and output devices. The differences existing among them are based on the internal eomplexity or construction governing the units. The speed with which information is made available, the quantity of data retrieved, and communicated in a given period, and finally the cost influences the choice. Studies conducted on the cost analysis and assessment on the functioning of these computers have revealed that a mini-computer could be obtained at not more than one fifth of the total cost of a main frame computer, and also prove that the performance level between them is equally efficient.

2. What validity exists in replacing the traditional catalogue (page, card, etc.) with computerised forms, specially in the Indian context?

Experts, who are commercially motivated in the western countries, assert that no library/information centre could ensure efficiency and satisfaction to its users in their demand for information without a computer as the growth of knowledge, and the production of books and documents as sources of information is fantastic and unmeasurable.

Justification for the use of computers for cataloguing in libraries exists in ample measures. Although the catalogue supported by a computer by itself presents benefits by way of speedy retrieval of information, saving of user's time, and larger quantity of information output a decision to replace the traditional manually operated cdard/other catalogues needs care and forethought by the management.

1. The size and type of library, 2. it a staff provision, and levels of competency, 3. financial commitments and 4. the computer availability in the neighbourhood are important factors, which need dispassionate study before going automative.

Libraries with limited resources, one man staffed as in the case of small branch libraries, a stock of less than 100,000 valumes, and a limited number of readers actively and regularly using the library, (less than 500) and restricted working hours as observed by branch libraries serving small population, specially in India, with book grants inadequate to cover the total demand of the readers, would hardly need a computerised catalogue nor would it be possible to install and maintain it. In reality, there are libraries which do not have even a typewriter. The reading accommodation is not adequate for all readers due to lack of floor space and furniture, as observed even in the libraries of states with public library laws governing their functioning. It is safe commonsense to drop the idea of installing com-catalogues in such institutions. Even the availability of a computer in the proximity with which the individual libraries cuuld share and integrate is remote.

Also big academic institutional libraries of universities, autonomous colleges, research centres also cannot, as a rule go in for com-catalogues. A change from the mannual to the com- catalogues is costly and the proven results of such a change do not warrant the adoption of com-catalogues, as they cannot increase the number of users, nor the books, nor the quality of information. In these circumstances, big university library systems, with more than one million volumes, and the faculty and students, more than 25,000 feel hesitant to devote the limited financial grants to be invested on the com-catalogues. As instances of not computerising the catalogues by big library systems, one might readily cite Manchester, Liverpool, and the National Library of India, which are quite big, continue the manual, catalogues, even though financial resources might be available.

Finally, the criteria for not computerising the catalogue of a library should be the measure of man power and talent available, comparatively at cheaper cost than automation cost. In countries, where the man power available is limited, its cost increases. In such cases, it is wise to opt for computerisation of the catalogue. But it should clearly be understood, that while the mechanisation reduces the quantity of tedious functions to be performed by library staff, does in no way improve the quality of work done by human intellignece. With all the revolution in electronic technology, it is only the human talent that retains this prerogative.

3. User's reaction to the retrieval of information from the com-catalogue is a significant factor, which will influence the decision to continue its maintenance or to revert to the traditional manually operated catalogue.

As early as 1955, the writer, while working with the British National Bibliography had observed, that the card catalogue of current British books produced from the B.N.B. entries was placed in the rotunda (reading room) of the British Museum. Most of the readers preferred to obtain the books or information by contacting the staff at the central enquiry tables, instead of from the card catalogue, as it appeared to them a new intruder on the time old practice. Perhaps time has changed the outlook of readers when the British Library had adopted computerised equipment for many of its operations, including Cataloguing. Usually the prevailing practice continues to hold its position, in spite of highly convincing arguments for the use of computerised forms. In India, the situation is yet to witness this transition. New large library systems have the advantage of exposing the readers to the computerised form even from the initial stages with the result that the readers take to it in an hospitable manner.

4. Financial resources play an important role in opting for computers in place of human power. The total investment in the case of a micro-computer involves 1. the cost of micro-computer itself, and 2. the peripheral devices, the input and output in the form of keyboards for input combined with cathode ray tubes (CARTS), and printers for output. In case of the first item, at present prizes, it would require approximately Rs. 1,50,000/- and for the second item Rs. 2,000/- monthly for maintenance. A Main- frame computer would involve at least Rs. 25,000/- for maintenance per month. These figures of expenses for computer equipment and monthly upkeep and servicing, appear beyond the resources available for the small libraries in this country. There is a doubt whether these items might not become obsolete after a few years due to advance in electronic research and technology.

The reported expenses of the Liverpool Polytechnique for using Com-catalogue (mini-computer) are the capital expenses £ 36,000.00 in 1984-85, recurring and maintaining £ 7,000.00. These figures are given to compare the possible expenses in Indian Libraries which may be contemplating to modernise their libraries. The central theme of the All India Libraries Conference recently held at Brarathidasan University Tiruchirapally, 1987 was 'Modernisation in Indian Libraries'. Although, the papers are a good number, none appears to have gone into the actual realities of the Indian set up of the Libraries. There is not much help that could be found on the pages of these papers on these issues. It also doubtful, whether the figures cited above include the expenses on the wages of staff, and replacement processes. However, the idea is to proceed cautiously and achieve appropriate results.

The on-line interactive cataloguing system favoured for adoption by big libraries, e.g. the British Library, is full of promise, but beyond the available resources for libraries in India, and other developing countries, of Asia, except Japan, which is fortunate to possess all the knowledge in electronics an it is and exception. Japan has the latest computerised cataloguing services.

5. Computer Literacy levels of competency expected of the library staff, and of the users of the com-catalogue is a reasonable factor to count with, when opting for computerised cataloguing services.

1. Library staff who were charged with the cataloguing processes, fixing author headings, added entries, subject headings, references, and filling the cards in the cabinet, and withdrawing entries for books lost and discarded have either to be replaced or educated for *programming* and allied work (KWOC entries), and instruct the users in using

the com-catalogues output on the computer screen.

Programming: The Computer needs instructions to carry-out various tasks, one by one, in the sequence determined and the programmer chooses the language in which the computer could be fed. There are several such languages-BASIC, COBOL, PLI, FORTRAN, and PASCAL. In order to facilitate machine coding, these intermediate *high level* languages have been devised. Even for the adoption of any of these languages, it requires a highly trained person and the job is arduous and tedious. See illustration on opposite page.

The programme written in a high level language gets translated within the machine by a master programme into machine code, which alone a computer can understand, and perform the tasks accordingly. This is also called the *compiler*.

The input programmes can be done either by getting the existing staff of a library specially trained to work on computer programming or by appointing new staff. In the case of new staff replacing the existing persons, they (the old) are usually deployed for other work, like assisting the readers, checking the list of new titles ordered with the catalogue etc.

The output/retrieval of information appearing on the screen of the computer is dependent on the high level language used and its translation into binary code/machine language, and the same is obtained by following search instructions provided by the side of the computer screen. For detailed study and understanding of how this is done by the computer, readers may refer to books on computer performance, and its adoption for library activities, and services. List of such works could be found at the end of this chapter. It is also possible to locate in a subject bibliography a number of such works.

A library may also become a partner in the *network* by having connecting terminals with other centres, and the information from outside libraries can be made available to the readers. This is more or less like the operation of teleprinters (telex services), which automatically supply the same information to different centres. An example of library cooperation can be seen in this kind of 'network' functioning. Well known networks are BLAISE, OCLC On Line Computer Library Centre Inc., Dublin (Ohio) and also in Birmingham., MEDLARS. ETC. There is certainly an advantage over the manual systems of catalogues, but at a price beyond the reach of the small and medium sized libraries.

An example of a Guide to the Readers in Using the Computer

Catalogue is provided, and alterations could be made to suit the type of catalogues.

The ultimate beneficiary of computerisation of the library catalogue, being the library users/readers, it is essential to impart instructions to them on computer literacy, without which all effort would be futile. A simple method is to provide a set of these instructions by the side of the computer screen, enabling them to search and locate the desired entry or information from the catalogue. Every Catalogue needs these directions in helping and educating the users, as to how to get at the desired book/document. Com-Catalogue is no exception. Perhaps, copies of these guide lines may be provided and freely distributed to the users.

There is one unanswered question, what to do with the card catalogue? Should it be maintained upto-date or not.? There are quite a few problems in its maintenance, first its cost, second utility after the advent of the Com-Catalogue. Com-Catalogue is susceptible to repairs and replacement of-parts, when it becomes inoperative.

There is no way of searching and locating the book, in the absence of the Card Catalogue. The management of the library should consider these issues before a decision is taken on the old time tested tool in unfolding the contents of the library.

It seems that computer print out Catalogue Cards could be used and filed in the Card Catalogue, which will not only provide continuous service, but also distribute the number of readers waiting to use the com-catalogue or it could be used as an official reference tool by the library staff.

Also students of library and information science may use it for comparison with the new tool and establish certain norms.

## Com-Catalogue

**Directions to the user to search and locate the desired information.**

1. Gently press the key "Start Over" to begin or end your search.
2. Touch the heading of the file "Author", "Title", "Subject", you want.
3. Touch the entry coming on the screen before the one you want: Numerical/Alphabetical.
4. Repeat the operation till you see "Browse, Reverse/Browse, Forward" at the screen's bottom and watch for the entry you desire to appear. If it is not in the library's holdings, it will not

be found. Sometimes a different spelling may require another similar operation.

5. By touching the heading of the term you wanted, the entire list of books under the same heading will appear one by one on the screen.
6. When the exact title required is visible on the screen, touch it again to indicate whether it is on the book shelf or on loan and also the information if it is in the Central Library/Branch Library. Now it is possible to note the call number of the book and obtain it by the procedure adopted in the library.
7. If your search is over, touch "Start Over", in order the fresh search may be undertaken.

Usually libraries, provide these instructions to the library users, in order they could get at the information through the computer catalogue. The reader may operate the Com-Catalogue and the screen, which looks similar to a teleprinter, *presents* these items. One could find from the set of instructions above that in case of manually operated Card-Catalogue (Dictionary/Simple Alphabetical) all the operations have to be done by the reader with the knowledge of the system of dialing the entries. Perhaps, the time taken is slightly more and somewhat tedious, which the com-catalogue aims to eliminate. An obvious advantage with the Com-catalogue is that the reader need not proceed to the shelf if the information on the screen tells that it is checked out or under repairs etc.

Titles mentioned below would yield further detailed information on this topic.

1. Fosdick, Howard, Computer basics for librarians and Information Scientists, London, Information Resources Press: 1981.
2. Fry, T.F., Beginner's guide to computers, 2nd ed., London, Newnes, 1983.
3. Hildreth C.R., On line public access Catalogue: the user inferface, O.C.L.C.; 1982.
4. Hunter, Eric. J., Computerized Cataloguing, London, Bingley 1985.
5. Rowley J.E., Computer for libraries, London, Bingley, 1980.
6. Viswanathan C.G., Elements of Information Science and Technology, 2nd ed., Lucknow, Print House, 1985.
7. Willis, Jerry, Computer for everybody, 3rd ed., Dilithium Press, 1984.

# 9

# VARIETIES OF CATALOGUES, THEIR SCOPE AND FUNCTIONS

The chief forms of Library catalogues in use are (1) the *alphabetical*, by authors, titles, and subjects, maintained in two or three different sequences or combined in a single sequence, when it is called a dictionary catalogue; (2) *the classed*, in which the arrangement of the entries follows the order of subjects predetermined in a scheme of book classification, which generally aims to bring together subjects related to each other in a logical manner; (3) *alphabetico- classed* in which the entries are arranged in a compromised order, which aims to combine the advantages of the *alphabetical* and the *classed* forms. These can as well be called the *internal forms of catalogues.*

1. *The Author Catalogue.* It is perhaps the oldest form of catalogue and also fundamental to all other forms and combinations.

The author catalogue is a list of books in a collection, entered under the names of the authors of books, the entries being arranged alphabetically. The heading for these entries consists of (i) the surname of the author, followed by (ii) his forename or forenames in complete or secondary fullness in the case of all western writers, with a few exceptions, *e.g.* Wells, Herbert George, exception, *e.g.* Augustine, Saint. In the case of eastern writers, the practice is to enter the authors under their personal names, followed by their surnames or family titles with a few exceptions, *e.g.* Radhakrishnan, Sarvepalli; Raman, C.V.; exception, *e.g.* Gandhi, M.K. The main object of such style of entry is to enter an author's name under the best known form. The body of the author entry contains the record of the title of his work, imprint and collation.

This kind of catalogue is of immense value and importance, because the author of a book is its origin and the fact is uncontroversial although opinions about the subject headins of a book may be different. There may be several books with a common title. But about the name of the writer of a book, little difference is likely to arise. As the works of a writer are entered under his name, it is specially valuable in yielding the information about all his works together, when one approaches the catalogue by knowing his name only and not his works. Without the author entry, it would be ncessary to look under the titles of his works or names of subjects dealt with in his works. The entries for titles do not come together as the works invariably have different titles and get filed under different letters of the alphabet; *e.g.* Oliver Twist; Pickwick Papers; Tale of Two Cities of Charles Dickens will have to be looked for in three places in the catalogue, if there were no author entry for each one of them under Dickens, Charles. In such a case, all these three works are brought together under one common form of an author heading. Such a close display of an author's works will also enable the catalogue to answer the question, quickly and without effort what works are there in a collection by a given author. Another simple enquiry, answered by the author catalogue is "Is there a particular work of a given author?"

Due to these reasons the *author catalgue* is given the first position in the hierarchy. There is common acceptance of the fact that no library catalogue can be completed without some form of an author catalogue.

It is alleged that the author catalogue suffers from the defects of incapacity to answer questions relating to subject or title. It is true that it cannot provide information about the subject of a book or the title of a book, as it is not designed to yield this type of information. In order to satisfy this adverse criticism the author catalogues are supplemented with alphabetical subject indexes, *e.g.* London Library (Author) catalogue has a subject index.

*Name Catalogue*. Sometimes the author catalogue is extended in scope to contain the names of persons as subjects of books, chiefly in autobiographies, biographies, criticisms, diaries, memoires, etc. When these entries of personal names as subjects are mixed with author entries it is called a name catalogue. The combination of author and subject limited to the person is of certain value, as under one alphabet and under one style of heading information about a person as author and as subject can be found. It is convenient to have in sequential array the works by and about an author. This form of catalogue is specially valuable for collections of literature, personal memoires, autobiographies. The distinction between the person as author heading and the same person as subject is maintained by adopting different typographic disposition of the heading or using different coloured ink, *e.g.*

| | | |
|---|---|---|
| | Dickens, Charles | David Copperfield. |
| | Dickens, Charles | Oliver Twist. |
| *Person as author* | Dickens, Charles | Pickwick Papers. |
| | Dickens, Charles | Tale of Two Cities. |
| | Dickens, Charles | A Critical Study by G.R. Gissing |
| *Person as subject* | DICKENS, CHARLES | The Soul of Dickens by W.W. Crotch. |

2. *The Title Catalogue.* It is a list of books in a collection in which the entries for books under their titles are arranged in alphabetical order. The heading for these entries consists of the title proper, followed by the date of imprint and the number of volumes, if more than one. The body of the card contains the author's name repeated in the form and fulness, in the next line, as in the heading for the author entry. *e.g.*

Vanity fair. 1903
Thackeray, W.M.

This form of catalogue is to help those approaching the catalogue in search of a specific title. In the case of works belonging to form classes and specially fiction, the title entries are essential and serve the reader in his approach. But in case of the general books (classed books) the approach to them is by their subjects as well as by their titles or authors. Economies in cataloguing sometimes require that title entries need not be made, as for the titles, *e.g.* Outlines of Entomology by Imms; Essays by William Hazlitt. A title catalogue, therefore, does not fully represent a record of every book in a collection, unless it is made strictly conventional and mechanical to provide a title entry for every book irrespective of its need and justification. For title entry, the title of the book is generally transcribed as it is given on the title page, the entry word being the first word, not an article, of the title. Further, if the terms used as subject headings for the book are identical with the words of the title, the title entry will be overlapping the subject entry and will, therefore, serve no genuine need. A *title catalogue*, by itself, will prove inadequate and will not function independently.

3. *The Alphanetical Subject Catalogue.* It is a list of books in a collection, each entered under the name of the specific subject of the book as a heading, the entries being arranged alphabetically. The body of the subject entry contains the complete record of a book in the same form and fulness as on its author entry. Several books on the same subject, having a common form and style of subject heading, will be brought together in the catalogue. When more than one book is there under one subject heading the author of the book is taken to determine the alphabetical order. If the author's name is common or spelt similarly for several books, the titles are sought to fix their order of arrangement, *e.g.*

BIBLIOGRAPHY – BEST BOOKS
Sonnenschein, William
Best Books.
ENGLISH LITERATURE – HISTORY
AND CRITICISM.
Saintsbury, George.
Outlines of English literature.
INDIA – POLITICS & GOVERNMENT
Jawaharlal Nehru.
Discovery of India.
INDIA – POLITICS & GOVERNMENT
Jawaharlal Nehru.
India on the march.
INDIC LITERATURE – HISTORY
Winternitz, Maurice.
History of Indic literature

This form of *subject catalogue* is called an *alphabetical subject catalogue*. If one approaches the catalogue with a view to finding a book or books on a specific subject it provides excellent service. The user has to refer to it like a dictionary, but the moment the user wants to find all the material on a field of knowledge in a systematic way, the catalogue fails to answer his enquiry, *e.g.* a book on physics will be entered under the subject heading PHYSICS and not under SCIENCE; nor a book on MAGNETISM under PHYSICS. One has, therefore, to look under separate headings at different places in the alphabetical arrangement, if all the material available on a given field of knowledge is to be gathered.

In small public libraries, its continued usefulness is maintained, because the average reader uses the library in fulfilment of his specific day to day needs, and refers to the specific subject headings to obtain quick access to the books. "In American libraries the alphabetical subject catalogue is the most common, although it is usually an integral part of dictionary card catalogue which includes, in one alphabetical order (though frequently with conventional departures from strict alphabetical order) all entries for authors, titles, and subjects. Within the last two decades, however, a number of libraries have introduced divided catalogues, separating authors and titles from subjects on the theory that the resulting catalogue is more easily understood and used."[1]

4.. *The Dictionary Catalogue*. It is a catalogue which consists of author, title, and subject entries arranged in one alphabetical order. The reference entries also find their appropriate location in the order. It has been styled after a dictionary as it is expected to function as simply as a dictionary. As one knowing the alphabet can use a dictionary, so also the dictionary catalogue in which the ruling factor is the alphabet is expected to prove quite simple in its reference and use.

This form of catalogue has been quite popular in American libraries. There has emerged recently a volume of adverse criticism, that the dictionary card catalogue has tended to become too complex and unwieldy. The *divided catalogue* which is considered a substitute, has not offered a complete solution. It is, however, expected that an average person using the dictionary catalogue can get at the desired information about authors, titles and subjects in a direct manner. By making the headings for these entries specific and consistent, it is possible to provide the information without resorting to any other file or list. If one wants to know what books are available in the library on "Horses", one should look for the heading 'HORSES" in its place in the alphabetical order. If the library has books on 'HORSES' they will all be found entered under the heading 'HORSES' which will furnish information about the author and title of the books and their location on the shelves. The reader need not possess the slightest knowledge that 'HORSES' is a subject which forms part of ZOOLOGY or part of 'DOMESTIC ANIMALS' or part of 'LIVESTOCK' or part of 'FARM ANIMALS'. But it does not mean that 'HORSES' as a subject is left unrelated to the other subjects, of which it is an integral part. The specific subject is linked up with the general and co-ordinate subjects by making use of *"See also" references*. The relation between synonymous and opposite subjects is estabilished by providing "*See*" *references*. The quickness with which information about the titles or authors on a specific subjects is obtained, is incomparable with any other form of catalogue. In order to achieve this end, the dictionary catalogue is constructed on the basic principle of entry under the specific subject heading. It is considered its strength as well as its weakness, *e.g.*, direct reference to 'HORSES' as subject, eliminate waste of time, instead of finding 'HORSES' under, DOMESTIC ANIMALS, and then under 'HORSES'. This direct and specific subject entry does not bring together related material in a comprehensive and logical manner, for each specific subject gets scattered under different letters of the alphabet, *e.g.* COLT under C, MARE under M, and STALLION under S. If one wants the whole range of material on 'HORSES' as a class one has to look under all the specific subjects adopted. The search is continued. This defect is not only true of the dictionary form, but it will be seen subsequently that no one form of catalogue can fully answer the entire needs of the reader.

Sometimes, it proves far superior to the classified catalogue as it groups like subjects together within limits which are governed by the incidence of the first word used in the heading. The alphabetical order adopted is not illogical; it is a system different from the numerical order of the classes in a *scheme of classification*. The *dictionary catalogue* is pragmatic and supplements the shelf order of books. But its value in a research library is discredited. "The dictionary catalogue is a public library tool and... as such has no proper place in a research library. The subject entries are an irritation rather than an answer to the researcher."[2]

"The dictionary catalogue has served American libraries well for fifty years. The next fifty years may well tell a different story if timely and adequate steps are not taken to make it an effective tool in library administration by introducing an element of logic and simplicity in ample measure in the arrangement of its entries. It would be courting disaster to go on in the second half of the twentieth century without fundamental rethinking of the nature and function of the dictionary catalogue. Multimillion card catalogues can be expected to double in size before the century ends. The difficulties will be far more than doubled if a large measure of control is not forthcoming."[3] This timely warning is a challenge to the talent engaged in *simplification* and *rationalization* of the *existing cataloguing practice*.

5. *The classified Catalogue*. The unwieldly growth in size, poor

response to the systematic approach of the user, and extended time in searching and locating information in the dictionary catalogue have contributed to its ineffectiveness. "It is this loss in effectiveness of the *alphabetic subject catalogue*, that has produced the growing dissatisfaction with the dictionary form. In general it may be said that as a collection grows in bulk and variety of subject matter the need for an adequate subject catalogue likewise increases, but the need for adequate subject coverage grows more rapidly than the volume of the collection."[4]

The second factor that has improved the prospects of the *classified catalogue* is the production of more satisfactory schemes of book classification during the twentieth century.

The third factor is the growing tendency towards the return and adoption of *printed book catalogues* to which the classified form of arrangement is traditional.

The classified catalogue is one in which the entries are arranged in a systematic order of subjects, the order usually being that of the scheme of classification used for the arrangement of books on the shelves. In this form of catalogue the arrangement of the entries for books is according to the class symbols. As the classes and subjects under it are usually arranged from general to specific at all levels in a classification scheme, its adoption for the arrangement of catalogue entries reproduces an identical order of classes and subjects, represented by the books. Its value depends largely on the soundness of the classification scheme used and on the extent to which the subjects are collected and the specificity of a subject attained in its schedules. The dependence of this catalogue for *the arrangement of its entries on the classification scheme* is so full and complete that it becomes a faithful representation of the scheme. If *a scheme of classification* is satisfactory in its structure, its adoption for a classified catalogue renders it equally satisfactory. If the system of classification lacks logic and utility, the unsatisfactory feature gets reflected in the classified catalogue adopting it. Therefore it is correct to state that the independence of a catalogue is not maintained by the classified catalogue. Instead of supplementing the order of arrangement of books followed, as is done by the dictionary catalogue the classified catalogue slavishly imitates the order of arrangement of books either for good or bad.

A book requires only a single *main entry* under its subject in a classified catalogue. It is considered an advantage and economy when compared to several entries (author, title. subject, reference) which are needed for a book in the dictionary catalogue. This is only a seeming advantage. The classified catalogue fails to serve those who approach it with a view to find the works of an author or a title of a work, or even a casual subject, unless they know where, under what class, sub- class and specific subject number, they can find it. As it is improbable that the library patrons possess a knowledge of the layout of *the scheme of classification* adopted, it becomes necessary to provide for quick reference and direction, an alphabetical index of authors, subjects and titles showing the symbol or class number under which a desired author, subject or the title could be found. The number of index entries of a *classified catalogue*, and the fullness of the entries and their style almost correspond to the added entries made for a book in the dictionary catalogue. The *main entry* is precisely the same in both dictionary and classified catalogues.

It can be amply proved by trying to find out from the shelf list of a library, which is essentially a classified catalogue, if there is a work by a given author, e.g. Henrick Van Loon: The Story of Mankind. No amount of searching will yield the information. Turn to the dictionary catalogue of the library. If one looks at the author's name or the title of his work it is readily available under the appropriate *alphabetical arrangement*. The entries contain the *call number of the book*, which renders it unnecessary to go to the classified catalogue, unless one requires to know what related works are available in the holdings of the library. The chief advantage possessed by the classified catalogue is that the main entry not only is found under the subject of the book but it lies in the neighbourhood of the entries for books on related subjects whether general or specific, *e.g.*

332.1 Banks and Banking
332.4 Money.
332.6 Stock Exchanges.
332.7 Credit.

This arrangement results in what is called a logical order. It will be unnecessary to look for books on Banks under B, Money under M and Stock Exchanges under S. All related headings of the subject Banks and Banking will be found together in a small compact group.

Sometimes the question whether the classified catalogue can bring together all the material on a country or any subject is raised. In fact, no kind of catalogue can do that completely and satisfactorily. Consider the HISTORY of a country. The classified catalogue can reveal together in a logical order, all the books in a library on the HISTORY of a country in general and on specific periods, cities and towns, kings and rulers, but this group or class of entries will not contain any information on the Geography, Literature, Art, Social Conditions, Religions of the Country. The enquirer will have to look for material under other classes. In the following specimen the comparative achievement of the classified catalogue and the dictionary catalogue may be seen.

A brief assessment of the advantages and *disadvantages of the Classified Catalogues* over other forms will be helpful.

*Advantages*

1. It reproduces the logical or systematic order of the scheme of classification used for arrangement of books in a library. This close identity of arrangement between catalogue entries and the books, tends to increase the reader's familiarity with a larger number of books than a dictionary catalogue.
2. It discloses the strength and weakness of a library by subjects.
3. Each group or class of books in it can be printed to form a complete catalogue of that group or class, which is unthinkable in the case of a dictionary catalogue because of the scattering of subjects throughout the alphabet.
4. The arrangement of the entries according to the notation of the book classification scheme renders it independent of language, which may lead to international standardization and ultimately co-operation in cataloguing.
5. The index entries to a classified catalogue are easier to refer to than the subject entries in a dictionary catalogue which become more and more complex with the growth of the catalogue.

*Disadvantages*

1. The notation by which the entries are arranged in the classified catalogue is not so commonly understood by the users as the alphabet.
2. The classified file, *i.e.* the main part of the classified catalogue, depends for its effective use on the alphabetical index entries which must be referred to first before using the classified entries. Hence two operations are involved, but in the alphabetical catalogues a direct and single reference to the heading will satisfy the user.

**CLASSIFIED CATALOGUE ENTRIES ADOPTING DECIMAL CLASSIFICATION NUMBERS**

| | |
|---|---|
| 954. | India – History. |
| 954.023 | India – History – The Moghuls. |
| 954.082 | India – History – East India Company. |
| 954.083 | India – History – Mutiny. |
| 954.084 | India – History – British Occupation – 1858-1947. |
| 954.085 | India – History – Republic 1947. |
| 954.1 | Calcutta – History |
| 954.7 | Bombay – History. |
| 954.8 | Madras – History. |
| 800 | Literature. |
| 891 | Indic Literature |
| 891.2 | Sanskrit Literature. |
| 891.4 | Hindi Literatue |
| 700 | Art. |
| 720 | Architecture, |
| 722 | Architecture, Oriental. |
| 722.413 | Architecture, Buddhistic. |
| 723.3 | Architecture, Muslim. |
| 200 | Religion. |
| 291 | Non-Christian Religions |
| 294.5 | Hinduism. |
| 294.553 | Sikhism. |
| 295 | Zoroastrianism. |

**DICTIONARY CATALOGUE ENTRIES ADOPTING THE ALPHABETICAL ORDER**

| | Scattering by Class Number |
|---|---|
| India – Army ... ... ... | 355 |
| India – Description and travel. ... ... | 915.4 |
| India – History ... ... ... | 954 |
| India – Languages. ... ... ... | 491 |
| India – Literature ... ... ... | 891 |
| India – Mythology. ... ... ... | 291 |
| India – Religions. ... ... ... | 291 |
| India – Sociology. ... ... ... | 309.154 |

3. Whenever there is a necessity of re-grouping the subject fields, the notation undergoes total change and hence that part of the *classified catalogue* also must undergo a corresponding change.

*This will require a complete remaking of the entries under the new numbers.*

4. The total dependence of the classified catalogue on the classification system for the arrangement of entries limits the autonomy of the cataloguer who cannot provide any more subsidiary entries than the system will permit. Even special

classification systems and analytico-synthetic schemes, which claim exhaustiveness and autonomy in classificatory operations, have been found to fail at times. But in alphabetical subject catalogues, no limit is set and any number of subjects as may be necessary to the book can be provided in order to guarantee adequate subject coverage.

6. *The Alphabetico-classed Catalogue.* It is a hybrid form of catalogue which has recently been introduced in some American libraries, as an alternative form of the classified catalogue and an improvement over the alphabetical subject catalogue. The aim has been to combine the advantages of both forms by arranging the major divisions alphabetically, with classified arrangement for subordinate subjects under each large group or arranging the major groups in classified order with the subordinate subjects in alphabetical sequence.

Instead of adopting a few main classes as in the classification scheme, a larger number of main classes are employed as a convenient expedient. These are arranged in alphabetical order, while subjects following under each one of these extended main classes follow the order of the classification scheme. For example 530 PHYSICS can be split up into and will have in addition the following large classes arranged in alphabetical order:

| | | | |
|---|---|---|---|
| PHYSICS | 530 | Classified order for subordinate subjects | |
| Dynamics | | HEAT 536 | |
| Electricity | | Theory | .1 |
| | | Nature | |
| Fluids | | Communication | .2 |
| Gases | | | |
| Heat | 536 | Action of bodies on | |
| Light | | heat | .3 |
| | | Effect, Action of | |
| | | heat on bodies | 4. |
| Magnetism | | | |
| Mechanics | | | .5 |
| Molecular Physics | | Temperature | |
| | | Calorimetry | .6 |
| Statics | | Thermodynamics | .7 |
| | | Applications | .8 |
| | | Tables Problems | .9 |
| | | Questions. | |

The advantage in this kind of arrangement of the specific subject entries under a major subject is that it enables one to get all the related material in a collection in a logical manner. But if one has no knowledge that CALORIMETRY is a part of HEAT and that a book on 'Calorimetry' will have to be seen first under Physics and then under Heat, it will not be obtainable, but in an alphabetical subject catalogue direct access to it is assured. In actual performance, it needs an alphabetical index, as much as the classified catalogue. This form of catalogue has not yet been fully experimented on a large scale. It has not gained favourable reception in Indo-British Library practice. A close observation and study of reader-use and reader-reaction to the alphabetico-classed catalogue will provide the basis for satisfactory appraisal.

A close study of the *varieties of catalogues* indicates that each one of them contains decided advantages, not possessed by other forms. Attempts to integrate all the advantages and eliminate all the disadvantages of each one of the forms into a new form of catalogue have not proved quite effective. The future of cataloguing practice is more certain to be pragmatic than idealistic in its outlook. Library catalogues will be 'finding lists' as well as control mechanisms of library collections and ultimately of knowledge.

## REFERENCES

1. **M.F. Tauber, Technical Services in Libraries.**, N.Y., Columbia University Press, 1953, p. 153.
2. **A.B. Berthold.** "The Future of the Catalogue in Research Libraries," **college and Research Libraries**, v.2,8, pp. 20.22,53, January, 1947.
3. **Andrew D. Osborn** and **Susan M. Haskins**, "Catalogue Maintencance." **Library trends**, v.2, No. 2 October, 1953, p. 288.
4. **J.H. Shera** and **M.E. Egan, The Classified Catalogue**. Chicago American Library Association, 1956, p. 11:

# 10

# SUBJECT CATALOGUING

The most interesting and perhaps the most intelligent part of cataloguing is the *subject cataloguing.* The cataloguer brings out the various subjects treated in the books in such a manner that no significant part of it remains unnoticed by the user of the catalogue. In a large number of libraries, the class of people who use the books by *subject approach is larger than the class of readers who require a specific book. It is more true of academic libraries*, where the students and teachers use the catalogue in search of material on a definite subject related to their study or research. As a good number of library patrons is interested in the subjects of their interest rather than in the authors or titles of books, it is essential to provide the required subject entries in the catalogue.

It is not quite easy to prepare a subject catalogue, because the term or terms employed to represent a subject may have more than one meaning and may be understood differently by different people. New concepts in science and technology have added to the difficulty in finding precise and appropriate *subject headings* to indicate them specifically. The past and present practice of subject cataloguing is yet to be codified. "There are libraries, for the most part academic libraries outside the United States, which do not possess subject catalogues. In most cases the explanation of this lack is to be found in the enormous difficulty of supplying a subject catalogue."[1]

All good schemes of *library classification*, when applied to books, result in a logical arrangement of the books on the shelves, the order being from general to specific ones. Such an arrangement is conventional and the habitual library patrons feel quite at home in such libraries where they find their way straight to the shelves and locate the books desired. But there is also a section of library users, who come to the library with the object of getting any good book on a specific subject and with no knowledge of how the books are arranged on the shelves. Such casual readers are indeed very frequently met with in public libraries. Perhaps they have neither the time nor the desire to know the method by which the books are arranged. All they expect from a library is that they get the needed book or books with least delay and effort. If a library provides the means to satisfy them, they will never worry about the order in which the books are displayed on the shelves.

The only satisfactory means by which provision to such casual readers could be made is the specific *subject catalogue* of the books. The subject catalogue is bound to serve them admirably. A subject catalogue, in which subject entries are made under appropriate subject headings, and filed alphabetically, undoubtedly supplements the classified arrangement of books on the shelves. This class of readers need not go to the shelves to find out the desired books. It is tiring and the effort in locating a desired book will not always be fruitful unless the reader looks for it in its proper location as determined in the schedules of the classification scheme followed in a library.

The *subject entries* (cards) in a catalogue of the alphabetical or dictionary type, will help the reader to find the call number, which takes him direct to the location of the particular book required with utmost quickness. Subject entries, therefore, provide a reference to the books on a specific subject and their exact location.

For example, a library patron, familiar with the arrangement of books in a library, wants to locate a book on "Gold Standard." He proceeds to the shelves marked 330 Economics, then further ahead to 332 Financial Economics, and on to 332.42 'Monetary Standards' and finally 332.422 'Gold Standard'.

But another patron who knows nothing about the arrangement of the books on the shelves, goes to the catalogue and looks under the name of the subject or topic, here 'Gold Standard', and finds a direct reference to a book or books classed in 332.422. It is therefore clear that the subject catalogue affords a direct approach to books on a specific subject. For a reader who knows of no book on the subject of his inquiry, author or title catalogues are useless. For him a subject catalogue is essential.

The principles of *subject cataloguing* should be concerned with such questions : "(1) What is the *purpose of subject cataloguing*? (2) What form is the subject catalogue to take? (3) to what depth shall subject analysis ordinarily be attempted? (4) what shall be the form of entry for the subject catalogue? and (5) what ought the language and *terminology of the subject catalogue* to be?"[2]

The existing practice in subject cataloguing is based on some of these principles, although diversity of opinion continues to exist on the effectiveness of the *alphabetic subject catalogues* as an independent unit or as an integral part of the dictionary catalogue. Bliss holds the view that "*Subject headings* are more complete, more inclusive, more expressive for many general concepts, more capable of minute and meaningful subdivision in many cases and more plastic in showing inter- relationships than are any of the classification systems presently known,"[3] *Classification and subject headings* are complimentary to each other. These principles are clearly stated and explained by *D.J. Haykin.*[4]

On the other hand *Dr. S.R. Ranganathan* advocates in his *Theory of Library Catalogue* with strong conviction that the subject headings used in the alphabetic subject catalogues or in the dictionary catalogues as well, have proved so completely ineffective and illogical that there is little justification for continuing the subject heading operations in cataloguing. According to him, a well developed and synthetic scheme of classification can offer as many class numbers as the subjects contained in the book, in addition to the specific class number, which may well replace the *subject headings* in alphabetical order. A unit catalogue card, with the class number of the subsidiary subject and a brief description of the book and a reference to the specific (class) notation in which the book is actually located can not only replace the alphabetic subject entries, which are filed in no logical order except the order of the alphabet, but also provides a convenient and compact grouping of the record of subject materials in an orderly manner.

Another view opposed to the view held by Dr. Ranganathan is: "Sure systematic order is very rarely found even in **systematic bibliographies**. In the schedules of **the Dewey Decimal Classification** and the **U.D.C.**, there is a continual confusion between classification (assembling objects in terms of likenesses or differences) and subordinating topics to the sciences by which they are studied. Very often the generic name is that of a scientific discipline while the species are objects and occasionally a class of objects includes the name of a scientific discipline. Most systems of "classification" suffer from this structural defect. Structurally the alphabetic subject catalogue is far superior to any type of systematic or "classified catalogue" that has yet been devised.

"All attempts to arrange subjects (or objects or ideas) in a logical, classified order (i.e. according to genera and species) have up to now failed and there are sufficient grounds for believing that all future attempts will fail. On the other hand the formation of headings referring to particular, definitely circumscribed entities, and the alphabetical arrangement of such headings has proved to be acceptable to practically all inquirers, not only in case of library catalogues but also in the case of encyclopedias and other reference works."[5]

Failure to secure a large measure of common agreement over these principles has given rise to a volume of controversial discussion on the utility and futility of subject catalogues. It seems to us that the delicate differential characteristics distinguishing a *subject index* to a *classified catalogue* from an *alphabetic subject catalogue* have either been ignored or subordinated in the battle between two opposing sections. The primary purpose of the *subject catalogue* is to indicate those books on a specific subject that are present in a library's collection, while the subject index to a classified catalogue aims to function beyond this by attempting to provide a direction to the notation of subject rather than a book and ultimately to a comprehensive coverage of material. For example, the subject index to the *British National Bibliography* guides the reader to all relevant material at several subject levels, and therefore aims at wider coverage than a simple alphabetic subject catalogue.

A more pragmatic approach concerns the user of the catalogue which should provide neither more nor less effective help to him than what is exactly needed. This will depend on the limits of specificity represented by the verbal statement and description of the subject. Although from Cutter onwards to date, every cataloguer admits validity of the principles of specific entry but how specific is not solved.

The abnormal growth of a *dictionary catalogue* and the complexity in using it, is sometimes chiefly attributed to a number of subject headings beyond the subjects indicated by the class notation and the '*See*' and '*See also references*' introduced with a view to make it a '*syndetic*' *catalogue*. The liberal provision of subject headings made with the purpose of securing full subject coverage of the contents of a book adds to the cost of cataloguing. If the huge expenditure is to be cut down, there should be a reduction in the number of subjects cards made. It is suggested by some cataloguers that as *descriptive cataloguing* and class notation can indicate the subject content of a book to some extent, additional subject entries must be kept down to the minimum or at best made when absolutely essential. The example furnished below indicates that a complete and full revelation of the contents of a book cannot be achieved, in several such cases, until more than one subject entry with an appropriate subject heading is provided, *e.g.*

332.43 Lutz, F.A.

L97 International monetary mechanisms; the Kevnes and White

proposals. Princeton University. 1943.
1. COINAGE, INTERNATIONAL 2. MONEY
3. CURRENCY QUESTION

It will be seen that in the above example, two more subject entries under 332.42 Monetary Standards and 332.5 Paper Money will be necessary in order to provide effective accessibility to the subject contents of the book as its location under 332.43 and its description fails to indicate and secure full coverage of the subjects.

*Subject Cataloguing* requires sufficient knowledge of the subject of the book, if it is to be adequately and appropriately analysed and placed under specific terms used as subject headings. As it is almost impossible to obtain the advice of subject bibliographers and experts in the subject field by all libraries and on all occasions, cataloguers themselves who possess a background study of the humanities and sciences generally perform this function, which is, by and large, acceptable to expert opinion.

It does not, however, mean that every individual cataloguer will practise subject cataloguing in his own way. Far from it. The subject entries should be made in accordance with the rules governing their choice, style and terminology. Any deviation from these rules will produce a subject catalogue with innumerable variations in the subject headings which will prove a positive hindrance to the public in their use of the library.

The making of an author and title entry is easier than making a subject entry, for the author's name and the title of his work are established facts clearly indicated on the title page of a book, or at any rate, frequently to be found in reference books. There are also codes governing the making of author and title entries. But the subject heading for a book has to be chosen for the book by the cataloguer himself most appropriately so as to be useful to the enquirer. The only guidance available to the cataloguer is the rules for choice of subject headings in *Cutter's Rules for a Dictionary Catalogue*, pp. 66-82, the *Vatican Rules* and the recognised *Lists of Subject Headings* like the *A.L.A. List of Subject headings, Sear's List of Subject headings for small libraries* and the more comprehensive *Library of Congress List of the Subject Headings*, for the form and style. It should be noted that on some occasions appropriate terms and forms for new concepts are not found in them. Libraries will have to make their own headings, with a view to consistency and specificity and record them in authority files or in the official copy of the list of subject headings for future guidance and adoption. Another consideration in the making of these headings is whether popular or scientific terminology should be adopted for expressing the subjects. A decision on this point will be influenced by the currency of the term used and the character of the library. Obsolete terms should be discarded.

Special libraries require highly developed and specific headings in a specific field of knowledge, e.g. public administration, chemical industries, etc. The A.L.A. Division of Cataloguing and Classification through its Board of Cataloguing policy and Research, is preparing to study the problem of integrating general and special subject heading lists. *C.J. Frarey* gives an excellent summary of the seven tentative assumptions on subject headings. "In other words, a workable plan for integration of general and special subject heading lists will recognize at the outset that if the reader is to be the focus, standards must take formal notice of individual differences."[6]

*Subject entries* are ordinarily required to be made for all classed books. When the book is a work of fiction, a single play, a literary essay or a poem, no subject entries are needed, for these books are more valuable for their form than for their matter. None of them is likely to be called for by its subject. It can, therefore, be seen that it is the specific need of readers, that influence the making or unmaking of subject entries. Readers also influence the form and style of subject headings and the best known form of subjects is adopted from the list of subject headings. In case the form of a subject anticipated by the reader were to be different from the form in the list of subject headings, provision of 'See' reference, helps to direct the reader to the form adopted, *e.g.* Political economy, see Economics; Moral philosophy, see Ethics.

We may define a subject heading as a term that indicates a subject-fully in all its aspects and forms as dealt with in a book, *e.g.* the subject heading for a book "lectures on Moral Basis of Politics" is Political ethics – Addresses, essays, lectures. The cataloguer must know the exact meaning of the term with which the subject matter of the book is indicated. Constant reference to standard dictionaries, both language and subject, is necessary in order to comprehend the meaning and significance of the terms used.

The cataloguer's technical reading of a book enables him to determine the subject, its scope and form as dealt with by the author. In order to maintain uniformity, consistency, and specificity in the subject headings chosen, the cataloguer verifies the choice from the list of subject headings followed and the authority list maintained in the library.

All groups, scholars and specialists, cataloguers and documentalists, have been closely watching and investigating the new techniques in the production of subject catalogues. *Classification schemes* recently adopted for coding the subjects or terms in the punched card system have led to vigorous thinking on the necessity and model of the *subject catalogues.* It will, therefore, be some time before definite decisions on the changing techniques and patterns of subject catalogues can be reached. "To effect the improvement sought in subject cataloguing will require; (1) that we find out more about who uses the subject catalogue, for what purpose, and in what way; (2) that we define the function of the subject catalogue in the light of this knowledge, and spell out a code of practice to facilitate the construction of subject catalogues for all types and sizes of libraries ; (3) that we develop both standard and specialised *lists of subject headings* in accord with this function and code; and (4) that we make use of our code and our lists to exploit the possibilities of cooperative cataloguing in obtaining more complete and more effective subject control of library materials at less cost"[7].

In the end, it must be admitted that it is unlikely that the alphabetic subject catalogue will totally be discarded from library administration and that a total withdrawal of the subject catalogue from library operations, if it takes place, will leave a gap which can at best be partially covered by compehensive classification schemes, mechanical devices, *open access, classified catalogues, and 'uniterm' analytical subject indexes.*

REFERENCES

1. **L. Jolley, The Principles or Cataloguing,** London, Lockwood, 1961, p. 100.
2. **Carlyle J. Frarey,** "Developments in Subjects Cataloguing", **Library Trends,** v.2, No. 2, October, 1953, p. 218.
3. **M.F. Tauber. Technical Services in Libraries,** N.Y., Columbia University Press, 1953, p. 157.
4. **Library of Congress, Subject Headings, A Practical Guide** by D.J. Haykin. Washington, D.C., U.S. Government Printing Office, 1951.
5. **P.C. Coetzee.** "Syntactics and Semantics of the Subjects Heading: An Essay in Catalogistics", University of Pretoria, 1957, **Mousaions** Nr. 21, pp.11-13.
6. **Carlyle J. Frarey** "Developments in Subjects Cataloguing", **Library Trends,** v.2, No, 2, October, 1953, pp. 229-230.
7. **Ibid.** p. 232.

# 11

# CATALOGUING DEPARTMENT: ORGANIZATION AND ADMINISTRATION

The primary *function of a cataloguing department* is to prepare the record of reading materials with a view to incorporate the information in the catalogue of the library to ensure quick accessibility to the collection. Efficient performance of this function demands that the work done in this department is properly planned, organised, directed, controlled, and co-ordinated in relation to the operations in the other departments of the library. Chief items of work done in the catalogue department are *classifying, shelf-listing, descriptive cataloguing, subject cataloguing, duplicating catalogue cards*, arranging and filing them. Finally, books are made ready for circulation and distributed to various departments and branches.

The organizational structure of the catalogue department of large libraries does not conform to the same pattern, because of the number and diversity of elements on which organization of cataloguing work depends. The more important elements that influence the organizational pattern of a catalogue department are: "(1) function; (2) subject: (3) language ; (4) form of type of material, (5) degree of difficulty of material; and (6) level of treatment to be accorded to various categories of material. Theoretically, the organisational work in catalogue departments along strictly functional lines seems both natural and logical. Yet few departments have set up separate divisions for classifying, descriptive cataloguing, and subject cataloguing."[1]

Some cataloguers prefer that classfying and subject cataloguing, because they require subject analysis, should be combined and placed under one group and *descriptive cataloguing* under another. But in actual practice prevailing in Indian and British libraries, we find that all these three operations are performed by each cataloguer, usually classifying and subject cataloguing processes preceding descriptive cataloguing.

There are libraries serving the readers in special subject fields as in universities. There are public libraries specialising in particular subjects, as a fruitful method of co-operation. In such libraries the division of work in catalogue departments is by subjects. This kind of division of work results in a higher degree of subject specialisation on the part of the *cataloguing staff* than in the division of work by functions. It is possible that knowledge and control acquired by a cataloguer in a subject may get reflected in the catalogue of that subject.

The cataloguing department of a library where the cataloguer and his assistants prepare the catalogue entries and arrange them for filing in the catalogue cabinets cannot be isolated from the other departments of a library. The work of the cataloguing department is intimately connected with that of the book order and accessions, reference, and lending departments. Constant inter-communication with them and a reference to the public catalogue, where there is no separate catalogue for the staff, makes it essential to plan the location of the catalogue departement in a convenient position, so as to economise the time and labour of the staff.

The layout of the library department shows the satisfactory location of the catalogue department.

Planning of available space, to secure maximum light and ventilation is called for. The work of cataloguing demands that plenty of light be provided to ensure accuracy and lessen the strain and fatigue of the cataloguing staff. In the calculation of floor space, it is necessary to consider the space needed for each person in the department on the basis of:

(1) the working table 5"×2 1/2" and the seating accommodation 3"×2"
(2) ample space for book trucks, 3 1/2"×1 1/2"
(3) space for book cases 4"×1 1/2"
(4) space for reference book shelf 4"×1/2"
(5) storage case for supplies, cards, stationary, etc. 4"×3".

Approximately every person working in the department needs to be provided 100 sq. ft. of floor space. Liberal planning and provision results in avoiding congestion and overcrowding as the library grows.

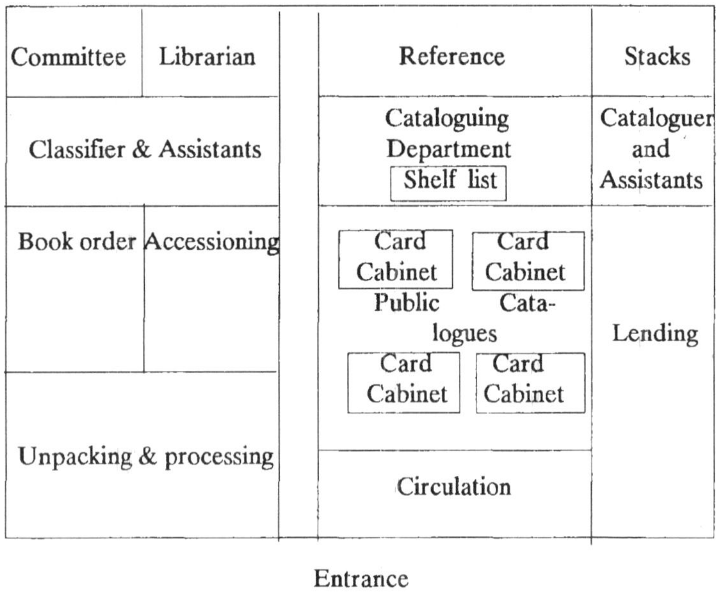


**Cataloguer's Tools and Equipment**

The daily work of a cataloguer demands constant reference to authoritative books in fixing the form and fullness of various entries. They are of the following types:

(1) Bibliographies of subjects uptodate
(2) Catalogues of important libraries
(3) Cumulative indexes of books
(4) Standard dictionaries of languages and subjects
(5) Catalogue codes
(6) Approved list of subject headings
(7) Classification schedules
(8) Authority lists

Provision should be made for their supply and maintenance.

The material of the entries is the standard cards, adequate stock of which should be maintained. Besides these cards, a set of guide cards, both readymade and blank, should be made available.

These cards when made, require to be arranged and kept in a tray. A liberal supply of trays to hold the cards in sequences is necessary.

The number and kinds of catalogue to be maintained has to be decided, for on them will depend the number and kinds of entries to be made. When a decision is made, a wise cataloguer takes into consideration the cost of cataloguing. Every additional entry, every duplicate card and every item of information in each entry, even a punctuation mark on the card, if not carefully chosen, in conformity with the need and the code followed, is likely to prove superfluous and add to the *cost of cataloguing*. Therefore, it is essential to lay down whether the cataloguing is to be full or simplified, having regard to what will be required of it by its users. The next step is to decide, if the catalogue is to be of the Dictionary or Classified type or both forms.

Attention is to be paid to the number of the cataloguers, character of the library and the degree of minuteness of work expected. Every person in the department should be assigned definite responsibility when several persons are employed in big libraries. Otherwise wasteful duplication and inefficiency are unavoidable. When more than one person work in the catalogue department, a chief cataloguer has to be chosen and empowered to direct and supervise the work of others. The chief cataloguer, who is an expert, should be given a free hand to plan and divide the work in the best manner without undue interference from the librarian or the committee or the readers. Various functions like choosing the author heading title heading and subject heading, must be assigned to specific individuals. The choice of subject heading should be put in the charge of an experienced and fully qualified cataloguer as it is often noticed that *subject cataloguing* calls for initiative, intelligence, correct appraisal, and thorugh familiarity with the rules governing their choice and adoption. It is advisable that the chief cataloguer should reserve this function to himself.

Revision of work has to be methodically carried out to avoid errors in copying the entries. No card should be passed on to the catalogue for filing before it is thoroughly scrutinised. It is found that mechanical duplication may eliminate such errors. Even if printed cards are used, scrutiny of the call number on each card is essential.

As the work of a cataloguer and his assistants is purely professional, the status of professional workers and the salary attached to such work should be provided to the *cataloguing staff*. Routine or clerical work like pasting and writing labels or arranging the books in the order of the call numbers may be however entrusted to non-professional men, whose salary will be less than that of the professional staff. As the work in a catalogue department calls for accuracy, uniformity and consistency, it can cause eye strain and fatigue. Therefore, unduly long hours of duty should not be insisted on. At best, continuous work for six hours with off time for rest for half an hour in the middle is a satisfactory duration.

*Routine in the catalogue department* is basd on : (1) the quantity of work to be done; (2) its proper distribution; (3) elimination of waste of time; (4) assurance of economy without sacrificing quality. The actual work falls into two main divisions: (1) to get all the books catalogued and made ready for shelving and circulation; and (2) to get the catalogue cards made and filed.

There are three groups of books forwarded to the cataloguing department: (1) books received by the book order department; (2) books received from the shelves for re-cataloguing ; (3) books and other ephemeral printed material received by the gift department.

These books may further be divided into: (1) rush books which are in immediate demand by the public; and (2) ordinary books that go to supplement the existing stock. These two broad divisions will include different types of books. In order to expedite their cataloguing, they may further be grouped into : (1) fiction; (2) non-fiction or classed books; (3) serials; (4) foreign language books; (5) added copies and later editions; and (9) pamphlets. Each group of books may be entrusted to the charge of an individual who will be responsible for the work.

Process cards or slips are made for each book, involving patient search and verification of previous entries in the catalogue. When a process slip is finally approved by the chief cataloguer, it is ready for copying. The number and kinds of cards indicated on it are made, compared, revised, arranged, and filed in the catalogue. The books go to the shelves and get properly arranged.

It is necessary to maintain statistics of every item of work done in the catalogue department, in order to review the work and include in the annual report to the library committee, as well as to assess the strength and weakness of the cataloguing department.

The following items require to be recorded daily and cuomulated so that final figures are ready for adoption:

Number of (1) main entry cards made
(2) added entry cards made
(3) analytical entry cards made
(4) series entry cards made
(5) former entries investigated

(6) cards revised
(7) volumes made ready for shelving
(8) volumes by classes or major subjects.

It should be noted that the quantity of work will vary in proportion to the quality. Quantity alone should not be taken into account to determine the ability of the various members of the cataloguing department.

In measuring the work of the *catalogue department*, both quantitatively and qualitatively, there is a tendency to place undue significance on the arrears in cataloguing and blame the catalogue department. No doubt, it is the responsibility and function of the staff of the cataloguing department to catalogue the books acquired from time to time. "It cannot hope to escape criticism for being behind in its work unless it has taken all steps necessary to maintain high efficiency. But if, despite good organization, sound procedures efficient techniques, and satisfactory morale, a catalogue department is unable to bring its accumulated arrears under control, the solution to the problems must be found in providing more cataloguing personnel or in adopting a more realistic aquisitions programme."[2]

The last, but not the least, important problem in the administration of the catalogue department is the maintenance of the catalogue.

Before the advent of the card form, printed or manuscript book catalogues were in common use in libraries. When new books were acquired, their entries were incorporated in current volumes as space admitted but when it became impossible to intercalate the entries, interleaving was tried. As this process proved unsatisfactory, supplementary and cumulative volumes were issued. During the stage of preparation, information of new reading material was not readily available to the users.

*Maintenance of card catalogue* poses different problems. They may be stated in the following order : "(1) Final preparation of cards of the catalogue, including minor revisions to printed catalogue cards, (if used), and the addition of call numbers and added entry heading to both printed and locally reproduced unit catalogue cards; (2) the reproduction of unit catalogue cards in sufficient quantity to meet the requirements of the library's catalogue system; (3) filing; (4) routine recataloguing of materials as necessary (5) editorial work on the catalogue to correct filing errors, reconcile differences in headings, correct or augment the reference structure, replace worn or soiled cards, and introduce new guide cards and labels as needed; (6) catalogue expansion and shifting as required; and (7) subject heading control and revision."[3]

Large scale use of printed catalogue cards obtain in the American libraries, because of the easy availability of *Library of Congress* and *Wilson Cards. Printed catalogue cards* are now issued by the British National Bibliography for current British publications. In India printed catalogue cards are seldom used, and the language element in the acquisition programme of Indian libraries makes it obligatory to prepare their own catalogue cards. Besides, the distance and time involved in obtaining such catalogue cards as may be used tend to discourage the adoption of printed catalogue cards. It is, therefore, necessary that Indian libraries, as well as libraries too distant from card producing centres, prepare their catalogue cards locally. Besides the typewriter, other duplicating machines can be employed in card reproduction.

*Filing the catalogue cards* is an important step in the maintenance of catalogues. As the catalogue grows in size and becomes older, the number of cards will reach the million range and the complexity of filing increases. It may be necessary to divide the catalogue in order to ensure ease of consultation, and when there is a revision of filing rules, the catalogue cards are removed, rearranged and filed again. Revision of subject headings is necessary to discard outmoded ones and rehabilitate the catalogue with current headings which are better understood. This process will need refiling the cards.

When books are lost or weeded out, the corresponding cards must be removed from the catalogue. If it is not done then and there, users are likely to ask for such books whose records are still found in the catalogue but which are not in the holdings of the library. A similar error is likely to be committed by the staff of the library, when checking the titles before ordering them.

Catalogue maintenance is a continuous item of work.

"Except in libraries that weed their book collections extensively the problem of **catalogue maintenance** will grow steadily worse, simply because an additional hundred thousand cards in a year means another million cards in ten more years. So a rehabilitation programme is necessary in the first insurance to get the catalogue in hand before it is hopelessly out of order. And thereafter provision should be made for a curator of the catalogue who has sufficient time and staff to make improvements, on a continuing basis.....Two co-operative measures can help. First studies in catalogue maintenance, as well as the development of new cataloguing rules and practices can be made on the basis of common experience and judgement. Second, the publication of book catalogues, in full or in part can be thought of as a joint venture."4

REFERENCES

1. **Arnold H. Trotier.** "Organization and administration of cataloguing processes.' **Library Trends,** v. 2, No. 2, October, p. 264.
2. **Ibid,** . p. 276.
3. **M.F. Tauber. Technical Services in Libraries.** N.Y., Columbia University Press, 1953, p. 245.
4. **Andrew D. Osborn** and Susan M.Haskins. "Catalogue Maintenance", **Library Trends,** v. 2, No. 2, October, 1953, p. 288.

12

# COST ANALYSIS OF CATALOGUING PROCEDURES AND SUGGESTED ECONOMIES

Modern trends in *Library Administration* are towards increasingly efficient and improved *library service* to the readers. *Cataloguing* is one of the chief and essential operations in all kinds and sizes of libraries, without which no library service can be considered. During the last one hundred years of library history, standards have been formulated for *cataloguing practice* and costs measured at different times and at different places. The gifted American librarian *Charles A. Cutter* put forward a vigorous defence of the American cataloguing system, and of its value and intellectual eminence. The very idea of measuring the expenditure on cataloguing in terms of money was loathsome to him. Dr. *W.W. Bishop* held the view that production standards could not be set but in any study of cataloguing costs the title, and not the volume, should remain the unit for calculation of costs. There is common agreement that the cataloguing of fiction costs less than non-fiction. The pre-war data provided by *Fremont Rider* for cataloguing operation at the Wesleyan University Library alone indicated unit cost per volume at $ 0.70 labour and $ 0.92 total cost. The cost of recataloguing also remained at the same figure. It must be noted that at present day prices, the cost is likely to be not less than 3 to 4 times that amount. One important factor in such cost accounting is that it is of local value and will have no bearing on library system outside the area, unless identical conditions exist.

*Work Measurement in Public Libraries* in New York by *W.O'D Pierce* provides data in terms of cataloguing time per title – fiction 16 minutes; non-fiction 34 minutes; periodicals 24 minutes. His report confirms the view that the financial impact of cataloguing on the total library budget is a small one. "Unit cost is a mathematical generalization and therefore does not do full justice to individual cases. Moreover, it is a quantitative measurement, and the quantitative imponderabilia which do not lend themselves to arithmetical calculation are unsatisfactorily considered. This is one of the reasons that most American libraries have been lukewarm about setting standards of production."[1] It is not only hazardous but also extremely arbitrary to lay down production standards in cataloguing, as long as men and women as cataloguers are not replaced by automations. The average cost of cataloguing during the years following the Second World War is assessed at $4.00 per title or $2.50 per volume in the American libraries, while the British Municipal Libraries spent 6 shillings per title or 4s. 6d. per volume.[2] There is still a persisting criticism that library catalogues are inadequate and that cataloguing practice should be simplified and rationalised to bring down the cost of cataloguing and improve its efficiency to the user. Some librarians maintain that present day catalogues are proving ineffective and inadequate, because no funds are voted to employ service staff to interpret the catalogue and that it is logical and necessary to increase cataloguing budgets instead of planning drastic cuts in cataloguing expenditure.

> "It is, in my opinion, more important for the library to assist self-education than for it to become directly educational. It is in the use of its resources that the library makes its greatest contribution, and it is essential that every student should know how to find the books he requires.... **Ranganathan** advocates that the tools of learning should be primarily for staff use in aid of readers. What a handicap he places on both the student and the librarian. Surely it is far better for the library to place all the evidence at the disposal of the students and allow them to exercise the liberty of choice."[3]

The entire criticism of increasing costs of cataloguing seems to have originated and developed from a hypothetical basis that readers do not use every item of information given on the card and since most of it remains unused by most readers, it is certainly uncalled for and adds to mounting costs and *arrearages*. But it must be borne in mind, that any proposal to cut down the details on the cards will certainly result in disappointment to a group of readers who expects to find the fullest details of books on the cards and will increase their dependence on the trained library personnel.

There is yet another proposal to reduce the cost by changing the policy in the provision of subject entries. Any proposed plan to reduce the subject approach to reading material will be a premium on the reference function of libraries. *J.C.M. Hansen* is convinced that substantial shortcuts in cataloguing would be economically unsound because "an honest and experienced librarian is not satisfied to meet a demand for reduction in cataloguing costs by saying that he has succeeded in cutting the costs twenty-five cents per title, without at the same time informing his trustees that the reduction had been achieved by omissions and curtailment which must necessarily reduce the efficiency of the catalogue and place additional burdens on other divisions of the library, notably the reference department not to mention the public."[4]

After considering the basic issues involved in a plan to reduce the cost of cataloguing, it will be interesting to observe the measures tried in actual construction of catalgues.

The technique of modern library cataloguing has been gradual in its development. Prior to the 20th century, printed and other related forms of catalogues show that the entry for each book was exactly a line in length of the printed page. Occasionally, it extended over two or three lines. The aim was to compress in a page as many entries as possible. The public who used these catalogues did not get the fullest information about the book or its subject. When unit cards replaced these earlier forms, they permitted fuller details to be incorporated. Further, library schools in U.S.A imparted such instruction in the cataloguing technique during the 20th century that the art of descriptive cataloguing almost became standardised and attained the level of a short standard bibliographic description. The fuller and more minute the particular, the greater is cost of preparing a catalogue entry.

Many library boards became greatly concerned over the cost of cataloguing. The cost analysis of cataloguing revealed that the descriptive part of cataloguing was responsible for nearly 50 per cent of the expenditure in cataloguing. A close scrutiny and observation of the advantages of providing full entries in the catalogue led to the conclusion that a bulk of the readers, were hardly interested in the minute details given in the entries. The time taken was necessarily more in conforming to the standard of fullest entries. Every library complained of arrears in cataloguing and wanted either more money or more staff to get through the mounting accumulation of work in the cataloguing department.

If new books are held up in the *cataloguing department* indefinitely, readers get impatient. Therefore, a method of reducing the cost of rushing the books to the shelves has been developed in the last two decades.

The first step is to provide entries in the catalogue only for such books as are likely to be used by the readers and thereby reduce the bulk of the catalogue.Fewer entries mean less time to make and file the cards. This is known as *selective cataloguing.* When selective cataloguing is decided to be adopted as a measure of economy, the library usually groups the books to be treated into:

(1) books, which should be fully catalogued, *e.g.* reference works, standard books of information and original works,
(2) books which may be partially catalogued *e.g.* text books, editions, translations and foreign language books, etc., and
(3) books, pamphlets, serials, etc. which are of passing interest to be kept aside without any entry in the catalogue.

Books falling under group (1) will be fully catalogued with main and added entries and cross references while books coming in group (2) will have only one main entry with no tracing of added entries, which are not required to be made. Materials in group (3) which are not to be catalgoued are kept sorted out roughly by the subjects and kept on the shelves at the end of catalogued books on the subject. There could be no order among these uncatalogued materials excepting the order of receipt. It is difficult to maintain this order on the shelves, nor is it in any way logical.

The selection of items for group (3) should be done with great care by the chief cataloguer lest a really valuable book or pamphlet or monograph of vital interest and value to the public be put into this disorderly lot.

*Selective cataloguing* did not fully solve the problem of reducing cataloguing costs. Therefore, another technique known as *simplified cataloguing* was put into practice. In simplified cataloguing the amount of detail given varies. Generally the author heading is given in secondary fullness, *i.e.* forename is given in full if only one; if more than one, only initials are given; no dates of birth and death, profession or designation added to the heading.

The title under the author heading is to include the main title proper with no information about introduction or foreword or preface and the imprint is to contain the date of publication and the collation is to be totally omitted except for books in more than one volume, when the number of volumes alone is indicated.

In the tracing of added entries only one subject heading is indicated; the other headings for editors, translators, etc. omitted, except for outstanding persons; the title heading is omitted when it is insignificant and too general. The *Title entry* is to contain the title proper in the heading followed by the date and the name of the author in secondary fullness. The subject entry is not provided with subdivision and other form divisions. By this limited approach the time and cost of preparing the entries is saved to a certain extent. It is very doubtful if reduction in the quality of entries, with a view to economise expenditure, will bring in adequate results. However, simplified cataloguing appears more satisfactory than the selective.

If *book selection* is done properly, it is unlikely to result in any great need of selective or simplified cataloguing at least with regard to the books and periodicals purchased by the library. Selective and simplified methods may be tried in respect of the material that comes into the library unasked and unwanted. Large libraries may find it necessary to practise both selective and simplified cataloguing for certain materials or departments.

Any evaluation of the *cost of cataloguing*, if it is to be realistic, must take into account: (1) the emerging catalogue; (2) the size of the collection; (3) the degree of minuteness and fullness of the entry; (4) the salaries and proficiency of cataloguing staff; (5) the element of language in reading material; (6) the closeness of classification adopted; and (7) the library service as a whole.

Cataloguing is and must be recognised as an intellectual activity and cataloguers have seldom been complacent about their performance and methods. It is our conviction that efficiency of the catalogue should remain the guiding factor in the reduction of *cataloguing expenditure.*

## REFERENCES


1. **Felix Reichmanm**, "Cost of Cataloguing," **Library Trends**, v. 2. No. 2, Oct., 1953, p. 307.
2. **S.J. Butcher**, "Cataloguing in Municipal Libraries," in **Cataloguing Principles and Practice; an Inquiry**; ed. by Mary Piggott. Library Association, 1954, p. 101.
3. **Ibid.**, p. 101.
4. **J.C.M. Hansen**, "Sound and Unsound Economy in Cataloguing," **Library Quarterly**, v. 4. January, 1934, pp. 65- 75.

# 13

# CO-OPERATION AND CENTRALIZATION IN CATALOGUING

Co-operation as a practising principle has produced admirable results in all fields of human endeavour. Co-operation in literary undertakings, of which cataloguing a library's collection is undoutedly one, is capable of reducing labour, time and cost. Co-operative measures in the field of cataloguing tend to relieve stringency, especially when libraries are hard-pressed for finance in reinforcing the reference and bibliographical services. The main object of co-operation is (1) reduce the cost of cataloguing by the sharing of expenses by participating libraries and (2) to eliminate wasteful duplication of the processes of cataloguing which have been once performed in an authoritative and accurate manner elsewhere.

A general review of the book stock of public and university libraries shows that there are several books, which are common to all these collections. Catalogue cards are made by each institution for itself. Consider a method by which readymade printed catalogue cards can be obtained at cost price from a common agency, which employs highly qualified professional cataloguers to prepare them. It is possible that a little over 60 per cent of the books in university libraries and 90 per cent of the books in public libraries can be provided with readymade catalogue cards. The rest of their stock which is a small percentage has to be catalogued in individual libraries.

But a scheme envisaging the distribution and use of such catalogue cards from a central cataloguing agency requires certain conditions for its successful operation.

1. The participating libraries should adopt identical rules of cataloguing, *e.g.* AACR.

2. *Standard sized cards* 12.5 cm. x 7.5 cm. should be used, as odd sizes do not fit in into a single catalogue.
3. Similarity of colour and weight, will obtain uniformity.
4. Timely intimation of the needs of individual libraries is to be conveyed to the cataloguing bureau.

Successful examples of such co-operation are found in the U.S.A. *The Library of Congress*, Division of catalogue cards Distribution, *H.W. Wilson, N.Y., John Crerar Library, Harvard University Library and Chicago University Library* have been printing and distributing catalogue cards at a little over cost price. The 1958 price of L.C. printed cards orderd by L.C. number is 7 cents for the first copy of the card and 5 cents for each additional copy. The average cost of 5 cards for 5 cents for each additional copy. The average cost of 5 cards for a book will be 27 cents. At current cost, it may be 60 cents. If each individual library were to catalogue the same book over and over again at different places and times it would be wasteful repetitive expenditure.

If a carefully worked out programme of ordering books and cards is practised, they can arrive very nearly at the same time. The moment the books and cards are received in a library (1) compare the cards and books, (2) place classification number uniformly at the upper left hand corner, (3) write or type the headings of subject and added entries as indicated, and (4) add accession number and special location or department mark. The cards are then ready for filing in the catalogue.

The advantages of such a co-operative effort are:

1. Efficient and adequate catalogue entries are available.
2. Printed cards wear well and present a uniform and neat appearance.
3. They are more legible and easier to consult.
4. Delay in cataloguing is reduced.
5. Libraries do not show diversity of entries for similar books.
6. It saves the time of the cataloguing staff to devote to the Readers Advisory Service, Extension and Display.
7. Being cheaper than indigenous cataloguing, it results in definite saving.

There are certain titles disadvantages present in the adoption of the scheme of which mention should be made:

1. Catalogue cards for certain titles of books cannot be supplied.
2. It may tend to decrease the number of skilled cataloguers being employed in individual libraries.
3. Familiarity with the subject of books on the part of cataloguers tends to grow less and less, as the work connected with readymade cards is largely mechanical.
4. Books will have to be sent to the cataloguing agency by the participating libraries if the cataloguing agency is not a copyright library, like the British Museum or the National Library, Calcutta, which is empowered by law to receive copies of every book printed and published in the country.

*The British National Bibliography*, which is based on the copyright deposit of British books at the copyright office of the British Museum is a recent example of centralized cataloguing, not limited to a library system, with good potentially behind its efforts. The British National Bibliography does all the work of cataloguing itself. The Libraries which buy and use its cards are not considered to have cooperated in making them.

According to Miss Morsch, Deputy Chief Assistant Librarian of Congress, H.W. Wilson Company, New York which prints catalogue cards for sale to subscriber, and the Library of Congress which prints catalogue cards for its own use but makes them available for sale to others, are centralized cataloguing agencies. She considers that *co-operative cataloguing* is a part of *centralized cataloguing* as long as it is coordinated by a central agency and its product is distributed by a single point. Whatever may be the closeness in similarity in the performance and objectives of co-operative and centralized cataloguing, there are some essential features that distinguish one from the other.

Centralized and co-operative cataloguing should not be confused because both methods involve a central cataloguing agency for production and distribution of catalogue cards.

> "The cataloguing of a large library system is often centralized, but it is not co-operative, except in a very insular sense. One simple form of co-operative cataloguing may be said to exist when a number of libraries take a share in the cost or work of providing and maintaining a centralized cataloguing bureau, and keep the benefits accruing from it, by being freed from the necessity of having to provide entries for such books as are catalogued by the central bureau."[1]

It is obvious that *centralized cataloguing* is a cataloguing activ-

limited to a library system, which has a number of branches or departments. There is no commercial basis involved in the production and distribution. The entire cataloguing processes are carried out at the central or headquarters library, just as the books for all the branches are purchased and distributed. Successful examples of centralized cataloguing can be seen in the Derbyshire County Libraries Headquarters, Derby, Middlesex country Libraries Headquarters, Hounslow, Manchester, Liverpool, sheffield and other big city library systems in the United Kingdom. The Delhi Public Library System is an example of centerlized cataloguing.

Besides *co-operative cataloguing* and centralized cataloguing, there is still another measure of economy and advantage in cataloguing which envisages a union catalogue. It is a combined catalogue of the books of the different libraries in a given area, compiled with the object of finding out the location of a book in one or more libraries of the region or country. The entries for the books are necessarily brief. But they contain enough information to identify a book. Examples of *union catalogues* can be found at the *National Central Library, London.*

Sometimes the union catalogues may be limited to periodical publications and serials. At the present day, union catalogues of periodicals are in greater demand. International organizations like *UNESCO* have taken up the compilation and publication of union catalogues of periodicals and serials as major bibliographical schemes. Other good examples are the British Union Catalogue of Periodicals and Union list of serials.

The U.K. Local Government Computer Committee has issued "Computer Applications in the Library Service – first Report on Cataloguing" submitted by the Working party of the Local and Public Authorities' Computer panel, in October 1967. Membership of the Working Party comprised of professional Librarians appointed by the Library Association, members of the Computers Panel, and Computer specialists. After considering the possible applications of the Computer to various branches of Library Service, the Working Party concentrated its attention on cataloguing as it was convinced that "the biggest dividends would accrue from a concentration of effort on the future methods of cataloguing" before it becomes unmanageable due to ever-expanding growth rate in book production by publishers, and acquisition of books by libraries.

The present state of catalogues is not standardised. Different views are held as to the desirable format and content of catalogues and the system of classification. Well meaning efforts for standardisation of these two processes failed, partly due to lack of flexibility, and partly to the local prejudices. Unless common standards are evolved and necessarily followed by libraries in the field of cataloguing, there would be remote chances for the use of computers in cataloguing which would benefit all libraries by releasing expensive professional staff for other branches of library service—specially reader/user- service—which cannot be provided for without professionally competent persons.

The working Party is of opinion that the computer is capable of editing, and selective dissemination of information, and information fields can be defined by selection for particular users. But it emphasises the difficulty of the lack of a unique characteristic to identify a book, and recommends that each publication be assigned a unique number; the number printed in and on the book by the publisher and invariably quoted in all pre-and-post-publication publicity.

The Working Party recommends the establishment of a central organisation to catalogue all books and provide for quick dissemination of information. It is also to be limited to non- fiction books. This would reduce the unnecessary cost of cataloguing by avoiding duplication of effort of the same type at various centres. A far-reaching recommendation of the party is that B.N.B. should be entrusted the responsibility of cataloguing all British publications and given full facilities in converting the current and post cataloguing data in machine readable form, these proposed recommendations are a prerequisite for the application of the computer for cataloguing.

It may be observed that with the anticipated advantages, there are equally disadvantages in this scheme. The one idea that the professional personnel engaged in cataloguing would be released for readers' service is certainly welcome, but a professional librarian who has not done enough cataloguing work, which gives him confidence to undertake other bibliographical services in a library, can never prove successful in users' service. It, therefore, will emerge that *computerisation of cataloguing process*, which involves coding, programming, feeding, and retrieval, would need certain fundamental thinking and intellectual processes before the work could be entrusted to the computer. Various experiments and attempts at automation of bibliographical processes in the U.S.A., Europe, and U.K. have taken place. Perhaps it would be appropriate to mention that the MEDLARS system (medical literature analysis and retrieval system) of the U.S. National Library of medicine is the first instance of successful application of computer potential to bibliographical control and indexing.

The next example of automation in this field is *Project MARC (Machine Readable Catalog)* of the Library of Congress and B.N.B.

## BLAISE

The British Library's Automated Information Services is a successful example of providing information from a number of databases involved in the cooperative information service to individuals and libraries. The four types of databases participating are:

1. the bibliographic databases holding citations to published literature of various types;
2. MARC databases having information on published works in a cataloguing format;
3. databases holding information on specific research projects, products, and materials;
4. dictionary databases compiled with a view to providing assistance in on-line searching.

BLAISE, a computerised information service located at Harlow, Essex, England for which access is available via a standard telephone linked up with a suitable terminal. This centre provides information internationally through the EURONET and IPSS communication channels. The information located after search is displayed on the computer terminal, which can be printed on demand.

After gaining an experience of operating the databases for approximately ten years, the British Library commenced the BLAISE records MARC service with a view to give easy access to an expanding database of machine readable records offering fast, efficient data delivery channels to the library community. The MARC Records service ensured significant cost benefits over the on-sight cataloguing by providing bibliographic records at an economically accepted rate. Perhaps, the processes like acquisition and circulation also might benefit by using this service instead of indigenous local preparation of these records which are costly in terms of staff resources. The databases, as they include U.K. MARC and L.C. MARC, become very comprehensive, and appreciable standards of bibliographic description of on line entries prove of real value to all the sharing libraries. This is truly a model of centralised bibliographic activity, including cataloguing. It would become popular in course of time and eliminate the repetitive operations performed in individual libraries, and thereby ensuring real economy.

The foregoing experiments and projects involving the use of machines in cataloguing have the primary object of reducing the cost of cataloguing and at the same time leading towards standardisation of the format and keeping the catalogue up to date and efficient in the service of the reader.

## CATALOGUING IN PUBLICATION

This facility (CIP) offered to the Libraries and to the compilation f bibliogaphies is also named as Cataloguing in Source of the publication, together with ISBN and following ISBD for the description aspect of the entry. This standardisation is intended to obtain uniformity in style and level of the entry and economise expenditure for all participants.

A recent study by the British Library Bibliographical Service Division revealed that the time taken to catalogue titles for which CIP entries are available is appreciably less than the time required, if the CIP entries were not present. The overall processing time for CIP material was found to be 7.8 minutes, and the titles without these entries required 15.8 minutes for each book. But the time taken for classifying a book with and without CIP entries was the same.

As individual publishers do not find it feasible and viable to employ a full time librarian to do this work of Classification and Cataloguing, etc., a group of publishers in a city, locality, or region engage a competent person and share the time and expenditure by mutual adjustment, for performing this work, at the time, and period suitable to the participants. The British Library Bibliographical Services Division has laid down the standards for adoption in making the entries in BNB and by others. The entries conform to AACR 2, level 2 for descriptive data, and contain full subject data for BNB. (Refer BNB weekly issue No. 1819, 2nd January 1985.) *see* fig. opposite (of Cataloguing in Publication Data Sheet). This data sheet in copies is distributed to the publishers who have enlisted for this cooperative achievement. The publishers usually print the CIP entry on the verso of the title page of the book. A specimen of these entries is reproduced from the B.L. News Letter No. 35- 2, Feb. 1985. (see page opposite)

As anticipated, the British Library received the fullest cooperation from the publishers, and supplied the full information of the book in the prescribed data sheet, in advance and made the CIP programme a complete success, benefiting the library community, Readers, Publishers, Book-sellers.

REFERENCE

1. **Henry A. Sharp, Cataloguing,** 4'th ed. London, Grafton, 1950, p. 266.

# UNION CATALOGUES AND SUBJECT SPECIALISATION

A *Union Catalogue* is a simple *'Finding List'* or Catalogue of the books, pamphlets, and other reading material held in the cooperating libraries within a region or country, in which the entries are arranged alphabetically by authors in a single sequence and indicate the location of every copy of the book available in the libraries of the area. Union catalogues are generally maintained in card form, occasionally in sheaf form. Union catalogues are not printed in book form except when they are limited to a subject or a form of literature, *e.g.* Union Catalogue of Science Periodicals in South Asia, the British Union Catalogue of Periodicals. There is an advantage in printing such union lists covering specific fields of knowledge as law or medicine or a foreign language. They are valuable as subject bibliographies to specialists and they may be distributed to any desired centre for reference.

There are still several other uses of the union catalogues, (1) "They help conservation, maintenance, and organisation of the country's book resources. A realistic approach to secure complete or at least adequate record of books owned by libraries in the country is possible through a union catalogue. When the union catalogue attains a shape, form and fullness, the entries can be checked with all sources of bibliographical information to spot out the titles of books not at all available in the nation's libraries. Immediate steps can be taken to obtain copies of such titles, if in print; if not, microfilm or photostat copies of these important titles can be obtained and preserved in some of the depository libraries."[1] (2) "They have helped to distribute the burden of inter-library loans, to reduce the need of several libraries purchasing rarely used materials, to diminish or prevent duplication of certain types of library materials, to indicate gaps in holdings of libraries within an area and suggest fields of purchases, to make co-operative purchasing practicable and feasible and to serve as useful bibliographical tools to various departments of libraries."[2] (3) Union catalogues speed up research, and ultimately advance knowledge. If all the nations of the world maintain dependable union catalogues and if a copy of every entry in the national union catalogues is combined and arranged in one alphabetical sequence by authors and located conveninently, it will certainly be a master union catalogue of the world's libraries' resources and approximate to a universal bibliography as was conceived by *Konrad Gesner*.

Union catalogues may be limited in scope (1) by locality, (2) by subjects, and (3) by form of reading material.

1. If a town or city with a number of independent libraries in the area compiles a catalogue of the entire resources, and uses it to common advantage, it may be called the city union catalogue. But the master catalogue at the headquarters of the city library system, containing entries of books distributed to its branches, should not be considered a union catalogue. City union catalogues are seldom found.

More common are the union catalogues for a contiguous geographical area and for the whole country. When it comprises a defined geographical area, it is called a regional union catalogue and when it comprises the whole country, it is termed a national union catalogue. In England and America there are regional union catalogues and national union catalogues. In Switzerland, perhaps due to the small area of the country, there is the national union catalogue only. In India, there is at present no union catalogue, either regional or naional, but when the proposed National Central Library at Delhi takes shape, there is bound to be a union catalogue, for without this tool no satisfactory bibliographical service or clearance of information and interlending can be guaranteed.

After nearly three decades, 1930-1958, of preparation, construction and organization, we find that in the United States, there are four regional catalogues—one in the Pacific North- west, one covering the Rocky Mountain Region at Denver, one at Cleveland and one at Philadelphia. The process of reproduction of catalogue cards of the co-operating libraries by making use of typewriters, specially built Recordak cameras and microfilming machines is interesting. The figures available up to 1962 indicate that the United States National Union catalogue and its supplements contain 1,327,000 entries. Subsequently the national union catalog was converted to MARC form and it is up to date.

"In England there are eight regions, including one for the Metropolitan Boroughs; Wales has two mutually co-operating regions; in Scotland cooperation now centres in the Scottish Central Library; in Northern Ireland the Belfast Public Library acts as a centre, and in Eire the Irish Central Library... Apart from the London Union Catalogue and South Eastern Region, which are conveniently located in the National Library of Wales, and the Northern Region which is based on the Newcastle Literary and Philosophical Society Library, the regional headquarters of Bureau are housed in the city libraries at Birmingham, Bristol, Cardiff, Leiceister, Manchester and Sheffield."[3] The National Central Library, London, maintains the National Union Catalogue and its supplements which includes the catalogue entries of 220 special libraries called 'outlier' libraries. The organisation and maintenance of regional and national union catalogues is based on voluntary association of co-operating libraries, which contribute towards its cost on an agreed rate. Overcentralization has been kept under check in order to avoid delays in bibliographical retrieval of information.

2. Union catalogues in select subject fields are sometimes found very useful by students, scholars, specialists and subject bibliographers. A recent example is that of the union catalogue of the British Institute of Education which is in two parts – one for Books and another for Periodicals covering the fields of education. The *subject union catalogue* may be arranged by author or subject. Usually, it is limited to a region or locality and helps locating material on a subject. When subject requests are received at the bibliographical centres, the subject union catalogue offers the best guidance. "Unless the subject field is a limited one, the sheer bulk of the material to be dealt with is bound to give rise to the question is it worth it?... Whether it is worthwhile compiling a subject union catalogue, on a national or regional scale, in a printed or index card form, must depend on the circumstances of each project and the purpose it is intended to serve."[4]

3. *Union Catalogues* of material in a given form, *e.g.* periodicals, or in a given language may also be considered. The British Union Catalogue of Periodicals, compiled by J.D. Stewart has been published by Butterworth during 1956-58. This is a fine example of a printed union catalogue covering the periodicals in the British libraries up to 1955. The union card catalogue of Russian books at the National

Central Library, London, has been compiled and arranged by authors. It is being continued, and the two cataloguers working on it are responsible for all Slavonic inter-library loans.

Preparation of union catalogues involves time and money, careful planning, and organization. Unless the co-operating libraries realise the necessity of providing regularly the information on standard cards or slips for new books added from time to time, the union catalogue cannot be kept up to date and reliable. Perhaps, co-operative cataloguing of books by a central agency for a number of participating libraries in the region might reduce the cost of maintenance of the union catalogues.

The methods of compilation of union catalogues are varied. the simple method as it obtains in the South Eastern Regional Bureau, England, is described, for it is suited to conditions in India and other similar countries.

The South Eastern Region is divided into seven circuits of libraries, which are 85 in number. The union catalogue is an author catalogue in sheaf form. Entries contain details of author, title, edition, date of publication, series, language of text if other than English and score for music. The joint code (Anglo-American) rules are generally followed.

Each slip (see illustration on next page) 8" × 4" is printed with numbered squares which are used for recording the location and edition of each copy in region. The upper half is blank enabling the typini of the particulars of the book and the four punches holes at the left margin help insertion into the sheaf holder. These slips are passed from one library to the next within the circuit enabling each library to mark its number indicating the availability and location of the copy described. When a complete round is made in the circuit the slips are passed on to the next circuit for similar procedure and finally to the Regional Union Catalogue Bureau for incorporation in the union catalogue. It is necessary that accurate details of every copy are given on the slips; otherwise it will become unreliable.

Additions to the *union catalogue* are notified once a quarter on 5" ×3" record slips (see illustration on page No.160) supplied by the Bureau on which are printed a set of location numbers. A little over 100,000 additions are received in a year. By the begining of January, April, July and October the libraries listed first in the seven circuits prepare record slips for the books added to stock during the previous three months. These are marked with their location number or library stamp, sorted into al-

Author.................................................................................
Title....................................................................................
Edition.................................................................................. Volumes..........................................................................................

| 1 | 2 | 3 | 4 | 5 | 6 | 7 | 8 | 9 | 10 | 11 | 12 | 13 | 14 | 15 | 16 | 17 | 18 | 19 | 20 |
|---|---|---|---|---|---|---|---|---|---|---|---|---|---|---|---|---|---|---|---|
| 21 | 22 | 23 | 24 | 25 | 26 | 27 | 28 | 29 | 30 | 31 | 32 | 33 | 34 | 35 | 36 | 37 | 38 | 39 | 40 |
| 41 | 42 | 43 | 44 | 45 | 46 | 47 | 48 | 49 | 50 | 51 | 52 | 53 | 54 | 55 | 56 | 57 | 58 | 59 | 60 |
| 61 | 62 | 63 | 64 | 65 | 66 | 67 | 68 | 69 | 70 | 71 | 72 | 73 | 74 | 75 | 76 | 77 | 78 | 79 | 80 |
| 81 | 82 | 83 | 84 | 85 | 86 | 87 | 88 | 89 | 90 | 91 | 92 | 93 | 94 | 95 | 96 | 97 | 98 | 99 | 100 |

Union Catalogue slip Recording Location and edition of each copy in the region.

The numbers within the squares are The Code numbers of cooperating libraries.

| **Author (name in full, surname first and in capitals** | |
|---|---|
| **Title** | **Date** |
| | **Edition** |
| | **Volumes** |

| | | | | | | | | | | | | | | | | | | | | | | | | | | | | | |
|---|---|---|---|---|---|---|---|---|---|---|---|---|---|---|---|---|---|---|---|---|---|---|---|---|---|---|---|---|---|
| 1 | 2 | 3 | 4 | 5 | 6 | 7 | 8 | 9 | 10 | 11 | 12 | 13 | 14 | 15 | 16 | 17 | 18 | 19 | 20 | 21 | 22 | 23 | 24 | 25 | 26 | 27 | 28 | 29 | 30 |
| 31 | 32 | 33 | 34 | 35 | 36 | 37 | 38 | 39 | 40 | 41 | 42 | 43 | 44 | 45 | 46 | 47 | 48 | 49 | 50 | 51 | 52 | 53 | 54 | 55 | 56 | 57 | 58 | 59 | 60 |
| 61 | 62 | 63 | 64 | 65 | 66 | 67 | 68 | 69 | 70 | 71 | 72 | 73 | 74 | 75 | 76 | 77 | 78 | 79 | 80 | 81 | 82 | 83 | 84 | 85 | 86 | 87 | 88 | 89 | 90 |

ADDITIONS TO THE UNION CATALOGUE NOTIFICATION SLIP

phabetical order and forwarded by messenger or registered post to the library next on the rota. The library receiving the slips checks them with its own record of additions during the same period, makes a circle round its locations during the same period, makes a circle round it location number on the slips for books already recorded, makes out slips for books not recorded and inserts them into the alphabetical sequence. Different editions of a work are recorded separately. A time-table accompanying the slips indicates the date on which each library should receive them, and it is important that the slips should be despatched so as to be received by the next library on the date shown. If it is impossible for a library's additions to be recorded in the time allotted, the sequence of slips should be passed on, and the entries for two quarters incorporated when the slips are next received. Otherwise only additions to stock during the previous quarter should be recorded in any circuit.

The notification of withdrawals to the Regional Bureau is made on 5"×3" slips or cards. Only when the last copy of a work in a library system has been withdrawn should the Bureau be notified. Many withdrawals are, in fact, recorded from the reports entered on application forms. When pressure of work permits, it will be desirable to check with the union catalogue, proposed withdrawals or, at least, the older books, to ensure that unique copies of books are not destroyed.[5]

The *Swiss Union Catalogue* has been in existence for the last 40 years, covering the select titles in the 350 libraries of the Swiss Union. It is interesting to note that the absence of a common code of catalogue rules has not proved an impediment in its compilation and maintenance. The Swiss Union Catalogue is in three parts; authors, anonyms and periodica. Author cards are filed according to the *Berghoeffer System*, which takes first surnames and then title into account, disregarding Christian names and initials. Reports indicate that it is satisfactory in performance, helping loction of over 66 per cent of requests.

The high cost of compiling and maintaining the union catalogues and in a few cases, the doubtful economic return for the cost involved, has led a group of American librarians to conclude that regional union catalogues are not necessary to be compiled and maintained, as long as there is an efficient and adequate national union catalogue. The American regional union catalogues are neither so closely allied to nor a necessary adjunct to the interlending system, as it obtains in the

United Kingdom. In America, the bibliographical details by a reference to the union catalogues while the actual inter-lending of books is done directly between libraries according to local codes. But in the United Kingdom, the policy has been to limit the field on the national union catalogue by devolving the responsibilities to a good extent on to the Regional Bureaux and Regional union catalogues which are a necessary part of the inter-lending process. The idea is to render the smaller areas, the regions, self-sufficient at least in British publications and make the National Central Library responsible for rare books and foreign publications.

There is no doubt, a great prospect awaits the national union catalogues in the future, but the extent of their success and usefulness will depend to a large extent on international library cooperation, a universal catalogue code and perhaps a universal classification system.

It will not be out of place to discuss here how far the union catalogues influenced new concepts in *library co-operation* subject specialisation, and bibliographic centres.

It is the union catalogue that can indicate the extent of duplication of material as well as the gaps in subject coverage by libraries. Libraries specially strong in one or more subjects can also be disclosed. With this data, a scheme for subject specialisation, distributing the coverage in an economic and practical manner, can be drafted and implemented.

Although the primary purpose of the union catalogues is to serve as finding Lists, experience has shown that they may also serve as efficient bibliographical tools.

REFERENCES


1. C.G. Viswanathan, "Library Co-operation in India." **Indian Librarian,** June 1956, pp. 1-7.
2. W.W. Bishop, " Union Catalogue", **Library quarterly,** v. 7. pp. 36-49, January, 1937.
3. **P.H. Sewell. The Regional Library System** : 2nd ed. Library Association, 1956, p 8.
4. D.T. Richnell, "Subject Union Catalogues" in **Cataloguing principles and Practices : an Inquiry** ; ed. by Mary Piggott. Library Association, 1954 pp. 78-79.
5. South Eastern Regional Library Handbook, South Eastern Regional Library System, London, 1948, pp. 15-16.

# 15

# CATALOGUING OF SPECIAL MATERIAL

The General Conception of Reading Materials in libraries limits itself to ordinary printed books and periodical publications. But almost all modern libraries, not to speak of special libraries, acquire a variety of reading material besides the printed books, in order to meet the demands of readers. Fortunately, the number of items of these special types of reading material is very small in comparison with books.

The special material will comprise (1) *Incunabula,* (2) *Maps,* *(3) Print and Pictures,* (4) *Manuscript,* (5) *Music,* (6) *Gramo-phone Records*, (7) *Films*, (8) *Microfilms*, and (9) *Coins* etc.

We are here concerned with the problem of cataloguing such material. The usual type of entry and description adopted for ordinary books is found inadequate and sometimes inappropriate for these special types of reading material. The reader does not get unrestricted access to these items on account of their rarity, cost and fragility, and therefore he has to depend more or less fully on the catalogue for identification, and retrieval of information, before deciding his choice. Another factor which will influence the cataloguing practice of these materials is that only a few special classes of readers, engaged in intensive and advanced study of the subject are likely to use them.

"Although there are generally accepted standards and rules for the handling of such material, and although these rules and standards are applicable in general as well as in special libraries, nevertheless the actual form and content of catalogue and index entries and the methods of filing are subject to the work which they must perform."[1]

*Incunabula*. This is a term signifying books printed before 1500. "Many copies of these interesting production of the fifteenth century presses possess an individuality which they share with no other copy of the same work; and for that reason we are of opinion that every library should describe in the fullest possible detail its own examples of such books, regardless of the fact that one are more copies have been described already either in some standard bibliography or elsewhere."[2]

Experience of great bibliographers like Hain, Pollard, McKerrow, Proctor and others, corroborates the conclusions that these early printed books are dominantly characteristic of individuality in the production of each copy. Reference to the *British Meseum Catalogue* of 15th century Printed Books and the *Berlin Gesamtkatalog der Wiegendrucke* and *Hain's Repertorium Bibliographicum* will be helpful and provide guidance in cataloguing the incunabula.

A large number of our libraries today and the cataloguers in them have little opportunity in doing this exciting task of handling and cataloguing incunabula. But scholarly libraries of universities and learned academies and large public libraries owning special collections will require knowledge of the methods of cataloguing this material.

Guppy in his cataloguing of incunabula has furnished specimen entries, full, shortened and a model for the card catalogue. The main items of an entry in order; (1) Heading (author, title, imprint) (2) Collation (size, format, as folio, quarto, etc., signatures, number of leaves, number of columns on a page, if more than one, number of lines to a page, kinds of type, headlines, catchwords, illustrations, printer's ornaments and devices), (3) Description (quotations from its title, incipit or some significant lines of text), (4) Refereces to well-known and recognized catalogues and bibliographies in which the item is described, (5) General note (brief description of literary contents), (6) Special note (on the particular copy, its binding, imperfections, illumination, ms. notes in margin, ownership, press-mark).

The study and treatment of incunbula is mainly the function of a historical bibliographer. But as libraries generally expect the cataloguers of printed books to deal occasionally with a few items of incunabula, it is worthwhile for the cataloguers to be well acquainted with the fundamental features of these early specimens of printing. The students of cataloguing will do well to read McKerrow's Introduction to Bibliography for literary students and Esdaile's Students' Manual of Bibliography; in order to appreciate the art of early printers and describe their products as faithfully as possible.

A-ACR 180-185 provides guidance for *descriptive catalogue of incunabula*, in a general catalogue.

One peculiar feature of a large number of incunabula is that they lack the title pages and very little information is available on author, title of the work, printer, place, date of printing, pagination, etc. In the absence of these details no satisfactory description of an incunabulum is possible. Although authorities like *Henry Guppy* are of the view that every library should describe its incunabula as fully as possible. A-ACR recommend a short title form of catalogue entry, on the pattern of Goff's entries as the main purpose is identifying one incunabulum from another, and as several libraries holding incunabula and reference sources have already provided detailed descriptions of them.

*Maps*. Cataloguers are conscious of the importance of maps and atlases as reading material in libraries. Maps are different from printed books in their format, their authorship and title. The common and primary approach of a reader to maps and atlases is by the geographical area covered and the type of information contained in it, *e.g.* Political map of India will first be referred to under the country India. Seldom is a reader found to apply for it under the name of the cartographer, (map maker) or publisher.

*The Anglo-American Code* and its revision A.L.A. catalogue rules, (No. 100 directs the entry of maps under the name of the cartographer; if not found, under one of the following in the order set out, editor, publisher, govenment bureau, society or institution; while A-ACR 210-11 provide for entry of maps under authors responsible for them.

*The British Museum* rules provide for the entry of atlas, map, chart, plan or view under the generally accepted name of the geographical or topograhical area covered by it, which should be full enough for identification. Subsidiary entries are to be made where possible, under the name of every author, whether draughtsman, surveyor or compiler.

Boggs and Lewis in their 'Cataloguing and Classification of Maps and Atlases', N.Y., Special Libraries Association, 1945, after a survey of American and British practice in cataloguing maps and atlases, recommend the main entry for maps and atlases, under the name of the geographical area, which is an obvious and significant characteristic of maps. Although this procedure is not accepted by the A.L.A.,[3] one must admit the logic behind the entry under the geographical area recommended by Boggs and Lewis. The only theoretical objection to such an entry to be filed in the midst of regular author entries is that it brings in the subject element in an author catalogue.

*R.L. Collison* holds the view that the actual engraver of an old map is of considerable importance while in the case of modern maps, which are the products of governments or firms specialising in their production, the mapmarker has ceased to occupy any significance in the identification of the map. 4 A complete catalogue entry for a map or atlas must contain the appropriate author heading, followed by the title (if none, one to be composed and written) edition, imprint, scale, collation, and description (insets, langauge, size, projection, the meridian, and the form-sheet, wall, roller, globe, etc.) on the body of the card.

A-ACR 210-11 provide directions for the choice of entries for maps, etc. under the author responsible for them, in order that these entries fall in line with other author entries for books in an author and title catalogue, while conceding the fact that most map libraries make the main entry under the name of the area depicted by the map. In formulating these rules, maps are considered on the basis of informational content: (1) *geographic maps* and (2) *Subject maps*. If a map represents both geographic and subject aspects, the one that predominates indicates the rules of entry to be followed. If it is decidely a subject map. *e.g.* a map of India showing the location of universities, the rules of entry, as for ordinary books and book like materials in chapter (1) are to be applied ; but if the principal aspect of the map is geographic, A-ACR 211 governs the entry.

A. The main entry, in accordance with this rule for a map, set of maps, or an atlas mainly geographic in its coverage, is made under the person or corporate body, which is shown as primarily responsible for its geographic content. Generally, the term 'compiled by' is indicative of its primary authorship. If the title of the map includes the name or part of the name of a corporate body, excluding a commercial firm other than a map publisher, the corporate author is taken as primarily responsible for the map, *e.g.* the map of India showing the physical features and rainfall issued by the Survey of India. The main entry will be India. Survey of India.

B. In case the primary responsibility for the authorship of a map is not explicit, the main entry is to be made in order of preference given below and added entries are provided for persons or corporate bodies that have a sizeable share of responsibility for the work.

1. The person who, by his survey, provides the basis for map-making;
2. The name of the *cartographer*;
3. The engraver, if known to be also a cartographer;
4. The corporate body, including a map publisher, that prepared the maps, e.g.

*Title*

Germany : Zones of occupation, map appended to the protocol of the European Advisory Commission, a document presenting conclusive evidence that Berlin in accordance with the Agreement, is an area "for which a special system of occupation is provided". Berlin, Press and Information Office, 1962.

Production: Hartmann Bros., Berlin.

*Main entry* under the headig for European Advisory Commission.

*Added entry* under Hartmann Bros.

A-ACR 212-215 lay down the procedure and details for the descriptive entry of *Maps, Relief, Models, Globes,* and *Atlases,* respectively. The last three differ with Maps, in physical form and shape.

The relief model is used to denote a three dimensional map, other than a globe and it is made of plaster, papier mache, rubber, plastic and similar materials. The collation includes this information, by using the term 'relief model' instead of map and the scale, first horizontal and then vertical, is given.

A globe is a spherical representation of the earth and the map is drawn on it. The treatment in describing a globe is similar to a map, except that the collation includes the term 'terrestrial globe' or 'celestial globe' instead of 'map', and the measurement of the diameter is given. If any special features are there, they are stated in a note.

The descriptive entry for an atlas differs from that of the ordinary book in giving its collation, the pages of text, and number of maps distinctly, and providing the scale as an item of notes.

It is important to arrive at a decision on the method of filing the entries in the general library catalogue or in a separate map catalogue. As the *maps* and *atlases* are used as illustrative and supplementary reading material to books, it is an advantage to file the entries for maps together with the entries for books in a classified order. It is advisable to get the entries for maps readily distinguished by using edge coloured cards or cards of different colour other than one used for books. The maps themselves will, of course, be shelved in a separate sequence in specially designed cases, which admit of horizontal or vertical location, the latter being more convenient to handle.

*Prints and Pictures*. Every library has to deal with prints and pictures, frequently as illustrative and supplementary reading and occasionally as original reading material as in the case of original drawings and engravings. Their physical form and their large number render it difficult to maintain them as individual units. The general practice is to group them by place or person or scene and keep them in boxes and mount a list of the prints or pictures contained. These collections can easily be located through an index but some libraries provide a separate catalogue. The entry for a picture should ordinarily contain the heading, the title, process (line engraving, woodcut, photograph, etc.) size and date. The entry for pictures by eminent artists, painters, engravers, which are valuable as works of art, should contain the names of the artists School libraries and junior libraries in a public library system will find it necessary to maintain a full scale record of picture collections, in order to answer the minute enquires of young readers. As most of this material is of passing interest, it will be unjustifiable to incur large expenditure in compiling their catalogues.

A-ACR 260 deals with the choice of entry of individual pictorial works, sets of such works, and photographic and photomechanical reproductions of the same. The main entry for these, is made in accordance with general rules for books in chapter I. The artist or the corporate body responsible for the work is considered as the author. In certain pictorial works the sole responsibility of producing a work vests in the owner holding the copyright, or printer or publisher or studio. In these cases the main entry is to be under the name of that person or body. Between an artist and a corporate body, prefer an artist as the author.

(*i*) Laxman, R.K.
The landscape of Kashmir in colour.

(*ii*) India. Department of Archaeology
Pictures of Buddhist architectural remains in North India.
(Engravings)

A-ACR 261 governs the choice of entry for copies made by artists. The main entry of a copy in the same medium, (oil or water, charcoal, etc.) by another artist is made under the name of the original artist and an added entry provided for the copyist. But a copy in a different medium is treated as an adaptation of the original and the main entry is under the copyist with an added entry for the original artist.

Samarendra Chowdhury
The Lanes of old Delhi, an oil colour painting by Mohammad

Hussain, reproduced in lithography.
I. Mohammed Hussain.

Lalit Kala Akademi, New Delhi
A Portfolio of contemporary
Indian Paintings, in loose
mounted reproductions – Shergil to Ramchandran. 1969
(Photomechanical process)

A-ACR 263 provides directions for the entry of collections of pictorial works assembled by an individual or corporate body or a library acquiring them for use by readers.

A. If the pictures in the collection is traced to a person or body as author, it is entered under the appropriate person or body.

(*i*) Price, Frank Earl
Laboratories of Engineering Faculty of the Illinois University and the U.P. Agricultural University, an album of photographic pictures, 1965-1967.

(*ii*) UNESCO
Collection of photographic prints of Public library building in Asia, Europe and Latin America.

B. Collections of pictures, whose original author is not known, is entered under the person responsible for collecting them, and the designation '*collector*' is added to his name in the heading.

Rajendra Singh, *Collector,*
Snow capped mountains all over the world, being fine
photographic pictures by various photo artists.

C. If the collection cannot be treated under A and B above it is entered under its title.

D. When there is no title for the collection, one is to be supplied by the cataloguer and enclosed in square brackets.

A_ACR 265-272 govern the descriptive entries of individual pictures and also are suitable with modifications, for describing groups of pictorial works. Among these rules, A-ACR 269 c lists terms for describing the medium of production of a picture and reproduction methods.

The descriptive procedure and the details to be included in the entry have been formulated for standard catalogue entries in order these can be filed in the catalogue for general books and other materials, but these rules are open to simplification or elaboration. The added entries also may be increased or decreased depending on the cataloguing policy of a library.

Provision of terms of technical processes followed in the pictures is certainly helpful for cataloguers, who cannot be expected to have knowledge of all these processes.

*Manuscripts*. The term manuscript has been used in the past to cover different reading materials. Even today the terms '*archives*' and '*manuscripts*' mean different things to different people. Some apply the term 'archives' only to records of government departments although they are produced just like manuscripts, thus limiting the coverage of manuscripts to isolated hand-written works of a private nature.

In the 16th and 17th centuries the term 'manuscript' was used to indicate a bound volume of hand-written material, comprising a book or collection of books and treatisets, or occasionally a collection of separate but related documents. Today the term 'historical manuscripts' refers to a loose collection of documents, charters, deeds, letters, and other non-literary records collected by or related to some great personality, organisation or institution. The application of the word '*manuscript*' in a restricted sense to bound volumes can be traced to the beginnings of English book collecting during the reign of Henry VIII. When monasteries were confiscated – the literary treasures in them faced the grave danger of disintegration and destruction. But *John Leland*, the king's chaplain and librarian, organised a movement to rescue them. He collected nearly 2,000 volumes of manuscripts, which later, (1759) became the King's Library of the British Museum. As these volumes were bound and looked like books, they were known as Ms. volumes. If the manuscripts were loose and scattered, they were commonly called 'papers' or 'sometimes records.'

A more satisfactory definition of 'Manuscript' according to *Seymour de Ricci* in his *Census of Medieval and Renaissance Manuscripts*, includes "written documents of every kind, with the sole exception of inscriptions on stone, metal, or other hard substances. Letters, charters, and deeds are included, but as often as not are treated in groups. To have described them singly would have more than trebled the bulk of this work, without adding to its usefulness in anything like a corresponding manner." The manuscripts of literary works in bound volumes are usually written in the book-hand of professional scribes, serving as models for the early printed books. A document or a letter, on the other hand, will be written in the cursive script and will be less legible and more difficult to read.

NOTICES OF SANSKRIT MSS.
*By*
Rajendra Lal Mitra
*Vols. I to IV*

No. 1273. शिशपाल-वधः

Substance, palm-leaf, 14 1/4 X 1 3/4 inches. Folio, 153. Lines, 4 on a page. Extent, 2,294 slokas. Character Bengali. Date, Sk. 1436. Place of deposit. Calcutta, Government of India. Appearance, very old, Prose Correct.

Sisupala-vadha. An epic poem by Magha, on an episode of the Mahabharata, the subject being the destruction of Sisupala, a sovereign inimical to the Pandu brothers. The work has been printed several times and is well-known, but the MS. under notice is a very old one, being dated Saka 1436-A.C. 1512, and contains many readings not to be met with in the printed editions. Its style of writing is shown on plate V.

Beginning. श्रियः पति. श्रीमतिशासित जगज्जगन्निवासो वसुदेवसद्मनि ।
वसन् ददर्शावतरन्तमम्बराद्धिरण्यगर्भाङ्गभुवं मुनि हरिः ॥१॥
End. सर्वेण सर्वाश्रय इत्यनिन्द्यमानन्दभाजा जनितं जनेन ।
यश्च द्वितीयं + + + + तीयो मुख्यः सतां गौणमवाप नाम ॥
श्रीशब्दनस्य कृतशब्दसमाप्तिलक्ष्म
लक्ष्मीपतेश्चरितकीर्तनमात्र + + ।
तस्यात्मजः स्वकविकीत्तिपुराशयो॰दः
काव्यं व्यधत्त शिशुपालवधाभिधानं ॥
Colophon. इति श्रीदत्तसूतोः श्रीमाघकवेः कृत्तौ श्रीलक्ष्मणि शिशुपालवधे महाकाव्ये
+ + + + + + : सर्ग समाप्तः ॥
विषयः । शिशुपालवधविवरणं ।

A Descriptive catalogue of the Samskrta and Prakrta Manuscripts
(Bhagvat Singhji collection & H.M. Bhandkamkar collection)
in
The Library of the University of Bombay; compiled by C.V. Devasthalli
Book II
Volume II parts IV-VII & Volumes III and IV, Bombay, University of Bombay, 1944
2249

शिशुपालवध of माघ
with सर्वंकषा by मल्लिनाथ

Foll, 28; size 12 1/4 in. by 5/1/4 in.; material thick yellowish paper ; fair, Devanagri character ; 8-12 lines in a page and 50 letters in a line.

The MS. begins on fol. 1 a and ends on fol. 27b. Foll 1a and 28b have the title and foll. 28a is blank. The text in red ink occupies the middle of each folio and the commentary both above and below it. The colophon is written in red ink. All folios are discoloured with damp and foll. 27 and 28 are slightly worm- eaten. The MS. is almost accurately copied in Saka 1764.

The work : Canto 1 of Magha's Sisupalavadha, with Sarvankasa, a commentary thereon by Mallinatha.

Dated:

शके १७६४ शुभकृन्नामसंवत्सरे आषाढ़शुद्धप्रतिपदा मन्दवासरे इंद पुस्तकं लिखितं समाप्तम् । श्रीकृष्णार्पणमस्तु ।। यादृशं पुस्तकं ।।

B.M.C. 102 19)

Catalogue of Sanskrit Manuscripts in the Bodleian Library, Vol. II begun by Moriz Wintermitz, continued and completed by A.B. Keith. Oxford, Clarendon Press, 1905.

1235 – MS. Sansk. d.84.

Magha's Sisupalavadha, A.D. 1474.

Contents : the Sisupalavadha, by Magha, complete in 20 sargas. It begins : svasti sriganesaya namah sriyah patih srimati & c. It ends; iti sisupalavadhe mahakavye Kavisrimaghakrtau mayuyuddham name vimsah sargah. The number of verses agrees with that in the edition printed at Calcutta, 1869 (samvat 1925, except in the following sargas; sarga II (ending on f. 14v); has 117 verses: vi (on f. 42) has 80; xii (on f. 92) has 70; xv (on f. 107v) has 102; XVI (on f. 114v) has 86; XVII (on f. 21 v) has 70; XIX (on f. 107 v) has 102; XVI (on f. 114 v) has 86; XVII (on f. 121 v) has 70; XIX (on f. 136v) has 125 verses. From. ff 1-15 v (-I, i-III, 13) the whole of the margin is covered with explanatory notes written in small characters by a Jaina. F. 44 is blank (VII, 17-30 missing). F. 120 (XVII, 53-63) is supplied by a modern hand.

Bought in 1887 from-Dr. Eugen Hultzsch (Ms. 84).

Size: 10 × 5 1/2 in. Material : Paper

No. of leaves: iii 146

Date: samvat (1530 = A.d. 1474) warse maghavadi i somavasare.

Written by order of His Majesty the Prince Suryasena (maharajakumaras-risuryasenad evalikhapitam).

The entry was afterwards deleted.

Character : Jaina Devanagri.

Injuries: the marginal notes on ff. 2-15 are slightly damaged in places, the last line of f. 118 is obliterated. A few words on f. 144 v are illegible, and the colophon is partly erased.

The chief differences between *manuscript books* and printed books make it necessary that different methods of cataloguing them are followed. "The cataloguer of printed books is dealing with a multiple and standardized product, and one of his objects – though not the only one or perhaps the most important one – is to describe the copy in front of him so clearly that any one else having another copy of the same edition may determine definitely that it is the same."[5] The information about the author, the title or subject is ordinarily available to the cataloguer of printed books usually on the title pages, and more often than not, is dependable.

But the cataloguer of a manuscript faces a different situation. Each manuscript assumes an individuality of its own depending on the scribe's performance. An entry in a catalogue of one manuscript of the work of an author will be dissimilar to the entry of another manuscript of the same work of the same author, *e.g.* Magha. Sisupalavadha – three different styles furnished (vide pages 158-160)

The method, treatment and objective of ***manuscript cataloguing*** by the professionally trained historians and scholars engaged in study and research in classical literature and ancient history and who hold the office of curators of manuscript collections, is not the same as those adopted by the professional librarians, who have to catalogue ordinarily extensive collections of printed books and occasionally some manuscripts, when their libraries may acquire them for special reasons. The former aim at an exhaustive and minute description leading to the literary evolution, usefulness of a manuscript, while the latter is content to provide such information on its entry as to help a reader to identify and locate it. Although manuscript cataloguing is an intellectual discipline of modern scholarship, the professional librarians, whom we have in view, are not so much concerned with it as they are with the cataloguing of printed books.

But, in order that manuscript cataloguing is done in an efficient and faultless manner, it is necessary that the cataloguer in a modern library gets familiar with the sense and application of the terms commonly used in the process.

Terms

| *Unfamiliar* | *Familiar* | |
|---|---|---|
| 'Titulus' | 'Incipit' | = Here begins 'text' |
| 'Prohemium' | 'Explicit' | = Here ends 'text' |
| 'Voces finium' | 'Colophon' | = Summit/Finishing touch put on a ms. by the copyist. |

The scribe's introductory statement as to what he is about to copy often begins with the Latin word 'incipit'. Sometimes it is mistaken for 'incipit' but it is appropriately called the 'titulus', while the opening words of the actual text is the 'incipit'.

The scribe's concluding statement as to what he has finished copying often begins with the word 'explicit'.

The word 'titulus' is the forerunner of the term 'title'. Just as the title of a work or book, which includes the name of its author, enables one to identify and distinguish it from another, the 'titulus', which is an identifying tag or label attached to a manuscript in early days did the same function.

The present-day cataloguer of early manuscripts will find it necessary to investigate the 'titulus', the 'incipit', the 'explicit' and the '*colophon*' before he sets out to describe a manuscript in the entry in the catalogue. If manuscripts, as they sometimes do, contain the colophon of the translator, the commentator, and the scribe, separately, the cataloguer should be careful in distinguishing one from the other. In India manuscripts, which largely contain commentaries in the fields of philosophy, religion and law, the cataloguers' task becomes increasingly difficult.

If the author of manuscript is known, it should be entered under his name; if anonymous, under the title by which the manuscript is known, provided it is distinctive; if not, then the entry is to be made under the designation or number in the collection to which it belongs.

Adoption of this procedure will tend to produce a catalogue of manuscripts of a general nature, which will serve the readers in a library as well as a catalogue of printed books. Experience in general libraries indicates that the catalogue of manuscripts, even when maintained separately, is used by fewer readers than the catalogue of printed books and the groups of readers using it is interested in historical sources of information, textual criticism and emendation of classical works.

The technique of cataloguing hand-written material, whether public or private, remains the same for both, "Whether collections of private records are categorized as archives or manuscripts, the technique of cataloguing them is similar to that for public records. In both cases, it treats the files of an agency as a group and employs such finding media as check lists, inventories, indexes, calendars and to a lesser extent card catalogs, and maintains the integrity of the original arrangement whenever possible. The chief difference is that certain additions are necessary for public records because they are inter-related and complex, whereas private ones are made up of unrelated series. The cataloguing of single documents such as letters, or the analyzing of isolated documents, likewise is similar.[6]

The *arrangement of the manuscripts* may be alphabetical, if the collection is chiefly personal ; if historical, a chronological arrangement is more appropriate; if miscellaneous, arrangement by numerical sequence is followed. It is a distinct advantage if the entries are filed separately from the usual library catalogue. Where a separate cabinet is not used, in view of the small number of the manuscripts in a library, a separate tray, either the first or last in the public catalogue, may be designated 'Mss catalogue'.

A-ACR 200-204 for entering and describing, a single manuscript and 205-207 for collections of manuscripts, provide detailed guidance in cataloguing this library material. For cataloguing purposes manuscript materials include works in handwriting, inscriptions on clay tablets, stone, etc. and works in typescript, although some authorities on manuscripts collection, description, etc. exclude inscriptions on stone, metal or hard substances. Libraries in general hold manuscripts written on vegetable substances and to a lesser extent on parchment or prepared leather. The chief manuscript collections in India are on palmyra leaves and hand-made paper of special oblong size that can accommodate a few lines, of text. In some manuscripts on palmyra leaves, ink is not used for writing, but the letters are inscribed by a sharp needle-like instrument provided with a wooden handle. This fact needs to be mentioned in the descriptive entry of such manuscripts to distinguish written and inscribed ones.

A-ACR 200 lays down the general principle that a single manuscript is treated on the same lines as a publication of identical content, *i.e.* the entry being made under the person who is responsible as its another and an added entry under the scribe. When anonymous, the provisions of A-ACR 103 are applied.

A-ACR 201 A. The description of a modern manuscript (mainly literay ones) follows the rules for describing printed books, with modifications. Instead of an imprint, the year or years of writing are given after the title; if no year is mentioned in the manuscript, an approximate date is supplied, if possible. Other details are to be given in a note.

B. Ancient, Medieval, and Renaissance manuscripts.

As regular title pages for manuscripts of the above categories are not provided, these are treated more or less like the early printed books (incunabula) whch do not contain title pages as specified for modern printed books, by adopting the title from a published edition of the manuscript or from a better known manuscript of the work, or even from a published catalogue of manuscripts. Square brackets are not used for the information supplied, as it is common to these manuscripts. Failing all previous methods of fixing the title, the cataloguer provides one, based on the text.

The description in the body of the entry following the title should include, the language of the text, if the title does not make it explicit, the date of writing or completion; the actual number of leaves, the number of columns, the number of lines on a page and the size in centimetres.

Notes should contain information on the scribe, place, illumination, ownership marks, etc.

Specific treatment of letters, speeches, lectures, sermons, etc. and legal papers in manuscript form is indicated in A-ACR 202-204 respectively, as they differ in subject content, purpose, and endurance from literary ones.

Collections of Manuscripts.

In the A-ACR a manuscript collection has been defined with great extension so as to include not only a conventional group of manuscripts but also typewritten materials formed by or around a person, family, corporate body, or subject. These materials may be in their original form or reproductions. Even letters, diaries, memoranda; business records, drafts the archives of a family or corporate body, etc. are also considered to be manuscript and treated under A-ACR 205 for the main entry, 206 for added entries, and 207 for descriptive entry.

A-ACR 205A. The main entry for a *collection of manuscripts* formed around a person, family, corporate body is under his or its name, if it contains material written by or addressed to the person, family, or corporate body.

Gandhi, Mohandas Karamchand.
  Letters to Jawaharlal Nehru, 1932-1942

B. Collection of manuscripts other than those in A above are entered in the following order of preference:

1. If the collection is known by the name of the person who made the collection, entry is under his name.

Durga Das (Collector)

Vedic manuscripts collected by Durga Das during 1901-1940.

2. If the collection has any other name the main entry is under the name of the collection.

Sankaradvaita Collection.

Advaita (Vedanta) collection of Sanskrit manuscripts in the Baroda Oriental Institute.

3. If no name exists for the collection, it is entered under the title supplied by the cataloguer.

C. A very large collection of manuscripts, if divided into smaller units, the main entry is under each unit, with an added entry under the name of the collection. The division into units, if by subject or language, can be better represented in the catalogue by following this rule.

D. If a collection contains a specially important set or group of manuscripts, on a subject of historical or literary interest, an identical entry may be provided for it in the usual form.

A-ACR 206 A collection with a name, if entered under author addressee or collector, is provided an added entry under its name, unless it begins with the surname of the person chosen for main entry.

A collection, whose name includes the name of a person, family or corporate body, if not chosen for main entry, is given an added entry.

A-ACR 207 provides detailed directions for making the descriptive entry of a manuscript collections, regarding the title, physical features, location, form, and note on scope and content, and reference to published sources.

*Music*. The average public library usually contains a few volumes of musical scores, and a few on the theory and history of music. The interest of the public in music has increased after the discovery of gramophone records and other mechanical reproductions of music. Special attention in cataloguing this material is necessary in order to provide accurate and dependable information for muscially minded readers. Cataloguing muscial scores is different from cataloguing ordinary printed books, whose title pages usually provide most of the information necessary for their entries.

There are three rules in the Anglo-American Code: (1) A musical work is to be entered under its composer, with added entries for editors, or arrangers, and with regard to operas, oratorios, cantatas, etc. added entry is to be made under the writers of the words; (2) A *libertto* is to be entered under the librettist if known; if not under the title. Added entry is to be made under the composer of the music. On this issue opinions are divided; some prefer to make the entry under the composer of the music to which the libertto belongs; (3) A *thematic catalogue*, in which the arrangement follows the opening themes of musical compositions, is to be entered under the name of the composer, if it is confined to a single one. These rules provide directions in a single way and the cataloguing of musical material follows the same pattern as for other books. What is required in the music catalogue is adequate description of the form, style, language, etc. and arrangement which will allow grouping by form, instead of a straight alphabetic order by composers. The cataloguers will do well to refer to Sharp's *Cataloguing*, pp. 232-237, where guidance and discussion on the treatment of Western music is provided.

A-ACR 230-243 replaces the rules in the A.A. Code and A.L.A. Rules on the choice of entry for works on music. Directions for descriptive entry of musical works are given in A-ACR 244-248.

*Oriental music*, particularly Indian music which has its Vedic origins, devotional and sacred background in the Sama Veda or Sama Gana has not been dealt with in any book on cataloguing practice. The Indian students of cataloguing and cataloguers of libraries attached to colleges and academies of music need some guidance. Although the chief rule of making the main entry for a musical work under the composer can be adopted, directions on the making of added entries, descriptive cataloguing and notes seem to be necessary.

In the catalogue entry for an Indian musical composition the cataloguer should furnish in the body of the card the following essential information:

1. Name of Raga (with Aroh and Avaroh).
2. Tala
3. Type (*i.e.*) Varnam, Kriti, Padam, Javali, Ragamalika, etc.
4. Time and occasion to be sung.
5. Language.

If the composition is anonymous, the first lines of the composition 'Pallavi' may take the place of author heading. Added entries for artists rendering the song may be made, if the artist is well-known and belongs to any particular school of music.

Information to be given on a catalogue entry for Western music includes:

"a. Medium of performance, including alternative and optional instruments,

b. Indication of whether, or not the work consists of score and/or musical parts for performance,

c. Statement that the work is an arrangement or other special version, with indication of the original form,

d. Name of the arranger,

e. Type of notation, if of a special nature,

f. Duration of performance."[7]

Poetry and music are closely related, but not identical. Some poems are meant to be sung and written by the original writer as musical compositions; *e.g.* Rabindranath Tagore's poems, specially lyrical poetry, sung as music, Suddanada Bhartis poems sung as music; but there are other forms of literature, dramas, stories, etc. which form the basis of musical compositions. The catloguer should distinguish between the two types of musical work in making the choice for the main entry of the work.

The general rules for entry A-ACR 1-16 are applicable to musical works also. The composer is normally taken as the author of the musical composition, allowing for certain exceptional cases, for which a title or uniform title or a corporate body is chosen for the main entry.

A-ACR 230 deals with the entry of musical works with authorship of mixed character.

A. Make the main entry under the composer of a musical work, embodying the work of a poet, playright (*e.g.* a song, opera or dance music, ballet, etc.). Author-title added entries are made for other persons sharing the responsibility for the work as a whole.

Gopalkrishna Bharti
  Nanda the Harijan saint, a
musical drama.

Thyagarja
  Pancha ratna kriti

The remaining rules directing the entry of musical works of special character are omitted in this work, as the need for their frequent application appears to be remote.

*Gramophone Records* Among the special reading materials, gramophone records must be considered a very useful and popular type. Most American libraries lend gramophone records to their readers just as they lend ordinary books and provide sound-proof rooms in the library building to play the records. If the reader does not want toborrow them. In some of the advanced public libraries in England also, *e.g.* City of Westminister libraries, good collections of gramophone records are maintained. It is advantageous tohave separate catalogues, as it its necessary to provide special shelving for them.

They differ from books in the following respects ; (1) the text of a gramophone records cannot be read, (2) the physical shape, colour, weight, etc. of several records look exactly similar and it needs close scrutiny of the label at the centre to distinguish one from another, (3) both sides of a record may be totally unrelated, being two different pieces of music of different composers, and therefore lacking the homogenous quality of a single book, and (4) the fragility of the records prevents direct access to the shelves. These features of gramophone records maket it essential that the readers and library staff depend entirely on the catalogue entries for the required information about them. "The catalogue, therefore, must be well constructed and contain as many cross references and added entries as possible, if the collection is to be exploited to the full. Although one usually thinks of records in connection with music there are many other subjects for which they are used, such as for speeches, language teaching, poetry readings, animal and bird sounds, and so on. The cataloguing of records of music is, however, the most important from the general point of view."[8]

The catalogue entry for a record will contain (1) the composer, (2) the title, (3) the artists and performance, (4) the instruments as accompaniment in case of vocal music, and (5) the musical form as essential items. Subsidiary information on the number of sides, size, make, and the time of playing in minutes, may be given, if the library can devote enough staff and time for cataloguing the records fully. Standards works of reference like Groves Dictionary of Music and Musicians, Thompson: the International Cyclopedia of music and musicians; 7th ed. 1956; Scholes: The Oxford companion to music; 9th ed. 1955 may be consulted for the form and fulness of the names of composers, etc. Besides the composers under whom the main entry is made, it is sometimes found useful to provide added entries for national anthems, folk songs and prayers. The arrangement of all these entries may be in one alphabetical sequence if a dictionary catalogue is maintained; but a classified arrangement by a given instrument or musical form is more advantageous.

In cataloguing non-music records, the need for making subject entries is recognised, *e.g.* a record of bird or animal sounds will be referred to by the names of birds or sounds rather than the recorders' name. So is the case with language teaching and learning records. When a classified catalogue is compiled for these records, the main entries will be arranged by the notationand index entries may contain a reference to the class notation and the accession number of the records as well, so that direct access to the records, which are usually arranged by the accession order, is ensured.

The Music Library Association and the American Library Association Division of Cataloguing and Classification have issued a '*Code for cataloguing Music and Phonorecords*' in 1958, which offers satisfactory guidance in cataloguing both musical works and gramophone records.

A-ACR'250-253 cover the entry and description of 'phonorecords', the term adopted for various types of aural records/media. The principles underlying the entry of books or book-like material also appy to the entry of phonorecords, with the addition of particulars necessary on account of their non- visual but audible character.

*Films* (*Motion Pictures, Film Strips*). The increased emphasis on the use of audiovisual aids for educational purpose has placed additional importance on the cinematograph film are acquired in good number, a special filim library ad a separate film catalogue are maintained.

Films are usually well-known by their titles and the main entry for a film should, thereofre, be made under its title, with added entries for the subject treated and for the producer, director cameraman, musical director and other collaborators provided such entries will be of eal help to the users of the catalogue.

The body of the entry should contain information on:

(1) Country of production,
(2) Year of release,
(3) Format (16 mm. 35 mm. etc.),
(4) Length and projection time,
(5) Type (Sound or Silent),
(6) Colour (if other than black and white),
(7) Script,
(8) Accession number and class number,
(9) Material – inflammable/non-flammable.

If the film is acquired as supplementary reading to the test of a book, this fact must mentioned, If there will be only a handful of films in a library, their catalogue cards may as well be amalgamated with the general catalogue of the library, but marked 'film' at the end of title, or cards of different colour may be used for entries for films, so that they may be readily distinguished from cards for books.

International standards for film cataloguing, evaluation, and data as to availability were discussed by the United Kingdom National Commission for UNESCO in England in 1953 and at a conference on International Standards for Film Cataloguing convened by the United States National Commission for UNESCO in Washington in the same year. The decision to adopt the rules of the *Library of Congress* and the British Film Institute as a basis for universal standards for descriptive catalogue entries was considered by *UNESCO*. The Cataloguing Committee of the Aslib Film Production Librarians Group has reached a remarkable measure of agreement, and only two alternative rules have had to be formulated. This is obvious from the *Film Cataloguing Rules*, Aslib, 1963.

A-ACR 220-229 governing the entry, and description of films (*motion pictures*) and *filmstrips* have subsequently been adopted for cataloguing the special library material.

It is very appropriately pointed out in the introductory note to these rules that the films, being commonly identified by their titles are to be entered under titles. Further particulars of the film, obtained from sources other than the film itself, are not documented.

A-ACR 220 directs the main entry of a film under the title under which it is released, regardless of the title of its original release, followed, after any alternative title or subtitle, by the designation (Motion Picture) or (Filmstrip).

Aradhana, a tale of sublime
  love and worship (*Motion picture*)
Valley of the dolls (Motion picture).

B. If the title is wanting or it cannot be ascertained, an appropriate title is supplied by the cataloguer.

The open field into a University.
  The origin and development
  of the U.P. Agriculture University.
  (Motion picture)

D. If two or more distinct motion pictures are presented in one reel, separate entry is provided for each title, with an appropriate note.

> Going to college and using the library
> (Motion picture )
> (two films presented on a single reel)

A-ACR 221 directs the making of added entries for films under:

(1) the director or person/s chiefly responsible for the subject content;
(2) author and title of a published work which is the basis or background tothe film;
(3) the individual or organization responsible for its production;
(4) distributor in the country concerned;
(5) alternative titles;
(6) variant titles (in different languages);
(7) title of separate parts mentioned in a note; and
(8) series title, if significant.

Film libraries may find it necessary to provide all these added entries, but a few films in a general library may require only a select few of these added entries.

A.ACR 222-229 cover the making of descriptive entry for films, which has been already explained. Among these rules, A-ACR 228 provides guidance in giving a factual summary of the content or text of film, in order to reduce to the minimum the necessity for exhibiting the film to know what it is about. The instructions folder accompanying standard films always contain a reliable text of the film, which can be briefly summarised on the catalogue entry.

*Micro Films*. Microfilmed copies of books and periodicals have been gradually coming into use because of (1) lack of space in libraries, (2) rarity and deteriorated condition of books, and (3) necessity to supply copies of extracts and articles from originals to distant libraries. Some American librarieans like Fremont Rider anticipated that a day will come when printed books will be rare and microfilmed copies of them common and plentiful in libraries. But the day is far distant.

"Cataloguing of microfilm is not very different from that of the originals they reproduce, consisting mainly of additions describing the physical form of the films and the technical problems which that form involves."[9]

(1) if the copy is positive or negative;
(2) full collatio of the original;
(3) number or reels, if more than one;
(4) length of the film, in feet;
(5) width of the film, 16 mm./35 mm. in order to adjust the type of reader;
(6) manufacturer's number in his catalogue or list;
(7) and the word 'MICROFILM' stamped boldly on the top or across the card in a distinctively coloured ink.

The microfilms are best preserved in metal (aluminium) containers and filed in the numerical order of their accession numbers, which will reduce their shifdting to the minimum. These accession numbers must be written on the entry, as a means of quick location.

A-ACR 190-191 on this topic may usefully be studied and applied in making the entry for the microfilm or macrofilm.

*Coins*. Some libraries specially devoted to numismatic, historical and antiquarian studies, acquire coins as original sources of information. Cataloguing the coins is a specialist's job, because of the difficulties involved in deciphering the script and emblem on the coins. No specific directions are available in the joint code on cataloguing coins.

The cataloguer will do well toenter the individual coin under the name of the country, followed by the name of the ruler, with the dates of his reign. This procedure has the advantage of briging the entries for coins of a copuntry or nation together. They can then be arranged alphabetically by the name of rulers, or chronologically.

The title must be provided, as Gold/Silver/Copper/Alloy coin followed, by date of mint and value if known. The collation should furnish information on the circumference, facts on obverse and reverse and weight in grams or fine ounces.

Added entries for names of rulers may be made, if important. rulers of a country or of different countries may follow the code rule for collections and be entered under the collector or library, as the case may be.

Further guidance on the descriptive cataloguing can be had from the standard catalogues of coins in the British Museum and other large libraries.

A-ACR is silent on the cataloguing of *coins* as library material but the foregoing directions are considered helpful for the purpose.

REFERENCES

1. **Robert L. Collison.** "The Cataloguing, Arrangement and Filing of Special Material in Special Libraries." **ASLIB**, 1950, p.1
2. Henry Guppy. Rules for the Cataloguing of Incunabula; 2nd ed. rev. reprint 1947.
3. The A.L.A. Code is for author and title entries only. The **area** covered by a map is certainly not the author not is it always the filing word of that. If entry is to be made under the place nam,e whch is surely a subject entry, it would be appropriate to have a separate catalogue of maps, speciall, if the collection is of any size.
4. Robert L. Collison. "The Cataloguing, Arrangement and Filing of Special Material in Special Libraries., **ASLIB**, 1950, p. 53.
5. **William Jerome Wilson. Manuscript Cataloguing.** Traditio, N.Y. Fordham University Press, 1956, v. 12, p. 468.
6. **Evelyn Hensel.** "Treatment of Nonbook Materials", Library Trends, Oct., 1953, p. 188.
7. **Library of Congress. Rules for Descriptive Cataloguing.** Washington, 1949, p. 75.
8. Robert L. Collison. "The Cataloguing, Arrangement and Filing of Special Material in Special Libraries." **ASLIB**, 1950, p. 34.
9. **ibid.**, p. 28
10. **F.r. Goff,** Incunabula in American libraries; a third census of fifteenth century books. N.V. Bibliographical Soc. of America, 1964.

# 16

# ARRANGEMENT, FILING, GUIDING OF CATALOGUE AND INSTRUCTIONS FOR ITS USE

The catalogue entries are made according to the form of catalogue decided. But the mere making of main and added entries for a dictionary catalogue and main and index entries for a classified catalogue, will not produce the results desired, unless the cards are arranged so that quick and convenient reference is possible.

In the case of a *dictionary catalogue* the entries are arranged either in a strict alphabetical order or with some modifications under certain groups; introducing the element of classification in order to render the arrangement more logical. There is ample guidance furnished by *C.A. Cutter* in *his Rules for a dictionary catalogue.* The A.L.A. has published the *Rules for filing catalogue cards,* 1942, which is mostly based on Cutter's rules. If the same heading is used as another, title and subject, it is desirable to follow the order author, subject and title, e.g.

| | |
|---|---|
| Jawaharlal Nehru,<br>Discovery of India. | (author) |
| JAWAHARLAL NEHRU, | (subject) |
| Jawaharlal and Gandhi. | (title) |

There are two methods for *alphabetisation:* (1) *Letter by letter* and (2) *Word by word.* The first is called 'all through' and the second is known as 'nothing before something'. It is preferable to adopt the 'word by word' method in which the unit is the word and not the letters, *e.g.*

| *Letter by letter arrangement* | *Word by word arrangement* |
|---|---|
| New | New |
| Newark | New Delhi |
| New Delhi | New England |
| Newel | New London |
| New England | New York |
| New London | New Zealand |
| Newly | Newark |
| Newness | Newel |
| News | Newly |
| New York | Newness |
| New Zealand | News |

In the case of a classified catalogue the arrangement of the main entries is according to the class number or symbol assigned to each entry. The order of arrangement can be called numerical or symbolic. It is far easier to evolve the arrangement of these entries, each class number determining its place quite specifically in the hierarchy of the classification system. Arrangement of entries within a class cannot be determined by the notation of that class, as the cards for several books on the same subject will have the same class notation. It will leave open the choice of arrangement, which can be decided on the need existing for it. The arrangement usually adopted is alphabetical by authors and if the author has more than one work classed under the same notation the sub-arrangement is by the title; but other modes of arrangement within a class are also possible: (1) chronological order by date of publication; (2) inverse chronological order in the case of scientific and technical books; (3) geographical order by country or locality; (4) by language ; (5) by form in literature. In order to maintain consistency, no two different modes of arrangement should be adopted in arranging the cards of a single class.

If any doubts were to arise a reference to the schedules of the classification scheme would easily determine the location and order. The index entries are arranged in alphabetical order. Authors, titles and subjects may be mixed together and arranged in one sequence or in separate sequences.

The quickness with which the desired catalogue entries are located, depends on the extent of guide cards placed in the catalogue. A *guide card* is a card with a projecting edge or tab on which a letter or phrase is written or printed. These guide cards are availbale in sets of alphabet and classes. The tabs are protected by celluloid or xylonite in order to keep the letter or numberss from fading due to wear and tear. One of these guides if lettered "how o use the Catalogue" and below the tab, specific instructions are printed. One such guide card is placed in front of each tray, so as to attract the attention of the user.

In the case of *classified catalogues,* a guide card should be provided for each major class number as well as or each one of its subdivisions used in the catalogue. A guide card should display the class number and the subject heading and scope. If there is a large number of cards under a single class number, alphabetical or chronologial guide cards must be used liberally.

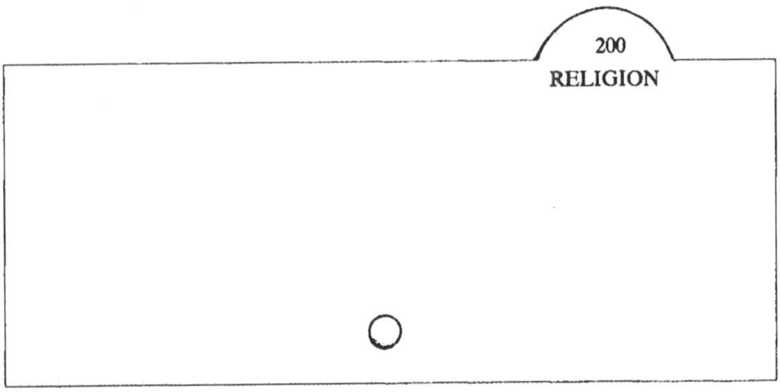


GUIDE CARD

Spacing the guide cards is a matter for individual decision for libraries. The larger the catalogue, the greater is the need for frequent guides in the catalogue. These guide cards not only save the time of a reader in locating a desired entry directly and quickly, but reduce unnecessary wear and tear of the catalogue cards, whose longevity is thereby increased.

In alphabetising, filing and guiding, accuracy extraordinary is required to an extent. The value of a catalogue card is only proved when an entry is readily found in the midst of thousands of cards. Therefore, accurate and consistent filing of these cards will alone bring forth the desired results.

The work of alphabetising and filing of catalogue cards should not be entrusted to persons who have not been disciplined in accurate methods. Before a card is filed, it should be reviewed as it stands on the self-locking rod to detect any error in alphabetisation.

Keeping the catalogue up-to-date is possible by filing that catalogue cards at the time a book is made ready for circulation as well as by taking out the cards for books withdrawn from circulation. Errors of inconsistent headings, different class numbers from similar books and varying forms of sub-division of subjects are brought to light when they are filed if they had escaped at the time of their preparation.

The final job connected with the making of a catalogue has, therefore, to be done with all care and responsibility to ensure satisfactory working of the catalogue.

When all the catalogue cards have been properly alphabetised and inserted in the catalogue trays of the cabinet with appropriate guide cards, the method of handling the various cards for the same book filed in different places or trays requires to be made clear to the public, for whose use they have been made and filed.

The layout of the catalogue, its internal divisions and location of entries, should be explained in simple terms. As there is a rule for every item of work connected with the production of a catalogue, the instructions for the public in the use of the catalogue should reflect the application of the rules by furnishing concrete examples of how to find a book, under the author's surname, under its subject or subjects, under its title, under its related subjects. The public should feel that the consultation of a *card catalogue* is no more difficult than referring to a word or term in a dictionary or encyclopedia.

Whatever may be the standard or perfection aimed at and achieved in compiling the catalogue, the public, who are expected to use it, still find the card catalogue to be more complex than a printed catalogue. Perhaps, the printed book catalogue appears self-contained. When the reader opens the book catalogue, he finds instructions on the system of classification adopted for arrangement of books on shelves and the order in which he will find the entries in the catalogue. The indexes at the end of catalogue enteries provide further facility to the reader in his task of location and identification.

But a dictionary card catalogue, by virtue of its physical size and shape, its unit cards, its cross references, and its complicated arrangement following the 'word by word' principle needs to be fully explained.

1. The *card catalogue* is a record of books in the library's collection.
2. Each book is represented by one card under the name of the

author, one under its title, one under the name of its subject; if a book deals with more than one subject, there are as many subject cards as the number of subjects contained in it; if the book contains more than one work of the same author or works of different authors, there are additonal cards.

3. Besides these author, title and subject cards there are cards, under the names of collaborators, *i.e.* editor, translator, joint author, commentator, etc.

4. There are cards which direct the reader from one heading to another. They are used to direct the reader from a heading which the cataloguer might have used for a particular book but which he has in fact not used because he has preferred a synonym, a combined heading or a term denoting a related subject. These are reference cards, which bear no notation. These reference cards are made for names of persons, subjects, and occasionally for titles.

5. There are alphabetical *guide cards* at convenient places and each tray in the cabinent is provided with a label indicating the inclusive range of cards contained in it, *e.g.* 'A-AE'.

6. If the author is known, look under his name, *i.e.* surname followed by forenames or initials, *e.g.* Shakespeare, William; Wells, H.G.

7. If the author is an oriental writer, usually look under his personal name, followed by other parts of his name, *e.g.* Narayan, R.K. Rajagopalchari, Chakravarty ; Lin Yu Tang. But there are a few oriental writers, who are better known by their family names or surnames. These are entered under their family nemes, followed by the other parts of the name, *e.g.* Gokhale, Gopal Krishna; Gandhi, M.K.

8. If the name of the author or the title of the book is unknown, look under the name of the subject on which you want material, *e.g.* if books on Television are wanted, look under Television; if there are books in the library's collection on the subject they will be found. The heading 'Television' will be written or typed distinctly, in block letters, or coloured ink and the author and title of the book given below on the card.

9. In case of fiction, look under author or title of the novel or story desired, *e.g.* Tolstoy: Anna Karenina ; Tale of Two Cities, Dickens.

10. If a work is known to belong to a series and if its exact author and title are unknown look under the name of the series as heading. If the volune is in the collection, it will be found entered on the series card. *e.g.* Story of the Nations: Lanepool: India.

11. Look up the names of persons, for their biographies,

autobiographies, diaries, and memoirs entered as headings on cards.

However, helpful may be the written instructions to the public in the use of the catalogue, the reader will still need the personal guidance of the library staff. The individual attention and personal guidance given to the reader is a sure step to better appreciation and use of the library by the public. The foundations of purposeful and effective reading are well laid in a *junior library*, where young readers should be given proper orientation in the use of catalogues and books, with the hope that when they become adults, they will become self-reliant in a larger measure.

# 17

# EDUCATION AND TRAINING OF CATALOGUERS

Surveys of *Teachnig Methods of Cataloguing and classification* have been conducted in the United States and to some extent in England. The idea was to arrive at a satisfactory method of teaching and to provide a comprehensive curriculum of cataloguing studies in order that good cataloguing personnel might be made available to libraries, whose cataloguing problems could be handled with realism. *The Humeston survey (1951)*[1] and *the Pettus survey 1952*[2] afford interesting and useful data on the content and method of teaching cataloguing. There has existed diversity in the methods as well as in the content of curriculum. But one common problem that has been before the teachers of cataloguing and that is yet to be solved is how much emphasis must be laid on (1) the principles and (2) how much on the practice of cataloguing. One section of teachers believe that the old pedagogic method of teaching by the rules of catalogue codes should be given up, as it renders cataloguing dry and unintellectual to the students. The students ultimately become more mechanical than sensible cataloguer and that is why cataloguing has not attained the same level of recognition, as other similar intellectual activities before the scholarly world. The other group of teachers believe with equal conviction that the proper understanding of the rules in the catalogue codes is the core of the study. If the rules are explained, about their purpose, and the context of their application to the students, they can compile satisfactory catalogues. After all the reader does not care to go into the intellectual calibre of a cataloguer, but tests it by the standard of efficiency attatined and displayed in the catalogues which he uses.

This controversy is based on cataloguing tradition. Professor *P.S. Dunkin* of the Graduate School of Library Service, Rutgers University, declares that "Crisis demands not a restatement of tradition, but a broad new outlook." Instead of a veneration for tradition , cataloguers should develop a "creative scepticism." He opposes the old form of drill and attention to technical details, which detour students from concern with the real problems of cataloguing. His proposed programme of instruction would involve, in addition to other things, introduction to principles in a few lectures, using audio-visual aids, and actual cataloguing in libraries which will work in cooperation with the library schools.[3]

New concepts on *teaching cataloguing* are coming up in recent years in an endless stream. It is almost impossible even for an up-to-date school of librarianship to discard the basic concepts of cataloguing in its curriculum, simply because they happen to be old. It seems to us, therefore, that in teaching cataloguing, balance between the theory and practice must be maintained.

A satisfactory course of instruction on the subject of cataloguing to post-graduate students undergoing a year's course at the Universtity Schools of Librarianship should include lectures on:

1. Nature, scope, and functions of library catalogues.
2. History of catalogues and cataloguing codes.
3. Varieties of catalogues and their distinguishing characteristics.
4. Arrangements of catalogues and rules of filing.
5. Personal author and corporate author.
6. Titles as main entries.
7. Need for added entries.
8. Descriptive cataloguing standards and purposes.
9. Subject cataloguing.
10. Relation of classification to subject cataloguing.
11. Relation of cataloguing to (other branches of library administration) documentation processes, and information storage, location retrieval, and presentation.
12. Problems of cataloguing foreign language books.
13. Cooperative cataloguing, union catalogues.
14. Reclassification and re-cataloguing.
15. Costing cataloguing processes.
16. Maintenance and editing of catalogues.
17. Mechanical appliances used in processing and duplication of

cards.

18. Studies of catalogues in relation to reader approach and use; idealism versus pragmatism.
19. Relation of catalogues to bibliographies.
20. Cataloguing of special materials.
21. International cataloguing practice.
22. Scholarly background to cataloguing work.
23. What is a computer ? Its structure and functions.
24. Is computer, both qualitatively and quantitatively superior to a care catalogue ? Can computerised Catalogue totally replace the traditional card and other forms of catalogues ?
25. Advantages and disadvantages of Com-catalogues and On- line retrieval systems.

The foregoing are some of the more important topics on which the students of cataloguing should receive adequate instruction. The limited duration of the course of a year will indicate tha desirability of concentrating on basic issues in cataloguing.

Besides the theoretical study, the students should be given ample opportunity to do actual cataloguing of different types of books, at least for an hour a day and should be able to participate in various other processes, like duplication, search verification, alphabetisation, arrangement, filing and discarding, etc.

The prevailing practices in a library or libraries which the students observe during their course influence to a large extent the standard and performance of these technical services to be done by them elsewhere. As no two libraries have exactly identical procedures or staff manuals, methods and procedures in practical cataloguing are bound to differ.

Finally, it must be admitted that any amount of theoretical study and intensive practice, will not shape a student into a good cataloguer, unless he has the aptitude and love for the work. The teacher should be able to observe the interests of the students and direct them to appropriate fields of specialisation in library work. An inquiring mind, a retentive faculty, a disciplined adherence to rules, an inherent capacity to be at home in the midst of books, old and new, and a spirit of service to the reader are natural traits in a cataloguer. "But a cataloguer must be something more than a scholar and a man of the world; he must be an organiser, an ardent and patient worker, and the possessor of more than the usual modicum of tact, common sense and good humour."[4]

The education and training of cataloguers should, therefore, be closely linked or shaped in conformity to these ideals and traditions of cataloguing practice. It is high time that the library administrators realise the value of cataloguing and make the cataloguing positions sufficiently attractive so that young men and women of high intellecutal calibre are attracted to the study of cataloguing.

Cataloguing mechanisation is gradually becoming popular in view of the increasing data/information acquired and stored in the catalogues. "The only difference between the current and the future is the medium used to impart cataloguing information. The point is that the cataloguing data that doesn't communicate with the public now will not merely through a change of medium do any better in the future."[5] This is a very apt comment full of sense that the content of information is more important than the media of communication.

"As new techniques develop which can be applied to library and information work, there is need to educate and train not only new entrants to the profession but also those who are already in mid-career. It is important to stress that any education or training should cover the techniques and how they may be used and should also cover how they can be managed."

"Initial professional education for librarianship is largely the province of the library schools and their task is to integrate a knowledge of the new techniques and heir effects into an already crowdedcurriculum, and while continuing to cover much of the traditional methods, new techniques and their applications should, it is suggested, become a core subject in every school teaching library science, and the first problem is to ensure that qualified instructors are available."[6]

The working staff in libraries certainly need attention in regard to the introduction, management, and understanding of the library users' problems as a result of the new technology adopted for the library. As library schools may or may not undertake to educate the library personnel, it is the responsibility of the individual libraries to provide for the inservice training, as otherwise the change brought about due to automation may not yield the results expected of it, but create a barrier between the books and their users.

"The main conclusion I reached as a result of these surveys is that one shouldn't be too much carried away by 'new technology as it is'; the major problem facing the teaching staff in the schools is generally not the availability of the computer or technological resources, but the time and effort required to harness this technology appropriately for the education of future librarians and information scientists." The difficulty in finding the software and to develop it is the general agreement among the teachers of new technology to students. The recommendation made is that a post of peripatetic programmer should be created by the British Library Research and Development Department for two years in the first instance. This would greatly help in the development of the teaching aids using new technology in the schools, particularly in the smaller schools which could not avail the funds of the British Library Research and Development Department.

The software for teaching On-line cataloguing and On-line searching should possess the following characteristics:-

1. Written in a commonly available high level language,
2. Machine independence as far as possible,
3. Well laid out so that others can easily see the structured in design,
4. Comprehensive of the topic,
5. Accompanied by good documentation,
6. Contain any comment/remark statements to explain the functions of the parts of the programme,
7. Well tested,
8. Not be too lengthy.

These recommendations are contained in the British Library Research Development 1981 Report No. 5616 by Lucy A. Tedd, after carrying out a survey of the situation in sixteen schools teaching Library and Information Science in the United Kingdom may afford guidelines in drafting the core curriculum for teaching this technology in the Indian Schools of Library and Information Science.

## REFERENCES


1. **E.J. Humeston.** "Teaching Cataloguing Today." **Jl. of Cataloguing and Classification,** v. 7, pp. 53-57, 1951.
2. **Clyde Pettus** " Teaching Cataloguing." **Library Journal,** v. 11, pp. 1770-1773. Oct. 15, 1952.
3. **P.S. Dunkin** "Petty Codes and Pedagogues." **Jl. of Cataloguing and Classification,** v.7, pp. 53-57, Summer 1951.
4. **H.A. Sharp, Cataloguing;** 4th ed. London, Grafton, 1950, p. 355.
5. Dickinson: The Card Catalogue : current issues, Scarecrow Press, 1981, referred to in Peter Gilman and Silvina Peniston: Library Automations: a current review. ASLIB, 1984, p.6

6. Library Association: The Impact of New Technology on Libraries and Information Centres, a report by the Library Association Working Party 1981-82 (L.A. Reports 38) p. 39, para 145 and 146.

18

# DOCUMENTATION: AN EXTENSION OF CATALOGUING AND CLASSIFICATION APPLIED TO ISOLATES

*Documentation* is a term which has recently been applied to the handling of mirco units of thought, specially in the fields of science and technology. It is the intensity with which every idea on every page of an article on a related subject is recorded and coded that distinguishes the work of documentation from traditional cataloguing. *A.D.Osborn* remarks that a *documentalist* is a "Perfectionist Cataloguer."

Mortimer Taube says "Documentation as the designation of the total complex of activities involved in the communication of specialized information includes the activities which constitute special librarianship plus the prior activities of preparing and reproducing materials and the subsequent activity of distribution."[1] He holds the view that publishing activity is part of documentation, for all printed material is published with the object of distribution to specialists. *The American Documentation Institute* has as its object the advancemnt of the principles and techniques of recorded information.

There is a clear statement about documentation, what it is and what it does and what it aims at in the outline of the course on documentation adopted by the Graduate School of Library Service, Rutgers University.

"Documentation is the identification, recording, organization, storage, recall, conversion into more useful forms, synthesis and dissemination of the intellectual content of print and other recorded materials, in relationship to the specialized needs of particular users and uses. The librarian initiates subject analysis in the cataloguing process, but when he moves into the intensive handling of the ideas contained in every page of every source he starts to function as a documentalist. And since the conversion or inversion into new forms is prerequisite, and the masses of objects to be handled is much greater when every idea and every page of every article must be subject to recall and manipulation, and since the transmission of information is requisite, the documetalist must be much more interested in the materials handling, converting, and transmitting systems than must the librarian or bibliographer who supply the raw material to the documentalist."

There is yet another brief definition of *Documentation* as "the group of techniques necessary for the ordered presentation, organization and communication of recorded specialised knowledge, in order to give maximum accessibility and utility to the information contained."[2]

Two basic types of bibliographical organization are (1) organization for 'retrieval' of information already known to the enquirer more or less exactly, and (2) organization for 'dissemination' by which enquirer can be kept informed of advances made not only in his special field of knowledge but in the related fields as well. Large collections in libraries containing the recorded information of use both to the general reader and the specialist have been classified, catalogued, indexed and abstracted by adopting the conventional library methods. These methods appear to be large scale operations, which have only partially served the needs of the highly specialised investigators in science and technology who require "pin-pointed" information of absolute specificity. Several industrial and technological establishments realised the necessity of developing their own specialised bibliographical services. The organization for specialised use of the innumerable scientific and technical reports and bulletins published during the last decade resulted in the formation and functioning of documentation centres, largely manned by scientific personnel. Their experience in the retrieval and dissemination of specialised information indicated that the ordinary book classification and cataloguing techniques if adopted for sorting and presentation of research reports, patents and other scientific data were uneconomic and "the grouping, as established by the classification system is at cross purposes with the search requirement. This means in practice that the classification scheme fails to provide some one grouping which may be consulted to meet the search requirements."[3]

The realisation of the limitations of the *Dewey Decimal Classification* even in its application to books stimulated librarians and documentalists to develop the *Universal Decimal Classification. The U.D.C.* also failed to get over the limitation of rigid combinations of concepts and ideas. Several U.D.C. number were necessary to be provided for a single patent in order to establish the relationship between generic and specific concepts. These sets of notations were not only time- consuming but sometimes confusing to the user.

At this stage Dr. Ranganathan seized the opportunity and and provided a classification with faceted notation. This is called *Colon Classification* and further researches into "Depth Classification" are being continued to help the organization, presentation and correlation of micro-units of thought. "Ranganathan, through his system of facets, main classes, divisions, etc., has contributed greatly in turning the spotlight on elements of rigidity in the U.D.C. and pigeon-hole classification systems and by so doing has pointed the way to coding systems whose flexibility corresponds to the complexity of the subject contents of present-day scientific and technical papers."[4]

It is, then, quite likely that a synthetic classification with complete autonomy for the classifier can in reallity by helpful in presenting the information in the form suited to the specialists. The classified catalogue, based on such a classification can very well indicate further development to the documentalist. Can we call documentaion 'subject bibliography of the hour or the moment'?

"*Bibliography* can hardly exclude cataloguing and indexing; this does not make a bibliographer a librarian, but high though this title, such as Director, and whatever else she or he does, she or he is not a librarian who is not, or is not able or at least willing to be a cataloguer and indexer."[5] Librarianship by tradition and practice was associated with only the collection, preservation and indication of literature to which new material "scientific and technical reports and non-book material like films and gramophone records have been added by necessity. The new technique "*documentation*", which has as its sole aim the speedy provision and presentation of current information, chiefly in the fields of science, technology and industry, in a "pin-pointed" manner, has been boosted out of all proportion, overlooking the basic fact that it has its origins and it has developed from cataloguing and classifying which has been accepted by great and small librarians in the past and present, as the core of the profession. Because of the growing tendency of some librarians to belittle and decry cataloguing, and classification, in preference to mechanical administration, and because of the failure of traditional methods of classification and cataloguing to satisfy the scientist, documentation, the offshoot of librarianship has gained such importance as to render librarianship less intellectual in the eyes of the scientists. *J.H. Shera* states "*documentaiton* lies at the very heart of librarianship, and the primary responsibility of the librarian is to make of himself an expert in bibliographic organization. Let librarians then, apply themselves to the problems of bibliographic organization, become once more the acknowledged leaders in the largely uncharted world of subject bibliography, and in the stern discipline of documentation, not only achieve a new professional self respect but rediscover their true purpose in society."[6] The above view of documentation and librarianship, would imply that librarianship, which certainly includes classifiers and cataloguers, has lost its significance and accredited place in society. Society, specially the world of learning and scholarship, is not solely or wholely constituted of scientists and industrialists, who form a small part of it. Documentation, as conceived can under no cicrumstances be a substitute for library cataloguing and classification. The chances of documentation centres displacing libraries are far remote.

It seems appropriate and interesting to reproduce a few of the assumptions of Metcalfe, which need thought and discussion : (1) "one is that there is no relevant difference between librarianship, documentation, and bibliography, and (2) another that bibliographyor cataloguing or indexing, with reference work as another form of literature and information indication, are the distinguishing characteristics of librarianship, bibliography and documentation as a profession, and (3) that for subject indexing, cataloguing, bibliography, and documentaion there can be and must be found a commonly accepted body of theory... and that this must must be a theory of their practice."[7]

*Cataloguing practice*, specially subject cataloguing of books and periodicals and the arrangement of various entries in the catalogue of a library, is certainly a sound background to the understanding and practice of documentation. Cataloguing, as has already been observed, aims at the communication of ideas embodied in books to readers in libraries, while *documentation* goes a step further in that these ideas in periodical publications, which are more current than those in books, are manipulated and synthesised into more useful forms, with the help of some mechanical aids, like machine-sorted punched cards, electronic machines, etc. "All the steps in classification from facet analysis to translation of isolate ideas into isolate numbers should be done by a classifier before the coding of numbers for the machineryare essential. The only step in classification not needed by machinery is that of arranging the facets in a preferred sequence and synthesizing the isolate numbers and the basic class number into the class number."[8]

In conclusion, we may state, that there is so close an identity of aims and operations between cataloguing, classification and documentation that it is difficult to draw a line of demarcation which will indicate where cataloguing stops and documentation begins.

## REFERENCES


1. **Mortimer Taube**, "Special Librarianship and Documentation. "**Special Libraries**, 43 : 206, July-Aug., 1952.
2. **James D. Mack and Robert S. Taylor**. 'A System of Documentation Terminology' in **Documentation in action;** ed by J.H. Shera and others. N.Y., Reinhold Publishing Corporation, 1966, p. 20.
3. **Marjorie R. Hyslop**. 'Inventory of Methods and Devices for analysis, Storage and Retrieval of Information, in "**Documentation in action;** ed by J.H. Shera and others. N.Y., Reinhold Publishing Corporation, 1959, p. 118.
4. **Ibid.**, p.120.
5. **John Metcalfe. Information Indexing and Subject Cataloguing**. N.Y., Scarecrow Press, Inc. 1957, p., 264,
6. **J.H. Shera**, "Documentation, its scope and limitation." **Library Quarterly**, 21: 13-26, Jan. 1951.
7. **John metcalf. Information Indexing and Subject Cataloguing**. N.Y., Scarecrow Press, Inc. 1954, p. 264.
8. **S.R. Ranganathan**, "Classification as a Discipline" in **proceedings of the International Study Conference on Classification for Information Retrieval, 13th-17th May,** 1957, Lond. **ASLIB**, 1957. p.10.

## 19

# CATALOGUE CARDS, THEIR STYLE AND REPRODUCTION METHODS

The entries in a catalogue are designed to perform certain functions assigned to each one of them. Therefore, the parts or items of information included in an entry are influenced by those considerations. The heading in each entry is the leading part. On the line of heading the *call-number* of a book is included and written on the top left corner in alphabetical arrangement of the entries and above the heading in a classified or numerical order. As one of the aims of an entry in a library catalogue is to help in the location of a desired book on the shelves, it is obligatory that these call-numbers find a place prominently and legibly on them.

The author entry, by agreed usage, will consist of a uniform style of author heading, usually surname, followed by forenames in the case of accidental writers and personal name followed by other parts of the name, in the case of oriental writers. On the line below, the title of the book, as on the title page, is given. If there are not more than three collaborators they are mentioned as a part of the title group, separated from the actual title by a semi-colon. The edition is also stated, unless it is the first. The next group is the imprint consisting of place of publication, name of publisher, and date of publication. Then follows the collation of the book, whch is given as a spearate group commencing at the second indention. If a book warrants it, special information about it may be given in a note in another group. Sometimes it may be necessary to provide contents as a group, when the title is not explicit or is composite in nature. Whenever the author entry is the main entry for the book, all the secondary entries which the cataloguer has decided to make are indicated in it at the bottom of the catalogue card in order to serve as a guide to the cataloguing department in the making and verification as well as withdrawal of these entries. Excepting this last part, known as tracing, the body of the catalogue card contains only such information as is vital to the reader for identification, location, choice, and study.

The secondary entries contain on the line of heading, the call number and the appropriate heading (title, collaborator, subject etc.) and the body of the card displays select items from the main entry in secondary fullness, because the heading of each entry and the call-number of the book satisfy a large number of the users of the catalogue in their approach to books, *e.g. Main entry.*

1 3 4<br>
320.1 laski, H.J.<br>
2 5 6 7<br>
L34 Grammar of politics; 5th ed. London<br>
8 9<br>
Allen and Unwin. 1948<br>
10<br>
xxvii, 672 p., 21 cm.<br>
11<br>
1. Political Science-Theory. 1. title.

Call No. (Class No.1 Imprint (Place 7, Publisher 8<br>
(Book No. 2 Date of publication 9)<br>
Author (Surname 3 Collation 10<br>
heading (Forename in secondary fullness 4<br>
Tracings 11<br>
Title 5, Statement of ed. 6

Secondary entries

Subject<br>
320.1 POLITICAL SCIENCE-THEORY<br>
L34 Laski, H.J.<br>
Grammar of politics ; 5th ed. Lomdon,<br>
Allen and Unwin, 1948.

Title<br>
320.1 Grammar of politics. 1948<br>
L34 Laski, H.J.

The reference entries are made from one heading to another and hold good for all books that belong to the headings in question. Therefore, these reference entries contain only three parts. (1) the heading referred from, (2) the direction *see* or *see also*, and (3) the heading referred to. The call number and the usual items of information about a book, which are present in the body of the regular entries are conspiciuously absent in these reference entries.

Reference entry "see" type

POLITICAL ECONOMY, **see,**
ECONOMICS

References entry "**see also**" type.

ETHICS, see also,
BEHAVIOUR

The style of a catalogue card which embodies the essential information about a book should be such as to make it easily intelligible to the reader when using the catalogue. Cataloguing tradition has become established with regard to the information that should be incorporated on a catalogue card. Although individual libraries adopt slightly varied standards of details on a catalogue card, it can be seen from the various specimens given below, that with regard to essential details, like author, title, subject, form and call number, there is uniformity.

1. **L.C. Catalogue Card.** (Printed).

Rose, Frank Xavier, 1914 –
Young people's book of jet propulsion. Rev. and enl. ed.
New York, Lothrop, Lee and Shepard, 1950.
163p. illus., port. 21 cm.
1. Jet propulsion. 2. **Rockets** (Aeronautics).
1. title.
TL709, R6 1950 629-13338 50-5805

**Library of Congress** 10

2. **U.P. Agricultural University Library Catalogue Card** (Type)

025.3 **Mann, Margret.**
M28 Introduction to cataloguing and the classification of books.
2nd ed. **Chicago, American Library Association, 1943.**
IX, 276p.
1017 1. **Cataloguing.** 2. **Classification (Books).**
1. title.

3.. **Wilson Card. (Printed).**

**Rose, Frank Xavier, 1914—**
Young people's book of jet propulsion. Rev. and enl. ed. Lothrop, 1950.
163 p. illus.
First published 1948. The 1950 edition has added new material on seven Air

Force planes, four Navy planes and one flying test tube. "The story of American jet-and rocket-powered aircraft, from its invention before the last War through its improvement during the War and after, to its present status. Illustrated with more than 50 half tones displaying the technical features of each model." Retail bookseller.

1. Jet propulsion. 2. Rockets (Aeronautics)
1. Title 629.13338
2-17-50 (W) **The H.W. Wilson Company.**

**4. Columbia University Library Card. (Typed).**

025.3 **Mann, Margaret**
M282 Introduction to cataloguing and the classification of books :
2nd ed. **Chicago, American Library Association, 1943.**
ix, 276p. illus., 24 cm.
"References" at end of most chapters.
O
**Cataloguer's Name or Initials**

**Tracing on Main entry (Reverse of Card)**
Cataloguing O
CLASSIFICATION-BOOKS
American Library Association

The items which are necessary to be provided on a catalogue card, are:

1. *The Call number*, consisting of the class number and the author number, showing the exact location of the book on the shelves. Specific and accurate call number ensures quick and correct location of the desired book.

904 Class Number
= Call No.
D44 Author Number

2. The *Author*, personal or corporate, responsible for writing the book. The author's name, if personal, follows the order surname, followed by forenames in complete or secondary fullness. The author, if a corporate (*i.e.*) body or organization, follows a different pattern, as it has no fore name and surname but only a corporate name which is to be given fully, *e.g.*

| | 1 | 2 | |
|---|---|---|---|
| *Personal Author* | Dickinson, | Lowes Golding | 1. Surname<br>2. Forenames in complete fullness |

| | 1 | 2 | |
|---|---|---|---|
| | Dickinson, | L.G. | 1. Surname<br>2. Forenames in secondary fullness |
| *Corporate Authors* | India — Ministry of Education.<br>Madras — Museum.<br>Banaras Hindu University, Banaras.<br>Ramakrishna Mission, Banaras.<br>Red Cross, New Delhi. | | |

The corporate author is given usually under the name of the locality and sometimes under the name of the body followed by location. This order is determined by the Catalogue rules, governing the different types of corporate authors. Therefore, a corporate author's name consists of two parts (1) name of locality, (2) name of body.

3. *The Title*, being an exact version of it as found on the title page of the book, but including a statement of the edition or editor, translation or translator and other collaborators like jt. author, illustrator, etc.

It should be noted that although the A.L.A.Catalogue rules define the title to include the name of the author, in actual practice the repetition of the author's name at the end of the title is considered not essential. In preparing the cards by writing or typing, the author's name need not be given as a part of it, even though printed cards adopt the practice of repeating the author's name as a part of the title.

*Title, including a reference to reviser or, editor, but omitting author's name, e.g.*

Soule, Richard.

Dictionary of English synonyms and synonymous expressions, designed as a guide to apt and varied diction; rev. and enl. ed. by A.D. Sheffield.

*Title, including a statement of the edition number only.*

Day, Clive.

History of Commerce; 4th ed.

*Title, including a statement of the editor only*

Dewey, John.

Intelligence in the modern world; ed. with an intro. by

Joseph Ratner.
*Title, including a reference to tr. and ed. in one.*

Freud, Sigmund.
Basic writings: tr.and ed. with an intro. by A.A. Brill.

*Title, including a reference to translation and translator.*
Thyagaraja .
Songs; English tr. by C. Narayana Rao.

*Title, including a ref. to. authors by repeating the name of the first author and a selection of important authors.*
Allen, John Stuart, and others.
Atoms, rocks and galaxies ; a survey in physical science by J.S. Allen, S.J. French and C.L. Hearnshaw and others.

*Title including a ref. to illustrator.*
Stiles. H.E.
Pottery of the ancients; illus. by Marion Downer.

4. *Imprint*, consists of 1. Place of publication, 2. Name of publisher (usually surname) and 3. Date of publication.

Dewey, John.
Experience and education N.Y. Macmillian, 1938.
1 2 3

5. *Collation*, which describes the physical features of the book – pagination or volumes, illustration and size in centimeters are commonly given.

Beven, Bernard.
History of Spanish Architecture. N.Y. Scribner,1939
199 p.,illus., maps, 21 cm.

6. *Series note*, contains the name of the series to which the book belongs with volume number if the publisher has assigned one to it.

Sharp, Dorothea.
Students's book of oil painting, N.Y., Pitman, 1938.
47p., illus., 22cm (Student's art book, 5).

The beginner should not confuse the number of volumes in which a book is published and the number of the book amongst other works in the series. The latter is given at the end of the series note, while the former is the first item of collation, when the book is in more than one volume.

7. *Notes,* about the origin and any bibliographical features not brought out by the previous six items in a catalogue card are given for certain books.

8. *Contents*, are necessary to be given for certain books when the title is not fully comprehensive, specially when the book is in more then one volume. Follow the order of the table of contents.

9. *Tracing or Indication*, of added entry cards and reference cards to be provided is usually given at the bottom of the catalogue cards (L.C. Model) or on its reverse. L.C. model saves time in turning over the card, especially when cards are typed or hand-written.

10. *Capitals, Punctuation, Figures,* are to be used when necessary and in accord with grammatical practice. Prefer arabic numerals to roman ones, which are used to designate rulers, kings, princes, popes and similar dignitaries.

The standard catalogue card is of the dimension 12.5 cm.in length and 7.5 cm. in height. It is filed erect in a drawer of the card cabinet by means of a uniformly punched hole at its bottom through which the self-locking rod passes and secures the cards in position. The cards are supplied to the specification by library supply houses. There are blank and ruled cards. There are light, medium and heavy weight cards. It is advisable to choose medium weight quality and ruled cards if the cards are written and blank cards, if they are typed.

The skeleton of a complete catalogue card 12.5cm. × 7.5cm. shows the order and position of the items, normally included in a catalogue entry. It is suggested that the accession number of the book though it has no bearing on the cataloguer's technique, may be given on the main entry at the bottom right hand corner or on the back, if many, to facilitate identification of copies or editions by the staff.

Skeleton of Main Entry Card

Call No. Author's surname, forenames.

Title.................................................................

......................., edition. Place. Publisher, Date

Collation.... ....(Series note)

Notes.

**Contents :—**

ACC. No. 1. Subject. I. editor. II title.

The printed unit cards in general use in the U.S.A. contain fuller details, while the cards made by individual libraries maintain a distinction between main entry and added entry cards by giving a shortened title and omitting all or part of imprint and collation. This practice is followed in many British and Indian libraries and has much to commend it.

**Skeleton of Added Entry Card for Editor**

Call No. Editor's surname, Forenames. Abbr. ed.
Author's surname, forenames.
Title..............................................Date.

**Skeleton of Added Entry Card for Title**

Call No. Title..............................................Date.
Author's surname, forenames

**Skeleton of Added Entry Card for Subject**

Call No. Subject heading
Author's surname, forenames.
Title..............................................
Place, Publisher, Date
Collation

The cataloguer should bear in mind that the object of the catalogue is to save the time and trouble of the readers in a library in the use of books. The catalogue cards made by him should perform this function. The best way for a cataloguer to make the catalogue cards which will satisfy the user is that he visualises the kind or group of readers for whom the book is being catalogued. The application of the rules tend to simplify the catalogue and to maintain uniformity, accuracy and consistency.

The regular procedure in practical cataloguing of a book is (1) read the title page carefully, (2) glance through the table of contents, (3) skim through the text, in order to obtain an accurate knowledge of the subject of the book, (4) decide upon the various entries or cards required to be made for the book (i.e.) the main entry and the added entries.

Generally, a book of non-fiction requires three to five cards and a book of fiction and literature, two cards.

The need for *reproduction of catalogue cards* is obvious, in order to provide entries in the catalogues to meet all possible approaches to books by readers. The methods of card reproduction are several, ranging from handwriting to xerography. Every method has its own advantages and disadvantages, but in choosing one of them, the requirements of the library, of a few or a large number of catalogue cards, should carefully be studied. A small town library with no branches, will not require more than one set of catalogue cards for its catalogue; while a large city central library with a numbre of branches and mobile libraries will need several sets of catalogue cards, besides the number requird for the master catalogue. As library budgets are limited, only equipment for card reproduction, which can justify the investment on it, should be chosen."Perhaps the cheapest is the flat bed duplicator which can be bought for about 10£; such a machine could produce good copies, filling the whole of a 5×3 in. card. At the other end of the scale are such installations as xerography coupled with offset lithography."[1] The typewriter, which is commonly used in libraries for reproduction of catalogue cards in India is slow and expensive in its output. It is time to discard copy-typing of cards and thereby release the funds for the provision of some kind of card reproduction equipment.

The chief varieties of duplicating machines adopted in libraries for reproduction of catalogue cards are:

(i) Wax stencil duplicators.
(ii) Spirit duplicators.
(iii) Offset Lithography.
(iv) Metal plate addressing machines.
(v) Stencil addressing machines.
(vi) Spirit addressing machines.
(vii) Microphotographic cameras.
(viii) Xerography camera.

A full description of the performance of these machines is provided by *Philip S. Pargeter* and *H.R. Verry* in their books.[2] Indian libraries will find that wax stencil duplicators of Gestetner Limited or spirit duplicators, Banda Model 10 or Ditto Model 9D-20 are suited to their purposes and within their available resources.

REFERENCES

1. Phillip S. Pargeter. The reproduction of catalogue cards. London, Library Association, 1960. p.11
2. H.R. Verry, **Document Copying and Reproduction Processes**, Fountain Press, 1958.

20

# WORK OF PERSONAL AUTHORS

The Anglo-American Cataloguing Rules (1967) are applied for making the entries, given as examples under each rule. The division of entries into Main and Added has been maintained, as adequate need and justification exists for their continued adoption. This has been fully explained in Chapter 5.

Most entries prepared for personal authors under A-ACR would fit in with entries already existing in any library which has been following the "no conflict principle". These new rules may, with least hesitation be implemented primarily for new authors and their works which libraries acquire, or by libraries cataloguing afresh their book collections. Established headings would remain as such and if necessary references may be provided to weld together the related headings.

The scope of each rule and the effect of its adoption for an entry is explained wherever needed. References to corresponding A.L.A. rules are also provided with a view to assist cataloguers and students of cataloguing to become easily familiar with A-ACR.

*General Pinciples*. Entry of the work of an author, whether a person or corporate body chiefly responsible for creating the intellectual or artistic content of a work, is made under the author.

Entry of a work is made under the editor, when there is no author, and when the editor is chiefly responsible for the work.

Entry of a collection of works by various authors is made under the compiler, who is mentioned on the title page.

Entry of other works, whose authorship is uncertain, unknown, or indeterminate is made under the title. The exception to this principle is the entry of serial works of diffuse authorship under corporate body.

**1. Works of Single Authorship**

*A*. Entry for a work, a collection of works, or selections from works by a single author is made under the person or corporate body that is the author, irrespective of the name appearing in the work or not.

(1) **Lewis, C.D.**
Enjoying Poetry; a reader's guide.

(2) **Cameron, W.R.**
David Copperfield in copperplate; forty-six illustrations for the famous Dickens novel augmented by interpretative short passages taken from the original text.

In the second example, the author chiefly responsible for the work is Cameron and not Dickens. The author entry is therefore made under Cameron. (cf. Illustrator rule ALA 19 E)

(3) **[Strindberg, August 1849-1912]**
Miss Julia.

In the third example, the author's name does not appear in the work, but has been established from other sources, and entry is made under the person responsible for the work as its author. The heading is enclosed in brackets to indicate that the information has been obtained from sources outside the book and supplied.

(4) **Shaw, G.B.**
Plays pleasant and unpleasant: a selection of Shaw's plays.

(5) **Maugham, Somerset.**
Collected works.

(6) **(The) Royal Asiatic Society, Calcutta.**
A Catalogue of rare books and manuscripts in the library of the Royal Asiatic Society, Calcutta till the end of the 19th century, 1952.

The main entry here is under the corporate body, that is its author.

*B*. Work of *attributed author*. If the authorship of a publication is erroneously or fictitiously attributed to a person, other than its actual author, the main entry is to be made under the actual author, with added entries for the attributed author, if he is a real person. Here the main entry is made under the actual author.

**David, John.**

Sayings of a mystic, (attributed to Lal Didi of Kashmir), collected, translated and edited by John David.
1. Lal Didi (Attributed author)

**2. Work of Unknown or Uncertain Authorship or by Unnamed groups.**

*A*. If the author of a work is unknown or uncertain, even by a body without a name, make the main entry under the title, and added entries under as many as three persons to whom authorship has been attributed, either in editions of the work or in reference sources. In a particular edition, which is being catalogued, an added entry for the attributed author in that edition is essentially called for.

The title of a work in such instances of unknown or uncertain authorship, being a more constant and reliable feature of the work, the main entry of the work is made under the title. This procedure will bring together different versions and editions of the same work, which may be attributed to several authors, none being certain of its authorship. Otherwise a scattering away of the work under different alphabetical incidence of the attributed authors' names will be found in the catalogue. To this extent this rule tends to be pragmatic and useful.

(1) **Prithviraj Raso**

An epic history of the Rajput Emperor Prithviraj, variously ascribed to Chand Bardayi, Prithvi Bhatt, and others.
I. Chand Bardayi II. Prithvi Bhatt.

In this example, the actual authors of the work being unknown or uncertain, the main entry is made under the title, providing for added entries under attributed authors.

(2) A Memorandum by leading citizens of Delhi to the Supreme Court of India to safeguard the constitutional privileges, special ly of freedom of voting.

Here the main entry is under the title of the work, as no definite name is found for the body, responsible for the work.

*B*. When reference sources reveal that a certain person is the probable author of such a work, however, the main entry is to be made under that person, with added entry under the title. If the work has also been attributed to one or more other persons, make author-title references under their names.

(i) **Shakespeare, William.**
Cromwell, the true chronicle historie of the whole life and death of Thomas Lord.
A play published in 1602, and included in 3rd and 4th Shakespeare folios(1663 and 1685).

(ii) **[Sturgis, H.O.]**
Tim, a delicate portrayal of a sensitive boy's devoted affection for an elder boy.
I. Title

*C*. For certain works, the only clue to authorship is the initials, some other alphabetical device, a characterizing word or phrase preceded by the indefinite article or a phrase referring to another work of the author, found in place of the author's name, on the title pages. In all these cases, the main entry is to be made under the title with added entry for the clue provided.

(1) **Robert and Emma: School days by J.E.B.**
I. J.E.B. II. B.,J.E.

(2) **Grow your garden** by an experienced gardener.
I. Gardener, Experienced.

(3) **Life's remorse:** a novel by the author of 'Molly Bawn'.
I. 'Molly Bawn', author of

If non-alphabetical typographical devices are found on the title pages of a work in place of the author's name, added entry under such devices is not necessary.

**Tales that have tickled a man in the street**. 1952.**
Here, the main entry under title is the only entry, as no added entry is useful under asterisks.

**3. Works of Shared Authorship**

The scope of this rule covers (1) a work produced by the joint collaboration of two or more authors, (2) a work in which different authors have severally but individually contributed, (3) an exchange (conversation, correspondence, debate, interview, symposium, series of addresses, lectures, etc.) written specifically for a given occasion or for a publication (not under the auspices or authority of a corporate body).

This rule is equally applicable for compilers, editors, revisers, translators etc., when they share the responsibility for the production of a work (*cf.* ALA rules 3-4). The distinction maintained between the works of joint authors and composite works in ALA rules is eliminated in A-ACR 3, as no useful purpose is served by providing different treatments to them.

*A. Principal Author.* If one of the collaborating authors of a work (joint production) is represented as the principal author, make the main entry under the principal author, whose name usually appears first, or is sometimes indicated as such by some typographical disposition on the title page, and added entries under the other authors, if not more than two, e.g.

Title Page

Plant classification by Lyman Benson, with the collaboration of Jerome D. Laudermilk.

Main entry

**Benson, Lyman.**

Plant classification, with the collaboration of Jerome D. Laudermilk.

I. Laudermilk, J.D.

*Main entry*

**Coben, S.** ed.

Essays in American culture by well-known authorities, ed. by S. Coben and L. Ratner.

IRatner, L. ed.

*B. Principal Author not indicated.* If none of the authors is represented as principal author and if there are not more than three authors, the main entry is made under the author named first on the title page, with added entires under the other authors, e.g.

**Field, Mary.**

See how they gorw: botany through the cinema by Mary Field, J.V. Durden, and F. Percy Smith.
I. Durden, J.V. II. Smith, F.P.

*A.* If such a work is in more than one volume, and the names of the authors appear in a different order on the title page of each individual volume, make the main entry under the name of the author mentioned first on the title page of the first volume, and added entires for the rest of the authors.

**Allen, F.B.**
First course in algebra, Book I by F.B. Allen, E.C. Douglas, and D.E. Richmond.
I. Donglas, E.C. II. Richmond, D.E.
Title page of book II the order of authors, E.C. Douglas, F.B. Allen, and D.E. Richmond.

*C.* If no mention of the authors is made in any edition of such a work, make the main entry under its title, with added entries for authors if found in reference sources.

If none of the authors is represented as the principal author, and there are more than three authors, the main entry is made under the editor, if mentioned on the title page; otherwise, under this title, with an added entry for the author named first on the title page, *e.g.*

*Main entry under Editor*

(i) **Berger, Morroe,** ed.
Freedom and control in modern society written in honour of Robert Morrison Maclver by Gardner Murphy and others; ed. by Morroe Berger.
I Murphy, Gardner.

*Main entry under Title*

(ii) **Farm management by**
John D. Black, Marion Clawson,
Charles R. Sayre, and Walter William
I. Black, J.D.

It will be seen in the two examples given above, there is need for making an added entry under the title in example (i) while it is uncalled for in example (ii) as the main entry is under the title of the work (*cf.* A-ACR 4).

**4. Works produced under editorial direction**

The scope of this rule will include works of multiple authorship, with an editor, responsible for directing the publication and exclude serial and corporate author publications.

*A.* Make the main entry under the editor of a work, provided (1) his name appears on the title page of the work, (2) the publisher's name is not part of the title , and (3) the editor is chiefly responsible for the work, as a whole. In all other kinds of multiple authorship works, the main entry is under the title, with an added entry under the editor, if his name is found on the title page. An added entry for the first of the authors given on the title page is also recommended.

(i) **Bentley, Eric.** ed.
The play; a critical anthology: one play each by Ibsen, Miller, Moliere, Rostand, Shakespeare, Sophocles, Strindberg, Wilde.
I. Ibsen, Henrik

(ii) **Hastings, James.** ed.
Encyclopedia of religion and ethics.
Edinburg, Clark, 1908-1926.
13 v.
I. title.

(iii) **Five gr3at modern Irish plays,** 1940.
Carroll: Shadow and Substance; Lady Gregory: Spreading the nes; O'Casey: Juno and the paycock; Suynge: the playboy of the Western World, and Riders of the sea.
I. Carroll, Lewis: Shadow and substances.

**5. Collection**

*A.* With collective title. Main entry is made under the editor of a work with a collective title, consisting of independent works by different authors (not written for a given purpose) when his name is found on the title page; otherwise enter it under the title.

Added entires are made for authors and titles of works included in the collection if there are not more than three; if there are more than three works, but not more than three authors, added entries for each author are to be made and the title added entry is considered inappropriate.

The directions governing the making or discarding the added entires in (A-ACR 5) do not appear to be based on specific reason or use. One may even drop out added entries for all authors and titles, or select one or two only according to the importance of his contribution.

(i) **Gruen, E.S.** ed.
The Image of Rome: a collection of speeches, writings, contemporary eyewitness opinions, and analysis by leading modern day historians on ancient Rome 1969
1. title.

(ii) **Palgrave, Francies,** ed.
The Golden Treasury. 1864.
Famous English anthology of short poems.
1. title.

*B. Without collective title.* If a collection of existing independent works of different authors is produced without a collective title, make the main entry under the author of the work, listed first on the title page. Make an added entry for the editor or compiler, if given on the title page. Added entires for other authors-titles may, according to the importance and need, be made.

**Bragg, William.**
Science lifts the veil by William Bragg; the Microscope by Allen Fergusson; Atoms and molecules by Robert Robinson; Cosmic rays by P.M.S. Blacket.

I. Fergusson, Allen: the Micropscope; II. Robinson, Robert: Atoms and Molecules; III. Blackett, P.M.S. Curious phenomena of cosmic rays.

**6. Serial**

(Note) These rules are also applicable to the series added entries that are made for monographs in a series, regardless of the series being numbered or not.

*A. Serials, not issued by a corporate body and not of personal authorship*. The kind of serials envisaged in this category are usually issued by a commercial publisher and have the characteristics of continuing indefinitely, regularly and successively being edited by different editors or compilers.

The main entry is made under its title, giving in parentheses the place of publication, and years of publication, to distinguish one serial from another, with identical titles. Added entries under editors or compilers, provided they are significant, may be made, e.g.

(i) **Statesman**, incorporating and directly descended from the 'Friend of India' (Calcutta, 1892–).
(ii) **Nature**, a weakly journal of science.
(iii) **British Books**, incorporating the 'Publishers Circular' and 'Booksellers Record'.
(iv) **Endeavour**, a quarterly review designed to record the progress of the sciences in the service of mankind.
(v) **The Writer's and Artist's year book**, a directory for writers, artists, playwrights, film writers, photographers and composers.

In the entry of a newspaper, references are made not only from the known forms of the title, but also from the title beginning with the name of the city served by the newspaper, when not so entered.

| | |
|---|---|
| Enter | Statesman. Delhi |
| Refer from | Delhi Statesman. |

*B. Serials issued by a corporate body*. This rule will apply to periodicals, monographic series, or a serially published bibliography, index, directory, almanac or yearbook, issued by or under the authority of a corporate body.

Make the main entry under the title of the serial, with an added entry under the corporate body.

But the main entry for a serial which includes the name of the corporate body in its title, is made under corporate body.

*Entry under title*

(i) **Yojana**, a fortnightly.
Issued by the Planning Commission.
I. India. Planning Commission.

(ii) **India** (a reference annual)
Issued by the Research and Reference Division of the Minis try of Information and Broadcasting, Government of India.

(iii) **Journal of Documentation**. ASLIB.

*Entry under corporate body.*

(i) **Library Association, London**
Library Association Record.
(ii) **Linnaen Society, London.**
Journal of the aLinnaen Society.
(iii) **Allahabad, University of Allahabad**
Studies.

2. A *serial* reporting the proceedings, actions, or transactions of a corporate body or one serving as a periodic report of the activities and functions of a body is always entered under the name of that body.
(i) **Institution of Engineers, India.**
Transactions.

(ii) **Library Association, London.**
Proceedings of the annual conference.

(iii) **Indian Statistical Institute.**
Annual Report.

(iv) **India. University Grants Commission, New Delhi.**
annual report

(v) **Delhi. University of Delhi.**
Handbook of information to students.

*C. Serials by a personal author.* When a person as its author is responsible for a serial publication the main entry is made under the name of the author, *e.g.*

**Govil, J.C.**
Annual income tax ready reckoner.

*D. Change of title, author, or name of corporate body.* Whenever changes occur in the title of a serial, or of the author, both personal and corporate issuing it, make separate entries for the issues appearing after the change.

(i) **Journal of Pharmacy and Pharmacology**
Monthly.
v.I. 1949 –
Preceded by Quarterly Journal of Pharmacy and Pharmacology upto 1948.

(ii) **Quarterly Journal of Pharmacy and Pharmacology – 1948.**
Continued as Journal of Pharmacy and Pharmacology.
Monthly from 1949.

The distinctions maintained between types of serials, periodicals, newspapers, almanacs, directories, yearbooks, etc. in ALA rules is overlooked, because their physical form and frequency of issue are their artificial characteristics. The only distinctive feature present in them is the 'problem of change of author or editor, or title'. Descriptive cataloguing of the Serials is covered in A-ACR 160 to 168, (see Chapter 6').

*Works with Authorship of Mixed Character*

The creation or production of a literary work involves intellectual and artistic efforts on the part of several collaborators, who contribute to the work as a whole. The term Authorship of mixed characters is used to cover writers, illustrators, translators, editors, revisers and commentators, etc. The authorship of a work, in which any or all of these collaborators have assumed a definite responsibility, becomes mixed in character. In determining the main entry of such a work, it is essential to lay down the relative importance of each one of them towards the contribution. The rules A-ACR 7-16 to provide general guidance in normal situations in determining the principal responsibility of a person or body for the intellectual or artistic content of a book. The typographic disposition of each one of these collaborators on the title pages of modern printed books makes easy the task of finding out the principal author of the work, and other collaborators, and accordingly enter them in the catalogue. In cases, where these functions cannot precisely be identified, the title of the work gets the place of main entry according to A-ACR 2A and 2C.

**7. Choice between Adapter and Original Author**

*A*. A work is an adaptation, when written in another style, or literary form different from the original book, *e.g.* paraphrase, adaptation for children, dramatization, novelization, versification. Make the main entry of an adapted work under the adapter, with an added entry under original author and title, except for entries for Bible and other Sacred literature, for which a form subject heading/entry is recommended, instead of an added entry under title. When the adapter is unknown,, the main entry is under the title, with added entry under the original author.

(i) **Lamb, Charles.**
Tales from Shakespeare by
Charles and Mary Lamb.
I Shakespeare, William. II. Lamb,
Mary. III. title.

(ii) **Shanta Rama Rau**
Passage to India by E.M. Foster, a radio adaptation.
I. Foster, E.M.: Passage to India

(iii) **Canterbury Tales for Children**
(Adapter unknown).
I. Chaucer, Geoffrey: Canterbury Tales.

**8. Choice between Artist and Author of Text**

*A*. Make the main entry under the artist, with an added entry under the author of the original text, when the performance of the artist is predominantly more significant than the author's contribution to the work. The A-ACR 8A recommends the making of the main entry under the one who is mentioned first on the title page, unless, the author's name is given greater prominence. In cases of doubt, the main entry is made under original author of the text, with added entry for the artist.

(i) **Caomeron, W.R.**
David Copperfield in Copperplate; fortysix illustrations for the famous Dickens novel, augmented by interpretative short passages taken from the original text.
I. Dickens, Charles.

*B. Illustrated work.* The main entry for a work containing the text of the author, and illustrations for elucidating the text by an artist, is made under the author of the text, with an added entry for the artist or illustrator only if the illustrations are significant.

**Brown, C.J.**
Travels across the Indian sub-continent; illustrated by Robert Smith.
I. Smith, Robert. illus.

*C Illustrations published separately*. When illustrations are separately published for a particular work or for various works make the main entry under the artist.

**Newman, C.J.**
Mathematical drawings of great mathematicians of the 19th century.

**11. Choice between Commentator and Author**

There are certain works, whose text require commentary or interpretation for the precise understanding of the thoughts embodied in them; *e.g.* Brahma Sutras. Upanishads, philosophical doctrines, and sayings of saints and early works of classical scholars. These abound in Indic Literature, and sometimes in western thought also.

If the title page of the work indicates that it contains a commentary to the text, which is comparatively less significant, make the main entry under commentary, with an added entry under the author and title.

This procedure will hold good, if the publication is not considered an edition of the work, with the text prominently displayed, and the commentary serving as footnotes.

(i) *Main Entry under commentator.*
**Radhakrishnan, S.** Comm.
Commentary on Bhagavad Gita.
I. Mahabharata. Bhagavad Gita.
II. Title.

(ii) *Main Entry under Author.*
**Kautilaya**
Artha Sastra; ed. with a comm. by
K. Sama Sastry,
I. Sama Sastri, K. II. Title

In cases of doubt, when equal importance is given to both the text and the commentary, make the main entry under the author of the text, with added entry for the commentator. The treatment will be similar, as in the case of an edition of the work.

**12. Praeses or Respondent**

Make the main entry of a dissertation written for defence of an academic disputation (according to the custom prevailing in the Universities of Europe up to 1800) under the praeses (the faculty moderator unless the authorship of the respondent, defendant, etc. can be well authenticated. Make an added entry under a respondent, etc. provided the main entry is not under him. Add the designations (praeses, respondent, etc.) to the headings for both main and added entries.

**Reil, Johann Charistian,** *Praeses*
Dissertati inauguralis botanica de fungorum origine. Halae, 1797.
Halle Medical Faculty Dissertation 12th April, 1797-Respondent Karl Ludwig Blottner.
I. Blottner, Karl Ludwig, *Respondent.*

If no one is mentioned as praeses, enter in the order of preference under (1) the proponent, (2) the defendant, or the respondent.

For a more detailed study on this topic, reference may be made to Wheatley's "How to catalogue a library", pages 105-121, and Watt's "On the improvement of the mind".

### 13. Choice between Reporter or Person Reported

*A*. Make the main entry under the reporter of an interview, discussion, conversation, or similar exchange, if the text of the report is in the works of the reporter. Added entries for the other participants are made, if limited to three only.

(i) **Pyarelal**
Conversation with Mahatma Gandhi on various subjects.
I. Gandhi, M.K.

(ii) **Purohit Swami**
Interviews with William Bulter Yeats.
I. Yeats, W.B.

*B*. If the reporter is a non-participant and the text of the report embodies the verbatim record of the persons engaged in discussion or conversation, etc. make the main entry under the participant mentioned first on the title page, or under the title of the report according to A-ACR 3. An added entry under the reporter, if stated in the work, is provided.

**Johnson, W.**
Report of discussion at the first Indian Agricultural Universities Workshop on Educational Policy between Dr. W. Johnson and Dr. N.K.A. Rao, and other participants ed. C.G. Viswanathan and K. Kanungo.
I. Viswanathan, C.G.

### 14. Choice between the Reviser and Original Author

*A*. Ordinarily, the main entry is made under the original author of the work, which has been revised, enlarged, abridged, condensed, etc., by another person, for whom an added entry is provided. If the new edition indicates that it is no longer the work of the original author, however, enter it under the new author, and provide an author-title added entry or an explanatory reference from the heading for the earlier work.

(i) **Brown, J.D.**
Manual of library economy;
7th ed. rev. by R. N. Lock
I, Lock, R.N.

(ii) **Winchell, C.M.**
Guide to reference books; 7th ed. based on the 6th ed. by Isadore Gilbert Mudge.
I. Mudge, Isadore Gilbert: Guide to reference books.

**15. Choice between Translator and Author**

*A*. The main entry for the translation of a work is made under the author of the original work, with an added entry for translator.

**Tolstoy, Leo.**
Anna Karenina; tr. by
Costance Garnett.
I. Garnett, Constance, tr.

In libraries, if foreing language works are represented in translations only, omission of the original form of title on the entry is recommended, *e.g.*

**Gorky, Maxim.**
The mother.

A collection of translations from various authors by one translator is treated according to A-ACR-5, and entered under translator.

**16. Choice between Writer and Nominal Author.**

*A*. A work is sometimes written or preferred by one person for another person in whose name it is presented. The main entry is made under the person who is purportedly responsible for it, with an added entry under the person who actually wrote it if his name appears in the work.

**Gandhi, M.K.**

To the students; speeches and writings arranged chronologically and presented by Nirmal Kumar Bose.

I. Nirmal Kumar Bose.

B. Occasionally a wrok is written by one person for another person to be presented as his own, but is never so presented. Here the work being erroneouly or fictitiously attributed to another person, it is termed a ghost written speech or the sprit or another person's ideas. In such cases, make the main entry under the person who actually writes the work. Not even an added entry is required for the attributed author.

**Namasivayam.**

Sermons and Sayings of the Tamil Saint-poetess Oowwaiyar.

**Related Works**

19. Related works, dealt with under this rule are continuations, concordances, indexes, manuals, sequels, special issues of serial, supplements, etc.

Adaptations, commentaries, editions, revisions, and translations are also related to the original work. As these related publications abound in larger numbers, and more significant in their use and value, separate treatment under appropriate rules (A-ACR 7,11,14 and 15) has been provided.

*A. Works with dependent title.* The main entry for a work, whose title is indistinctive and dependent on the title of another work, is made under the same author and/or title of the work to which it is related, provided the related work will be one of three types: An auxiliary, a suppelement in nature or continuation, a subseries and serial supplement.

An auxiliary work, that can be used only with the main work, and so its dependency on themain work is a characteristic of this category of a related work, e.g.

(i) **National council of educational research and training, New Delhi.**

First course in algebra, teacher's commentary to the student's text.

(ii) **Storer, T.I.**
Laboratory manual for the text "General Zoology" by T.I. Storer.

2. Supplements that are continuations of the main work, except for a supplement by a different author, whose entry will be under its own author, as an independent work, *e.g.*

**Mellor, J.W.**
Comprehensive treatise on inorganic and theoretical chemistry. 16v.
– Supplement II to Mellor's comprehensive treatise.
**British Veterinary Codes, 1953**
– same, supplement, 1959.

**Bartlett, J.**
Complete concordance to dramatic works of, Shakespeare.
I. Shakespeare, William.

**Vishwa Bharati**, quarterly. –
v. 25 – 40
v. 41 Special supplement devoted to Abanindranath and his paintings.

*B. Other related works*. Make the main entry for any other related work (not covered by the previous rules) under its own author and/or title as if it is an independent work. Added entry under the author and title or under title of the work to which it is related is made.

**Willing, E.P.**
Index to American Catholic pamphlets.
I. American Catholic pamphlets.
**Cumulative book index** : a world list of books in the English Language............supplementing the United States Catalog.

I. The United States Catlog.

**Angel, J. L.**
Troy : the human remains.
Supplementary monograph to Cincinnati University.
Troy: excavations, 1932-1938; ed. by C.W. Blagen and others.
I.Cincinnati University. Troy.

# 21

# CHOICE AND ENTRY OF PERSONAL NAMES

After the main entry for works of personal authors is determined in conformity with A-ACR 1-16, the next step in cataloguing is to decide the *form of name* or part of name of the author, which should be adopted as author heading, on the main entry card.

The A.A. Code (1908) rules 23-57, and A.L.A. Cataloguing rules (1949) 36-70 provided the directions for this part of cataloguing, prior to the publication of the Anglo-American Cataloguing Rules, (1967). It will emerge after comparison that A-ACR 40-58 squarely face the 'actual situation', the name and form of the name by which an author is commonly identified in his works and render it easily possible for the cataloguers to select the least controversial form of name for entry. "Finally, construction of heading has been treated as a problem of name. This problem of name is reduced to its own sub-problems: first the choice of a particular name and a particular form of that name; second, the conformation in which the name should be presented as a catalog heading. In general, rules for determining this conformation are based on considerations of morphology, language, and custom that determine the entry element of the name, considerations of the possible dependence of the name on another name, and considerations of the relationship of the name to other headings in the catalog."[1] These rules are expected to result in consistent and uniform style of *author headings* in a greater measure.

*Headings for Persons. General Rules*

40. **Basic Rule**

This directs the entry of a person under the name by which he is commonly identified, whether it is his real name, or an assumed name, nickname, title of nobility, or other appellation. It is essential to follow this practice, because a person has to be represented in the catalogue under one particular name, with a view to consistency and uniformity and quick access to the information. Make references from all other names to the one selected for entry in the catalogue. 'x' before an element is a direction to make a 'see' reference from it to the heading chosen.

**Goldsmith, Oliver**
Shaw, George Bernard
x Shaw, Bernard

**Wavell, Archibald Percival,** *Ist Earl of*
x Percival, Archibald, *Ist Earl Wavell*

**Bacon, Francis,** *Viscount St. Albans*
x Verulam, Francis Bacon, *Baron*
x St. Albans, Francis Bacon, *Viscount*

**Twain Mark**
x Clemens, Samuel Langhorne

The cataloguer can ordinarily determine the form of name of an author, editor, translator, etc., from the manner or style, it appears in his works, issued in his language. If the author's name appears in the form of initials on the title page of his work, entry under the names for which the initials stand is made, when known; otherwise entry of the work is made under the title followed by the initials in title page order (*cf.* A-ACR 2c).

(i) **Shaw George Bernard**
x G.B.S.
x S., G.B.

(ii) **Stevenson, Robert Louis**
x R.L.S.
x S., R.L.

(iii) **Robert and Emma: Shool days by**
J.E.B.
I J.E.B. II B., J.E.

If the *form of names* of persons, not primarily known as authors, is found in reference sources, that can be adopted in the heading.

**Russell, George**
x A.E.
x E., A

## 41. Choice among Different Names

When an author is not commonly identified in his works by one particular name, entry is made in the following order of preference:

(i) under the name by which he is generally identified in reference sources;
(ii) under the name by which he is most frequently identified in his works;
(iii) under the latest name used by him.

If, however, the name of a person undergoes a change by the adoption of a new name due to conferment of peerage, title of nobility (as in the U.K.) or a change in title enter under the latest name, or form of name or title, unless an earlier one is expected to continue to be better known.

(i) **Wavell, Archibald Percival,** *1st Earl of*
x Percival, Archibald, *1st Earl Wavell*

(ii) **Bronte, Charlotte**
x Nicholls, Charlotte Bronte
x Bell, Currer

(iii) **Bacon, Francis,** *Viscount St. Albans*
x Verulam, Francis Bacon, *Baron*
x St Albans, Francis Bacon, *Viscount*

## 42. Pseudonyms

In every country and literature, there are cases of authors, whose works are issued under assumed names, instead of the real names. Sometimes, an author is found to use both his real name and an assumed name. In such cases it is necessary to adopt one form of his name by which he is commonly identified in his works and provide references from other forms of his name, in order to establish a uniform style of author entry in the catalogue. If a person is best known by a pseudonym, it is appropriate to adopt that form of name, instead of his real name, in the entry of his work in the catalogue. This was Cutter's approach, because he realised that 'The catalog is made for the reader, not for the cataloguer'. The Library of Congress has been following this principle.

*A.* If all the works of an author are presented under one pseudonym, enter him under that pseudonym and refer from his real name or other names.

**Eliot, George**
x Cross, Mary Ann Evans

**Premchand**
x Dhanpat Rai

**Twain, Mark**
x Clemens, Samuel Langhorne

**Aunt Daisy**
x Basham, Maud Ruby (Taylor)

*B.* If an author's works appear under several pseudonyms or under his real name and one or more pseudonyms, enter him under the name by which he is primarily identified in modern editions of his works, and in reference sources. If in doubt, use the real name for entry.

**Irving, Washington**
x Knickerbocker
x Oldstyle, Jonathan
x Wagstaff, Launcelot
x Crayon, Geoffrey

**Dodgsons , Charles Lutwidge**
x Carrol, Lewis

## 43. Uniformity and Fullness

*A*. Fullness of an author's name sometimes varies on the title pages of his works. With a view to adopt a uniform style of author's heading for entry, use the fullest form of his name appearing in a prominent position (*e.g.* title page, half title, etc.) except that a rarely used initial of an unused or non- existent forename, is ignored.

Enter **Dickens ; Charles**
Ignore unused forenames *John Huffam* from
Charles *John Huffam* Dickens

*B*. If the fullest form of name contains one or more forenames represented only by initials, spell out the forenames, if necesary, to distinguish one name from another having the same initials. If the surname is common always spell out the first forename. Make reference from the form customarily used by the author, where it differs from the form adopted in the heading.

**Wells, Herbert George**
x Wells, H.G.
**Wells, Horton Gregory**

*C*. When need arises for further differentiation, give dates of birth and death, (and profession/calling).

**Sullivan, J.W.N.**
**Sullivan, J.W.N.** 1886 – 1937
**Sullivan, J.W.N.** 1886 – 1937, Musician.

44. **Language**

*A*. *Names in Roman alphabet*. If a name is found in different language forms, use the one that has become most firmly established in reference sources.

**Tolstoy, Leo**
x Tolstoy, Count Leo

(1) Use the Latin form of name for authors who write in Latin and who flourished before 1400

(i) **Marcus, Aurelius Antonius**, 121-180 A.D.

(ii) **Boccaccio, Giovanni,** 1313-1375 A.D.

For later writers, the vernacular form is used.

**Machiavelli, Niccolo,** 1469-1527.

(2) Authors writing in more than one language sometimes adopt their names in different language-forms. Choose the form corresponding to the usage in the language of most of his major works. If in doubt, follow the form predominant in the reference sources of the country of his residence or activity.

**Suniti Kumar Chatterji**
x Suneeti Kumar Chattopadhaya

3. **Persons with names established in an English form**

*A.* Use the English form of name for a person entered under given name or by-name, of a Roman or Classical times, whose name has become firmly esablished in an English form, due to common usage in English-speaking countries. This provision holds good chiefly to writers of ancient and medieval times, and to others, who are unknown primarily as authors. If in doubt, prefer the vernacular or the Latin form.

**Vergil**
x Publius Vergilius Maro
x Vergilius Maro, Publius

**Ovid**
x Publius Ovidius Naso
x Ovidius Naso, Publius

**Frederick, the Great**
x Frederick, the Great.

*B.* Adopt *an English* form of *name* for sovereigns *and* ruling princes, who come in numerical series of rulers of the *same* name in the same country if, that form is firmly established for them.

**Elizabeth I.** (*queen of England*)
**Elizabeth II** (*queen of England*)

4. **Other Persons.**

Follow *the form* mostly used in the reference sources of the *country* of residence or activity of *the writers.*

**44. B. Names not in the Roman alphabet.**

Use the form most frequently found in English language translations and reference sources.

**Chin ku Chi Kuan**
*Systematic romanization* : Chin, Kuchi Kuan

**Pu Sung-Line**
*Systematic romanization* : Pu Sung-Ling

**Rabindranath Tagore**
Systematic romanization : Ravindranadha Thakura

*Names of Biblical characters.* Enter under the form found in the Authorized version of the Bible.

**John,** Saint, the Divine.
**Peter,** the Apostle

**d. Authors writing in a vernacular of a country or territory presently or formerly under British rule.** Adopt the form found in any work of *the author published in the country* or in any English speaking country. This treatment *will not* apply to *writers* in Arabic or Chinese *languages.*

**Suvaminatha Iyer, U. Ve.**
x Swaminatha Iyer, U. V.
**Rajagopalachari, C.**
x Rajaji
x Chakravarti Rajagopalachari

Finally, the form of *name* that gets established through common usage in *English language* reference sources, may be adopted, for a large number of writers.

**Alfred, the Great**

**Charles I, King of Spain**
x Carlos I, King of Spain

**Dumas, Alexandre**
x Dumas, Alexander

45. **Spelling.**

When different spellings of an *author's name* are found, prefer the one which is most used. If in doubt, follow the spelling used for the first work catalogued.

*Entry of Name* (*General*)

There are several elements in a name by which a person is identified as the author of his work. It, therefore, is essential to choose the element/part of the name or title under which the entry has to be made in the catalogue. When a person's preference to a particular form other than the normal is known, adoption of that form is recommended, as his name tends to be quickly identified by that method. The following rules cover the types of entry under surname, given *name,* prefixed *name,* title, etc. The cataloguer is expected to correctly analyse the *name* into its component elements and then determine the element/part under which he should make the entry. When this process is completed, the rest of the elements follows the order in the heading, as indicated below.

1. Entry under the first element/part of the *name,* presents the heading in direct order as it appears.

**Jainendra Kumar**
**Tara Shankar Banerjee**

If the first element/part, under which the entry is made happens to be a surname, insert a comma before the next element except for Vietnamese names, which are entered as they appear, with a reference from the last part; *e.g. Chinese name* entered under surname as the first element.

**Pu, Sung-Ling**
Vietnamese name:
**Ho-chi-Minh**
x Minh, Ho-chi-

2. If the first element of *the name* is not chosen for *entry, the elements of the name* are transposed, in order that the entry element is placed in first position.

**Mill, Johan Stuart**
Name: John Stuart Mill, transposed above to bring the entry element first.
**Ibn Rashid, Abd al-Kasim**
Name: Abd al-Kasim Ibn Rashid,
transposed above to bring the entry element first.

3. When the proper name in a title of nobility is selected as entry element, place the personal name in direct order, after a comma, and then give the designation of the title indicating rank.

**Mersey, C.C. Bigham,** *2nd Viscount*
x Bigham, C.C. *2nd Viscount Mersey*

46. **Entry under surname.**

If the name of a person contains a surname, and who is primarily identified by it make the entry under the surname followed by the other parts of his name in the form and fullness commonly used by him. Occasionally one finds the surname alone or with the title of the person in his work. Provide the fullness in the heading from reference sources.

It will be seen that the aim of *this rule* is essentially practical. A number and variety of *rules* in A.L A. cataloguing rules 36, 37, 50-42 governing the entry has been replaced by A-ACR 46.

*A*. In certain countries, *e.g.* Arabic speaking areas, and Indonesia, a new trend in usage of surname of persons has been observed. The last element of the name is adopted as surname. It will be appropriate to enter such names under the last element by transposing it in order to bring it first in position.

**Hatta, Mohammed.**

**B. Compound surnames.**

A compound *surname* consists of two or more proper names usually connected by a *hyphen*, and infrequently without it. Most of *the English* compound surnames are hyphenated; while the European and other compound surnames omit the connecting symbol. It, therfore, is difficult to distinguish these compound surnames from single surnames. The following rules help determining the correct form of entry for these names. Refer from the parts of the compound surname not chosen for entry.

1. **Preferred or established form known.**

When a particular part/element of the *compound surname* is known to be the personal *preference* of the writer, enter him under that element/part; if this preference is unknown adopt the form found in reference sources, preferably in the language of the person.

| | |
|---|---|
| (English) | **Horton-Smith, Lionel Graham Horton** |
| | x smith, Lionel Graham Horton- |
| (spanish) | **Cervantes Saavedra, Miguel de** |
| | x Saavedra, Miguel de Cervantes |
| (Welsh) | **Lloyd George, David** |
| | x George, David Lloyd |
| (Dutch) | **Rijen, Adolf Josep Hubert Frans Van** |
| | x Frans van Rijen Adolf Josef Hubert |
| (French) | **Fabre-Luce, Alfred** |
| | x Luce, Alfred Fabre- |
| (German) | **Becker-Trier, Hanz** |
| | x Trier, Hainz Becker- |

2. **Hyphenated surnames.**

Enter under the first part of the compound surname, in which the elements are connected by a hyphen.

**Quiller-Couch, Arthur T.**
x Couch, Arthur T. Quiller-

3. **Other cases of compound surname.**

The entry element/part is determined according to the normal usage in the language of the person concerned.

*a. Persons, other than married women.*

*Compound surnames*, excluding those of married women, are entered under the first element/part unless the person's language is Portuguese, in which case enter under the last element.

(*spanish*) **Perez Galdos, Benito**
x Galdos, Benito Perez

(*Portuguese*) **Fogaca, Marizabel Xavier de**
x Xavier de Fogaca, Marizabel

*b. Married women.*

A *compound surname* of a *married women writer*, containing both the maiden *surname* and the husband's surname is entered under the husband's surname, excepting the women writers whose languages are Czech, Italian or Spanish, in which cases entry is *under the* first surname, regardless of its derivation.

**Ward, Elizabeth Stuart Phelps**

**Gaskell, Elizabeth Cleghorne Stevenson**

**Curie, Marie Sklodowska**
x Curie-Sklodowska, Marie
x Curie, *Mme* Pirre

*E. Surnames with separately written prefixes.*

Broadly these surnames can be grouped into (1) surname with a prefix, which is a preposition, an article, or both combined, and (2) surname with a prefix, which is neither a preposition nor an article.

1. Enter these *prefixed surnames* falling in the first group, *under the part* most commonly used in the reference sources in the *language* of *the person* involved.

(English) **De la Mare, Walter**

**Defoe, Daniel**

(French) **Le Porrier, Herbert**
**La salle, Bertrand de**
**Liniers, Jean de**

(German) **Goethe, Johann Wolfgang von**
Von Ender, Erich

(Italian) **La Stella, Enrico**
De La Fere, Ntala

2. Enter the *prefixed surnames* falling in the second group, usually under the prefix

**Mac Donald, Ramsay**
**Fitz William, Maurice**
**O'Hara, C.W.**

*F.* Sometimes the prefix is combined with the surname and appears as one word. Enter such names *under the* combined or hyphenated form, and make reference from the other part.

**Delacroix, F.V.E.**
**Le Bourdois, D.M.**
**Dekobra, Maurice**

An exception is recommended in the case of Russian surnames, preceded by the hyphenated *prefix fon,* derived from the German *Von*, which are to be entered under the part following the prefix.

*G. Titles of nobility, honour, addresses, etc. added to the name.*

1. A nobleman who is commonly identified by *his surname,* rather than by the title, *is entered under his surname.* In such *cases* give the title in vernacular after *the name and* refer from the title. In the *case* of the wife of a nobleman, the title corresponding to that of her husband is used.

**Rutherford Ernest,** 1st *baron* Rutherford of Nelson
x Rutherford of Nelson, 1st baron
**Disraeli Benjamin,** *Earl of Beaconsfield*

x Beaconsfield, Benjamin Disraeli, *Earl of*

2. **British title of honour.**

Add the terms of honour before the forenames in the headings; *e.g.* Sir, Dame, Lord or Lady, used in conjunction with the names of British baronets and knights ; dames of the order of the British Empire and the Royal Victorian order ; younger sons of dukes and marquesses: and the daughters of dukes, marquesses, and earls, respectively.

**Arnold,** *Sir Edwin*
**Hailey,** *Lord* Malcolm
**Montague,** *Lady* Mary Wortley

Add after the forenames the titles of rank, *bart or lady,* in the cases of a baronet and of the wife of a baronet or knight, who is not entitled to the prefixed title of "Lady" by virtue of her father's rank, respectively.

**Duff-Gordon, Lusie Austin,** *Lady*

3. **Terms of address of married women.**

When a woman writer is identified only by her husband's name, give the term "Mrs." after the husband's surname, the entry element.

**Ward,** *Mrs.* Elizabeth Stuart Phelps
**Ward,** *Mrs.* Humphry

49. **Entry under given name or by-name.**

*A. General rule*

1. If a person's name does not contain a surname, and if he is not indentified by a title of nobility, make the entry under the part of his name by which he is primarily identified in reference sources. Ordinarily the entry element is the first part in the name. It is desirable to include any by-names, (*i.e.* secondary name acquired informally, such as a nickname, epithet, sobriquet) that appear as integral parts of the name in reference sources.

**Solomon the Wise**
**Surya Kant Tripathi 'Nirala'**

**Bana Bhatta**
**Appayya Dikshita**
**Bhavabhuti**
**Panini, the Grammarian**

*B. Royalty*

Give the title in English, and the name of the state or people governed after the name of monarch (King, Queen, Emperor, Empress, Prince, Princess, Sultan, Maharaja, Maharani).

**Charles I** *King of spain*
**George VI** *King of Great Britain*
**Ashoka, the Great,** *Emperor of India*
**Edward,** *prince of Wales*
**Sayaji Rao Gaekwad,** *Maharaja of Baroda*

*C. Saints*

The word 'Saint' is added after the name of a Christian saint, unless the person happens to be a king or pope, in which case he is entered as such.

**Paul,** *Saint*
**Thomas a Kempis,** *Saint*
**Augustine,** *Saint*

Non-Christian Saints, (Hindu, Buddhist, Jain, Sikh, Parsi, Sufi, Mahommedan, etc.) may be treated like-wise by adding the corresponding word/term for Saint, found in the reference sources of the language of the person involved. In India, the terms commonly used for saints, are Rishi, Muni, Sadhu, Swami. These may be adopted according to the form frequently used or found in reference sources.

**Viswamitra,** *Rishi*; **Narada,** *Muni*

*D. Popes*

Add the appropriate designation, in English, after the pontifical name of a pope or anti pope.

**Gregory II,** *Pope*
**John XXIII,** *Pope*
x Roncalli, Angelo G.
x Joannes XXIII, *Pope*

*E. Bishops, Cardinals, etc.*

Give the title in English if possible, after the name of a bishop, archbishop, cardinal, metropolitan, or other such high ecclesiastical dignitary who is entered under given name or by- name. If the official has had more than one title, use the one of the highest rank. Abbreviations, –*Abp* for archbishops, *Bp* for bishops, may be adopted. The word *Cardinal,* is used for all cardinals. The name of his 'See' is included as part of the title for a diocesan bishop or archbishop.

**Gasquet,** *Cardinal*
**Thomas a' Becket,** *Abp of Canterbury*
**Makarios,** *Bp of Nicosia*
**Paulus,** *Bp of Nisbis*

F. *Other persons of religious vocations.*

When entering any other person of religious vocation under his given name or by-name, add the vernacular term of honour or address or title in the heading.

**Pranavananda,** *Swami*
**Kasyapa,** *Bikshu*
**Vimalendra,** *yati*
**Prakasha Vijaya,** *Tirthankara*

A-ACR 52 Dates, and 53 Distinguishing terms, Provide directions for general additions to name headings. Dates of birth and death are added, as the last element in the heading to distinguish persons of the same name. If the identifying dates are not available, add a term of address, title, position or office, the initials of an academic degree from reference sources, to the heading to distinguish one name from another.

**Graham, James,** 1895 – 1955

**Graham, James,** 1901 –
**Graham, James,** *Historian*
**Graham, James,** *Rev.*

*Special rules for names in select languages.*

Although it is expected that the A-ACR 40-53 governing the entry of names in headings, would, by and large, be sufficient to meet the needs of all groups of writers, whose names are not written in the Roman alphabet or in a non-European language, but written in the Roman alphabet, it is found in actual practice that the entry of oriental names calls for special treatment, because of the structure and combination of elements in names, quite different from those of western writers. Due to this reason A-ACR 54-58, have been provided for the treatment of (1) names in the Arabic alphabet, (2) *Burmese names,* (3) *Indic names,* (4) *Indonesian names,* and (5) *Thai names*, respectively.

A detailed discussion of Indic names their peculiar features, and their treatment is provided with a view to supplement the coverage of the topic under A-A ACR 56.

A few works on cataloguing by Western writers contain some elementary guidance on the entry of oriental names, but the treatment is found inadequate to the needs of the cataloguers in India and other regions of Asia, who have to enter a large number and variety of Indic names in the catalogues.

It is common custom with oriental writers that each one of them has a personal name, with which he is commonly identified in his works rather than the surname of the title. The family name and title of an oriental writer generally indicates the caste or tribe or place or the ethnic group to which he belongs. These will be unhelpful in distinguishing one name from others of the same name, without adding the personal name.

It is of utmost importance that a sound knowledge of the structure, order and usage of Indic names is expected of the cataloguing staff.

The practice and style of entering the names of persons in India differs in different parts of the country, *e.g. North Indian names.*

1. Ramchandra Shukla
2. Tulsi Das
3. Gulabrai
4. Jaya Shankar Prasad
5. Mahadevi Varma

6. Maithili Saran Gupta

An analysis of the structure of these names is interesting. The first name is in two words, of which the first is the personal name and the second refers to the caste or sect to which the bearer of the name belongs.

The second also is constituted of two words, but both together represent the personal name of the writer. The second word of this name does not refer to the caste or sect as it does in example number one.

The third name is in one word only and does not indicate anything about title or caste. It is a simple personal name.

The fourth is of three words, all forming the personal name. No title or sect is represented in it.

The fifth is of two words, of which the first word is the personal name and the second the sect or caste to which the bearer of the name belongs.

The sixth is made of three words, the first two being the personal name and the third indicating the caste of the bearer of the name.

It will be seen that there is no uniformity in the number of words that a personal name consists of and that several personal names do not contain any indication of the title or caste of the persons.

In the case of *East Indian names,* chiefly of Bengal and Orrisa, similar characteristics as in North Indian names are visible, with some additional features relating to tittle or sect, *e.g.*

| | |
|---|---|
| Enter | **Subhas Chandra Bose** |
| Refer from | Subhas Bose |
| ,, | Bose, Subhas Chandra |
| ,, | Vasu, Subhas Chandra |
| ,, | Basu, Subhas Chandra |

| | |
|---|---|
| Enter | **Hem Chandra Ray Chaudhury** |
| Refer from | Ray Chaudhury, Hem Chandra |

In the above example, the name of the person consists of four words, of which the first and second constitute the personal name and the third and fourth represent the ancestral title.

| | |
|---|---|
| Enter | **Surendra Nath Das Gupta** |
| Refer from | Das Gupta, Surendra Nath |

In this example, the name of the person is made of four words, the first and second forming the personal name, and the third and fourth the caste to which the person belongs. The words indicating the caste or title may be of one or more words following the personal name.

There is a new characteristic in respect of *West Indian names, e.g.*

| | |
|---|---|
| Enter | **Anant Sadasiv Altekar** |
| Refer from | Altekar, Anant Sadasiv |

Here the name consists of three words, the first being the personal name of the bearer, the second his father's personal name and the third, ancestral name used from father to son and so on . This may also indicate the caste to which the bearer of the name belongs.

| | |
|---|---|
| Enter | **Gandhi, Mohandas Karamchand** |
| Refer from | Mohandas Karamchand Gandhi |
| " | Gandhi, *Mahatma* |

In this example the order of entry is the patronymic name, followed by the personal name of the bearer of the name and his father's personal name.

The inversion conforms to the Western practice of entering under the surname followed by the forename.

*South Indian names* consist of Telugu, Tamil, Canarese, and Malayalam names. The Telugu people (Andhras) usually have a surname, followed by the personal name, and sometimes the name of sect or caste to which one belongs. As in the case of other Indic writers these persons are commonly identified in their works by their personal names. The entry will therefore be under the personal name, followed by others parts of the name, *e.g.*

| | |
|---|---|
| Enter | **Radhakrishnan, Sarvepalle** |
| Refer from | Sarvepalle Radhakrishnan |
| Enter | **Suryanaryana Sastri, Malladi** |
| Refer from | Malladi Suryanarayana Sastri |
| Enter | **Krishnaswami Ayyangar, S.** |
| Refer from | Ayyangar, S. Krishnaswamy |

In the last example above, the name is made of the personal name, the caste or sect name and the initial of the father's personal name.

One common characteristic of all Indic names is that the person is commonly identified in his works by his personal name, except in some cases in which the person is identified by the last part of the name rather than the other parts. In such cases it is preferable to enter the person according to his usage.

56. **Indic names.**

*A. Early names.*

The directions are that a person with an Indic name who flourished prior to 1850 be entered under the first word of his name; while ancient and medieval sanskrit authors and Jain authors of Prakrit texts are to be entered under the Sanskrit form of the name, with reference from significantly different forms; and Buddhist authors of Pali texts under the Pali form of the name, with reference from significantly different forms.

The line of distinction maintained among these three groups of writers seems arbitrary, as all of them are Indic writers, and almost all of these wrote either in Sanskrit or Prakrit, and they were commonly identified by their forenames or personal names, which ordinarily was the first word of the name. The use of surname or title as one of the elements/parts of the name of Indic writers was unknown in ancient, medieval or early modern writers of Indic languages. A number of these authors had only one monosyllabic word used as the name. The need to enter the names under the first word and in the Sanskrit form is obvious, and the rules make it only explicit.

Further, the Buddhist authors of Pali texts are to be entered under the Pali form of the name. This rule does not include non- Buddhist authors of Pali texts, and there are several in this category, who have written in Sanskrit or English or German or Tibetan languages.

Early names, *e.g.*

Goutama
Bhodayana
Atri
Jamadagnl
Kasyapa
Vasistha
Vyasa

Sanskrit writers, *e.g.*

Harsha
Bhavabhuti
Kalidasa
Bhaskaracharya
Agnimitra
Asvaghosa
Katyayana

Pali writers, *e. g.*

Varahamihira
Vajradanta
Milinda
Dhammakitti
Malalasekhara

These examples of Indic names will indicate that no other form of entry is possible for them.

*B. Modern names.*

Directions are given to enter Indic names of writers flourishing after 1850, under the surname or name that a writer is known to have used as a surname; otherwise under the last name, (which means the last part of the name).

As explained earlier, the surname is not a characteristic feature of Indic names and it is inappropriate to consider the last part of the name as entry element under the assumption that it performs the function of the surname.

It is more appropriate to enter Trilok Singh, under the first part of the name, as it is his personal name by which he is commonly identified instead of Singh, Trilok. This principle would apply to all such names except for a few writers who have used consistently initials only in place of their forenames and given the last part of the name in full on the title pages of their works, *e.g.* Raman, C.V.

*Names in South Indian languages (Kannada, Malayalam, Tamil, Telugu).*

Directions are provided in the A-ACR 56 B to enter the name in any of these languages under surname, if it is an element of the name or any part of the name known to have been used as surname by the person; otherwise to enter under the given name.

As already pointed out in the preliminary discussion among the names in these South Indian languages, the names in Telugu have a surname and even then the person is commonly identified by the personal name. Therefore, to enter these names under surname would be inappropriate. In the case ot the names in the rest of three languages, Tamil, Malayalam, and Kannada personal names are significantly predominant. The entry will, therefore, be most appropriate under the personal name. The only care that should be taken to analyse the name into its component parts – the given name or personal name, father's name or initials, the caste or sect name, and occasionally the ancestral place name to which the person belongs.

| | (1) | (2) | (3) |
|---|---|---|---|
| Tamil name | Ariyakkudi | Ramanuja | Ayyangar |
| | 1. Ancestral place name | | |
| | 2. Personal name | | |
| | 3. Caste name | | |
| Enter | **Ramanuja Ayyangar, Ariyakkudi** | | |
| | (1) | (2) | (3) |
| Malayalam name | Pennathur | Madhavan | Nair |
| | 1. Ancestral place name | | |
| | 2. Personal name | | |
| | 3. Caste name | | |
| Enter | **Madhavan Nair, Pennathur** | | |
| | (1) | (2) | (3) |
| Kannada name | Mysore | Vasudeva | Char |
| | 1. Ancestral place name | | |
| | 2. Personal name | | |
| | 3. Caste name | | |
| Enter | **Vasudeva Char, Mysore** | | |
| | (1) | (2) | |
| Telugu name | Sarvepalle | Radhakrishnan | |
| | 1. Surname | | |
| | 2. Personal name | | |
| Enter | **Radhakrishnan Sarvepalle** | | |

REFERENCES

1. **C. Sumner Spalding.**, Introuction to Anglo-American Cataloguing Rules,. A.L.A. 1967. P. 4.

# 22

## WORKS OF CORPORATE AUTHORS

Besides *the individual* or *personal author publications*, there is a large variety of literary productions by bodies or groups of people, having official names, which appear on the title pages of their works, in place of the *personal author*. During the 20th century the number and variety of such corporate productions have become innumerable and posses authoritative value, as sources of information, data, and statistics. Therfore, no library can be an exception to hold a few or many of them in their collections. Much of the stock of printed material in government departmental libraries and national libraries, consists of such corporate author productions. If the National Library, Calcutta were to possess all the government documents of the Central, State, and Local governments, the humble village panchayat library will contain the annual reports on the working of the Panchayat Board.

These corporate publications, have one common characteristic of subordinating the individuals who actually write them, in preference to their corporate name. Even if the names of persons were to be found on the title pages of these *corporate author* works, they are not usually considered as authors of those works.

The student of library science and the new cataloguer should be able to readily mark the difference between personal and *corporate authors* and make the entries appropriately. The types of works usually issued by a corporate body as the author is contained under *A-ACR 17-18*. These require entry under *corporate body*.

A discussion on the merits of this procedure for entry of corporate authors, will impress on the new cataloguer the inadvisability of entering these publications under the names of individuals found in the book.

The Library Journal (Bowker and Bowker) volume 21, pages 493-4 contains an article, opposing the principle of *corporate authorship*, as a library superstition and it recommends the practice of the German libraries and others in the neighbourhood, like Austria, Switzerland and Holland, which consider all works issued by corporate bodies as anonymous for purposes of entry, when they have no individual author. Its main entry is made under the title. Where an individual name appears on the title page, the writer is regarded as its author, irrespective of his performance, either in his official or private capacity and the entry is made under his name, as for simple *personal author* productions. This principle is adopted in the rules of *Dziatzko*, 1886 and is continued in the *Instruktionen fur die alphabetischen kataloge der preussischen bibliotheken*, 1908, popularly known as the *Prussian code*, e.g.

(1) The annual report on the general administration of the Government of the Uttar Pradesh for 1950 by the Chief Minister, Pt. Govind Ballabh Pant, submitted to the Legislative Assembly.
(2) The Report on the working of the Jails Department, U.P. for 1949.

If the Prussian code rules for the entry of these two corporate author productions are applied, the main entry for the first book will assume the form:

Govind Ballabh Pant.
The Annual report on the general administration of the Government of Uttar Pradesh for 1950.

The second one will be entered under the title as there is no name of the compiler. It is considered anonymous.

The Report on the working of the Jails Department, U.P., for 1949.

In an alphabetical or *dictionary catalogue*, the first report will be found under the letter 'G' and the second under 'R' thereby getting separated far apart from each other, although both reports are issued by the Government of U.P. in its different branches of administration. Secondly, with every change in the incumbent, the author heading will vary. The purpose of the catalogue in bringing together the works of the same author will remain unattained. No doubt, *the procedure* of the

*Prussian code* saves much time and trouble in determining the form of entry for corporate author, by the catalouger. But it is not the fundamental object of the catalouge. It is to save the time and trouble of the user.

"To sum up briefly, the complications attending *the entry* of *corporate bodies* are due to the fact that their publications are usually prepared by various agents, that they often have no proper self-sufficient names by which they can readily be identified, that they are subject to various transmutations, that they are productive of other bodies which assume *individual* characteristics and functions and that they are sometimes vague in their existence. The principles desired may not always admit of easy or sharp criteria, but it must be remembered that the criteria are an instrument to facilitate the application of the principles, not a substitute for them. To abandon salutary principles because of the difficulty of defining sharp criteria is to jettison one's compass in the wilderness because of the obstacles encountered on the indicated course."[1]

*Cutter* in his Rules for a Dictionary Catalogue (prior to rule 45) convincingly argues the case for corporate authors. Just as all well meaning cataloguers agree on all basic issues in cataloguing, we are one with Mr. *Lubetzky* in pointing out the unreasonableness of maintaining the distinction between the entry of *'societies'* and *'institutions'*. CCR has harmonised the treatment of societies and institutions by providing a uniform style of entry and a common set of rules for both.

## 17. **Choice between corporate author and personal author**

Works issued by or bearing the authority of a corporate body, but written or edited specifically and openly attributed to one or more *persons*, *by name* or offcial designation will be treated according to *these rules*. The spirit of *these rules* is that every *corporate body* shall be entered *under the name* by which it is identified in its works, and also in the form adopted by it. The past practice of entering such *corporate bodies* sometimes under place, and sometimes under the name of the body as laid down in A.A. Code, and *A.L.A. Rules* has been replaced by the new approach of *A-ACR*, which seems decisively simpler and more logical.

"The most obvious difficulty to the user posed by this change is that a great congestion in the catalog might occur under common generic names such as *'Institute'*, *'University'*, *'Museum'*, *Public Library'*. (Miss

L.C. Colvin in the working paper "Entry of All Institutions under Name Rather than Place" presented at the Institute on Cataloguing Code Revision, Stanford Univeristy, 1958 has proved by sampling four hundred entries that the congestion expected to result will considerably be less than that which now exists under the names of places). Another undoubted disadvantage that is bound to result from the elimination of entry under place is the loss of the file of works under the name of the Library's own locality, which has hitherto been a most useful reference aid.

"But all disadvantages actual or possible, are overbalanced by the advantages which this policy of consistent entry under name rather than place will certainly bring about."[2]

*A. Work of corporate authorhip*

Make the main entry under the corporate body, with an added entry for the writer named first, for a work that by its nature necessarily expresses the thought content or activity of the corporate body. The types of works which will be included in this category are:

Official documents and reports, statements, studies, and other communications about the policies, operations, or management of the body made by the employees of the body in their official capacity.

Single reports, however, that are written by employees containing the results of scholarly investigation or scientific research are not dealt with under this rule, unless the report is by three persons, and none of whom is identified as the principal author. Reports made by advisory experts or consultants to the corporate body are also beyond the scope of this rule, as these reports do not convey official views and the persons writing it are non-officials.

(*i*) **Library Association, London**
The charter and bye-laws of the association.

(*ii*) **Indian Science Congress**
Proceedings of the Conference held at Delhi, 1962.

(*iii*) **National Library, Calcutta. Bibliography unit**
Indian national bibliography.

but, enter under person.

**Pargeter, P.S.**
The Reproduction of catalogue cards.
London, Library Association, 1960.

**Blacket, P.M.S.**
Report to the Prime Minister of India, on the Atomic Energy Plant.

as the authors are consultants, who prepared these reports for the corporate body, in their personal capacity.

2. A work describing the body, its functions, procedures, facilities, resources, etc. or an inventory, catalogue, directory of personnel, list of members, etc. is enterd under the corporate body with an added entry for the person whose name is associated with its preparation.

(*i*) **Library of Congress, Descriptive Cataloging Division.**
Rules for descriptive cataloging in the Library of Congress, with a foreword by Lucile M. Morsch, Chief of the Descriptive Cataloging Division, Wash., L.C., 1949.
I Morsch, Lucile M.

(*ii*) **British Museum.**
The catalogues of the printed books by F.C. Francis, Director and Principal keeper of Printed books in the British Museum 1952.
I Francis, F.C.

*B. Works not of corporate authorship*

Sometimes one comes across works seemingly corporate author productions, which create doubts in the minds of catalogurs, if or not they should be treated as corporate author publications. In such cases, make the main entry under the personal author or editor or title, as the case may be with an added entry under the corporate body referred to in the work.

(*i*) **Randhawa, M.S.**

Roses of India by M.S. Randhawa, Director, Indian Council of Agricultural Research. New Delhi, I.C.A.R.

(*ii*) **Dictionary of American Biography**. Under the auspices of the American Council of Learned Societies; ed. by Allen Johnson.

I American Council of Learned Societies.

II Johnson, Allen.

*C. Work by Chiefs of State, Heads of Government, etc.*

The following rules cover the entries for government, documents or communications, excepting Acts, Laws, Statutes, and other legal publications dealt with under A-ACR 20-A.

**1. Official communications**

(**a**). An address to parliament, a message to a legislature or governing body, a proclamation, an executive order by a chief of state, *e.g.* President of India; a head of government, *e.g.* Prime Minister of India; or a head of an international inter-governmental body, *e.g.* Secretary-General, United Nations, are considered in this group. The main entry for a work of this nature is made under the corporate heading or the office held by the official concerned. In case of doubt about the official character of the document, entry is made under rule 2 below:

(*i*) **India, President, 1969 – 1974** (*V.V. Giri*)
Address to Parliament, after oath-taking ceremony.

(*ii*) **Gt. Britain, Sovereign, 1952 –** (*Elizabeth II*)
Proclamation of Ghana's independence.

(**b**). The main entry of a communication acompanying or transmitting a document to legislative or governing body is made under the heading appropriate to the docummnent. An added entry is made under the name of office held by the Chief of states, etc.

**India. Ministry of Home Affairs**
Memorandum to the President submitted by the leaders of opposition parties to enquire into the working of big business concerns with which some cabinet ministers are alleged to be interested, accompained by his directions to investigate the charges.

I. India. President. 1969– *(V.V. Giri)*

*C.* A collection of official communications of more than one Chief of State, etc. is entered under the heading for the office held.

**India, President.**
A collection of Presidential Messages to Parliament, from the first to the 4th President.

**2. Other speeches and writings**

Works considered in this category are not official documents but those for which the person holding the office of Chief of State, etc. is individually and personally responsible.

(*i*) **Radhakrishnan, Sarvepalle**
Speeches of Dr. S. Radhakrishnan delivered at cultural functions issued by the Publications Division

I. India Ministry of Information and broadcasting. Publications Division.

6. A collection of such speeches of writing of more than one incumbent of the office, is treated as an ordinary collection of works under A-ACR 5 (if monographs) or under A-ACR 6 (if serial) in character.

(c). A mixture of official as well as personal writings and speeches of one incumbent of the office is considered a work of personal authorship while a collection of such publications of several incumbents of the office is entered under the compiler.

(*i*) **Sukumar Sen**
Speeches of the Indian Prime Ministers from 1947-67 delivered at University convocations.

(*ii*) **Rajendra Prasad**
Complete collection of speeches (both official and non-official) compiled by the Publications Divison.

I. India President. 1950 – 1962 (Rajendra Prasad)

**18. Choice between corporate body and subordinate unit.**

A. If a corporate author publication is precisely attributed to a subordinate unit, make the main entry for the work under the heading for the subordinate unit.

But the omission of the subordinate unit as a part of the corporate author heading is recommended, when it plays a minor or insignificant role in the production of the work.

(*i*) **India, Ministry of Education. Scholarship Division.**
List of overseas scholarships available for Indian students.

but

(*ii*) **India. Ministry of Information and Broadcasting.**
China's betrayal of India, background to the invasion. Issued by the Publications Division, 1962.

In example (*ii*) the subrodinate unit is omitted in the heading, because it has acted as a publication agent only. Perhaps a reference from the division to the heading adopted may be useful and recommended.

**B.** If, in preparing the work, the responsibility of the subordinate unit is not openly disclosed or if the subordinate unit cannot be identified, make the main entry for the work under the parent body.

**India. Ministry of Food and Agriculture.**
Report on marketing farm produce by task force on marketing.

C. If two or three subordinate units are stated to share the repsonsibility for the work, entry is made under the one indicated as principal author; otherwise under the one named first on the work. Added entries are made for other sharing units.

The procedure is similar as in case of personal authors sharing the responsibility for the work (*cf.* A-ACR 3 B1) and (*cf.* A-ACR 3c2).

REFERENCES

1. **Seymour Lubetzky. Cataloguig Rules and Principles.** Library of Congress, Washington, 1953. pp.54-55.
2. **Effie C. Astbury.** Implications for the Refrence Librarian. **Wilson Library Bulletin**, v. 36,6 February 1962 pp. 450-451.

# 23

# LEGAL PUBLICATIONS

Government publications, specially legal ones, have a distinctive feature, not found in the works of other corporate authors. The chief distinguishing feature is the area or the jurisdiction over which the government extends. In other respects they resemble the works of other *corporate authors,* and are treated as such.

**A-ACR 20. Laws, etc.**

Legislative enactments and decrees that govern political jurisdictions are treated *under this rule,* while administrative regulations legally applicable are covered by A- ACR 21; *constitutions* and *charters* by 22; *court rules* by 23; annotated editions of laws etc. by 24; *treaties and agreements* by 25.

*A*. Make the main entry for legislative enactments and decrees, etc. of the Chief Executixe issued in lieu of legislative enactments under a heading consisting of the name of the jurisdiction governed by the law followed by the appropriate sub-heading as directed. Added entries under names of persons and corporate bodies (except Legislatures) responsible for compiling or issuing the laws, are made.

| | *Juridiction* | *Sub-head* |
|---|---|---|
| (*i*) | Country, State, City-State, Province or equivalent *jurisdiction.* | Laws, Statutes, etc. |
| (*ii*) | *Local jurisdiction* (*e.g.* A country or municipal jurisdiction in the U.S.A.) | Ordinances, local laws, etc. (This form of sub-heading is recommended for adop- |

| | |
|---|---|
| | tion by the local governments of the U.S.A. only). |
| (*iii*) [*e.g.* A country or municipal area (in the U.K. and commonwealth countries) and District (Urban/Rural) Municipal area, Panchayat area, etc. in India.] | *Laws, bye-laws, etc.* |

Examples of headings for main entry.

(*i*) **India.** *Laws, statutes, etc.*
A collection of civil acts governing procedure in civil law courts; comp. by Sanjiva Rao.
I Sanjiva Rao.

(*ii*) **Madras.** *Laws, statutes, etc.*
The local boards, and Panchayatraj acts, for the State of Madras (Tamil Nadu).

(*iii*) **Delhi (Union territory).** *Laws, statutes etc.*
The secondary education acts.

(*iv*) **New York (City).** *Ordinances, local laws etc.*
Traffic regulations, acts.

(*v*) **London.** *Laws, bye-laws, etc.*
Motor vehicles parking regulations within the metropolitan city area of London.

(*vi*) **Ramnagar.** *Laws, bye-laws, etc.*
Public Sanitation rules for the village of Ramnagar in force from 1960.

*B. Laws governing more than one jurisdiction*

1. Make the main entry for a compilation of laws governing each of two or three jurisdictions under the one first named, with added entry for the others,

Title page : Citizenship laws of Goa, Pondicherry, and Manipur;
Comp. by Bernard Pinto.

*Main Entry:*

**Goa.** *Laws, statutes etc.*

Citizenship laws of Goa, Pondicherry, and Manipur; comp. by Bernard Pinto.

I Pondicherry, *Laws statutes, etc.*
II Manipur, *Laws, statutes etc.*
III Pinto, Bernard, *Comp.*

2. Compilations of laws pertaining to more than three jurisdictions are entered under the personal or corporate compiler if their names are found on the title page; otherwise make the main entry under the title.

**India.** *Southern Road Transpot Council.*

Road transport laws and regulations of the states of Andhra, Kerala, Mysore and Tamil Nadu (Madras); Comp. by southern road transport Council.

C. *Bills and drafts of legislation*

Make the main entry for legislative bills under the appropriate legislative body; but the drafts of legislation are to be entered under the personal or corporate author.

(*i*) **India.** *Parliament. Lok Sabha.*
Bills to amend the existing banking laws.

(*ii*) **India.** *Ministry of Home Affairs.*
The draft of an act governing strikes by essential services staff.

*D. Ancient laws, certain medieval laws, customary laws, etc.*

Make the main entry for laws of ancient jurisdictions, laws of non-western jurisdictions prior to the adoption of legislative institutions based on western models, customary laws, tribal laws, etc., and early or traditional compilations of such laws under the title, if any, by which the law or compilation is identified in reference sources, or in the absence of such information, under the title as adopted on the title page of the work; make added entries or heading and title references under promulgators or compilers.

(*i*) **Manu Dharma Sastra;**
the code of ancient laws governing the society in Arya Varta; commentary on the text by P.V. Kane.
I Panduraga Vaman Kane.

(*ii*) **Hammurabi's laws** of ancient
Babylonian empire, on the rights and duties of citizens, professional ethics, trade, etc.

(*iii*) **Marumakhal Thayam**; the law of inheritance of property in Malalayam (Kerala).

It seems very appropriate to reproduce the observations made in the second edition of this work , on A. A. Code 1908 rule 62 and the A. L. A. Code 1949 rule 83, on the entry of ancient laws.

"The general rule No. 62 for '*laws*'does not provide for exceptions, which are necessary. There are laws of ancient countries, like Egypt, Babylonia; India, and Rome which are easily best known under the name of law-giver, or law-maker, *e.g.* Hammurabi of Babylonia; Manu of ancient India; Justin of ancient Rome. It would be unnatural to enter these ancient laws under the country with sub-divison '*states*' for these laws will be called for by the names of individuals. Therefore, exception in entering them under the individual names has to be made, *e.g.* Manu Yajnavalkya, and a '*See also*' reference from the usual form may be made *e.g.* India. Statutes, see also Manu.

The second edition of the A. L. A. Code, 1949, has provided for such entry in its rule 83."[1]

The A-ACR 20 D embodies the views of the writer, and lays down the procedure accordingly for the entry of ancient laws, etc.

**21. Administrative regulations**

*A*. Make the main entry of regulations, rules, etc. promulgated by an agency, authorised to do so by legislative enactment, under the agency. If there is indication in the document that the regulations relate to a particular law, make author-title added entry for the law.

**India.** *Ministry of Commerce*

Important policy of the Government of India for the fiscal year ending.......

*B* Make the main entry for a work containing both laws and regulations pertaining thereto, under the group first mentioned in the title, adopting the appropriate form of heading, with added entry for others.

**India.** *Laws, Statutes etc.*
Currency laws of India, and regulations governing the foreign exchange of money.
I. India. Ministry of Finance.

22. **Constitutions and charters**

*A*. Political jurisdictions Make the main entry of a constitution or charter of a political jurisdiction under the jurisidiction followed by the sub-heading constitution or charter, as appropriate. A 'see' reference from the name of the jurisdiction, followed by the vernacular title of the document as a sub-heading, and from the jurisdiction followed by the vernacular title of the document as a title is to be made. A 'see also' reference from the name of the jurisdiction followed by one of the appropriate sub-headings: Laws, statutes etc.: ordinances ,local laws etc.: or laws, etc. is called for.

(*i*) **India.** *Constitution*
The constitution of India adopted by the Constituent Assembly in November, 1949.

x India. *Samvidhan,*

x Bharat. *Samvidhan,*

x India. : *Samvidhan,*

xx India. *Laws, Statutes, etc.,*

It will be clearly evident that all possible forms of reader's approach to the document in the catalogue have been provided for by directing the provision of 'see'and 'see'also' references. The A. A. Code(1908) rules 68-70 contained more or less similar directions for the treatment of constitutions, constitutional conventions, charters, without specific directions for the making of references x, and xx.

If the document is issued by a jurisdiction, other than the one goverened by it, make a 'see' reference from the name of the jurisdiction from which it emanates, followed by the sub-heading *Laws,* statutes etc. and the title of thé act.

(*i*) **India.** *Laws, statutes, etc.*
The India independence act, 1947, passed by the parliament of Gt. Britain.

(*ii*) **Gt. Britain.** *Laws statutes etc.*
The India independence act, 1947.
x India. Laws, statutes, etc.: India independence act, 1947.

A charter granted by soverign or other chief of state is entered under the name of the political jurisdiction to which it extends, with a reference (x) from the corporate heading used for that official followed by the vernacular title of the document.

(*i*) **Gt. Britain** *Charter*
The Magna Carta or the great Charter.

(*ii*) **Gt. Britain.** *Sovereign* 1167-1216 (*John*)
The Magna Carta.
x Gt. Britain. Charter.

If there will be several charters for the same jurisdiction, each one is distinguished by adding the year of adoption to the heading.

*B.* The *constitution, charter* etc. of other bodies (governmental, inter governmental, or private) are entered according to the rule that would apply if they did not have this special character. An exception, however, is made in respect of the Charter of the United Nations and the

Covenant of the League of Nations: *e.g.*

(*i*) **United Nations.** *Charter.*

(*ii*) **League of Nations.** *Covenant.*

Main entry for the charter of a private corporate body.

**The Library Association, London,** *Charter.*
*The Royal charter of incorporation, granted by Her Majesty the Queen of England, Victoria, the Great.*

*C.* The draft of a constitution or charter is entered under the personal or corporate authors responsible for it.

**India.** *Constituent assembly.*

The draft of the Indian constitution prepared by Alladi Krishnaswamy Aiyar, and others for consideration.

*D.* An amendment to or a separately published part of a constitution or charter is entered under the heading for the document as a whlole. If the title of the document is mentioned as sub-heading, state the number or designation of the particular part being catalogued.

(*i*) **India.** *Constitution.* 2nd Amendment
An amendment to article 216 or the Indian constitution.

23. *Court Rules*

*A.* By opting for the American practice, the main entry for court rules is made under the name of the jurisdiction from which the court derives its authority followed by the sub-heading court rules, and the name of the court governed by the rules. A '*see also*' reference from the heading for the court according to rule (3) is required. An added entry under the promulgating body, if it is other than the court governed by the rules is recommended.

**India.** *Court rules.* **Supreme Court.**
xx India. **Supreme Court.**

The main entry for court rules by adopting the procedure laid out in the British text of this rule will be

**India Supreme Court.** *Rules*

This form of heading for the main entry brings the corporate body next to the political jurisdiction, and lastly the form of work. Perhaps, the readers will apreciate this arrangement of the elements of the heading to be more compact, and reasonable than in the form arrived by following the Amercian style of interpolating form of work betwen political jurisdiction and corporate body.

*B.* If the rules apply to all the courts of a certain name, adopt the name in its plural form.

(*American form*)

**Tamil Nadu.** *Court rules,* **District Judges Courts.**

Rules of conduct and procedure of business in all the courts of district judges in Tamil Nadu, aproved by the state government and the High Court of Judicature.

(*British Form*)

**Tamil Nadu. District judges courts.** *Rules.*

*C.* If the publication deals with rules governing two or three courts or group of courts with different names, the main entry is made under the name of the court first given on title page, with added entries for other courts.

**Uttar Pradesh (Hill Area)** *Court rules.* **Judicial Magistrates Courts.**

Rules for the courts of judicial magistrates, district magistrates, and munsiffs, on the working hours, vacations etc. of the hill area of the state of U.P.

I. Uttar Pradesh. *Court rules.* District Magistrates Courts.

II. Uttar Pradesh. *Court rules.* Munsiffs Courts.

*D.* If the American practice is followed, the main entry for the work containing the rules governing more than three courts or groups of courts with different names, all of the same jurisdiction, is made under the jurisdiction, with only the sub-heading Court rules. Added entries under the promulgating body, if limited to one, and under the compiler, personal or corporate, if given on the title page are made.

**Nainital district.** *Court rules.*

Rules of procedure for the courts of Hony. Magistrates, Sub- Magistrates, Panchayats, and Mobile Magistrates, etc. in the district of Nainital as approved by the High Court of Judicature Allahabad.

I. Uttar Pradesh. High Court of Judicature.

The British practice calls for the main entry for such a work, under the promulagting body, if limited to one, the personal corporate compiler mentioned on the title page, or the title, in the above order of precedence. A unified or standardised heading for the main entry of such documents, made possible by this variant procedure resulted in a more helpful order in the catalogue.

**Uttar Pradesh. High Court of Judicature.**

Rules of procedure for the courts of Hony. Magistrates, Sub- Magistrates, Panchayats and Mobile Magistrates, etc. in the district of Nainital as approved by the High Courts of Judicature, Allahabad.

24. **Annotated Editions and Commentaries.**

*A. Annotated Editions.* Make the main entry of an edition of a legal source (*e.g.* law, decree, constitution, court rules) that is accompanied by citations to, or quotations from related court decisions, administrative rulings, or other legal sources, current or superseded, under the heading appropriate to the legal source, with an added entry under the annotator, if his name appears on the title page.

**India.** *Laws, statutes, etc.*

The Central sales tax act, 1956, section 5 (taxation by the

states of sales in the course of import, amended in view of the supreme court's decision in K.G. Khosla & Co. *vs* Deputy Commissioner of Commercial taxes: annotated by G.S. Pathak.

I. Gopal Swarup Pathak.

*B. Commentary accompanying legal source.* Make the main entry for the commentry accompanying the legal text, under the commentator, if the work consists of largely the explanation, or interpretation of the legal source by the commentator or if the title page explicitly states that the publication is a commentary to the legal text, with an added entry for the legal source. In case of doubt treat the publication as an edition of the legal source, making the main entry under the author of the legal source and an added entry for the commentator, *e.g.* Main entry under commentator, with added entry under author of legal source.

(i) **Kashi Prasad Jayaswal**. *Comm.*

(The Institutes of) Manu and Yajnavalkya; comparison and a contrast : a treatise on the basic Hindu law.

Sanskrit text dispersed all through the commentary in English.

I Manu : Dharma Sastra. II Yajnavalkya :Amriti *e.g.*

Main entry under author of legal source with added entry under commentator.

(ii) **Patanjali**

Yoga-sutras of Patanjali; Sanskrit text and English translation together with an intro. and an appendix, and notes on each Sutra based upon several authentic commentaries, all in English by M.N. Dwivedi; rev. and ed. by S. Subrahmanya Sastri.

I. Manmathanath Dwivedi, Comm.II. Subrahmanya Sastri, ed.

This rule has been omitted from the British text, because of the fact that such edition of, and commentaries on, legal materials are dealt with by rule No 11. It will be worthwhile to note that this rule offers an extended practice over A.A. Code 1908, rule 13.

25. *Treaties, Inter-governmental Agreements*, **etc.**

*A. International Treaties, etc.*

1. **Bilateral and Trilateral Treaties.** Treaties and other international instruments (other than a peace treaty) embodying an agreement between two or three countries will be covered under this rule.

Make the main entry of a bilateral or trilateral treaty, other than a peace treaty, or any other bilateral or trilateral instrument consisting of a formal agreement between two or more countries in the order of preference given below:

(*i*) Under the home country, if it is a signatory; (the home country is taken as the country of the library for which the cataloguing is done).
(*ii*) Under the party on one side of a bilateral treaty, if it is the only party on that side and there are two or more parties on the other side.
(*iii*) under the party whose catalogue heading is first in alphabetical order

Give the sub-heading *Treaties etc.* after the name of the country. In the case of treaties between two, parties only, add the name of the party on the other side to the heading followed by the date of signing of the treaty at the end of the heading in all cases. If the treaty is signed on various dates, give the earliest. Added entry is made for the other party of the treaty in the form corresponding to the main entry.

If there are more than three parties to a treaty, normally one added entry only is to be made under the country publishing the edition of the treaty, provided it is not the one under which the treaty is entered.

In the case of a treaty between two parties entered under the home country, make a general reference, instead of an added entry, under the name of the other country followed by the sub-heading *Treaties, etc.* and the name of the home country, to serve for all instances of treaties between the two countries entered under the home country.

(*i*) *Bilateral-Home country a signatory.*

**Great Britain** *Treaties, etc.France,* January 30,1951.

Agreement between the United Kingdom of Great Britain and Northern Ireland, and the government of the French Republic regarding rights of fishery in the areas of the Ecrchos and Minguiers, London, 30 January 1951.

*General reference*

France. *Treaties, etc. Great Britain, see* Great Britain. *Treaties, etc. France.*

(*ii*) *Bilateral, tripartite – one party on one side and two or more parties on the other side.*
(and home country not a signatory)

**Germany.** *Treaties, etc.*

Conventions between the governments of the United States of America, the United Kingdom of Great Britain and Northern Ireland and French Republic of the one part and Federal Republic of Germany of the other part, with accompanying instruments, Bonn, 26th May, 1952.

I.U.S. *Treaties etc. Germany, May 26, 1962. II Great Britain. Treaties, etc. Germany, May 26, 1952. III France. Treaties, etc. Germany, May 26, 1952.*

(*iii*) Bilateral – Home country not a signatory entered under party whose catalogue heading is first in alphabetical order.

**China Treaties.** *Treaties, etc. Nepal, June 1952.*

Agreement between the kingdom of Nepal and Peoples Republic of China regarding road construction on North East border, signed in June 1952.

I Nepal. *Treaties, etc. China, June 1952.*

In addition to the above directions for the treatment of treaties etc. the British practice provides for making a '*see*' reference from the name of a treaty by which it is generally known to the heading under which it is entered according to the rules. This (x) reference would cover the reader's approach to the document by its title by which it may be popular.

2. **Peace Treaties and Multilateral (other than trilateral) Treaties.**

(a). General rule. Make the main entry of a peace treaty or a multilateral treaty (other than trilateral), convention or agreement under a uniform heading by which it is known, preferably in English followed by the first year of signing in the case of a peace treaty, and in other cases, the year, if there is more than one treaty, under the same name. When the treaty is the outcome of an international conference, make a '*see also*' reference from the heading for the Conference to the heading under which the treaty or convention is entered.

In the case of peace treaties, make (x) references from the signatories in appropriate form to the heading chosen for the main entry. In the case of multilateral (other than peace) treaties make a (x) reference from the home country, if it is a signatory,in the form that would otherwise be used as heading. Also a reference is made from any other signatory, when the edition is issued as a treaty of that party.

**The Italian peace treaty, 1947.**

Treaties signed at Paris on February 10, 1947 between twenty members of the United Nations and Italy.

x Russia. *Treaties, etc. Feb.*10, 1947.

x Great Britain. *Treaties, etc. Feb.*10, 1947.

x U.S. *Treaties, etc. Feb.*10, 1947.

(*b*). *Treaties with a group name.* If the name of a treaty is adopted to cover a series of separate bilateral agreements, make the main entry of the collective publication under its name, while individual agreements will be entered as treaties in their own right, with '*see also*' reference from the collective name used as heading for the main entry.

**North Atlantic Treaty, 1949.**

x x U.S. *Treaties, etc. Germany, 1949.*

*B. Agreement contracted by inter-governmental bodies.*

1. Make the main entry of a formal agreement signed between an inter-governmental body and a country or between two inter-governmental bodies in the same manner as for bilateral treaties, but the exception being the entry for agreements between the United Nations or the League of Nations and another inter-governmental body, which are always entered under United Nations or League of Nations.

**India.** *Treaties, etc. World Bank, Aug.* 10, 1967.

Agreement between the Government of India and the world Bank on Tarai Development Corporation, Aug. 10, 1967.

I World Bank *Treaties, etc., India, August 10, 1967.*

2. **Agreement with other bodies.** Make the main entry of a formal agreement signed between an inter-governmental body and a jurisdiction or corporate body (other than a country) or another inter-governmental body, under the inter-governmental body, with an added entry under the other party. If more than one inter- governmental body is party to the agreement, the main entry is made under the one whose name falls first in alphabetical order. The entry under the United Nations or the League of Nations, in the event of either of the two being a party to the agreement is always an exception to the general procedure.

**International Bank for Reconstruction and Development.**

*Treaties etc. Tata Iron and Steel Company Feb.* 20, 1968.

Loan agreement between the International Bank for Reconstruction and Development and the Tata Iron and Steel Company for Development of Steel Plant, February 20, 1968.

I Tata Iron and Steel Company. *Treaties, etc. International Bank for Reconstruction and Development, February 20, 1968.*

*E. Protocols, amendments, revisions, etc.*

1. **Modifications of agreements entered under name.** Make the main entry of a separately published protocol, amendment, extension; or a revision of a treaty, under the heading for the original treaty,

followed by the terms *'Protocols, amendments, etc. or Revision',* as appropriate, and the date for Protocols,and the year for revision.

**North Atlantic Treaty, 1949.** *Protocols, amendments, etc.*
April 10,1952

U.S. Convention on relations with the Federal Republic of Germany and a Protocol to the North Atlantic Treaty.

**India,** *Treaties etc. Nepal. Revision,* 1969.

A revised agreement between India and Nepal on the military stations in the border, 1969.

26. **Court decisions, cases, etc.**

*A. Law reports.*

1. **Reports of one court.** Make the main entry for law reports of a particular court under the jurisdiction exercised by it, and the name of Court, as sub-heading with added entries for reporter or annotator.

(*i*) **India** *Supreme Court.*

The Supreme Court reports, 1968;
annotated by Ramnath Chopra.
I Ramnath Chopra. *Reporter.*

(*ii*) **Uttar Pradesh.** *High Court of Judicature, Allahabad.*

Indian law reports: Allahabad series, 1949.

2. **Reports of more than one court.** The main entry of reports of two or three courts is made under the name of the court mentioned first (on the title page) with added entries for others; while reports of more than three courts are to be entered under the title of the publication, with an added entry under the first mentioned court. In all cases added entries for reporters/annotators are called for.

(*i*) **Madhya Pradesh.** *High Court of Judicature.*
Reports of election cases adjudicated in the High Court at Bhopal, and on appeal in the Supreme Court of India, 1968.
I India. Supreme Court.

(*ii*) **Cases on Indian income-tax law.**
Decided by High Courts of India, Burma and the Privy Council, with select English cases, 1937, reported by A.N. Aiyar.

I Bombay. High Court of Judicature.
II Aiyar, A.N., *reporter.*

*B. Citations and digests*. Make the main entry of citations to, digests and indexes of, court reports, under the citator, digester or indexer, if his name appears on the title page; otherwise under title. When entering under title, provide an added entry for the corporate body, if any, responsible for the work.

(*i*) **Narayana Aiyar, A.**
Sales tax digest; being a digest of the cases on Indian sales tax law decided by the High Courts and the Supreme Court, 1965.

(*ii*) **General index to the Supreme Court reports, 1966.**
I India. Supreme Court.

*C. Particular cases.*

1. **Proceedings, etc.**

(a). *Civil suits* (*i*) Actions in the first instance. Make the main entry of the proceedings of actions in the first instance of civil suits, including contested election cases, under the name of person or body taking the action, followed by the appropriate legal designation for that party (plaintiff, complainant, contestant, etc.). If more than one person or body is responsible for the action, entry is made under the one mentioned first, with added entry for others with designation, provided there are only two. The first named person or body opposing the case is given an added entry (if not more than two) followed by the appropriate legal designation (defendant, respondent, etc.). Also make an added entry for the Court or other adjudicating body and the reporter.

**Bagchi, A.P.** *Plaintiff.*
The case of A.P. Bagchi versus Hrishikesh Sanyal and others, in the High Court of Allahabad.
I Hrishikesh Sanyal, defendant. II Uttar Pradesh, High Court of Judicature, Allahabad

2. **Appeal actions.**

Make the main entry of the proceeding of an appeal action, whether published alone or with the proceedings of the action in the first instance, hyphenate the legal designation appropriate to the appeal (*e.g.* appellant or appellee) to the party preferring the appeal.

**Bagchi, A.P.,** *complainant-appellee.*

A.P. Bagchi, complainant, appeal to the supereme court against Hrishikesh, Sanyal, defendant-appellant.

*b. Actions prosecuted by the States.* Make the main entry of the proceedings and records of actions prosecuted by the State (criminal trials, impeachments, court-martial, courts of inquiry, etc.) under the name of the person or body that is prosecuted, followed by the appropriate legal designation (*e.g.* defendant libellee). Added entries with designations, are made for specifically named associated parties, if limited to two, and also for the court, and the reporter.

(*i*) **Nathuram Godse,** *defendant.*

The trial of Nathuram Godse for the assassination of Mahatma Gandhi before the special Magistrate Court, New Delhi.
I Delhi. Special Magistrate Court.

(*ii*) **Karanjia,** B.K. *libellee.*

Report of the trial of B.K. Karanjia, editor of the weekly *Blitz.* for contempt of Court, in the Bombay Presidency Magistrate's Court.

(c). *Judical decisions.* Make the main entry of a judgement or other decision of a court in a particular case under the court, with added entry with designation under the first named party on each side.

**India Supreme Court.**

Judgement delivered by a Special Bench of the Supreme Court on the election appeal made by D. P. Mishra, against the judgement of the M. P. High Court.

I Mishra, D. P.

*f. Judicial opinions.* Enter an opinion of a particular judge under his name as author, with added entry with designations under the first named party on each side. No added entry is required for the state conducting the prosecution.

(*i*) **Harish Chandra,** *Judge.*

The opinion of Harish Chandra, Judge, in the case of A.P. Bagchi *vs*. Hrishikesh Sanyal, and others at the Allahabad High Court, May 13, 1948.

I Bagchi, A.P., *complainant.* II Harishikesh Sanyal, *defendant.*

(2*b*.) *Court room argument.* Make the main entry of a court room argument presented by a particular attorney under the attorney, with added entry under the party represented, with designation (except of the state as party).

**Gopinath Kunzru.**

Argument of G.N. Kunzru in the case of A. P. Bagchi *vs*. Hrishikesh Sanyal and others in the High Court of judicature, Allahabad, 1948.

I Bagchi, A.P., *plaintiff.*

REFERENCE

1. C. G. Viswanathan Cataloguing Theory and Practice; 2nd ed. London, Blunt, 1959. pp. 218-219.

## 24

# CHOICE OF HEADINGS FOR CORPORATE BODIES

A-ACR 17-32 provide guidance in determining the authorship of corporate works while the following A-ACR 60-99 direct the choice of the *form of heading* for the *corporate author; i.e.* under which part of the corporate authors name, entry should by made.

A-ACR 60 is a basic rule directing the entry of a corporate body directly under its name, except when a specific rule stipulates its entry under a parent body of which it is a part or under the name of the government of which it is an agency.

**Indian medical Association**
**Chemical Society, London**
**American chemical society**
**University of Madras**
x Madras University
**Indian chamber of commerce and industry**
**Annamalai University**
**British Council**
**State bank of India, Delhi**
x Imperial Bank of India, Delhi

**61-62**

The name of a corporate body adopted in reference sources sometimes differs from the form of name used on the publications. In such case, adopt the form given on the publications. If the form of name varies from publication to publication, use the name as it appears in formal presentations (at the head of the title, in the imprint, and in formal author statements) except for local religious institutions (governed by A-ACR 98). If the body is well known and identified by, a conventional name, prefer it in place of other forms of name, (*vide* A-ACR 63). In the absence of uniformity in the form of names given in the formal presentations, follow the guide-lines in sections A and B of A- ACR 62.

**Institute of Chartered Accountants of India.**

(Name used on its publications)

x Indian Charterted Accountants Insititute

(Name given in reference sources)

**Ten Downing Street, London**

Conventional form of name for the British Prime Minister's Lodge/House/Residence.

x Official residence of the British Prime Minister
x British Prime Minister's Lodge

**Birla Mandir (Temple), New Delhi**

x Lakshmi Narayan Mandir, New Delhi

If different forms of the corporate name are used in the formal presentations, adopt the form in the order of preference given below:

*A. Brief form.* Among the various forms apearing in formal presentations, choose one which is brief, as it will adequately identify the author.

**Dolls Museum, New Delhi**

x International Museum of dolls and toys for children
x Toys museum, New Delhi

**Book Trust**
x National book trust of India

x Indian book trust

1. **Initial letters of the name.** If a corporate body uses a brief form of name, made up of initial letters of its name, use this form, if written in capital and lower case letters, or if reference sources contain the brief form.

**Iaslic.**
x Indian association of special libraries and information centres

2. **Syllables of the name.**

**Agrivarsity**

x Uttar Pradesh Agricultural University

B. *Official form.* If a brief form that can indentify the author is not found among the variant forms, adopt the offical form available from any source.

*C-D.* When no information exists about the brief form or the official name, adopt the form predominantly used in the publications. In case of doubt, choose the most recently used.

These two rules are so general in scope that they eliminate the need for several rules of A.L.A. 103-114.

63. **Conventional name.**

*A.* If a conventional form of name found in the reference sources is able to frequently identify a body, prefer this one to the official name and other forms of name found in its publications.

**Writers' building, Calcutta**
x West Bengal government secretariat offices

B. Adopt the English form of name of body of a ancient origin or of international character, if the form has become finally established in English language irrespective of the other forms found on its publications.

**Quakers**

not Society of Friends

**Jesuits**

not Society of Jesus.

64. **Language**

If the name of a body appears in different languages, adopt the form in the official language; if more than one official language exists, and one of which is English, prefer English.

**Bibliotheque Nationale de Paris**

not National Library, Paris

**National Library, Calcutta**

x Rashtriya Pustakalya (H)
x Desiya Noolnilayam (Ta)

If, among the official languages, English is not one, or if no information about the official language is available, choose the form in the language most dominant in its publications; if in doubt, prefer English, French, German, Spanish, or Russian in this order.

*A. International bodies.* If the name in English of an international body is found on its publications adopt this form.

**International Traders Association, Hongkong**

**International Federation of Library Associations**
x Federation internationale des
associations de bibliothecaires

*B. Romanization*

1. Use the Roman alphabet for the heading, by following the appropriate transliteration or romanization system for library purposes, for publications not in Roman alphabet.

**Khadi aur gram udyog ayog**

2. If the publication provides its own romanized form of name, use that form, with reference from the standard library form.

A-ACR 65-68 are very general in scope and character, and are intended to make the corporate headings more specific, and distinguish one from another, by addition of local place name, country, State, year of foundation etc. by omission of initial articles, adjectives denoting royal privilege (except in English) phrases citing honours; modification of name, and change of name. The cataloguers will be able to adopt these directions without any further elucidation and standardise the headings.

A-ACR 69-71 govern the entry of subordinate and related bodies. These rules envisage boards, trustees, and other governing agencies as subordinate elements to the corporate bodies they govern, but a body merely founded, owned or, controlled by a parent body is not treated as subordinate to it. Also characteristic of subordination is not to be applied to higher units in the corporate hierarchy, which are associated with it as affiliated or collateral. If the parent body's name forms part of the name of a subordinate body, it is certainly treated as subordinate.

69. **Bodies with names implying subordination.**

The following six types of subordinate bodies are treated according to this rule which directs entry under the higher body with the name of the subordinate body as sub-heading.

(*i*) The complete name of the higher body forming part of the name of the subordinate body.

**U.P. Agricultural University. Agricultural Experiment Station.**

x Agricultural Experiment Station of the U.P. Agricultural University.

*but*

**Delhi School of Economics**

x University of Delhi. School of Economics.

**University of Calcutta. Library**

x Library of Calcutta University

*but*

**Bharat Kala Bhavan**

x Banaras Hindu University. Bharat Kala Bhavan.

(*ii*) The name of the subordinate body including terms – 'branch', 'bureau', 'department', 'division', section, etc. indicate subordination.

**Indian National Cooperative Union. Banking Dept.**

**University of Madras. Department of Telugu**

**Indian Art Society. Bengal Branch**

(*iii*) The name of the subordinate body containing terms implying administrative subordination to the higher body, *e.g.* 'Panel' 'Committee'.

**Indian Standards Institution. Book Production Standards Committee**

**Export Trade Council of India. Raw Materials Committee**

(*iv*) The name of a University College/School limited to a particular branch of education.

**University of Chicago.** *Graduate School of Library Science*

**Banaras Hindu University.** *College of Medical Sciences*

(*v*) The name describing the functions of the subordinate body, as well as common to both subordinate bodies and independent bodies, *e.g.* 'Institutes', Centres', 'Laboratories' etc. of Universities.

**University of Punjab.** *Centre of Advanced studies*

**Council of Scientific and industrial Research.** *Central Road Research Institute*

**Banaras Hindu University.** *Institute of Technology*

(*vi*) The name of a subordinate body, which can be identified only with the name of a higher body.

**University of Delhi.** *Academic Council*

**National School for the Blind.** *Braille Research Laboratories*

*A. Direct or Indirect heading.* When a corporate body has several subordinate bodies in a hierarchical order, the lowest subordinate body is entered as subhead under the one above it that may be entered independently. Intermediary subordinate units which are non-essential to disclose the functions of the smaller unit are omitted in the heading. If in doubt give the intermediary unit above it with a view to render the heading adequate for identification.

**National Council of Eductional Research and Training.** *Text Books production section*

Hierarchy : N.C.E.R.T.

Publication Unit

Text Books Production Section

**Indian Institution of Engineers.** *Electronics Division. Education and Training Deptt.*

In this example the interposing element is essential as similar Education and Training Departments exist under other branches of engineering, e.g. Mechanical Division, Civil Division, etc.

*B.* If the name of a subordinate body is found in various languages on its publications, follow the languages on its publications, follow the language form adopted by the parent body.

*C. Addition to names.* Conferences, congresses, etc. Provide the number, place, and date (according to A-ACR 89-91) in the heading for a particular conference, congress, convention of an association or other corporate body, resulting in a specific heading which will help quick and direct identification of the work.

**Theosophical Society,** *Convention, 51st. Banaras,* 1946

**Indian Manufacturers Association.** *Conference, 2nd, Bombay 1959.*

**Inter-University Board of India.** *Conference of Vice- Chancellors, 15th, Delhi, 1962.*

70. **Other subordinate bodies**

Any other subordinate body beyond the scope of A-ACR 69 will be entered directly under its own name in accordance with the provisions for corporate bodies in A-ACR 60-68

**Miranda House**
x University of Delhi. *Miranda House*

**Secondary School Teacher's Association**
x Indian Federation of Teachers' Association. *Secondary School Teacher's Association*

71. **Related bodies**

*A. General rule.* A society, association or other body that is auxiliary or otherwise closely related to another body is treated as subordinate and entered as a subheading under the name of the body to which it is related, provided its name (1) includes the complete name of the body to which it is related, (2) is inadequate for identification, without the name of the related body or (3) is usually known only with the name of the body to which it is related need not be repeated in the subheading.

**Banaras Hindu University.** *Music and Drama Society*

Name : Music and Drama Society of the Banaras Hindu University.

**Indian Floriculturists Union.** *Rose-growers Division.*

Name : Rose growers Division of the Indian Floriculturists Association.

*B. Joint Committees,* commissions, etc. When representatives of two or more corporate bodies constitute a joint committee or commission, make the entry under the name of the Joint body.

**Joint Commission of Inquiry on the working of the National Research Laboratories of India.**

x India. Council of scientific and industrial research. Joint Commission on the working of National Research Laboratories of India.

x University Grants Commission. Joint Commission on the working of the National Research Laboratories of India.

Other directions are that the name of the parent bodies may be omitted in the heading under the joint body, if, by itself, it is adequate for identification. If the parent bodies themselves are subordinate to another common parent body, and would be entered as subheadings under that body, entry of the joint body is made in accordance with the provisions of A-ACR 69.

*Geographic Names*

The corporate author headings usually contain the name of the locality, country, state, province, city, town or other area as an esential feature, because the generic terms that constitute the corporate names, without the geographical names, cannot be distinguished one form the other. A standardised form of geographical name and language is essential for the sake of uniformity and universal understanding. The A-ACR 72-77 provide directions fully covering the needs of the American, European, and other western countries, in regard to geographical names, administrative districts, and language. As far as the Indian geographical names are concerned, it will be appropriate to use the names given in the Indian Gazetteers, provincial (State) Gazetteers, and District Gazetteers, and adopt the roman spellings provided in these authoriative reference sources. Besides, the cataloguers may refer for more up-to-date information on this subjct in the latest Census Reports, the Indian Constitution (Text) and the official languages acts.

*Government Bodies and Officials*

All modern governments are vested with legislative, judicial, and executive authority. In order to facilitate the smooth discharge of these responsibilities, a number and variety of agencies are appointed by the government which carry out these functions according to the policy and directions of the government. These agencies and the persons attached to them are subordinate to the government and therefore given us subheadings under the heading for the government. A line of distinction should, however, be drawn between these bodies and institutions created and controlled by the government to advise them, to provide expert guidence and to supplement its performance.

A-ACR 78 provide directions to the cataloguers as to what types of corporate bodies created and controlled by a government are to be entered under their own names, and what other categories of corporate bodies are to be entered as sub-headings under the headings for the government.

*A*. A corporate body created and controlled by a government is treated according to A-ACR 60-71, regardless of its official nature, or its subordination, or otherwise, to a government agency, and entered under its name as heading, if it is one of the following types :

1. Organizations engaged in commercial, cultural, or scientific pursuits or promoting similar interests.

**Sahitya Akademy**

**Commonwealth Agricultural Bureau**

**British Council**

**Indian Council of Agricultural Research**

**National Council of Educational Research and Training**

**National Productivity Council**

2. Institutions (typically with their own physical plant)

**National Library (of India)**

**National Physcial Laboratory (N.Delhi)**

**Indian Standards Institution**

3. Installations and Parks

**Botanical Garden, Calcutta**

**Palam International Air Port**

**Brindavan Gardens, Bangalore**

**Peoples Park, Madras**

4. Bodies created by inter-governmental agreement

**Southern States Regional Food Council**

**Bengal-Bihar Boundary Commissions.**

5. Authorities and Trusts for the operation of utilities and industries.

**Damodar Valley Authority**

**India Coffee Marketing Board**

**Punjab State Electricity Board**

**Bombay Port Trust**

6. Banks, Corporations, Manufacturing plants, Farms, and similar specific enterprises.

**Food Corporation of India**

**Hindustan Machine Tools**

**Reserve Bank of India**

**India. Railway Board**

**Suratgarh Central Farm**

**Tarai Development Corporation**

7. Established Churches

**Church of England**

**The Greek Church**

*Exceptions :*

The following types of bodies are stated as exceptions to the applications of the provisions under 78-A :

1. Bodies designated as Ministries, or a foreign equivalent, or by terms denoting that they are component parts of a unit *e.g.* 'department', 'division', 'branch', and their foreign equivalents. If the parent body would be entered independently under this rule, however, apply the provisions of A-ACR 69.
2. Libraries, archives, and other government bodies functioning as service units of a particular agency of a government and if their names include the name of the agency and without which, they cannot identified.

**India.** *Ministry of Finance, Library.*

Name : Finance Ministry Library.

**India.** *Ministry of Defence, Electronics Laboratory.*

Name : Defence Electronics Laboratory

These bodies included under the exceptions to A-ACR 78-A, will be treated under A-ACR 78-B.

*B.* A government body which will not fall into any one of the seven types described under A, or in case of doubt, is entered as a subheading under the heading for the government, according to the provisions of the A-ACR 79-86.

**India.** *Ministry of Education and Youth Services*

**India.** *Ministry of External Affairs*

**New Delhi.** *Municipal Board*

**Punjab.** *Governor*

**Lucknow.** *City Corporation*

**India.** *Parliament. Lok Sabha*

**Uttar Pradesh.** *Legislative Assembly*

A-ACR 78 is so broad based that it replaces several specific rules of ALA 103-104. it is not only logical, but a decided advantage that non-governmental bodies find a place with rules for other corporate author.

79 **Subordinate Agencies and Units**

*A. Direct Subheading.* If an office or agency of a government, according to A-ACR 78B, is subordinate to another such body, its entry is made as a direct subheading under the name of the government, provided no other agency in the same administrative jurisdiction will similarly be named.

**India.** *Patent Office*

x India. *Ministry of Commerce. Patent Office*

**India.** *Bureau of Mines*

x India. *Ministry of Mines and Natural Resources. Bureau of Mines.*

*B. Indirect Subheading.* A government body outside the scope of A above, or a doubtful case is to be entered as a subheading under the lowest unit in the hierarchy that can be directly entered under the name of the government. Other intermediary units, not essential for identification are omitted in the heading.

**India.** *Ministry of Commerce and Industry. Company Law Administration Dept.research and Statistics Division*

In the above example the two intervening units are essential for identification of the lowest units.

**India**. *Bureau of Education. Adult Eduction Division*

But in the second case,the intervening agency 'Ministry of Education' is omitted, as the lowest unit could be identified as sub-heading under 'bureau of Education' entered under the heading for the name of the government.

**India**. *Tariff Board.Sugar Industry Panel.*

Here also the intervening elements 'Ministry of Food and Agriculture' and 'Consumer and marketing Division' are omitted, and only one element is interposed between 'India' and 'Sugar Industry Panel'.

80. **Government Officials**

This rule will apply to Countries/States Flourishing in post medieval times.

*A. Chiefs of State etc.*

1. **A king, queen, (Common Designation to both *'Sovereign'*)** President, Governor, Emperor, Empress, Princess, and any other equivalent vernacular form of Chief of State, in his official capacity as the author/subject of a work, is entered as heading in the following order of elements:

(i) the title or his office in English or equivalent vernacular term,

(ii) the inclusive years of his reign or incumbency (separate heading for each period, if more than one),

(iii) his name in parenthesis in brief form as sub-headings under the name of the government. The common term 'Sovereign is used, in case of countries, where both King/Queen are eligible to be Chief of State.

**Great Britain**. *Sovereign*, 1952-(*Elizabeth II*)

**India**. *President*, 1950-1962, (*Rajendra Prasad*)

**U.S.** *President*, 1968 - (*Nixon*)

**West Bengal** (*State*). *Governor*, 1969-(*Dhawan*)

If a Chief of State is also a writer or subject of a work in his personal capacity, give explanatory references under each heading, vide A-ACR 121 B.

2. When a heading for Chief of State will cover more than one incumbent, dates and names are left out in the heading; e.g. collections of addresses to Parliament of the Presidents of India.

**India**. *President*

**Radhakrishnan**, *President of India*

Under the second heading private communications, public speeches, and collections, that include both private and official communications, are entered.

Official acts of the President's address to Parliament, proclamations, etc. will be entered under the heading :

**India**. *President*, 1962-1967, (*Radhakrishnan*)

Works before assumption and after relinquishment of the office will however, be entered according to A-ACR 1A. In order to establish a link to the other works, make "See also" reference to the headings indicated above.

*B. Heads of governments*. Terms usually used for heads of governments are Prime Minister, President of the Council of Ministers, Chief Minister, Mayor, Chairman, for their respective jurisdictions.

The headings for a head of government who is not also a Chief of state in his official capacity will consist of the name of government followed by the title of his office as a sub-heading, without date and name.

**India.** *Prime Minister*

but

**Burma.** *Chairman of the Revolutionary Council* 1962-(*Ne Win*).

In this case the person is both Chief of state and Chief of government, and the heading is as for the Chief of State.

**Madras.** *Chief Minister*

**Lucknow.** *Mayor*

**New Delhi.** *Chairman, Municipal Board*

*D. Other Officials.* The heading for other officials of a government (not covered by above sections) is under the ministry or agency to which he is attached.

**India.** *Ministry of Education*
x India. *Educational Adviser*

**India.** *Ministry of Defence*
x India. *Scientific Adviser (Defence Ministry)*

If, however, the official does not form part of a ministry or agency of the government or the designation of the official is the only name by which he is known, the heading will be under the name of government, with the title of his office given as sub-heading.

**India.** *Attorney-General*

**India.** *Election Commisioner*

81. **Legislative bodies**

*A.* Chambers of legislature are entered, each one separately, as sub-heading under legislature.

**India.** *Parliament. Lok Sabha*

x India *Lok Sabha*

**India.** *Parliament. Rajya Sabha*
x India *Rajya Sabha*

*B*. Committees and other sub-heading units of a legislature of a particular chamber, are entered as subheadings under the appropriate body.

**India.** *Parliament. Joint Committee on freedom of the Press*

**India.** *Parliament. Lok Sabha Library*

*C*. The number and the year or years of a legislature numbered consecutively are added to the heading; if the sessions are also numbered, the heading will provide this information also.

**India.** *Ist Parliament*, 1947-1952

**India.** *2nd Parliament, 1st Session*,1952

82. **Constitutional conventions**

A constitutional convention is directly entered under the name of the country (Jurisdiction)or which the constitution has been drafted, with the year of the convention.

**India.** *Constituent Assembly*, 1946

If, however, the name of the constitutional convention of the same jurisdiction varies from time to time, and if the official language is English, use the term. '*Constitutional convention*'.

83. **Courts**

A court is entered under its name, as a subheading, under the name of the country, state or other jurisdiction, over which its authority extends.

**India.** *Supreme Court*

**Uttar Pardesh.** *High Court of judicature.*

84. **Armed Forces**

The entry for each of the principal services of the armed forces of a government is made under its name, as a direct sub-heading under the name of the government.

**India.** *Army*

**India** *Navy*

**India** *Air Force*

A component branch, command, district, or military unit is entered as a direct sub-heading under the heading for the service, unless its name begins with the name of the services or its adjectival form. In the latter cases, enter it directly under the country.

**India.** *Army Medical Corps*

**India** *Air Force 12th Squadron*

*but*

**India.** *Naval Headquarters*

**India** *Marine Engineering Corps*

85. *Embasies, Legations, etc.*

An embassy, legation consulate, high commission etc. which represents the government of one country in another, is entered as a sub-heading under the name of the country represented, in the language form of the country. A distinction in the form of heading between an embassy or legation and a consulate is maintained. Mention the name of the country to which an embassy or legation (including High Commission) is accredited, as the last element in the heading in parenthesis; while in the case of a consulate or local office,give the name of the city where it is located.

**U.S.** *Embassy (India)*

**Mexico,** *Embajada, (India)*

**India.** *High Commission (Great Britain)*

**Great Britain.** *High Commission (India)*

**Germany, West** *Trade Consulate (Calcutta)*

86. **Delegations to International and Inter-governmental Bodies**

An official delegation, mission, etc. which represents the government of a country in an international conference or inter- governmental body is entered as a sub-heading under the country represented, and in the languages of the country; if the name of the delegation is not certain, form a name of it in the country's language with the help of terms found in the work to be catalogued; in doubtful cases, whether it is or not an *official delegation* of the county, entry is made directly under its name.

**India.** *Delegation to the United Nations*

**India.** *Delegation to the General Assembly of the United Nations*

An explanatory referene from the inter-governmental body would be very appropriate.

**United Nations.** *Missions*

Delegations, missions, etc. from member nations to the United Nations and to its subordinate agencies, will be found entered under the name of Country/Nation with the name of the delegation as sub-heading.

**India.** *Delegation to the international copyright conference, Washington, 1969*

*Conferences, Congresses, Meetings, etc.*

The introductory note in both the British and the North American

Text under this heading attempts, each in its own way to define these bodies and to distinguish similarly named bodies or organizations from these unnamed or ad-hoc bodies treated under A-ACR 69.70. The North American text excludes the general meetings of organizations called 'Convention' from the scope of this rule as, such assemblies have no corporate character of their own. The note in British text specifically states that "These rules (87-91) apply to meetings of persons, either as individuals or as representatives of various bodies, for the purpose of studying, discussing, or acting on a particular topic of common interest". In order to make it easier for the beginner, or student of cataloguing it may be elucidated that a conference meeting, etc. implying subordinate to a higher body is not to be treated under these rules, for it will normally be entered as sub-heading under the name of the body to which it is attached".

87. General rule directs the entry of a conference, congress or other meeting under its name, followed by number, place and date.

**Conference of Cardiologists.** *1st, New Delhi 1969.*

88. Variations in the formal presentation of the name of a conference require that the name or abbreviation of the name of a sponsoring body or another associated with the meeting is included in the heading as the first element.

**Insdoc conference on Cataloguing and Reprography**

90. **Place**

The name of the place, where a conference is held is given in the heading, after the number, adopting the forms for geographical names, indicated in A-ACR 72-74.

**Workshop on Soyabean,** *1st, Pantnagar,* 1967.

If, the heading is to cover a series of conferences, the name of the place is left out in the heading, in order the same heading could be appropriate for changes in the venue of the conference.

**Hybrid Maize Research Conference**

If the name of place forms part of the name of a conference, it need not be mentioned again in the heading.

**Madras Conference On Tamil, 1966**

**Cold Spring Harbour Symposium on Biology**

*B*. The name of the institution at which a conference is held, is preferable to the place, provided it results in better identification of the heading.

*C*. When a conference is held at two places, give both the names in the heading; if more than two places are involved, give only the principal or the first mentioned one.

**Indian Philosophical Conference**, *Banaras and Calcutta*, 1959.

91. **Date**

Give the years of the conference at the end of the heading, for a single conference only. Specific dates may be given, if necessary, to distinguish one conference from another.

**Religious Bodies and Officials**

The treatment of religious bodies is similar to other corporate bodies, with the exception of specific types covered in

A-ACR 92. Church Councils

93. Patriarchates, dioceses, etc.
94. Bishops patriarchs, etc. as Ecclesiastical officials

95. Administrative offices of the Catholic Church

96. Religious orders and societies

97. Local Churches, etc.

From a pragmatic consideration, so far Indian conditions demand, A-ACR 97 (British Text) is more likely to be used than the rest of the rules, and it, therefore, is explained in detail.

The corresponding rule in the North American text is 98, which differs from the British practice, as the entry for these corporate bodies is under the place of location (i.e. city, town, village, etc. whether incorporated or not), unless the first word of the name of the body is the name of the place in its catalogue entry form. In the latter case only, its entry is made under its name. "The most significant departure of the rules from the Paris Principles lies in special exceptions (98-99) for certain bodies of an institutional nature. These exceptions exempt the specified bodies from the principles of entry under name (9.4)* and substitute the rule of entry under the name of a place. They were made in response to the Association of Research Libraries recommendation and they have the effect of greatly reducing the impact of the Paris Principles on existing catalogues which are heavily infused with entries for corporate bodies under place names in accordance with all preceding catatloguing rules"

While the Amercian practice of entering these bodies under the place seems to have been influenced by expediency-the past cataloguing tradition which certainly has certain validity from the economic point of view, the British practice of entering under the name of these bodies, with select exceptions, in accordance with general rules A-ACR 60-64 appears convincingly logical, as in a large number of instances, these bodies are predominantly known and identified by their names, instead of the place of location e.g. St. Paul's Cathedral is unlikely to be looked for under London; Nataraja Temple under Chidambaram. There is also provision for entry under the prediominant form of name, when variant forms of name of the body appear in formal presentations. In case no one form of name predominates, choosing a form in the following order of preference is laid down :

1. a name containing the name of the person, persons, object, place or event to which the church or temple is dedicated, or after which it is named ;
2. a name beginning with a generic word or phrase describing the category of the church or temple;
3. a name beginning with the place name,where it is located

**Mahavira's Temple,** *Sravanabelgola*

**St. Mary's Cathedral,** *Delhi*

---

*Vide **Paris Principles** : (9.4) the International conference on cataloguing principles held in Paris in 1961. In Cataloguing Theory and Practice; ch. 5. pp. 53.

**Buddhist Monastery,** *Rajagriha*

*Sreerangam* **Ranganatha's Temple**

98 * **Radio and Television Stations.**

The rule directs the entry of a radio or television station under its call letters, followed by the terms Radio,(Television)station in parenthesis,and theplace with which the station is identified,if the call letters are the primary or the only identifying element of the name.Otherwise these bodies are entered under the name according to general rulesA-ACR 60-71 with provision to add the name of the place at the end of the heading,if it does not form part of its name.An explanatory reference under the terms "Radio (Television)Station"is provided in the catalogue for the guidance of users.

**AIR** [*Radio (Television)Station*], *Delhi*

**BBC** [*Radio (Television) Station*], *London*

**Radio** *Ceylon, Colombo*

**Radio** *Moscow*

REFERENCE

1. Sumner Spalding. Introduction to Anglo-Amercian Cataloguing Rules,London,Library Association,1967.p,3

*This serial number is according to the British text,and the corresponding rule in the North American Text is numbered 97.

25

# WORKS OF UNKNOWN AUTHORSHIP : ENTRY UNDER UNIFORM TITLES

Not all books that are catalogued in a library are works of personal or corporate authors. Some of them do not provide any information on their authorship. Even reference sources fail to reveal the author, responsible for the work. In such cases, the only means of identifying a work is its title, but the task is rendered difficult, as certain works, their edition or translations, are presented under varying titles which are obscured by the wording on the title page. There are a select few works in the category of early anonymous works, and sacred books, which have conventional titles, and are identified by those titles only.

Works of corporate bodies which may not reveal the names of persons actually writing them either on the title page or anywhere in the books should not be a valid reason of entering them under their titles. These would be treated in accordance with the provisions under A-ACR 17-A1, and 60-64.

The following A-ACR 100-119 governing the entry under uniform titles are "stated in terms of general applicability, since all uniform titles are based on the same general principles and are formed according to the same general procedures".[1]

The A.A. Code 1908 rules 112-129 dealing with the title as main entry may be compared to appraise the effect of A-ACR.

The types of works falling in this category of entry under uniform titles are :

Anonymous works, early chronicles and literary works: early compilation of ancient laws and customs, creeds and confessions common to different religious bodies:

Liturgical works

Early collections to be entered under title.

100. **Basic Rule**

*A-B*. When the editions (excepting revised editions as specified in *E* below), translations, versions etc. of a work are presented under varying titles, one of them is selected as the uniform title, to serve as a heading, under which all of them will be entered. Reference entries are provided in the catalogue, from varying titles, to the one selected as uniform title. An added entry is preferable to any title of a particular edition, rather than a reference to the uniform title itself.

*C*. If a publication of the work appears with a title varying from the one chosen as uniform title, place the uniform title between the heading and the transcription of the title page. References are to be made to the heading and title from the variant forms of the title.

*D*. Roman alphabet is to be adopted for the uniform title.

*E*. A uniform title is not necessary for cataloguing an edition, which is a revision of the original work or which is brought up- to-date under a different title. Give a note on each entry, earlier and later, linking the two editions.

**Rutley, Frank**

Elements of mineralogy, 1915.

24th ed. published in 1947 under title:

Rutley's Elements of mineralogy.

**Read, H.H.**

Rutley's Elements of mineralogy; 24th ed. 1947.

A complete revision of the original text 1915, which is re- written with modifications and brought up-to-date.

**Choice and Form of Title**

101. **Works written after 1500**

*A*. *General rule*. In choosing the title, the title of the original edition is preferred for a work written after 1500; unimportant phrases or words, and the initial article (without distortion) preceding the title proper may be left out in the heading. Exceptions to this rule are indicated in rules *B*, *C*, and *D* below.

**Hodgson, Gregory**

The Chinese: their manners and customs, etc.

The preceding phrase "An account of" is omitted.

*B.* If a later title or form of title of a work is better known in use or in reference sources, it should be adopted for entry in preference to the earlier or original title.

**Shakespeare, William**
[Macbeth]

The tragic history, life and times of Macbeth of scotland.

*C. Simultaneous publication under different titles.*

1. A work that is published simultaneously in the same language under two different titles, requires guidance as to which of the two titles should be used in the entry. The rule directs the use of the title of the edition published in the home country of the library, or when the country is not involved, the title of the edition received first in the library.

The need for application of this rule is expected to be infrequent as under normal conditions of publishing such instances of multiple titles of a work in one language are rarely met with.

(1) **Jawaharlal Nehru**
The light is gone: the funeral speech on the demise of Mahatma Gandhi.

(2) **The Sun sets in India** by Jawaharlal Nehru.

Rangoon, ............1948.

*see his* The Light is gone.

2-3. *Work of a corporate body published simultaneously in various languages and under different titles, and none of them is known to be the original title and language*

Choose a uniform title on the basis of the title in the language in which a corporate body's name is entered in the catalogue. If no title exists in that language, choose the title in the order of preference English, French, German, Spanish, or Russian.If none of these languages is used, form a title appropriately taking into consideration the language of the users of the library, the official language of the country in which the work was published and the language in which the majority of works of the author (personal or corporate) is written.

*D. Titles of laws*. The rule directs the entry of an individual legislative enactment, using the headings in the order of preference noted:

1. the official short title or citation title;
2. an unofficial short title or citation title, the use of which has become established in legal literature;
3. the official title of the enactment;
4. any other official designation, e.g. by number or by date.

**India**. *Laws, statutes, etc.*

Employees provident fund act,1952.

**India**. *Laws, statutes etc.*

S.B.I. act, 1955

**India**. *Laws, statutes etc.*

West Bengal appropriation (No. 2) act, 1968.

102. **Works Written before 1501**

*A*. This rule is general and directs that the title in the original language, by which a work written prior to 1501 is identified in references source is to be used; if reference sources do not provide the information, adopt the form of title used in modern editions, early editions, or manuscript copies, in this order. Beginning words or phrases of the title, whose omission will not affect the identification of the title proper, and the initial article, where ever possible, are left out in the title.

**Beowulf**

**Chans on de Roland**

x Song of Roland

x Roland's song

**Njal**

x Burnt Njal Saga

**Mahabharata**

x the Great Indian Epic

x the story of Pandavas and Kauravas

**Ramayana**

x Valmiki Ramayana

**Puranas**

x the Great Indian Puranas

*B. Classical Greek Works*. If there is a well established English title for a Greek classic, adopt it for entry; otherwise use the Greek title after romanization.

**Aesop**

Fables

**Aristophanes**

Knights

**Aristophanes**

Lysistrata

**Sophocles**

Oedipus Rex

*C. Anonymous Works*

1. Omission of initial articles and introductory phrases, whenever possible, from the title and using the title proper for entry is already provided for in A-ACR 102 A. The slang for such procedure is 'omit puffs' in the title.

*An Anglo-Saxon epic of the heroic deeds of the legendary hero* Beowulf

The part of the title in italics can be omitted, with least distortion to the title proper, Beowulf by which the work is identified.

2. **Works not written in the Roman alphabet**. The rule directs entry of an early anonymous work written in non-Roman alphabet under an English title, if one is available.

The original title of Arabian Nights in Persian is Hazar Afsana, but it is unfamiliar to large groups of readers. The English title of this early anonymous work "Arabian Nights" is preferred.

3. **Collective entries for stories with many versions.** Early anonymous basic stories are found in different versions and in various languages. It is essential to relate the versions in the catalogue. A uniform title, which is well established in English language reference sources, is adopted and the name of the language of the book is added at the end; e.g. legends of king Arthur, the numerous Icelandic, and Norse medieval tales, and the oriental legends Hitopadesa, Panchatantra, Katha Sarit Sagara, etc.

**Hitopadesa**, *English.*

**Hitopadesa**. *German.*

4. **Cycles.** Early poems, romances, etc. centering around the name of a person, event or object in the same language, are termed Cycles. If such a cycle has been given a title, more or less specific this title is adopted for the collections of the works in the cycle. In the absence of a title for it, treat it under A- ACR 5 for ordinary collections.

**Akbar-Birbal Stories**

**Tenali Rama's Tales**

103. **Work of unknown authorship without title**

The rule directs the entry of an anonymous work, a composite manuscript. i.e. a codex or manuscript containing more than one works, or a manuscript group, i.e. manuscripts known by the name of the group, e.g. Gilgit manuscript which is wanting in a title, under a uniform title or a uniform designation, observing the order of preference stated below:

*A*. Adopt a title given to the work subsequent to its writing.

**Vijaynagara Samrajya Vamsavali**

*B*. If the work cannot be identified except by the name of the manuscript containing it, use the name of the manuscript. The name of designation by which a group of manuscript is known, is used as uniform title. If the group or collection of manuscript is known by the name of the repository, refer from that designation in a form used for the heading for the repository followed by *Mss* and the designation.

**Lhasa Monastery Tibetan Collection** *Mss*

*C.* In the absence of a name for such a manuscript or group manuscripts, use the heading for the repository followed by the abbreviation *Mss* and the repository's designation for the manuscript or the group.

**University of Bombay.** *Library Mss Bhagwat Singji collection*, 257.

*D.* A non-English language manuscript without a name is to be provided with a name followed by the name of the language, and the year of its writing or approximate time.

**Prayer to Sun God.** *Prakrit* 3000 *B.C.*?

**Other General Rules**

104. **Qualifications added to the title**

*A. Clarification of heading.* In order to distinguish the title heading chosen, from another similar one in the catalogue, add in parenthesis after the uniform title an explanatory designation.

**Vikramaditya**, (*Emperor*)
**Vikramaditya**, (*Play*)

*B. Identification of work.* Distinguishing designations are to be given in parenthesis for the uniform title of different works that have the same title.

**Ramayana** (Sanskrit Verse)

**Ramayana** (Play in Hindi)
**Ramayana** (Tamil Prose)

*C. Indentification of version.* An appropriate designation is provide in parenthesis to the uniform title of a work to distinguish one version from another.

**Saiva sidhanta** (*Kashmir Version*)

**Saiva sidhanta** (*Southern Version*)

105. **Translations**

*A.* The name of the language of translation is added after the uniform title of a work if it is translated. Further designations like old English, Prakrit, Anglo-Saxon, etc. may be adopted.

**Vedas.** *Yajurveda, German*
**Puranas.** *Vayupurana,Hindi*
**Puranas.** *Vayupurana, Bengali*

*B. Text in two or three languages*. State all the languages on the heading of the uniform title; if one of these is the original language of the text, it is given last. The order of languages on the heading will be English, French, German, Spanish, Russian and other languages in alphabetical order. If the text is in more than three languages the term 'Polyglot' is used.

**Mahabharata. Bhagavadgita***Hindi and Sanskrit.*

**Aditya Hridayam.** *Polyglot*

(Prayer to Sun in Sanskrit. Telgu, Malayalam, Hindi, and Canarese language)

106. **Parts of a work**

*A. Single parts*. Voluminous works, specially early epics, classics contain distinctive parts, Each part has a title of its own and also is issued separately. The treatment given to these parts depends on its closeness, relation to the whole work, as well as its individuality. Normally a single part has to be treated as subordinate element in the heading for the work as a whole. But sometimes a single part attains an individual status and gets established under its own title, by which it is identified. In order to provide satisfactory guiandence in cataloguing the parts, these rules have been formulated as liberally as possible to acommodate all categories.

1. Whenever a single part of a larger work has appeared with its own title or designation, before any of the other parts has been issued with a distinct title, and also if the other parts do not have distinct titles, give its title as a subheading of the uniform title of the whole work; in case of doubt, apply rule 2 below. A heading title reference is made from the title of the part to the heading and uniform title of the part.

**Mahabharata.** *Bhagavadgita.*

x Bhagavadgita

If the part is numbered, give the number in Arabic before the subheading, and use English terms for parts, if available.

*Aristophanes*

[Plays, 1. the Clouds]
x his the clouds

2. In this section, directions, as to when the title of the part itself

should be adopted as the uniform title are available.

1. If the part is a unit of a loosely organized series, trilogy or the like;
2. If it is a unit with a well-established title of its own;
3. If it is an anonymous cycles; or collection of stories or other works.

Provide references from the heading for the larger work to the heading for the parts, catalogued as independent works.

**Dos Passos, John**

U.S.A. For separately published works, in this trilogy, *see his* The 42nd parallel. 1930

Nineteen-Nineteen. 1931
The Big Money. 1937.

**Hawthorne, Nathaniel**
The Scarlet Letter.

**Hawthorne, Nathaniel**
The Portable Hawthorne.

For separately published novels included in this work, *see his* the Scarlet Letter; the House of the Seven Gables (etc.)

**Ali Baba and forty Thieves**
**Arabian Nights**
For separately published stories in this anonymous work, *see*

Aladdin and the Wonderful Lamp

Sindbad the Sailor (*etc.*)

*B*. Several parts. Give inclusive numbers for consecutive parts, that are identified numerically, considering them to be a single part.

**Dante Alighieri**
(Divina commedia. *Books* 1-3)
1. Inferno
2. Purgatorio
3. Paradiso

107. **Collected editions, etc.**

An author's works, if more than one, appear in the form of
(1) complete works.

(2) partial collections, consisting of

(a) Various literary forms-essays, letters, plays, poems, speeches etc. and

(b) a single literary, form e.g. plays only or poems only.

There are also publications which contain parts of various works, extracts, quotations from different authors and issued under a collective title . This should be distinguished from the above forms and the term "selections" is used for this category. In accordance with the directions use the terms "Works" for *e.g.*

(1) **Shakespeare, William.**

[Works]
Comoplete plays and sonnets.

the terms "Selected works" for (2a) and (2b),

(2a) **Eliot, T.S.**

[Selected Works]
Plays, Poems, and Essays-a selection.

(2b) **O'Casey, Sean**

[Selected Works]
Collected plays, containing eight well-known plays of the Irish playwright.

**Bentley, Eric, ed.**

[Selections]
The plays; a critical anthology; one play each by Ibsen, Miller, Milloere, Rostland, Shakespeare, Sophocles, Strindberg, Wilde.

**Stevenson, Burton**
[Selections]

Home book of quotations, 75,000 quotations from ancient and modern literature.

**Special Rules for Bible and other Sacred scriptures**

A-ACR 108-114 govern the entry of the Bible and its parts, the language of the text, the version, the translation, and the date of the edition.

**108.** The uniform title 'Bible' is to be adopted for the Bible as a whole, and for any of its parts, adding the appropriate designation of the part, and other distinguishing features of language, version year etc.

to the subheading, as specified in the rules 109-114.

If the text of the Bible is in more than two languages, the term '*Polyglot*' is used as subheading without stating the version.

If the text is in two languages, give the name of one in the heading, and make an added entry for the other.

For detailed instructions, and scheme of subheading refer to the A-ACR pages 132-138. However, the more common forms of heading for adoption in general libraries is given below :

**Bible**
**Bible.** *N.T.*
**Bible.** *O.T. Revelation*
**Bible.** *O.T.*
**Bible.** *O.T. Pentateuch*
**Bible.** *N.T. Greek*
**Bible.** *O.T. Hebrew*
**Bible.** *N.T. Gospels. English Authorised*

If passage from a book of the Bible is better known by its title than by the uniform title Bible, an exception is made and it is entered under its title. Such exceptions are limited, *e.g.*

**Lord's prayer.**
x Bible *N.T. Mathew vi;* 9-13

**Ten commandments.**
x Bible. *O.T. Deutoronomy v.* 6-21

**Non-Christian Sacred Scriptures**

The treatment of other sacred books is largely on the model on which the Bible and its parts ate entered :

115. **Jewish Sacred works.** 'The Jewish Encyclopedia' provides information on the choice and form of title for parts of the main work Talmud.

*A*. There are two versions of the Talmud : (1) the Babylonian Talmud, and (2) the Palestinian or Jerusalem Talmud.

The uniform title for the first "Talmud" and for the second "Talmud Yerushalmi," and for parts of these works is adopted. The name of language is given as subheading for translations but when the text in original language is followed by a translation in a single volume, no mention is made of the language of translation on the heading but added entry is provided for the translation.

**Talmud**

An authorised Hebrew text of the Babylonian Talmud, with an English translation .

I Talmud. English

**Talmud Yerushalmi.** *Selections*

Selections from the Palestinian edition of the Talmud.

It would be advantageous to make the following references also :

Babylonian Talmud, *see*

Talmud.

Palestinian Talmud, *see*

Talmud Yerushalmi.

Jerusalem Talmud, *see*

Talmud Yerushalmi.

*B. Mishnah and Tosefta.* These two Jewish scriptural works and their parts are entered under the uniform title:

**Mishna**

**Tosefta**

The procedure for translations of these works remains the same as for Talmud.

However, an exception is made in respect of the tractate *Aboth*, which is to be entered directly under its name, instead of as a subheading under the larger work. This is because *Aboth* is well known and identified under its name .

*C. References*. Provide references from the titles of orders and tractates of the Talmud, Mishnah, and Tosefta, to the forms under which they are entered in the catalogue.

**Baba Kamma,** see

Mishna Baba Kamma

Talmud. Baba Kamma

General references from the heading for orders to the headings for their tractates are also provided.

**Talmud Nezikin,**

For separately published tractates belonging to this order,

*see*

Talmud [name of tractate] *e.g.*
Talmud, Baba kamma

116. **Buddhist Sacred Works.**

The chief Buddhist scriptural work is **Tripitaka**. It contains the part :

**Abhidhammapitaka**

**Dhammapada**
**Suttapitaka**

**Vinayapitaka**
**Jatakas**

The uniform heading for a collection of all these works is **Tripitaka**. If there is a translation of the original Pali text, the name of the language of translation is given as subheading.

**Tripitaka**. English.

As the parts are very well identified under their own names, they are directly entered under their own names and reference (xx) from Tripitaka to its parts Vinayapitaka, Suttapitaka, (etc.) is provided in the catalogue.

Tripitaka, *see also*

Abhidhammapitaka
Suttapitaka

Vinayapitaka
Dhammapada

Jatakas

117. **Hindu Sacred Works**

The foremost sacred book of Hinduism is **Veda**. It has four divisions (1) Rigveda (2)Yajurveda, (3)Samaveda and (4)Atharvaveda. A collection of Vedic texts is entered under the uniform Title:

**Vedas**

The name of the language into which the original Sanskrit/Prakrit text is translated is stated as a subheading.

**Vedas.** *German*

**Vedas.** *English*

Each division of the Veda, is entered as subheading under the uniform title.

**Vedas**. Rigveda
**Vedas.** Yajurveda

**Vedas**. Samaveda
**Vedas**. Atharvaveda

and the version of the text given in parenthesis.

The Vedas have certain auxiliary texts known in Sanskrit as Vedangas,menaning thereby the limbs. These are specifically known as Aranyakas, Brahmanas, Upanishads, and help the study and understanding of the Vedic texts, being a sort of commentary.

The uniform title for collections of these auxiliary Vedic texts is:

**Aranyakas.**

**Brahmanas.**

**Upanishads.**

The parts of each one of these works is given as subheading under the uniform title.

**Aranyakas**. *Aitareyaranyaka*
**Brahmanas.** *Satapatabrahmana*

**Upanishads**. *Svetasvataropanisad.*

There is again a third category of Vedic text known as Sutras, which are in the nature of aphorisms, embodying the highest and subtliest philosophical doctrines in a nutshell. Volumes have been written, on the basis of each one of these Sutras, e.g. Brahma Sutra. The uniform title for a collection of the Sutras is

**Sutras**

and its divisions are entered as subheading under the uniform title.

Sutras. *Brahmasutra*

Besides the Hindu Sacred works there are two other scriptural works relating to Jainism and Sikhism.

The Jain Canons are entered under the uniform title.

**Sidhanta**

and the seven standard collections of Jain canons ar given as subheadings under the uniform title, and the title of each individual text as further subheading.

**Sidhanta.** *Anga*

**Sidhanta.** *Anga. Acarariga*

The Sikh scriptural works are entered under the uniform title.

**Adi-Granth**

perhaps, a reference x from Guru Granth, and Granth Sahib, may be provided in the catalogue.

Guru-Granth, *see*
Adi-Granth.

Granth Sahib, *see*
Adi-Granth,

*F. Avesta.* The Zoroastrian scriptural work is collectively known as Avesta. Sometimes it is also referred to as Zend Avesta,

Use Avesta as the uniform title for a collection of Zoroastrian Scriptural texts and its parts are given as subheadings to the uniform

**Avesta.**

**Avesta.** *Yasna*
**Avesta.** *Khordah Avesta*

An individual work of the part is entered as a further subheading.

**Avesta.** *Yasna. Gathas*

In all the above instances references from individual titles or designations of work not entered under their names but entered as subheading under the uniform title, are provided to the chosen form of entry.

Atharvaveda, *see*
Vedas.*Atharvaveda*

Kenopanisad, *see*
Upanishads. *Kenopanisad*

Zend Avesta, *see*
Avesta.

118. **Mohammedan or Islamic Sacred Works**

What Bible is to Christianity, Koran is to Mohammedanism, The uniform title for the Koran and its parts is

**Koran**

**Koran.** *Hindi.*
**Koran.** *English.*

The titles of chapters (Suras) are given as subheadings, commencing with the term Surat; references are made from the Sura numbers in the form of subheadings to the uniform title and its subheading.

**Koran.** *Surat al-baqarah.*

x Koran. *Sura II*

It is suggested that reference (x) is made from alternate spellings of the work Quran, Quoran, and Qoran to the form of spelling adopted for the uniform title.

Quran, *see*

Koran

119. **Liturgical works.**

The A-ACR preliminary note under this topic is highly pragmatic and sensible. Although the adoption of a Uniform title for cataloguing purposes is desirable, it is certainly wise and frank to omit faulty uniform titles for such liturgical works on which authentic and accurate guidance is not available and use the titles of the works themselves, in place of uniform titles.

A detailed set of instructions on entering the liturgical works pertaining to Christianity is provided in A-ACR 119. The principles underlying the directions in the sections A-D of this rule may appropriately be adopted for liturgical works of religions and sects, whenever the need may arise.

REFERENCE

1. Anglo-American Cataloguing Rules (British Test) Ch. 4., p. 123.

# 26

# ACCESS POINTS TO BOOKS AND META-BOOKS BY A-ACR2

It is considered appropriate to pay attention to A-ACR2 (1978) after the smoke, din, and bustle coming out from both toy pistols and auto-machine guns of criticism has subsided during the subsequent few years and to provide some working knowledge of this code of Cataloguing and also to include certain directions to libraries in following the rules in this code for either revising the existing catalogue or for commencing the preparation of a new catalogue for fresh collections of books in the new libraries that are in the making. It is not that this new set of rules provides a solution to all library cataloguing issues, but because the code is produced after great care and deliberation, in order that the library catalogues governed by the rules in it are expected to serve the readers in a more satisfactory way than the previous ones. Let it be remembered that A-ACR 2 is a continuation of its predecessor A-ACR-1967, and libraries which have followed the ( A-ACR-1967) would have least difficulty in adopting A-ACR2.

A-ACR2 has only two parts-Part-1 Description and Part-II Headings, Uniform Titles and Reference, in place of three parts in A-ACR1-Part 1. Choice of entry (Author Headings) Part-II Choice of the form of headings and part III-Descriptive cataloguing. This does not mean that A-ACR2 does not provide rules for the choice of the form of headings; chapter 21 with which Part-II begins deals with the choice of main and added entries, chapters 22-25 with the form of headings and uniform titles, and chapter 26 with references. As usual the order of rules in each chapter is that general rules precede the special rules, with directions that where no specific rule exists for a specific problem, the more general rule should be applied. All the rules in Part II apply to works and not generally to their physical manifestation, even though the character of an idividual publication (printed, non-printed and other media) is considered in certain instances. Also the rules in this part apply to all kinds of library materials, irrespective of their published form or medium or whether they are in the category of serial works or finished works. Another special feature of A-ACR2 devotes a separate chapter-23 for the choice of geographic names, because these names create a separate problem, even though they normally form part of corporate headings. In all cases the cataloguer's care and attention in distinguishing between the problems of establishing geographic names according to a standard and of deciding the corporate headings involving such names is essential. (A-ACR-2 contains rules (22.18 to 22.20, for addition to names used as headings designating the functions, *e.g.* Captain, Magician, Rev., Baron, Solicitor, and dates of birth and death). These function-indicating terms are to be added at the end of the name in a catalogue heading, in order to distinguish between otherwise identical name headings in a catalogue. The library of congress printed catalogue cards used to contain these distinguishing features with a view to provide the fullest bibliographic data regarding the author of a work. In machine readable catalogues these would normally be provided for, with these fullnesses of name headings. Generally, terms like compiler, editor, commentator, translator, illustrator in their abbreviated form are used at the end of a person's name as heading, in order to indicate the differing functions of the same person and to bring together in the catalogue, a persons' works as main author, compiler, translator, together, one after another.

## Identical Features

The rules in this chapter—*Basic Rule* 21 contains 39 sub-rules, with specific rules under each one of them—provide directions for the choice of Main Entry, usually under the persons, the corporate body responsible for the creation of the work, and Added entries for other possible or likely approaches to the work. In this respect, the pattern of choice in determining the author of a work remains the same as in A-ACR 1. More explicit illustrations are provided under each rule applied to a large number and variety of examples, with a view to elucidate the scope and comprehensive character of the rule governing the choice of access points.

**21.1 A. Works of personal authorship.**

A personal author is defined as the person chiefly responsible for the creation of the intellectual or artistic content of a work, *e.g.* R. L. Stevenson, who conceived of '*The Treasure Island*' and wrote the book is a personal author; Thiagaraja, who composed *Kirtanas* in thousands in Telugu language in praise of *Lord Rama* and *His consort Sitamma* and also sang them, example '*Ma Amma Sitamma, Sri Ramudu Ma Thandri*' is a personal author of his musical compositions; similarly an artist-Picasso, who created exquisite paintings is a personal author of his paintings; R. K. Laxman is a personal author of his cartoons. But in the case of certain performers of sound recordings, films, they are treated as personal authors, vide 21.23C. *e.g.* M.S. Subbulakshmi is considered a personal author though a performer of a sound recording, containing the musical compositions of Annamacharya, Thiagaraja, and Sankaracharya all together in one disc.

The main entry, therefore, is made according to the rules for this form of name headings vide 22.1 to 22.28.

**Work by one or more persons, General rule, (21.1A2.)**

Make the main entry under the heading for personal author, vide 21.4A, the principal personal author, vide 21.6, or the probable personal author, vide 21.5B.

In certain cases of shared personal authorship vide 21.6 (shared responsibility), and mixed personal authorship vide 21.8-21.27 (mixed responsibility) entry is made under the person named first and added entries for others as directed in 21.19-21.30.

Shared responsibility in the creation of a work is collaboration between two or more persons or bodies, performing the similar kind of activity, (1) the contribution of each being distinct and separate in the work or (2) the contribution of each being inseparable from the rest. (Why not designate the first type of shared responsibility as 'composite authorship' and the second real' 'Joint authorship'.?)

Also adhoc events such as, athletic contests, exhibitions, expeditions, fairs and festivals, ships, and spacecrafts are considered to be corporate bodies.

Main entry for the work emanating from one or more corporate bodies is made under the heading for the appropriate corporate body, provided it can be classed in one or more of the following categories:

(General rule 21.1B2) itself.

(a) Administration of the corporate body (policy, procedure, operation, finance, staff, and resources-catalogues, inventories, membership lists.)
(b) Legal and governmental works; (such as laws, decrees (21.31). regulations (21.32), treaties (21.35), court decisions (21.36) and legislative hearings).
(c) Collective thinking and decisions of the body (Committees, commissions).
(d) Reports of conferences-proceedings, papers, etc.—results of expeditions—events relating to exhibitions, fairs, and festivals, provided these are stated explicitly in the records.
(e) Sound recordings, films, video-recordings relating to the collective activity of a performing group as a whole, including its production, performance etc. (21.2)

In certain cases of shared responsibility (21.6) and mixed responsibility (21.8-21.27) make the main entry under the first named corporate body, and added entries as directed in 21.29- 21.30

In doubtful cases of works, which may not fall within the above categories, treat them as non-corporate author works. (21.1B3).

If a work is the responsibility of a subordinate unit/agency of a corporate body and if it is prominently stated in the work, make the main entry under the name of the subordinate unit (21.1c (a); if the subordinate unit is not given any prominence in its work (either not mentioned or no specific name given to it) then make the main entry for the work under the name of the parent corporate body.

**Main entry under title (21.1c)**

Make the main entry under the title of a work, in case

1. the person as writer or author is unknown (vide 21.5)
2. it is diffuse (vide 21.6C2)
3. it cannot be determined, and
4. it does not emanate from a corporate body,
5. it is a collection or a work prepared under the direction of an editor or board of editors (vide 21.7.),
6. though a corporate body is responsible for it, but it does not fall

into any of the categories stated in 21.1B2, and it also is not a personal author work,

7. it is one of the approved sacred scriptures, (vide 21.37)

In all the above cases, added entries according to 21.29 to 21.30 are to be made. Adopt a uniform title, as instructed in chapter 25.

**21.2 Changes in titles proper.**

21.2A. A title proper of a work is considered to have changed,

(1) if the change occurs in the first five works, except an initial article in the nominative case *or*

(2) if any important words (nouns, proper name, or initials used for proper names, adjectives etc.), are added, deleted or changed (inclusive of spelling changes ) *or*

(3) if the order of words has undergone a change. While all other changes, including capitalization and punctuation are not construed as changes in the title proper and these minor changes may be given in a note (vide 1.7B4)

21.2B **Monographs.**

21.2B1 If a monograph in one physical part (volume) discloses changes between one edition and another, a separate main entry for each edition is required (vide 25.2 in deciding the use of uniform titles in order to bring together in a group all the editions).

21.2B2. Monographs in more than one physical part (volume) reveal a change between parts (volumes) adopt the title proper or the first part for all the parts (volumes). In case, another title proper of the later parts (volumes) predominates, adopt that title for all the parts (volumes).

21.2C **Serials**

If the title proper of a serial changes, make a separate main entry for each title.

21.3 *Changes of persons or bodies responsible for a work;*

21.3A *Monographs:*

21.3A1 Make the main entry of an original edition, that has been modified by a person or corporate body, other than the person or corporate body responsible for the original work, according to instructions in 21.9 to 21.23. (The general rule 21.9) governing modified works appears to be a more liberal adaptation and extention of the appropriate rule 14 A-B in A-ACRI governing reviser and original author).
21.3A2 Make the main entry of a multipart monograph in which there is change in the responsibility between parts, under the heading appropriate to the first part. If, however, a different person or corporate body is found to be predominently responsible for the later parts, change the heading appropriate to them, with an added entry for the person/corporate body responsible for the earlier part/s. Further, if more than three persons, or corporate bodies are responsible for the complete work, and none of them is predominently responsible, the main entry is made under the title of the work. (vide 21.6)

21.3B *Serials*

Even if the title proper of the serial remains the same in all volumes, a new (Main entry is called for: 1) when the name of the person or corporate body under which a serial is entered undergoes a change; (vide 22.2B or 24.1B or, 2) if the main entry of a serial is made under personal or corporate heading , and the person or corporate body responsible for the serial changes.

**21.4 Works for which a single person or corporate body is responsible.**

21.4A *Works of single personal authorship*

Make the main entry of a work, a collection of works, or selection from one or more works by one personal author under the heading for that person irrespective of his name being stated or not in the work.

1. Goldsmith, Maurice.
   Sage: a life of J. D. Bernal.

2. [Strindberg, August 1849-1912]
   Miss Julia

In example two, the personal author responsible for the work is not stated in the work, but the information is obtained from sources outside the book and supplied. The heading is enclosed in square brackets to indicate it, by following the customary practice in descriptive cataloguing of books, though A-ACR2 does not specify this method.

3. Shakespeare, William

   Complete collection of dramatic works.

4. Shaw, George Bernard

   Plays pleasant and unpleasant, a selection of Shaw's plays.

21.4B. *Works emanating form a single corporate body*

Make the main entry of a work, a collection of works, or selections from a work or works emanating from a corporate body, including a reprint, reissue of such a work under the heading for the body, provided the work/s could be classed into one or more of the categories stated in 21. IB2. (General rule)

1. Administrative

2. Legal and governmental

3. Collective deliberations and decisions

4. Reports of conferences

5. Sound recordings, films, video-recordings

Indian Library Association, Delhi.
The Constitution and bye-Laws.

Indian Standards Institution, Delhi.
A collection of patents issued for the period 1960-1970.

Geological Survey of India.
Report on Cauvery delta oil exploration.

Uttar Pradesh Intermediate and High School Education Board.
Programme of Examinations for 1982.

India. Ministy of Finance.
Incomme tax laws revised to 1982.
Indian Science Congress
Proceedings of the conference held at Bangalore, 1982.

World Book Fair
Catalogue of books, exhibited by the National Book Trust, and other government agencies during the V fair, 1982. New Delhi.

21.4C Responsibility for works, erroneously or ficititiously attributed to a person or corporate body.

21.4.C1. By popular notion and tradtion, a work is sometimes erroneously or fictitiously attributed to a person other than the actual author. In such cases, the main entry is made under the actual personal author or under title, when the actual personal author remains unknown. An added entry under the heading for the person to whom the work is attributed is also made, unless the attributtd author is not a real person.

*Actual author, e.g.*

Gopalkrishna Bharathi

The Harijan saint Nanda's prayer to Lord Nataraja (Dancing Siva) rendered into musical compsotion by Gopalakrishan Bharathi.

*Attributed author, e.g.*

*Attributed author added entry, e.g.*

Nanda, the Harijan Saint

Gopalkrishna Bharathi,

Prayer to Lord Nataraja.

21.4C2. *Responsibility for works erroneously or ficititiously attributed to a corporate body.*

Because the name of a corporate body is too often and specifically mentioned in a work, which is the responsibility of a person or persons, it sometimes is erronously entered under the heading for the corporate body. But a correct main entry for such a work is made under the heading for the person or persons, even though the corporate body and its activities form the subject matter of the work.

*Actual author*, e.g.

Haldron, Robert,
  A Critical assesment of the programme and activities of the I. B. M. Computers Ltd.

*Attributed author added entry* e.g.

I. B. M. Computers Ltd.

Haldron, Robert.
  A Critical assesment of the programme and actitivities of the I. B. M. Computers Ltd.

21.4D. Works by heads of state, other high government officials, popes, and other high ecclesiastical officials.

21.4D1 *Offcial communications.*

(a) Emanating from heads of state, heads of govenment, and head of international bodies, *e.g.* an address to Parliament by the President of India; Directions to Chief Ministers of State on implementation of adult literacy programe by the Prime Minister of India. Message of the Secretary General, U.N. to member states on the Human Rights Day; (b) Issued by Popes, patriarcs, bishops, etc. (including religious heads of other religious and other high dignitaries of those religions, *e.g.* Sankaracharya of Kamakoti Pitam.).

These are entered under the corporate heading for the official concerned, *e.g.*,

India. President 1969-1975 (V.V. Giri)

Opening address to parliament (joint session of Lok Sabha and Rajya Sabha) after the oath taking ceremony.

India. Prime Minster, 1977-1984 (Mrs. Indira Gandhi)

Directions to state governments not to resort to overdraft during the remaining period of the sixth Five Year Plan, as approved by the National Development Council of India, at its meeting on 14th March, 1982.

**United Nations**. Secretary General, 1980 (Kurt Waldheim)
Message to memeber states on the Human Rights Day.

The main entry of a communication accompanying or transmitting a document (by the Head of state/Head of government to a department, governing body, or other state legislatures, etc.,) is made under the heading for the department or the govenring body concerned.

India. Ministry of Information and Broadcasting.
A document on sharing broadcasting time by various political parties on the eve of elections to parliament, and state legislatures, communicate with an endorsement by the Prime Minister to Information and Broadcasting Ministry, Government of India.

21.4D2. *Other works.*

Main entry for all other works of such a person is made under the heading for the person responsible for the work. When the work is not an official document, but personal, e. g. Univerisity Convocation addresses, Inaugural address to Book Exhibition, or Address as a special invitee to a Citizens' Forum, etc.,

Radhakrishnan, Sarvepalli

Collected works comprising addresses to Oriental Scholar's Conference, Buddhist Congregations, etc. from 1940-1960.

An explanatory reference entry from the corporate heading to the personal heading is to be provided.

India. President, 1964-1968, Sarvepalli Radhakrishnan
Under this heading will be found all his works (official) in his capacity as president,
but *see* under the heading.
Radhakrishnan, Sarvepalli for his personal writing, speeches, etc. e.g.

Radhakrishanan, Sarvepalli
Upanishads, a commentary
—same
Hindu view of life.
—same
Idealist's view of life.

21.4D3. *Collections of official communications and other works.*

Make the main entry for a collection of official communications and other works by a single person under the personal heading , and an added entry is made under the corporate heading.

Jawaharlal Nehru,
Important official documents and popular addresses to citizens, and students of India and selected passages from his books 'Discovery of India, and World History, brought together for quick reference in a single volume.

(I. India Prime Minister, 1952-1968 (Jawaharlal Nehru).

21.5. *Works of unknown or uncertain authorship or by unnamed groups.*

21.5A Make the main entry of a work, whose personal author is unknonwn or uncertain or if it emanates from a corporate body without a precise name or identity, under its title.

Antartic expedition of 1982.
A popular account of the Antartic expedition, 1982, led by . Singh and others, by a student of oceanography.

Memorandum to Indian parliament, 1976
Freedom loving citizens, including Jayaprakash Narayan and others, present a Memorandum to Parliament demanding restoration of freedom as laid down in the constitution.

*Attributed author*

An added entry may be made for the person or persons or corporate bodies, if such a work is attributed to them either in editions or reference sources.

*Added entry*

Jayaprakash Narayan

Memorandum to Indian Parliament, 1976
Freedom loving citizens, including Jayaprakash Narayan and others present a Memorandum to Parliament demanding restoratio of freedom as laid down in the constitution.

21.5.B. *Probable author*

Probable authors of works by unknown or uncertain authors or by groups or bodies lacking a name, indicated in reference sources are treated as main entry headings and an added entry is made under the title.

[Shakespeare, William]

Cromwell, the true chronicle historie of the whole life and death of Thomas Lord.
A play published in 1602, and included in 3rd and 4th Shakespeare folios (1663 and 1685)

[Sturgis, H. O.]

Tim, a delicate portrayal of a sensitive boy's devoted affection for an elder-boy. (In both the examples above, the personal author heading is indicated in reference sources).

21.5C. In case, the name of a personal author is unknown and the only indication of authorship is a characterising word or phrase or of a phrase naming another work by the person, in place of the author's name in the chief source of information (title pages), make the main entry under the word or phrase (in the form given in 22.11C) in direct order as on the title page of the wrok with an added entry under title.

Experienced Gardener
  Grow your garden, by an experienced gardener.
  I title.

Author of Molly Bawn
  Life's remorse; a novel by the author of Molly Bawn

If, in place of author's name on the title page of a work, a predominantly non-alphabetical and non-numeric device is used, make the main entry under the title. No added entry under the device is necessary.

Tales that have tickled a man
  in the street by***
This is the only entry for such works.

21.6 **Works of shared responsibility.**

21.6 A In this rule, the nature and type of works that should be dealt with, are explained:

(i) Two or more persons responsible for producing the work (in which a person's individual contribution cannot be identified).
(ii) Different persons writing separately for a work or works.
(iii) Two or more persons exhanging their writing as in correspondence, debates.
(iv) Two or more corporate bodies responsible for the work.
(v) Works in (i-iii) above, containing contributions from one or more corporate bodies.
(vi) Works produced by collaboration or exchange between a person and corporate body.

These categories of works will also include shared responsibility production among adapters, arrangers, commentators, reporters, etc.; whose main entry is made under the headings for persons according to rules 21.8.-21.27. However, a work in which different contributors' writings have been brought together under editorial direction of a person or wrok which is merley a physical grouping or togetherness of already existing works, should not be dealt with as per this rule.

21.6B *Guidance for apprisal of principal responsibility in work of shared responsibility.*

21.6B.1 In case a work of shared responsibility discloses by means of wording or typographic distinction on its tilte page, that one person or a corporate body is chiefly responsible, make the main entry under the heading for that person or body. If, however, a different name of a person or corporate body is placed first in position on the title page, merely make an added entry for that person or body. Also, if other person or bodies are involved in such a work, added entries for them may be made, provided their number is not more than two.

*Main entry*

Carskadon, Thomas
Measure of a nation: picturing in charts and graphs America's needs and her human and material resources with the collaboration of Rudolf Modley.

I Modley, Rudolf, II title.

*Main entry*

Huxley, Aldous
What I believe; essays by well known writers and thinkers, and philosphers—C.E.M. Joad, Bertrand Russell, J.B. Haldane, and others.

21.6C *Principal responsibility not stated.*

21.6C1 If two or three persons or bodies share the responsibility for a work and none of them is indicated as the principal author, make the main entry under the name of person mentioned first and provide added entries for others.

*Main entry*

Field, Mary

See how they grow; botany through the cinema by Mary Field, J. V. Durden, and F. Percy Smith.

I. Durden, J. V. II. Smith , F. Percy.

21.6C2. If more than three persons or corporate bodies share the responsibility, and none of them individually or jointly indicated as principal authors, make the main entry under the title, with an added entries for the person or body named first on the title page.

*Main entry under title*

Farm management

By John D. Black, Marion Clawson, Charles R. Saayre, and Walter William.

I. Black, John D.

If no mention is made of the names of the persons in the work, an added entry for the first name found in a previous editon of the work is made; if no earlier edition exists, then under the name of the heading which comes first in the English alphabetic order.

**21.7 Collections and wroks prepared under editorial direction.**

21.7A This rule will cover the following categories of collections in (i & ii) and also (iii & iv) for which the editor/s is responsible.

(i) Independent works of different persons or bodies, brought together;
(ii) Extracts (selections) from independent works by different persons or bodies;
(iii) Works consisting of contributions by different persons or bodies produced under editorial direction;

(iv) Works partly of independent works by different persons or bodies and partly of contribution produced under editiorial direction.

This rule will not be applicable to the proceedings of conference, which are treated under A-ACR21. 1B2.

21.7B *Works with collective title*

If a work has a collective title and if it can be classed into any one of the above categories in 21. 7A, make them entry under its title, with in added entries under the heading for compilers or editors, if they are not more than three, and if they are also distinctly named. There may be more than three compilers or editors for certain works with collective titles; in such case, an added entry is provided for the principal editor/compiler or one named first.

*Main entry*

Five great modern Irish plays, 1940 contaning Shadow and substance, by Lewis Carroll; Spreading the news by Lady Gregory; Juno and the paycock by Seen O'casey: the Playboy of the Western world: Riders to the sea by J. M Synge.

*Main entry*

The play; a critical anthology; One play each by Ibsen, Miller, Moliere, Rostand, Shakespeare, Sophocles, Strindberg, Wilde; ed. by Eric Bentley.

I. **Bentley**, Eric. ed.

*Main entry*

Journal of medical research by Indian council of medical research, 1980.

I. Indian council of medical research.

21.7C *Works without collective titles*

In case, a work falling under the categories in 21.7A above lacks a collective title, make the main entry under the heading appropriate for the first work stated on the title page. Added entries for editors/compilers may be made, if prominent.

*Main entry*

A work without a collective title,

Bragg, William.

Science lifts the veil by William Bragg; the Microscope by Allen Ferguson; Atoms and molecules by Robert Robinson; Cosmic rays by P. M. S. Blackett.

I Ferguson, Allen: The Microscope
II Robinson, Robert; Atoms and Molecules.
III Blackett, P. M. S. ; Cosmic rays.

(Name title added entries are made for the works other than the first one).

21.8 **Works of Mixed Responsibility.**

21.8A A work produced by different persons or bodies each one performing a different function, in order to render the work comprehensive, can be defined as mixed in character. Writing the text, illustrating it, commenting the passage, editing, translating, adapting and even indexing are some of the important functions to create the work as a whole. Each one of these functionaries are authors to the extent of their contribution.

Works of mixed responsibility fall into two basic groups:
1. a previously existing work, that is modified by adaptation or translation or revision, and 2. a new work or which different persons make contribution like illustrating, collaborating by writing certain special chapters or reporting a debate or interview or corespondence.

In these cases, the relative importance of a person's contribution to the work should be determined in order to make the main entry under the person or body as the heading.

## 21.9 **General Rule (Modifications)**

This is a general rule, which provides directions for making the main entry for works modified: (1) which have undergone substantial changes in nature and content from the original and also the expression has been altered, and (2) which have been subjected to minor changes-updating, abridgement, revision, rearrangement. Usually the title page reveals the degree of modification to serve as a deciding factor. The main entry for the first category is made under the heading appropriate to the new work, while the main entry for the second category would be made under the heading appropriate to the original.

(This rule leaves scope for the subjective judgement of the cataloguer in deciding, which work should be grouped under the first and which one under the second. Is not re-writing and revision of the text embodying current thinking in place of the previous theories a substantial change; e.g. Brown's Manual of Library Economy, rev. 2 ed. by R. N. Locke, which bears little resemblence to the previous revison by W. B. Sayers of the original? If a clear cut demarcation in distinghuishing the original and modification for purposes of main entry is not indicated, it would result in variation of the same work being entered inconsistently. No uniform practice of entry could be expected in library catalogues).

## 21.10. **Adaptation of texts**

Adaptation of texts is given a wide connotation to cover paraphrasing, rewriting, adaptation for children, or version in a different literary form, e.g. drama, novel, verse. The main entry for such a work is made under the heading for the adapter; if the name of the adapter is not known, the mainentry is made under its title. Also a name title added entry is made under the heading for the original work.

*Main entry under the adapter*

Shanta Rama Rau
Passage to India by E.M. Foster,
a radio adaptaion.

I. Foster, E.M.: Passage to India.

Somervell, D.C.
A study of hisotry, an abridgement preserving the method, atmos-

phere and texture of the original in a different style, of the original.
–Arnold J. Toynbee: A study of history

I. Toynbcc, A.J.: A study of history.

*Main entry under title, the adapter's name being unknown.*

Canterbury tales for children

I. Chaucer, Geoffrey: Canterbury tales.

*Main entry under the heading for original work, being a doubtful case.*

Aesop.
Fables: storics of animals inculcating morality in children's mind made easy by Reginald Hunter.

21.11 **Illustrated Texts.**

21.11A. The general rule directs that the main entry of a work, containing the text, with illustrations by the artist to elucidate the text, is made under the heading appropriate to the text with an added entry for the illustrator, as instructed in 21. 30K2.

Brown , C.J.

Travels acorss the Indian Sub-continent;
illus. By Robert Smith.

I. Smith Robert, illus.

21.11B. If a wrok containing illustrations for a text or for several texts, by a single artist, is separately published, make the main entry, under the heading for the artist. Make an added entry for the work(s) illustrated if not more than three. If, however, the illustrations happen to be related to more than three works by the same writer, make an added entry under the heading for the writer.

Maugham, Somerset

69 gravure illustrations, and brief bibliographical texts of old

Master's by Herman J. Wechsler.

I. Wechsler, Herman J. Old

Masters: brief biographical texts.

21.12 **Revision of Text.**

21.12A. Make the main entry of a revised, enlarged, updated, abriged, etc., of a work under the heading for the person or body responsible for the original work, if the chief source of information indicates that the original writer continues to be responsible for the revision also. An added entry for the reviser, editor, etc., is to be made.

Brown, J.D.
Brown's Manual of library economy; 6th ed.
rev. by W.B. Sayers.

I. Sayers, W.B. rev.

21.12B. Make the main entry under the reviser, if there is indication in the chief source of information that the original person or body responsible for the work is no longer considered responsible for the revision. Make a name-title added entry under the heading for the original.

Winchell, C.M.
Guide to reference books; 7th ed. based on
the 6th ed. by Isadore Gilbert Mudge.

I. Mudge, Isadore Gilbrt: Guide to reference books.

21.13 **Texts published with commentary.**

21.13A. Works consisting of text or texts by the same person or body, and a commentary or interpretation of the text by a different person or body are covered by this rule.

21.13B. *Commentary emphasised*

Make the main entry under the heading for the commentator, if the chief source of information indicates its predominance or importance, more than the accompanying text of the work.

Such instances in which the commentator's contributions of greater importance than the original work are found in plenty in Indic literature and sometimes in western literature also.

Panduranga Vaman Kane. Comm.

Hindu Dharma Sastra: a critical commentary on Manu Dharama Sastra.

I. Manu : Dharma Sastra.

Care must be taken to see before making the main entry under the commentator, that the work is not a revised edition of the original, where the commentary would be supplementary to the text.

Radhakrishnan, Sarvepalli. Comm.

Commentary on Bhagavadagita.

I. Mahabharata: Bhagavadgita.

21.13C. *Edition of the work emphasised*

In case the presentation of the work, as disclosed on the title page or else where, is only an edition of the original work, (and the commentator's contribution auxiliary,) make the main entry of the work under the heading appropriate to the person or body responsible for its production with an added entry under the heading appropriate to the commentary.

Schopenhauer, Arthur

Philosophy; ed. with critical interpretation on pessimism and romanticism combined in a philosophy of life struggle, ed. by Irwin Edman.

I. Edman, Irwin. Interpretor.

Kautilya

Arthasastra; ed. with a commentary by K. Sama Sastry.

I. Sama Sastry, K. Comm.

21.13D. *Chief source of information ambiguous*

Provision to make the main entry under the heading appropriate to the commentary or the edition (original) as indicated in:

(1) the prefatory material
(2) the typographic display of the text and commentary
(3) the relative extent (space/volume) occupied by the text and commentary in this order of preference.

The importance of the commentary over the text which may be given in a scattered form or in a smaller type, and the pages of the work (space) provided for the text and commentary would be helpful to decide the main entry in case of doubt.

**21.14 Translations.**

21.14A The main entry of a translation is made under the heading appropriate to the original, and an added entry is made under the heading for the translator, as directed under 21.30 K1.

Koestler, Arthur

Darkness at noon; tr. into Tamil by S. Selvam.

I. Selvam, S. tr.

Omar Khayyam

The Rubaiyat; tr. from the Persian into English by Edward Fitzgerald.

I. Fitzgerald, Edward. tr.

Zola, Emile

Nana; tr. from the French into Hindi by Amar Chand Joshi.

I. Amar Chand Joshi, tr.

If the translation of the original work is in the nature of a free rendering (not literal translation) it is governed by 21.10 as an adaptation.

21.14B A collection of translations by different authors in treated under 21.7 because of its presentation as a collection of independent works, though in translation form. Either this could be entered under the title, if it has a collective title, or under the heading appropriate to the first work, if it has no collective title.

Waley, Arthur, tr. comp.

Translations of Chinese poems.

Yuasuda, Kenneth

Pepper Pod: Classic Japanese poems, together with original Haiku; tr. from the Japanese into English from the 15th century to the present.

These two entries above are examples of translations of various authors' works brought out in collective form, and so treaed under 21.7.

**21.15 Texts published with biographical/critical material.**

21.15A. Make the main entry of a work, in the nature of a biography or critical assessment of the life of another person, as indicated in the chief source of information, under the heading appropriate to the biographer or critic, (vide 21.1-21.7), and provide an added entry under the heading for the person who is the subject of biography.

Gopal, Sarvepalli

Biography of Jawaharlal Nehru: a critical account of his life and work.

I. Jawaharlal Nehru.

(The added entry in this case could be more appropriately provided for in the catalogue, as a subject heading (entry, as the person whose life is told is the subject matter of the work).

**21.16 Art works – Adaptation**

21.16A. Adaptation of art works envisaged in the context of this rule are paintings, engravings, photogrpahs, drawings, sculptures, etc., and any other creative work that is represented in picutre form, e.g., ceramic designs, tapestries, fabrics, etc.

Make the main entry of an adaptation from one medium of the graphic arts to another under the heading for the person responsible for the adaptation, but entry is under its title, if the adapter's name is unknown. Also make a name-title added entry for the original work.

Burton, Alfred

Paintings in oil on canvas of Khajuraho temple sculptures.

Ramakrishna Sastry.

Civilization through the ages in Litho of the bronze images of the South Indian Temples.

21.16 B. Make the main entry of the reproduction of an art work (e.g., photographs, including photomechanical reproduction, or a reproduction of sculpure) under the heading for the original work. Added entry for the person or body responsible for the reproduction is also made.

Ravi Varma.

Original paintings of Hindu Gods and Goddesses; reproductions in colour photography by Siva Raman.

I. Siva Raman.

Frescoe paintings of Amaravati and Ellora caves; reproduced in lithography by Ananda Murthy.

I. Ananda Murthy.

### 21.17 Reproductions of Two or More Art Works

21.17A. Make the main entry of a work consisting of reproductions of the work of an artist, without accompanying text, under the heading for the artist.

Nand Lal Bose.

One hundred original paintings in oil reproduced in water colour with no text.

21.17B. Make the main entry of a work consisting of reproductions of an artist's creative work accompanied by a text about the work/artist/both under the heading appropriate to the text, if the person responsible for the text is represented in the chief source of information, as the author of the work, with an added entry under the heading for the artist. Otherwise the main entry should be made under the artist. In case of doubt, enter under artist. In such a case, provide an added entry under the heading for the person, who is the author of the text, if his name appears in the chief source of information.

*Main entry under author of text*

Bangdel, Lain S.

The early sculptures of Nepal; illus. with 156 photographs of rare and hitherto unknown images.

*Main entry under original artist*

Da Vinci, Leonardo, 1415-1519

The Notebooks; text and drawings representing the genius of Leonardo as painter, sculptor, architect, engineer, inventor; tr. and ed. by Edward Mc Curdy.

I. McCurdy, Edward. tr. and ed.

21.18-21.22 **Musical Works.**

These rules, their scope and application are found hardly applicable to Oriental Musical works, specially Indian. So they are omitted from formal study. However, the need for cataloguing works on Indian music is not over ruled.

Guidance to the cataloguing of Indian Musical works provided under "Special Material" in the [illegible] reasonably comprehensive in dealing with works on Indian Music, and therefore, are retained as such.

The uderlying principles of the A-ACR2 stated above appear to have been formulated only for Western Music, and a glance at the specific rules for the cataloguing of divisions of Western Music would easily reveal the lack of identical features and characteristics between these two kinds of music-Oriental and Occidental. Perhaps, this is an area for the experts in both kinds of music to conduct research and establish identity, if at all it could be located.

The detailed instructions provided for on pages for catalouging Indian Musical Works need little revision at this stage, and can be adopted by libraries for the cataloguing of books, manuscripts, and other documents of this subject.

21.23 **Sound Recordings.**

21.23A Make the main entry of a sound recording of one work (musical compostions, texts, etc.,) under the heading appropriate to that work. Added entries are to be made for the principal performers (singers, readers, instrumental accompanists, orchestra, etc.,), if they are only three. If more than three, make an added entry under the one named first.

The directions in respect of added entries for Indian music, specially Carnatic music needs to be amended, as more than three accomapanists support a singer in several instances, in order to provide an entry for every accompanist to the vocal singer, because each one of them is of equal importance in the concert; e.g. a sound recording of Thiagaraja's kritis, performed by M.S. Subbulakshmi with accompaniments-*violin* by Lal Gudi Jayaraman, *Mridangam* by Murugabhupathy, *Ghatam* by Vinayakram, *Ganjira* by Dakshinamurthy, and *Morsing* by Hariharan would need added entry under each one of them, as no one of them is less improtant than the other. The restriction of three added entries needs to be modified and added entries are directed to be made for all of them.

Thiagraja

Pakkala nilabadi (karaharapriya) sung by M.S. Subbulakshmi, with accompaniments violin by M.S. Gopalkrishanan, mridangam by Murugabhupaty, ghatam by Vinayakram, ganjira by Dakshinamoorty, and Morsing by Hariharan.

I. Subbulakshmi, M.S. *performer*
II. Gopala Krishnan, M.S. *violin*
III. Murugabhupathy. *mridangam*
IV. Vinayarkram. *Ghatam*
V. Dakshinamurthy. *ganjira*
VI. Hariharan. *morsing*

21.23B. Make the main entry of a sound recording consisting of two or more works by the same person (s) or body (bodies) under the heading appropriate to those works. Added entries are made for principal performers, unless there are more than three. If more than three principal performers are there, an added entry for the one named first is made.

Note. In Carnatic music (vocal) not more than two principal performers would be found. It is the same in Hindusthani music (vocal). Chorus music/kavvali is excepted.

Thiagaraja

Pancharatna kritis: sung by

M. Balamurali.

All India Radio
Five orchestral performences;
directed by T.K. Venkatarama Iyer,
and Emani Sankara Sastry.

I. Venkatarama Iyer, T.K.
II. Sankara Sastry, Emani.

Gandhi, Mohandas Karamchand

Sarva Dharama talks: read
by Shiva Sagar Misra,
Sound disc, 30 min.

I. Shiva Sagar Misra

21.23C. Make the main entry of a sound recording containing works by different persons, under the heading for the person or body indicated as principal performer. If more than two or three persons or bodies are stated as principal performers, make the main entry under the heading appropriate to the first one, and added entries for others.

Vasant Kumari, M.L.

Compositions of Muthuswamy Dikshidar, Thiagaraja, and Purandara Dasa.

Sound disc, 60 min. both sides.

21.23D. Make the main entry of a sound recording containing works by different persons or bodies performed by more than three principal performers, or with no principal performer under title.

Pawai Nombu Collection
Thiruppavai, Thiruvenpavai,
and Godastuti devotional songs
specially sung by unmarried girls;
performed by Mani Krishnaswamy,
Rajeswari, A.P. Komala, and D. Swaminathan.
Sound disc – 60 min. 2 sides

21.24. **Collaboration between artist and writer.**

This rule is not to be confused with the rule 21.11A which deals with the work in which the text by its author is supplemented or elucidated by the illustrator, in which case the illustrator is always secondary to the writer of the text, who is responsible for the work, and therefore an added entry is provided for the illustrator.

But there are some works in which the collaboration between the artist and the writer is of equal importance and doubts arise, who between the artist and writer is primarily responsible for the work. The main entry of such works is made under the name of the person given first in the chief source of information, unless the other's name is given greater prominence by the wording or lay out. An added entry is made for the one, who is not considered for main entry.

*Main entry under writer*

Salim Ali
A Guide to Bombay birds; coloured
illus. by Ramakrishnan.

I. Ramakrishnan. *Illus.*

*Main entry under artist*

Mona Kapoor
Paintings of the flower valleys of the Himalaya
mountains; brief notes of botanical importance by
G.K. Randhawa.

I. Randhawa, G.K.

21.25. **Reports of inverviews of exchanges.**

21.25A. Make the main entry of a work in the nature of a report, if it is essentially confined to the words of the person (s) interviewed or of the participants in an exchange (other than the reporter), under the principal participant, first named participant or title as directed in 21.6. An added entry is to be made for the reporter under the heading appropriate to him, if he or she is openly named in the work.

Quasim, S.Z.

Report of an inverview with
S.Z. Qasim, Leader, Antarctic
Expedition, 1982, by A.K.
Chatterjee of The Times of India.

Chatterjee, A.K. *reporter*

Swaminathan, M.S.
Discussion on world rice production between
M.S. Swaminathan and other representatives of rice
producing countires of the world; reported by
Maharaj Singh, 1982.

I. Maharaj Singh, *reporter*

21.25B In case the report of an interview or discussion is in the words of the reporter, make the main entry of such a work, under the heading appropriate to the reporter, and added entries for the other persons involved, if they are not more than three; if more than three, make the added entry under the name of the person given first.

*Main entry under reporter*

Viswanathan, C.G. *reporter*

Summary of the discussions of the Vice-Chancellors and Deans of Indian Agricultural Universities at the first Workshop on Agricultural Universities of India on Teaching and Teaching Aids; presided by Dean W. Lambert of Illinois University.

I. Lambert, William

21.26 **Spirit Communications.**

Make the main entry of a work in the nature of a Communication presented as having been received from a spirit under the heading for the spirit (22.14), and give an added entry for the medium or other person who records the Communication.

Jeevan Mukta Yatindra Swamy
Past and future life of human beings, metaphysical concepts communicated while in a trance; recorded by Sivananda Saraswati.

I. Sivananda Saraswati

21.27. **Academic Disputations.**

Make the main entry of a work, in the nature of a written document (thesis) for defence in an academic disputation (according to the custom prevailing in the universities before the nineteenth century, and followed in some universities thereafter) under the heading praeses (faculty moderator) unless the authorship of the respondent, defender, etc., can be established. Make an added entry under the heading for whichever of the praeses, etc., is not chosen for main entry It is optional (better) to add the designations-praeses, respondent defendent, etc., as appropriate to the heading. No added entry is made for a person designated as opponent.

Bisheswar Dayal. *Respondent.*

Solid state physics; Disputation (viva-voce) recorded on Ph. D. thesis of the respondent; praeses: C.V. Raman.

I. Raman, C.V. *praeses.*

If no one is named as praeses, enter under (in the order of preference) (1) The proponent, (2) The defendent or respondent.

21.28 **Related Works**

21.28A Scope: the following varieties of separately catalogued works bearing a relation to another work are dealt with:

Continuations, Sequels

Supplements

Indexes

Concordances

Incidental music to dramatic works

Cadenzas

Scenarios, Screenplays, etc.

Choreographies

Librettos and other texts set to music

Subseries

Special numbers of serials

Collections of extracts from serials

Work that has only a subject relationship with another work should not be considered to fall within the scope of this rule.

Particular types of relationship (adaptation, revision, etc.,) are dealt with elsewhere (21.8-21.27).

21.28B. Make the main entry of a related work under its own heading (personal author, corporate body or title) according to the relevant rule (21). An added entry (name-title, or title as appropriate) is made for the work to which it is related.

Storer, T.I.

Laboratory manual for the
text 'General Zoology' by T.I. Storer.
I. Storer, T.I. : General zoology.

Bartlett, J.

Complete concordance to dramatic
works of Shakespeare.
I. Shakespeare, William

Viswa Bharati, qly.

Abanindranath and his paintings, special supplement as v. 41 of the quarterly.
I. Abanindranath: Paintings

Willing, E.P.

Index to American Catholic
pamphlets.
I. American Catholic pamphlets.

Cumulative Book Index: a world list of books in the English language...supplementing the Unitd States Catalog.

I. The United States catalog

Angel, J.L.

Troy: the human remains.
Supplementary monograph to Cincinnati University: Troy excavations, 1932-1938; ed. by C.W. Blagen and others.
I. Cincinnati University: Troy excavations, 1932-1938.

21.29. Added Entries-General rule and its sub-rules 21.29A to 21.29G are in the form of guide lines to the provision of added entries. These directions could be seen in chapter 27 of this work, and the cataloguers would find that coverage is ample enough to direct them appropriately in the making of added entries.

21.30. **Specific rules for added entries.**

The sub-rules 21.30A to 21.30K2 provide directions on the basis of their categories and characteristics for two or three, and more than three persons or bodies, collaborators, writers, editors, and compilers, corporate bodies, related persons or bodies, related works, titles, translators, who or which should or should not be considered apporpriate for an added entry. These instructions together with specimen types as examples are also given in the same chapter 27.

21.30L. *Series -- Added entry.*

Directions to make a series added entry (more liberally) separately for each work of the series catalgued, and a general series entry for all works of the series in a restricted manner are given in and chapter 30 of this work, wherein a full and detailed treatment has been provided, which hold good even now.

Several cataloguers would prefer more a series entry than an added entry under the name of the series as heading for each work of the series catalogued.

Users' reaction to the change adopted in A-ACR2 is yet to be tested, before one could positively state that the change is more effective in the retrieval of information.

21.30M. Analytical entries are again a form of added entries to bring out to the usesr's notice information, which has not been fully covered by the description of bibliographic details in the main entry. A full and detailed study of analytical entries are provided for in chapter 29 of this book.

21.31 – 21.36C9 **Legal Publications**

These rules cover cerain legal publications, and as a uniform policy the scope of such works is stated in the beginning of each main rule followd by specific rules. Cataloguers are directed to refer chapter 23 dealing with 'Legal Publications' in order to observe the relationship, identical treatment, and differences in the procedure as well, between A-ACR1 and A-ACR2.

Administrative regulations having the force of law 21.32;

Constitutions and Charters, 21.33;

Court rules, 21.34;

Treaties and similar formal agreeemnts are dealt with under a separate rule, 21.35;

Apply 21.13 to annotated editions of laws and commentaries.

Adoption of 'Uniform Titles' has superceded the practice of providing sub-heads under the heading of the main entry for legal publications/works, e.g. India. Laws, statutes, etc.,
Tamil Nadu. Ordinances, local law.: France. Laws. will now be the name of the jurisdiction where the laws are in force followed by the 'Uniform title, e.g. France

Laws

The option to follow this change or to continue the previous practice as in A-ACR1 is a sound decision of the A-ACR2 Joint Steering Committee.

21.31.B. *Laws of modern Jurisdictions*

21.31.BI. *Laws governing one jurisdiction.*

Make the main *entry* for laws under the *heading* for the jurisdiction governed by them. Provide added entries under the heading for persons and corporate bodies (other than legislative bodies) responsible for the compilation and issue of the *laws*. Add a uniform title as directed in 25.15A to the main entry. Apply 25.15A1 for collections of laws and 25.15A2 for single laws.

*Main entires. Examples.*

(1) A collection of laws, e.g.

India. Laws, etc.

A collection of civil acts governing
procedure in civil law courts of India; comp.
by Sanjiva Rao.

I. Sanjiva Rao. Comp.

(2) A collection of local laws, e.g.

Tamil Nadu Laws, etc.

The Local self government and the
Panchayat Raj act, 1950-1980; comp. and
edited by Sundaram Iyengar.

I. Sundaram Iyengar. comp.

(Make 'see reference' from Madras to Tamil Nadu)

(3) A collection of local rules and regulations, e.g.
New Delhi Laws, etc.

Traffic regulations and rules approved
by the New Delhi Municipal Board from 1970-1980.

(4) Laws relating to particular department of
government, e.g.

Uttar Pradesh Laws codes
The Education code of Uttar Pradesh;
revised and brought to date; annotated
by Bhairavanth Jha.

I. Bhairavanath Jha. annot.

21.31B2. *Laws governing more than one jurisdiction.*

Make the main entry of the compilation of Laws governing more than one jurisdiction as a collection applying 21.7. Added entries are to be made under the heading for the jurisdiction governed, if limited to two or three. If more than three, make an added entry under the heading for the first one named in the chief source of information. If all the laws are enacted by a single jurisdiction, make an added entry under the heading for the enacting jurisdiction. Add a uniform title as directed in 25.15A to the added entries.

*Main entry under title, e.g.*

Citizenship laws governing Goa, Pondicherry, and Manipur enacted by Indian Parliament; comp. by Bernard Pinto.

I. Goa: Laws, etc.: Citizenship laws. II. Pondicherry: Laws, etc.: Citizenship laws. III. Manipur: Laws, etc.: Citizenship laws. IV. India: Laws, etc.: Citizenship laws of uninon territories, Goa, Pondicherry, and Manipur, enacted by parliament.

21.31B3. *Bills and drafts of legislation*

Make the main entry of a legislative bill under the heading for the legislative body (24.21). Other drafts of legislation are treated as instructed in 21. I to 21.7 under the heading for personal or corporate author of the draft of an act.

India. *Parliament. Lok Sabha*
Bills and drafts of legislation,
42nd Amendment bill to the
constitution of India.

Tamil Nadu. *Legislative Assembly*
Bills and drafts of legislation
A Draft of law on religious endowments
in the state.

Ramesh Bhandari
A Bill to abolish Capital
Punishment placed before the Lok
Sabha for consideration.

21.31C. *Ancient Laws. Certain Medieval Laws, etc.*

Make the main entry for laws of ancient jurisdictions, laws of non-Western jurisdictions prior to the adoption of legislative institutions based on western models; customary laws, tribal laws, etc. under (in the order of preference).

(1) a uniform title consisting of the title by which the law or the early compilation of law is known (25.15B),
(2) the title proper of the work being catalogued.

Manu Dharma Sastra
[Laws, etc.]

The Code of ancient laws (Manu Smriti) governing the society of Arya Varta; comm. on the text by P.V. Kane.

I. Panduranga Vaman Kane. comm.

Hammurabi

[Laws, etc.]
Laws of ancient Babylonian Empiure on the rights and duties of citizens, professional ethics, trade, etc.

Marumakkal Thayam

[Laws, etc.]
laws of inheritance of property in
Malayalam from ancient times to date;
ed. with notes by A. Pandalai.

I. Pandalai, A. ed.

**21.32. Administrative regulations, etc., promulgated by government agencies.**

21.32A1. Make the main entry of regulations etc., issued by government agencies or agents authorised by law, under the heading for the agency. If the regulations are issued by an agency other than the promulagating agency, make an added entry under the heading for the issuing agency. If the regulations are derived from a particular law, make an added entry under the heading and unifom title (25.15A) for that law.

India. Comptroller of Imports and Exports.

[Imports and exports Policy, India.]

Handbook of Import policy of the government of India, for the fiscal year ending 1988.

India. Ministry of Commerce: Imports and Exports Policy.

21.32A2. Make the main entry of a work, containing a law or laws, and the regulations, etc., derived from it, if published together, under the heading appropriate to whichever is mentioned first in the title elements. Provide an added entry under the heading for the other. If only one, either laws or regulations, is mentioned on the title page, make the main entry under the heading for the one mentioned, and an added entry for the other. In case of ambiguity or inadequacy of information, make the main entry under the heading for the law or laws, with an added entry for the regulations.

India. Ministry of Finance.

[Laws, etc.]
Currency laws of India, and regulations governing the foreign exchange of money.

I. India. Ministry of Finance: Regulations governing foreign exchange of money.

21.32B If administrative regulations, etc., that are laws in the jurisdiction, make the main entry for it as instructed in 21.31. Provide added entries under the heading for government agencies or agents promulagating or issuing them. In case the regulations derive from a particular law, make an added entry under the heading and uniform title for that law as instructed in 25.15.A.

Madras City.

[Laws, etc.]
Bye-laws for the regulation of motor vehicles in the city of Madras and sub-urban areas including a code of regulations for the drivers.

I. India. [Laws, etc.]: Motor Vehicles Act, 1972.

21.32C. A collection of regulations enacted by more than one agency or agent is to be treated as a collection as directed in 21.7.

Krishanaswamy Rao. *Comp.*

Regulations promulgated by the Town Planning department and the Traffic departmemt of the city of Madras for information of the city population.

I. Madras. City Corporation:
Regulations.

21.33. **Constitution, Charters, and other Fundamental Laws**

21.33A Make the main entry of the Constitution, Charter, or other fundamental law of a jurisdiction, under the heading for that jurisdiction : amendments to the constiututíon are treated likewise.

If the document is issued by any jurisdiction other than the one governed by it, provide an added entry under the heading for the jurisdiction issuing it. Add the appropriate uniform title, as directed in 25.15A to the added entry, if the document is a law.

India

[Constitution]

The Constitution of India adopted by
the Constituent Assembly in November 1949.

India

[Laws, etc.]
The Indian Independence Act, 1947, passed by the parliament of the United Kingdom.

I. United Kingdom [Laws, etc.]: The Indian Independence Act, 1947.

India

[Laws, etc.]
Charter granted by H.M. the Queen Victoria to the governor of the East India Company.

I. United Kingdom. Sovereign (Victoria): Charters

21. 34 **Court Rules**

21.34A. Make the main entry of court rules governing a single court (regardless of their official nature e.g. laws, administrative regulations) under the heading for that court. If the rules are laws, make an added entry under the heading for the jurisdiction enacting the law, and add a uniform title to the added entry. Make an added entry under the the heading for the agency or agent promulagating the court rules.

India. Supreme Court.

Court rules
Rules of practice and procedure of the Supreme Court of India, issued by the Registrar of the Court.

I. India. Supreme Court. Registrar.

21.34B. Make the main entry of a collection of rules governing more than one court of single jurisdiction, but enacted as laws of that jurisdiction as directed in 21.31. Enter all other such collections of court rules, under the heading for the agency or agent promulgating them.

Provide added entries under the headings for the courts governed by the rules, if there are two or three. If the rules are applicable to more than three courts, make an added entry under the heading for the first one named in the chief source of information.

Uttar Pradesh. High Court of Judicature.

Rules of conduct and procedure of business in all the district judges' courts, and other sub-ordinate courts – Munsiffs', City Hony. Magistrates', etc.

I. Uttar Pradesh. District judges Courts.
II. Uttar Pradesh. Munsiffs Courts.

21.34C. Make the main entry of a collection of court rules that are the laws of more than one Jurisdiction, or that are promulagated by more than one agency or agent as a collection. (Follow 21.7.) Make an added entry under the heading for an openly named corporate body involved in the compilation, unless it functions solely as a publisher.

Uttar Pradesh. Bar Council. *comp.*

A Collection of select civil laws of the Centre and State legislatures, and rules of procedure in civil courts, promulgated by the High Court of Judicature, Uttar Pradesh, brought to date.

I. Uttar Pradesh. High Court of Judicature.

21.35 **Treaties, Inter-governmental Agreement, etc.**

21.35A. International Treaties, etc.

21.35A1. Make the main entry of a treaty or any other formal agreement between two or three national governments under (in this order of preference).

(1) the heading for the government on one side, if it is the only one on that side, and there are two governments on the other;
(2) the heading for the government whose catalogue entry heading (14.3E.) is first in English alphabet

Provide added entries for other government(s), and give a uniform title (25.16BI.) to the main and added entries.

Germany

[Treaties, etc.]

Conventions between the governments of the United States of America, the United Kingdom of Gt. Britain and Northern Ireland of the one part and the Federal Republic of Germany of the other part with accompanying instruments. (Bonn, 26th May 1952)

I. United States: Treaties, etc.
II. United Kingdom: Treaties, etc.

China

[Treaties. etc.]
Agreement between the kingdom of Nepal and the Peoples Republic of China regarding road construction on North-East border, signed in June 1952

I. Nepal : Treaties, etc.

21.35A2. Make the main entry of a treaty or any other formal agreement between more than three national governments under title either the title proper or uniform title as instructed in 25.16B2. Make an added entry under the the heading for the home government (i.e. the government of the cataloguing agency) if it is a signatory. Provide an added entry under the heading for any other government publishing the item being catalogued, if that government is a signatory. An added entry is to be made under the heading for the government named first in the chief source of information, if it is neither the home government nor the publishing government. If the treaty is the product of an international conference, make an added entry under the heading for the conference. Add a uniform title (25.16BI.) to the added entries for parties to the government.

India

[Treaties, etc.]

Agreement between Australia, Burma, India, Indonesia, Singapore, and Sri Lanka on keeping the Indian Ocean a peace zone, arrived in 1981. Colombo, 1981.

I. Sri Lanka. [Treaties, etc.]
II. Australia. [Treaties, etc.]
III. Indonesia. [Treaties, etc.]
IV. Singapore. [Treaties, etc.]

Charter of the Book, (1972)

Agreement adopted by the International Community of Booksellers' Association, Confederation of societies of Authors and Composers, Federation of Documentation, Federation of Library Associations, Federation of Tanslators, PEN., and Publishers Association at Brussels, 1971, to implement Books for all promulagated by UNESCO in the International Book year. Paris, 1972.

(make added entries for participating bodies, as directed in 21.35A2.

21.35B. *Agreements contracted by international inter-government bodies*

Make the main entry as directed in 21.35 A of an agreement between an international inter-government body and one or more (1) other international inter-government bodies or (2) national governments.

India

[Treaties, etc.]

Agreement between the government of India and the World Bank on Tarai Development Corporation, August 10, 1967.

I. World Bank. [Treaties, etc.]

Make the main entry of an agreement between an international and inter-government body and one or more (1) jurisdiction other than national governments, or (2) other corporate bodies. In these cases, no uniform title is to be given for any entry.

International Bank for reconstruction and development.

Loan agreement with Tata Iron and Steel Company for the development of the steel plant, February 20, 1968.
I. Tata Iron and Steel Company.

21.35D. *Agreements contracted by jurisdictions below the national level.*

21.35D1. Make the main entry of an agreement between two or more jurisdictions below the national level, or between a national government and one or more jurisdictions within its country as instructed in 21.6C.

Tamil Nadu.
[Treaties, etc.]
Momorandum of agreement between the government of Tamil Nadu and the central government of India on implementing prohibition laws in the state of Tamil Nadu, 1972.

I. India. [Treaties, etc.]

Karnataka.
[Treaties, etc.]
Joint agreement between the state of Karnataka and Tamil Nadu on sharing of Kavery river water, 1978.
Tamil Nadu. [Treaties, etc.]

21.35E. *Protocols, amendments, etc.*

Make the main entry of a separately published protocol, amendment, extension or other agreement ancilliary to a treaty, etc., under the heading for the basic agreement. Give uniform title (25.16B3).

A treaty, etc. which has been generally revised is considered as an independent work. So an added entrty is made for the original treaty revised, if the two headings differ; add a uniform title as appropriate.

United States.
[Treaties, etc.]
North Atlantic treaty, (1949).

U.S. convention on relations with the
Federal Republic of Germany and protocol
to the North Atlantic treaty.

I. North Atlantic Treaty, 1949.

India
[Treaties, etc.]
A revised agreement between India and Nepal
on the Military stations in the border, 1969.
I. Nepal. [Treaties, etc.]

21.35F1. *Collections*

21.35F1. A collection of treaties limited to the same two parties is entered in the same way as for a single one between them. If a compiler is openly named, make an added entry under the heading for the compiler.

India
[Treaties, etc.]
A collection of treaties between India and
the U.S.S.R. on economic cooperation signed
during the period 1960-1980.
I. U.S.S.R. [Treaties, etc.]

21.35F2. In the case of a collection of treaties signed by one party and two or more other parties, the main entry is made under the heading for the one party. Added entries are made under the headings for the other parties, if only two. Adopt a uniform titile for both main and added entries. If there is an openly named compiler to the collection , make an added entry under the heading appropriate to it.

India
[Treaties, etc.]
A collection of international agreements and treaties contracted
between India and France and Italy on cultural exchange of persons,
economic and technical subjects during 1970-1980; compiled by the
editor Foreign Trade Review, 1981.
I. France. [Treaties, etc.]

II. Italy. [Treaties, etc.]
III. Editor, Foreign Trade Review.

21.35F3. All other collections of treaties are treated as genereal collections dealt with in 21.7.

21.36. **Court decisions, cases, etc.**

21.36A. *Law Reports*

21.36A1. *Reports of one court*

Make the main entry of law reports of a single court, that are not ascribed to a reporter/reporters by name under

1. the heading for the court, if issued by or under the authority of the court;

   or

2. title, if they are not so issued.

An added entry is called for an openly named editor or compiler. Also an added entry is required, under the heading for the publisher, provided the responsibility is much more than publishing only.

Uttar Pradesh. High Court of Judicature.
Indian law reports: Allahabad series, 1970; ed. by Ramesh Chandra.
I. Ramesh Chandra. ed.

Important reports of cases of the
Supreme Court of India, 1981;
compiled by the Calcautta Eastern
Law Company.

I. India. Supreme Court.
II. Eastern Law Company, Calcutta.

Make the main entry of report of one court ascribed to a reporter (s) by name under the heading for the court, or under the heading for the reporter, or first named reporter, according to whichever is used as the basis for accepted legal citation practice in the country where the court is located. If that practice is unknown, or not possible to determine, enter under:

(1) the heading for the court, if the reports are issued by or under the authority of the court;

or

(2) the heading for the reporter or the first name reporter, if they are not so issued.

Make an added entry under the heading for the court or the reporter, whichever is not chosen for the heading for the main entry. Make an added entry under the heading for the publisher, if its responsibility extends more than that of publication.

India. Supreme Court.

Reports of cases filed by the state of Tamil Nadu for decision-during 1970-1971; reported by Anand Agarwal. Madras, Law Journal Press.

(Cited as Supreme court decisions in legal practice)

I. Anand Agarwal. reporter

21.36A 2. *Reports of more than one court*

Enter reports of more than one court, under the heading for the reporter, for the main entry, if responsible for all the cases reported: if there is more than one reporter, follow the instructions in 21.6.

If the reporter (s) is not responsible for all the reports, make the main entry under the title; provide an added entry under the heading for the reporter named first in the chief source of information.

Make added entries under the heading for the courts, if there are two or three. If more than three courts are involved, an added entry under the heading for the court mentioned first in the chief source of information is called for.

Editor or compiler if openly mentioned, or a corporate body involved in the publication, unless its function is limited to publishing only, are provided added entries.

***Main entry under reporter***

Anant Lal Sharma. *reporter*

Reports of election cases adjudicated in the High Court of Judicature, Madhya Pradesh argued, and decided on appeal in the Supreme Court of India, 1968, with notes by the publisher. Bhopal, Central Law House, 1970.

I. Madhya Pradesh. High Court of Judicature.
II. India. Supreme Court.
III. Central Law House, Bhopal.

*Main entry under title as the reporter is not responsible for all the reports*

Cases on Indian Income Tax law, decided by the High Courts of India, Burma, and the Privy Council, with select English cases, 1937; reported by A.N. Aiyar.

I. Aiyar, A.N. reporter

21.36.B. *Citations and Digests, etc.*

Make the main entry of citations to digests and indexes, of court reports under the heading for the person responsible for them, if he is openly named; otherwise under title. An added entry for an openly named corporate body is made, if it functions beyond the publishing responsibility.

Narayana Aiyar, A.
Indian Sales Tax digest; being a digest of the cases on Indian Sales Tax law decided by the High courts and Supreme Court. 1975.

General Index to the Supreme Court reports, 1978.
Calcutta, Eastern Law House, 1979.
(Index entries made and compiled by the Eastern Law House)

I. Eastern Law House, Calcutta.

21.36C. *Particular Cases*

21.36.C1. *Proceedings in the first instance. Criminal proceedings.*

Make the main entry of the official proceedings and records of criminal trials, impeachment, court martials, etc., under the heading for the person or body prosecuted. In case more than one person or body is prosecuted, follow the directions in 21.6. Optionally, the appropriate legal designation (e.g. defendent, libelle) to headings of persons or bodies prosecuted may be added at the end. Provide an added entry under the heading for the court or other adjudicating body, and also under the heading for an openly named reporter. No added entry is required for the jurisdiction launching the prosecution.

Nathuram Godse, *defendent*
The trial of Nathuram Godse for the assasination of Mahatma Gandhi before the Special Magistrates Court, New Delhi; reported by Upendra Bajpai.

I. Delhi. Special Magistrate's Court.
II. Upendra Bajpai. reporter

Karanjia, B.K. *libelle*
Report of the trial of B.K. Karanjia, editor, Blitz Weekly in the Bombay, Presidency Magistrate's Court.

1. Bombay. Presidency Magistrate Court

21.36C2. *Proceedings in the first instance: other proceedings*

Make the main entry of the Official proceedings and records of civil and non-criminal proceedings in the first instance (including election cases) under the heading for the person or body taking the action. If more than one person or body is responsible for the action, follow the procedure in 21.6c. Added entries for persons or bodies on the opposing side are made under the heading appropriate, if they are limited to three; if more, an added entry for the one mentioned as first is made. It is optional to add the appropriate designations (e.g. plaintiff, complainant, contestant, defendent, respondent, contestee) to the headings for the parties. Also, the court of other adjudicating body is provided an added entry. If a reporter is openly named, an added entry is made under the heading for the reporter.

Bagchi, A.P. *plaintiff*
The case of A.P. Bagchi versus Hrishikesh Sanyal and others in the High Court of Allahabad.
I. Hrishikesh Sanyal. *defendent*
II. Uttar pradesh. High Court of Judicature.

Rajnarain. *contestant*
The parliamentary election suit of the Rae Bareilley constituency, brought against Indira Gandhi before the high Court of Judicature, Allahabad; reported by Naresh Jain, 1977.
I. Indira Gandhi. *contestee*
II. Uttar Pradesh. High Court of Judicatue.
III. Naresh Jain. *reporter*

21.36C3. *Appeal proceedings*

Make the main entry of official proceedings and records of appeal proceedings in the same way as the proceedings in the first instance. It is *optional* to add the appropriate designations (e.g. defendent; appellee, defendent-appelllant).

Bagchi, A.P. *complainant-appellee*
Appeal to the Supreme Court of India, against Hrishikesh Sanyal (*defendent – appellant*)

1. India. Supreme Court.

21.36C4. *Indictments are entered as instructed in 22.36C1.*

21.36C5. *Charges to juries*

Make the main entry of a charge to a jury under the heading for the court. Provide an added entry under the heading for the judge delivering the charge. Make added entries for the first named party on each side, except for the jurisdiction in cases prosecuted by the jurisdiction. *Optionally* add legal designations, as stated in 21.36C1 to 21.46C3, to the added entry headings.

Delhi High Court of Judicature.
Charge of S.K. Kumar (ex. Judge)
against Justice Prakash Narain
Chief Justice, Delhi High Court, for defamation
on the Alleged bribery levelled. against him.
I Kumar. S.K. plaintiff-appellant.
II. Prakash Narain. Defendent.

21.36C6 *Judicial decisions*

Make the main entry of a judgement or other decision of a court in a case under the heading for the court. The first named party on each side is given an added entry, except for the jurisdiction in cases prosecuted by the jurisdiction. It is optional to add the legal designations, as appropriate to the headings.

India. Supreme Court.
Freedom of the press, in the case against the
daily Indian Express brought before it by Ram Krishna
Seth, and the court's decision.
I. Indian Express. *defendent-appellant*
II. Ram Krishna Seth. *plaintiff-appellant*

21.36C7. *Judicial opinions*

Make the main entry of the opinion of a judge under the heading for the judge. The first named party on each side, except for the jurisdiction in cases prosecuted by the jurisdiction, is given an added entry under the appropriate heading. It is optional to add the legal designations to the headings for parties to the action. Make an added entry for the lawyer concerned.

Tuljapurkar, A.N. Judge
Dissenting opinion in the case
Independence of judiciary over the Parliament
(legislature) and the Executive; argued by advocate
S.K. Garg on behalf of the Bar Council before the

Constitution Bench of the Supreme Court, opposing the stand of the government of India

I. Garg, S.K.

21.36C8. *Records of one party*

Make the main entry of a brief, plea, or other formal record of one party to a case under the heading for that party. If the proceedings of the trial would not be entered under the name of that party, make an added entry under the heading for the other party. It is optional to add entry under the heading for the other party. It is optional to add legal designations to the headings for the parties to the action; also provide an added entry to the lawyer concerned.

Bagchi, A.P. *respondent-appellant*
Brief of appellant in the case of A.P. Bagchi *vs* Hrishikesh Sanyal and others, in the High Court of Judicature, Allahabad; attorney for appellant G.N. Kunzru.

I. Gopinath Kunzru. *attorney*

The court room argument presented by a lawyer is entered under the heading for the lawyer; an added entry under the heading for the party represented is also made. If that party is not the one, under which the trial proceedings would be entered, make an added entry under the heading for the other party; *optionally*, add legal designation to the headings for the parties to the action.

Gopinath Kunzru.
The argument in the case Bagchi vs Hrishikesh Sanyal and others in the High Court of Judicature, Allahabad, 1948.

I. Bagchi, A.P. *plaintiff*

21.36C9. *Collections*

Make the main entry of a collection of the official proceedings or records of trials as a collection according to 21.7. Added entries for persons or bodies who are parties to the trials, if not more than three, are made. It is optional to add legal designations to the parties.

**Certain Religious Publications**

21.37. **Sacred Scriptures**

Follow the method and treatment of Sacred Scriptures, specially Hindu, and other Oriental ones, as stated on pages 302-307

21.38. **Omitted, as it would not apply to Indian theological structure.**

21.39. **Liturgical Works.**

Follow the directions for dealing with Liturgical works given on pages 302-307

# 27

# A A C R 2 1988 Revision: Choice of Access Points To Name Headings and Uniform Titles

In AACR 2 1988 Revision, descriptive cataloguing has been assigned chapters 1-13 of Pt. I, while choice of access points to works and names of persons as authors occupies Pt. II. With regard to main and added entries, reference may be made to the previous chapter and chapter three dealing with 'Catalogue Codes'. In this chapter, form of name headings and uniform titles (rules 22-25), references (rule 26 has been studied. It will be seen that chapters 14-20 have been left out blank, perhaps for future use to accomodate any changes without dislocating the preceding and succeeding chapters. As usual general rules precede specific or special rules. When there is no specific rule for a specific problem, the more general rule is to be applied.

It is important to know that all rules in Pt. II apply to works, and not to physical descriptions of those works. All library (reading) material, irrespective of the medium in which they are published, serial or non-serial in nature are to be catalogued as in rules in Pt.II. Rule 23 governs the entry of geographic names or their inclusion as a part of headings. In rules 22, 23, and 24 additions to names used as headings are dealt with. Wherever needed, examples and illustrations under the rules are given with a view to their elucidation and application in libraries. Guidance is provided for making 'see x' and 'see also xx' references under rule 26.

## HEADINGS FOR PERSONS

After determining the responsibility for a work as to 'who is the author of this work' it is not only reasonable but also essential to decide 'under what part of his or her name the heading should be made. The entry element followed by other parts of a name are entered in direct order (as found on the title page of his/her work. Reference sources may also provide useful guidance.

In order to guide cataloguers, AACR 2 1988 revision provides detailed rules governing the choice of names, entry element 22.1 to 22.3, additions to names 22.4 to 22.11, additions to distinguish identical names 22.17 to 22.20. This is followed by special rules for names in certain languages 22.21 to 22.28.

## CHOICE OF NAME

### 22.1. General Rule

22.1A The name by which he or she is commonly known should be the basis for choice of the name of an author. This may be the real name of a person or pseudonym, title of nobility, nickname, initials, or other appellation. A roman numeral associated with a given name, (as for example-Popes, Royalty, and Ecclesiastics) should be considered as part of a name, e.g. Pope John II; King Edward VII; Ruricius I, Bishop of Limoges, Gracias, Cardinal I of India; Shakespeare, William, and not the Bard of Avon.

22.1B Authority or sources for determining the common name of a person for adoption in the heading are:

1. Works of the person, issued in his or her language,
2. When the person is non-verbal as painter or sculptor or is not known primarily as an author, the reference sources issued in his or her language, or country of residence or activity. Even books and articles written about a person may also be referred to. e.g. for 1. refer Cambridge History of English literature; Who's who in English literature. for 2. refer any book on Indian Art.

22.1C. Include any titles of nobility or terms of honour, (xx) 22.12 or words in phrases (xx 22.B and 22.15) that commonly appear in association with the names either wholely or in part. Guidance for other terms in association with the name (x 22.19B,) e.g. Mother Teresa, Sister Nivedita, Duke of Wellington.

22.1D2 Hyphenated Names. Retain hyphens between given names, if they are used by the bearer of the name; e.g. Sun-Yat Sen; but omit a hyphen that joins one of a person's forename to the surname; e.g. Lucien Grausc, which appears as Lucian-grausc. The entry would be only Grausc.

22.2. **Choice among Different Names**

22.2A. *Predominant Name*

22.2A1. If a person is known by more than one name, choose one of them by which he is commonly known or referred to. Otherwise, choose one name or form of name in the following order:

1. the name appearing most frequently in one's works;
2. the name appearing most frequently in Reference Sources;
3. the latest name used by the writer.

This rule stands comparison with Rule No, 41 of 1967 Code; e.g. Bertrand Russell, not Earl Russell

22.2B. *Pseudonyms*

22.2B 1. One pseudonym. If all the works of one person are issued under one form of pseudonym, choose it for the author heading. In case his real name is known, make a x reference from this to the chosen pseudonym; e.g. enter Twain, Mark and refer by a x reference from his real name Clemens Samuel Langhorne. This is the same procedure laid down in 42A pseudonyms in AACR 1967.
22.2B2. (Separate Bibliographic Entities) e.g. Fiction, poetry, drama, essays, etc., If a writer uses one form of pseudonym for each type of works, choose that form of heading for all works in that group.
Make xx references to link all the different forms of name (entry) adopted.

This procedure results in scattering the same person's works, and leaves in doubt, when different groups should be overlooked, and only one form of pseudonym adopted for all his works.

22.2C. *Change of Name*

22.2C1. If a person (not using pseudonym) has changed his or her name, choose the latest form of name used by him, or her, unless he/she

is positively better known by earlier form(s) of his/her name. This procedure will also apply to the choice and entry of nobility.
e.g. Muhammad Ali, refer from Cassius Clay (x) to the changed name. Disraeli, Benjamin, (better known earlier name.), so refer from Beaconsfield, Earl of (x) to earlier name. This direction is also found in Rule No. 41 of AACR 1967.

## 22.3 Choice among Different Forms of the Same Name

### 22.3A. *Fullness*

22.3A1. Among varying forms of fullness, choose the form that is commonly found on the title pages of an author's works. Make references, if necessary.

e.g. Enter Dickens, Charles
Refer x Dickens Charles John Huffam

Enter Valera, Juan
Refer x Valera y Aleala Galiano Juan
x Galiano, Juan Valeray Aleala

If no one form predominates, choose the latest form. If doubtful regarding the latest, choose the fullest form.

### 22.3B. *Language*

22.3B1. If more than one language is used by persons for the name choose the form corresponding to the language of most of his works.

e.g. Enter Mikes, George
Not Mikes, Gyorgy
Tolstoy, Leo
Not Tolstoy, Count Leo

22.3B3. Also adopt the English form of a person's name and refer from the forms in Latin and Greek.

e.g. Enter Horace
Not Quintus, Horatius Flaccus

Enter St. Francis of Assisi
Not San Francesco of Assissi

22.3C. *Names written in non-Roman Script*

22.3C1. Persons entered under given name. Choose the form of name, that has been well established in English language reference sources for a person entered under a given name and whose name is in a language written in non-roman script. In case of different forms, choose the one that is most commonly used in reference sources.

Enter Homer
Refer x Horatius
Enter Ramachandran, P.S.
Not P.S. Ramachandran
Refer x Iramachandiran, P.S.

Enter Confucius
Refer from x Kung-tzu

22.3C2. Non-roman surnames. Persons whose surnames are in non-roman script should be romanised by adopting language schedules;
e.g. Enter Nasser, Gamal Abdel
Not Nasir, Jamal Abd al

Enter Dayan, Moshe
Not Dayan, Mosheh

ENTRY ELEMENT OF THE HEADING

22.4 General Rule.

If a person's name consists of several parts, choose that part of the name adopted in alphabetical lists (like Who's Who, and not Telephone Directories, and similar publications) in the person, language, country of residence, activity. In implementing this rule, directions in rules 22.5- 22.9 should be followed.

22.4B1. Order of elements. If the entry element is the first one, enter the name in direct order/title page order.

Enter Rama Narayana Sarma

22.4B2. When the first element is a surname, enter under that part followed by a comma.

e.g. Sarvepalli Radhakrishnan
Entry would be Sarvepalli, Radhakrishnan

This rule is inconsistent with the rule of Predominant/most commonly known forms. Further, being an Indic name, the rational approach is to enter under the given name or forename by which people ask for or search the author's works under Radhakrishnan and not under Sarvepalli. Choosing Radhakrishanan as entry element is most rational and in conformity with the rules for the entry of Indic names, which provide for a few exceptions of Indic writers who follow the Western practice of adopting the surname/the last element in the name as the choice for entry in the heading.

22.4B3. If the entry element is other than the first, enter under that element followed by the preceding elements after a comma.

e.g. Robert Hammersmith
  Enter Hammersmith, Robert

The entry under *surname*, which usually is the last part of the name of Christian/Western writers has been followed in the earlier editions of the code. Refer Rule 45.3 (1967 Code)

22.4B4 The entry of Noblemen are to be made under the title, which is generally a popular name. In this case the preceding parts are given in direct order.

e.g. C.C. Bingham, 2nd Viscount Mersey
  enter Mersey, C.C. Bingham 2nd Viscount
  refer x Bingham, C.C. 2nd Viscount Mersey

There is nothing new in the amplification. See AACR 2 1967 Rule 41.

22.5 **Entry Under Surname**

22.5A. *General Rule*

22.5A1. When a person's name consists of a surname and other elements/only a surname, enter under the surname. Exceptions to the procedure are dealt with in rule 22.6, 22.20, 22.28.

e.g. Edward Fitzgerald
  Enter Fitzgerald, Edward    enter Edwin, Arnold
  (the title page order being
  Arnold Edwin)

It is very rarely that a surname is stated by an initial with one or more elements of the name preceding it. In such cases, enter under initial with one or more elements of the name preceding it. In such cases, enter under initial and after a comma give forenames in direct order.

e.g. Jeoffrey M.
enter M., Jeoffrey

This form of entry under initial seems peculiar and practical utility of reader approach to the initial is doubtful or very less.
22.5B1 This rule of entry of a supposed surname, in the absence of a real surname as an element of the person's name seems too artificially designed. There is nothing to indicate the cataloguer, if a real surname is present/not. It seems more sensible to enter a name under the most commonly known element, irrespective of it being a given name/surname.

| e.g. Daniel Joseph | Enter Joseph, Daniel |
|---|---|
| Muhammad Ali | Enter Ali, Muhammad |

22.5C. *Compound Surnames*

22.5C1 Preliminary rule
Compound surnames, i.e. two or more proper names, and names that may or may not contain compound surnames are dealth with under the following rules. Refer from the part of compound surnames not chosen for entry.

e.g. T. Quiller-Couch
Enter Quiller-Couch, T.

e.g. David Lloyd George
Enter Lloyd George, David
Refer x George, David Lloyd

22.5C2. Preferred or established form known.
Enter a compound surname under that element by which the person bearing it prefers to be entered. In case the person's preference is unknown, adopt the form of entry given in reference sources, in the language/country of residence/activity of the author. (Refer to rule 46B

of AACR 1967 also)

e.g. Joaguim Maria Machado de Assis
Enter, Machado de Assis, Jaochim Maria

22.5C3. Hyphenated Compound Surnames
Compound surnames with a hyphen connecting both elements are to be entered under the first part of the compound surname. (a see x reference from the part not chosen is to be made)

e.g. Lionel Graham Horton-Smith
enter Horton-Smith, Lionel Graham
x Smith, Lionel Graham Horton-,

e.g. Miguel de Cervantes-Savedra
enter Cervantes-Savedra, Miguel de
x Savedra, Miguel de Cervantes

22.5C4. Other Compound Surnames except those of married women whose surname consists of surname before marriage and husband's surname/maiden name and surname of husband both adopted.

Enter such compound surnames under the first element of the compound surname, unless the person's language is Portuguese; in which case the entry is made under the last part of the person's name;

e.g. Adolf Hungry Wolf
Enter Hungry Wolf, Adolf

Portuguese language: Ovidio Saraiva de Carvalo e Silva
Enter, Silva, Ovidio Saraiva de Carvalo e

22.5C5. Compound surname of married women, who were not covered by the previous rule. Enter under the first element of compound surname (regardless of its nature), if the persons's language is Czech, French, Hungarian, Italian or Spanish. In all other cases, enter under the husband's surname.

Enter, Fabre-Luce, Alfred (French)
Becker-Trier, Hanz (Hungarian)

22.5D. *Surnames with separately written Prefixes*

22.5D1. Articles and Prepositions
Surnames include sometimes articles, and somether times prepositions or both. In these cases of surnames, enter under the element most commonly used as entry element in alphabetically arranged directories, etc., in the person's language/country of residence/activity. For examples of entry element, see the AACR 2 1988 revision. Even in the 1967 code also the entry is similar;

e.g. Jean de la Fontaine is entered under
De la Fontaine, Jean and x references as needed are made.

22.5D2. Other Prefixes
If the prefix is neither an article nor a preposition, nor a combination of the two, enter under the prefix.

| e.g., Ramsay Mac Donald | C.W. O'Hara |
|---|---|
| Enter, Mac Donald, Ramsay | O'Hara, C.W. |

22.5E. Prefixes Hyphenated or Combined with Surnames Enter the name under the prefix.

| e.g. Maurice DeKobra | F.V.E. Delacroix |
|---|---|
| Enter, DeKobra, Maurice | De LaCroix, F.V.E. |

Make a x reference from the name element after the prefix.

22.5F. *Members of Royal Houses entered under Surnames*

22.5F1. A member of a royal house no longer reigning or of a royal house that has lost/removed its throne, and who is no longer identified as royalty is to be entered under the surname or part of the name by which he or she is identified in his/her works or identified in reference sources. Add the titles the person continues to use.

e.g. Vibhutinarayan Singh, former Maharaja of Kashmir.
Enter, Vibhutinarayan Singh, Maharaja
e.g. Otto Archduke of Austria
Enter, Habsburg, Otto

e.g. Henri, Count of Paris
Enter, Paris, Henri Comte de

22.6. **Entry under Title of Nobility**

22.6A. *General rule*

22.6A1 Enter under proper name in a title of nobility (including courtesy titles), if the person is commonly known by that title. This rule is applicable to those persons, 1)who use their titles rather than their surnames in their works, 2) listed in reference sources under their titles. The order of entry would be:

1. Proper name in title;
2. Personal name in direct order;
3. The term of rank in vernacular.

Omit the surname and rank, if the person does not use it. Refer from the surname (x) unless the proper name in title is the same as surname e.g. George Gordon Byron, Baron Byron
enter, Byron, George Gordon Byron, Baron.

22.8. **Entry under Given Name, etc.**

22.8A. *General Rule*

22.8A1. Enter a name that does not include a surname, not identified by a title of nobility as listed in reference sources.

e.g. John, the Baptist
Leonordo, da Vinci x Vinci, Leonordo da
Panini, the Grammarian Bhavabhuti

22.8C. *Names of royal persons*

22.8C1. Enter the name of a royal person (royal house, dynasty, temporal designation or a surname by which he/she is known) in direct order.

e.g. Louis Bonaparte
Chandragupta Maurya
Madhav Rao Scindhia

22.9A. Roman names before A.D. (476). Enter under the part of the name mostly used in reference sources.

e.g. Caesar, Gaius Julius
Antonius Pius

22.10. **Entry under Numerals, Initials, Letters**
Enter a name consisting of initials, separate letters, or numerals in direct order.

e.g. Enter H.D.
x D., H.
Flowering of the rod.

D.S. Master
x S.D., Master
x Master, D.S.

22.10 to 22.28 cover more details of additions or deletions to name of entry, and may be referred to in the text AACR 2 1988 revision.

23. **Geographic Names**
This is a new chapter in AACR 2 1988 revision, and spells out the complexity of using geographic names in distinguishing one from another, as the same name is used for headings of corporate bodies, conference names, government names, etc. The five sub-rules deal with form, changes, additions, jurisdiction.

24. **Corporate Bodies.**
This chapter deals with headings for corporate bodies. The rules are simple directions in detail regarding corporate bodies and other forms as headings. in 1967 these have been dealt with, and here they provide directions for greater precision of the headings.

25. **Uniform Titles.**
The entry and procedure of uniform titles, as stated in earlier editions of AACR still hold good, as the revision of AACR 2 1988 reveals little

alterations and distinctive changes. The rule maybe adopted according to the edition followed.

**26 References**

The direction to follow and make general references and to make one, when in doubt seem to be the only additional information appearing in the rule. Otherwise, the rules governing the references in earlier editions of AACR hold good and may usefully be adopted.

Time of use of AACR 2 1988 revision by libraries will indicate the extent of alterations and amendments and deletions required in future editions.

1.

Binder's title.

A title referred on the cover of an item by a binder, as distinguished for a title on the publisher's original cover.

2.

Caption title.

A title given at the beginning of the first page of the text, or in the case of a musical score, immediately above the opening bars of the music.

3.

Colophon.

A statement at the end of an item giving information about one or more of the following: the title, author(s), publishers, printer, date or publication or printing. It may include other information. (In case of manuscripts specially Oriental, this term has greater significance, in helping the search for the original).

4.

Compound surname.

A surname consisting of two or more proper names, sometimes connected by a hypen, or conjunction, or a preposition.

5.

Computer file.

A file (data and or programmes) encoded for manipulation by computer.

6.

Direct access. (Computer files)

The use of computer files via carriers (e.g. discs, cassettes, cartridges) designed to be inserted into a computer, or its auxiliary equipment by the user. *see also* Remote access (Computer Files)

7.
Element.
A word, phrase, or group of characters representing a distinct unit of bibliographic information.
8.
Format (Texts).
The number of times the printed sheet has been folded to make the leaves of a book. (e.g. Folio One fold giving two leaves; Quarto, two folds giving our leaves and so on.)
9.
Half title.
A title of publication appearing on a leaf preceding the title page.
10.
Issue.
Copies of an edition forming a distinct group that are distinguished from other copies of that edition by minor but well defined variations (e.g. a new impression of a book for which minor revisions have been incorporated into the original type image.
11.
Pseudonym
A name assumed by an author to conceal or obscure his/her identity.
12.
Remote access (Computer files)
The use of the computer files via input/output devices connected electronically to a computer.
13.
Respondent (Academic disputations).
A candidate for a degree, who, in academic disputations defends/opposes a thesis proposed by the praesis, also called the defendent.
14.
Verso I
The left hand page of a book, usually bearing an even number. The side of a printed sheet intended to be read second.
15.
Videorecording
A recording on which visual images, usually in motion and accompanied by sound, have been registered., designed for play back by means of a television set.
16.
Volume

1. In the bibliographic sense, a major division of a work, regardless of its designation by the publisher, distinguished from other major divisions of the same work by having its own inclusive title page, half title, cover title, or portfolio title, and usually independent pagination foliation, or signatures. This major bibliographic unit may include various title pages and or paginations. 2. In the material sense all that is contained in one binding, portfolio, etc., whether as orginally issued or as bound after issue. The volume as a material unit may not coincide with the volume as a bibliographic unit.

# 28

## SUBJECT ENTRIES

The need for making subject entries for the subjects dealt with in a book and to file them in a catalogue has been fully established. Here the practical aspect of their making is covered.

There has been a large volume of opinion that subject cataloguing is an art which can be practised successfully and effectively by those having the ability and aptitude towards it. It does not mean that it has no technique which can not be stated and taught. The usual method of training subject cataloguers in various schools of liabrary science are limited to the practice of referring to some standard list of subject headings and applying them on books. New thoughts in certain fields of knowledge like science and technology, has indicated the limitations of even the most comprehensive of the list of subject headings, which fail to provide the appropiate headings. This kind of training does not help the students to obtain a correct conception of the basic principles. Instead of rendering it a fascinating, intellectual performance, subject cataloguing is reduced to a mechanical business. The subject cataloguer can no longer depend solely on these aids, but he has to summon his intellectual resources into constructing suitable subject headings.

Subject cataloguing, on the other hand, is an adventure in discovery of the exact subject or subjects contained in a book which is being catalogued. One should have a clear conception of what he is looking for, where to locate it, and how to communicate what has been discovered in an unequivocal manner.The process of discovery, when reduced to a function, will be a verbal statement and description of the subject comprising all its dimensions. This is commonly understood as the provision of a subject heading.

Derivation of the subject statement can ordinarily be obtained by an examination of the book, the jacket, the title page, the table of contents, the preface, the introduction, and the text. The titles of some books are so direct as to readily indicate the subject of the book, whithout involving further examination of the other means; while some other titles require a careful study of all available sources of information plus a reference to an expert or scholar in that field of knowledge.

The subject statement consists of some parts, which bring out the characteristics like, (1) the exact meaning of the term used as primary subject of the book which is governed by, (2) space, (3) time, (4) bibliographic form, e.g., outlines, dictionaries, collections, histories, etc., (5) literary form e.g., poetry, drama, fiction, etc., and (6) relation to other branches of knowledge or subjects. As there has not been any agreed uniformity of the order in which these characteristics are to be used in the formation of the subject headings they reveal diversity in their presentation. As far as possible, a fixed order, if arrived at, will not only provide uniformity among subject catalogues, but will help complete coverage of all the characteristics involved in each subject heading. As books vary in the treatment of the subject with regard to their scope, aspect, relationship, and language so must the combination or use of these characteristics, in the subject statement differ.

As the chief function of a subject heading in the catalogue is to serve as a point of reference by the inquirer, it will, therefore, be advantageous to place first the terms having the highest potency as points or reference and then the other parts of the subject statement in a convenient order, which is normally indicated by the author in his work, *e.g.*, A Dictionary of British Surnames. In this, the desirable order for the subject heading will be *Surnames, British Dictionaries.*

The beginner in cataloguing needs to remember that a work may require one or more subject entries, while it will have only one main entry under its author. The more composite a book is in its contents, the larger will be the number of subject entries that it requires. Besides the character of the book, the necessity for liberal provision of subject entries, will be felt more keenly in special libraries than in general libraries. The subject analytical entries will be an outstanding feature in the catalogues of special libraries.

An erroneous tradition had persisted that the subject headings chosen for a book should be limited to the words forming its title or to the terminology of the class numbers provided for the book. Both methods are to be deprecated, as they set limitations over the choice of appropriate subject headings. No scheme of book classification of a standard variety has found it possible to provide a class number for a book representing its subject to the fullest extent. Therefore, the correct procedure in fixing the form and fullness of subject headings for a book is to "Enter books under the words which express their subject, whether it occurs in the title or not" and whether the terminology of the classification used contains its indication or not.

The "fundamental concepts" [2] in the choice and making of subject headings are (1) the reader as the focus, (2) uniformity in style and terminology of the subject headings of all the books on the same subject, (3) usage of common and popular terms, (4) English terminology, except when no words in the English vocabulary could express the subject, fully and appropriately and (5) specificity of all subject headings to the extent exactly demanded by the scope and treatment of the subject in the book.

The most general rule and also a fundamental one governing all kinds of subject headings in a dictionary catalogue is based on the principle of "Specific Entry". "Enter a work under its subject heading not under the heading of a class, which includes that Subject", [3] *e.g.*, a book on "Arts" should be entered under "Ants" and not under 'Insects' nor under 'Zoology'.

The other rules for making subject headings are of two kind: (1) those covering the choice of the terms to be adopted and (2) those governing the structure and style of the headings.

1. *Choice of the terms*

(i) *Between Person and Country* : In choosing subject headings for books on the history of a country, the cataloguer faces the problem of entering it under the name of the country or under the name of the ruler or king or under both. The directions of Cutter are that if the book is a biography of the ruler or a work dealing with the period of his reign only, it should be entered under his name. *e.g.*, "Asoka," by J.M. Macphail should be entered under **Asoka, the Great**, *Emperor of India*. If there is a book which covers the whole or part of the history of acountry not limited to a single ruler, it should be entered under the country as its subject, *e.g.*, **History of India** by V.A. Smith, will be entered under the subject heading **India** *History*.

As the former book "Asoka the Great" and the later "History of India," are related to each other, the subject headings of both, even though they will be found under different alphabetical places in the catalogue are connected by providing a "*see also*" reference from the general to the specific subject, *e.g.*, **India.** *History, see also*, **Asoka, the Great**, *Emperor of India*. Instead of making individual reference to rulers, from each period sub-division of the history of a country, a general reference may be made *e.g.*, **India.** *History see also,* under the names of individual rulers, e.g., Asoka; Akbar; Chandra Gupta I; Hastings, Warren; Rajendra Prasad, 1st President, Republic of India, 1950-1962.

Perhaps a more logical method would be to enter all lives, personal memoirs and accounts of rulers of a country under the country with a reference from the names of rulers with the result that general histories of countries and personal history of the rulers of the country come together under one uniform subject heading of a country subdivided by *History. Peroid and ruler.* The only valid objection to it would be that the principle of specific entry is overlooked by the adoption of this method.

(ii) *Between event and country*: Cutter advocates the entry of events of periods in the history of a country which have a proper name, under that name with a reference from the country, e.g., **Plassey, Battle of; the Mauryan age** to be entered under their names, with reference from India. History. Period subdivision.

If the event or period is known by common or general names, the entry is to be made under the country, e.g., Medieval history of India; Independence of India, will be entered under **India.** *History. Medieval period:* **India.** *History. Independence* 1947.

(iii) *Between subject and country*: The only satisfactory procedure, according to Cutter is double entry under the subject and place. The method of double entry is superfluous in regard to certain subjects and costly in respect of all, e.g., Progress of Chemistry in India. In this title, the subject **Chemistry.** *History* is dealt with and there is no information on the country, India. It is very unlikely that any reader would look for this book under India. Therefore, it is sufficient, if one subject heading under the subject **Chemistry** is provided. In order to obtain the required specificity it may be subdivided by locality and form *i.e.* Chemistry. India. History.

The suggestion of Mann, in her *Introduction to Cataloguing and Classification*, chapter on Subject headings, for dealing with subject versus place, is worth considering. She advocates the entry of works on science and art limited to a locality, under the subject subdivided by the name of the locality and of works on the history, geography, politics, economics, and other social subjects related to the place under the name of the place with the subject as subdivision, e.g., Indian social conditions. The subject heading for this title would be India. Social conditions.

Modern practice followed by several leading libraries is to enter the scientific and technical subjects, artistic and literary subjects under the subject even though limited to a place and social, historical, religious and philosophical subjects under the name of the place subdivided by subject, e.g. entry under subject subdivided by place.

**Mines and mineral resources.** *India.*
**Coal mines.** *Bihar.*
**Agriculture.** *Punjab.*
**Printing,** *Indian.*

*e.g.* Entry under place, subdivided by subject.

**India.** *Politics and government.*
**India. Foreign** *relations. Russia.*
**Uttar Pradesh.** *Economic conditions.*
**Madras (City).** *History.*
**Mysore.** *Geography.*
**India.** *Religions.*

But sometimes doubts arise, in the choice of headings for books on education, philosphy, whether they should be entered under subject or place, e.g. "Indian Philosophy" by S. Radhakrishnan, is not entered under India. Philosophy, but under Philosophy, Indian. Similarly, Education in India by Anathanth Basu, is not entered under India. Education, but under Education. India. Both subjects, belong to the social or general group of subjects, but yet the practice of the Library of Congress (vide List of Subject Headings; 6th ed. 1957) is to enter them under the subject with place as subdivision.

Therefore, the beginner in cataloguing will find it necessary and safe to check the heading chosen by him from the L.C. List of Subject Headings or Sear's List of Subject Headings, so that uniformity is maintained.

(iv) *Between overlapping subjects:* The direction of Cutter is that among subjects which overlap, the one that preponderates should be chosen for the entry with reference from others, e.g. physiography and art overlap with regard to landscape, medicine and psychiatry overlap with regard to therapeutics. In such cases, the view point of the author, his credentials and profession help the cataloguer to find out the more dominating aspect of the subject under which the entry is to be made, e.g. An assessment of human values. A title like this will have as its subject heading Value (Philosophy). On the order hand a title like Economic values of the 20th century, will be entered under Value (Economics).

2. *The Structure and style of the headings.*

(i) A subject heading should be in English language as far as possible; when no English word appropriate to the description of the subject can be found, a foreign name can be used, e.g. Vedanta; Karma; Yoga; Vaishnavism; Dharma.

(ii) Between two synonymous names, choice should be made of one, with reference from the other; e.g. Agricultural implements and Farm implements; Adwaita and Vedanta; Reincarnation and Pre- existence; Dealth penalty and Capital punishment.

**Adwaita,** *see*
**Vedanta**
**Agricultural implements,** *see*
**Farm implements**
**Implements, Agricultual,** *see*
**Farm implements**
**Implements, Farm,** *see*
**Farm implements**

In the choice between synonymous headings the one that is (1) most familiar to the class of people who use the catalogue and the library, (2) most used in other catalogues, (3) most intensive in its meaning, is to be preferred.

Of two opposite names one should be adopted with reference from the other, e.g. Temperance and Intemperance. If the rule is followed, a reference, Intemperance, *see* Temperance will have to be made, when Temperance is chosen. Between Free trade and Protection, if Free trade is chosen, a reference in the style, Protection *see* Free trade, has to be made. When there is a book in which the case for Protection is dealt with, it would look unreasonable to enter it under the subject heading "Free trade", although the disadvantages of Free trade might be discussed in the book.

Therefore, instead of choosing one of two opposite terms, as the subject heading both may be adopted according to the necessity and a *see also* reference may be made to link them together. Or the subject heading may combine both opposite terms and a *see* reference may be made from one of the opposite, terms e.g. Between Good and Evil, if a combined heading like "Good and Evil", is chosen, it will be found appropriate to the kinds of books one on 'Good', and another on "Evil." A reference in the style Evil, *see* Good and Evil, has to be made.

(iii) *Formation of the heading*: (1) The simplest form of subject heading is surely a single noun made of one word, *e.g.* Chemistry; man; soul;

(2) compound subject headings consist of a noun preceded by an adjective, *e.g.* Moral Philosophy; Religious psychology; Vocational education. In such subjects, the inverted form as Psychology Religious, may be adopted. When the inverted form is used, a *see* reference form the uninverted form is made to the form chosen. When a different term is used as Ethics, instead of Moral philosophy; a *see* reference from the compound subject heading is made, both from inverted and uninverted forms, *e.g.* Moral philosophy, *see* Ethics; Philosophy, Moral *see* Ethics:

(3) a noun preceded by another noun e.g. Death penalty; Book trade. As such usage is wide and popular, a *see* reference from the second noun, inverting the first or followed by the prepositions of and in, is uncalled for. Therefore do not make a *see* reference in the form Penalty, Death, see Death penalty, Trade in books *see* Book Trade;

(4) a noun connected with another noun by a preposition, *e.g.* Figures of speech; Conduct of life. Here, a reference, Speech, Figures of *see* Figures of speech is calleld for;

(5) a noun joined by the conjunction 'and' *e.g.* Belief and Doubt; State and Church; Science and Religion; Colleges and Universities. A *see* reference from the inverted form is necessary, *e.g.* Religion and Science, *see* Science and Religion; Universities and Colleges, *see* Colleges and Universities;

(6) a phrase or sentence, *e.g.* First aid in illness and injury; Geographical distribution of animals; A *see* reference from the last noun or nouns after the preposition is necessary to be made, *e.g.* Illness and injury, First aid in, *see* First aid in Illness and injury; Animals, Geographical distribution of, *see* Geographical distribution of animals.

Generally, a compound subject name is to be entered under its first word, unless some other word is more significant, when an inverted form is obviously needed.

(iv) *Personal names* are used as subject headings for books of biography, autobiography, diaries, memoirs, criticism, etc. *e.g.*, Gandhi, Mohandas Karamchand will be the subject heading for his autobiography "Experiments with Truth". The form of name of a person used as subject heading may in general follow the A-ACR.

Personal names used as subject headings can further be subdivided by the terms 'Anecdotes; Cartoons, Satire, etc.; criticism and interpretation'. The subdivisions adopted in the L. C. List of Subject Headings; under voluminous authors like Shakespeare, William may be used for similar authors or persons. The subdivision helps in obtaining necessary specificity and grouping the material in logical arrangement under a person.

(v) *Corporate names* also may be used as subject headings when books contain their history and progress and their organisation and function. Their names used as subject headings should conform to the form used as author entry according to the A-ACR *e.g.* "The origin and growth of Red Cross" will have "Red Cross. History" as its subject heading; the annual report of the Banaras Hindu University will have "Banaras Hindu University. Annual report" as the subject heading.

(vi) *Proper names* of things and places etc. can be used as subject headings, e.g. The Himalaya mountains; the Taj Mahal; the Ganges etc. Even names of literary works, sacred books may be used as subject headings, with subdivision, commentaries, criticism and interpretation, etc. *e.g.* Hamlet. Criticism and interpretation; Vedas. Commentaries.

(vii) *Subdivision of subject headings* can be by (1) geography, (2) history, (3) form and (4) aspects or view points, *e.g.* Geology. India; Philosophy. 20th century; Education. Addresses, essays, lectures; English language. Indian authors.

(viii) *Form used as subject heading* is common in these field of literature; *e.g.* Sanskrit poetry, German Drama; French essays, Common forms are Poetry, Drama, Essays, Satire, Letters, Bibliography and Collections etc. Sometiems thsese forms are used as subdivision, *e.g.* Folklore. Bibliography.

General or Common form subdivisions which may be used under any subject are;

*Addresses, essays, lectures*
*Bibliography*

*Collections*
*Dictionaries*
*Directories*
*Encyclopedias*
*Handbooks, manuals*
*History*
*Outlines*
*Periodicals*
*Societies*
*Statistics*
*Study and teaching*
*Theory or Philosophy*
*Travel and description*
*Yearbooks*

The subject heading is written in bold letters or in red ink, in order to make it distinctive. A line is left blank below the heading and before the repetition of the heading of the main entry on the body of the card. The subject entry usually contains the same details about the book, as the main entry has except the tracings.

Subject entry.

**English language.** *Dictionaries*
Wyld, H.C. ed.
The Universal dictionary of the English language. Lond, Routledge, 1952.
xx, 1447p., tables, diagr., bibliography, 29cm.

Cutter in his rules for a Dictionary Cataloguer recommends that a form heading 'Periodicals' be made for periodicals. In very big libraries, the adoption of this form heading will bring together all titles of periodicals in an alphabetical order of their names, and may not necessitate looking for each periodical under different alphabets. But periodicals of a subject cannot be brought together, as they will be arranged in alphabetical order of their titles. This is due to lack of a specific subject entry for the subject or subjects covered by the periodical. In order to bring the periodicals of a subject together, it is suggested that the subject entries for periodicals be made with form division 'Periodicals' as subheading. This procedure will bring the periodicals of a subject together in the catalogue under one consistent subject.

Added entry under the subject with 'Periodicals' as form division, given as subheading.

**Chemistry**. *Periodicals*
Faraday Society, London.
Transactions.

REFERENCES

1. Cutter Rule No.172, in his **rules for a Dictionary Catalog.**
2. Library of Congress: **Subject heading**, a practical guide,1951;ch.II
3. Cutter Rule No.161 in his **Rules for a Dictionary Catalog.**

# 29

## ADDED ENTRIES OTHER THAN SUBJECT ENTRIES

Added entries are made in order to supplement the main entry by providing additional direct access to bibliographical information displayed in the catalogue.

Added entries are secondary entries to the main entry of a book. Usually in handwritten and type written catalogue cards, selected items of information only are given on these various added entries, while the fullest record of the author and his work is given on the main entry. If printed cards like the L.C. cards, are used, both main and added entry cards, contain the same items of information, with the addition of the appropriate heading on the added entry cards.

No limit to the number of added entries for a book can be fixed. The character and scope of each book will influence the number of added entries, required for it. Usually they are made for (1) jt. authors, (2) editors, (3) illustrators, (4) commentators, (5) compilers, (6) translators, (7) series, (8) titles and (9) subjects.

In all these types of added entries, the author heading, the title proper, the date of publication and number of volumes are invariably included. Each added entry has a definite function to perform. Based on the function, the particulars in the entry are determined.

The headings for all added entries, except the series entry (which is dealt with in a subsequent chapter) commence from the second indention on the top line. The heading for the main entry is written on the line below commencing from the first indention, in the same style and fulness as on the main entry. The title is written on the next line commencing from the second indention, subsequent line of title coming out to the first indention, till it is completed. The imprint follows the title on the same line, leaving four letter spaces, after the title. If sufficient space is not available on the same line, it is begun from the first indention on the next line, so as to make a paragraph. Collation, if given, is commenced on the next line from the second indention.

Added entry for jt. author

Heffernne, R. F.jt.auth.
Perls, F.S. and others.
Gestalt therapy: excitement and growth in the human personality by F.S.Perls, R.F. Hefferline and Paul Goodman.
N.Y. Julian Pr.,1952
xii, 466, 22cm.

Added entry for translator.

Connel, Brian, tr.
Papen. Franz von.
Memoirs tr. from the German by Brian Connell. London.
Deutsch, 1952.
630p., front (port) 4pl., 22cm.

Added entry for editor.

Dimmock, F.H. ed.
Burnham, Roy,
B-P's life in pictures; the story of Lord Baden-Powell of Gilwell; ed. by F.H. Dimmock, drawings by Kenneth Brookes. Lond., Boy Scouts assoc.,1952.
60p., illus., 22.5cm.

Added entry for illustrator.

Brookes, Kenneth, illus.
Burnham, roy.
B-P's life in pictures:the story of Lord Badden-Powell of Gilwell; ed. by F.H. Dimmock, drawings by Kenneth Brookes, Lond., Boy Scouts Assoc., 1952.
60p., illus., 22.5cm.

Added entry for compiler.

Spark, Muriel, comp.
Bronte,Emile Jane.
A selection of poems; Comp. by Muriel Spark, Lond., Grey-walls pr., 1952.
62p. 19cm.

Added entry for commentator.

Mallinatha, comm.
Kalidasa.

Raghuvamsa; with commentory 'The Sanjivini' by Mallinatha. Bombay, Nirnaya Sagara Pr., 1904.
276 p., 212cm.

Added entry for title.

B-P's life in pictures. 1952.
Burnham, Roy.

The directions to make an added entry are contained in the rules, and in 'The Principles of Cataloging' given in Chapter 5 but the cataloguer has to assess the value and use of such added entries before automatically making them.

The added entries are based on the information contained in the main entries. If the author heading of a main entry is incorrectly fixed, all added entries repeat the same incorrect form. Therefore, the student of practical cataloguing is advised to bestow sufficient care over the making of main entries. The usual order of indicating the added entries on the main card is (1) subjects and (2) other added entries in the order (i) joint author, (ii) editor, (iii) translator, (iv) compiler, (v) commentator, (vi) illustrator, (vii) series and (viii) title.

A-ACR 33 states the general principles for making added entries. These entries may be made for a personal or corporate author associated with the publication, if the reader use of the catalogue would justify their provision. When the main entry is made under a corporate author or under a title, there will be increasing need for providing the added entries for persons connected with the work.

The final section [P.] of this rule contains the exceptions for which no title added entry will be required. These directions will be specially helpful to students and beginners of practical cataloguing, because unwanted title entries could be eliminated.

(i) Works with common titles that are incomplete or meaningless without the author's name, *e.g.* "Collected works", "Autobiography," "Letters", "Diaries", "Memoirs", "Bulletin", "Proceedings", "Report", "Transactions", etc.;
(ii) Works having unusually long titles and indistinctive;
(iii) titles which will alphabetise at the same place as the heading for the main entry or subject entry;
(iv) title provided by the cataloguer, and enclosed in square brackets;

The categories mentioned above will not require title added entries.

# 30

# ANALYTICAL ENTRIES

An analytical entry is defined as "the entry of some part of a work or some article contained in a collection (volume of essays, serial etc.)"[1] including a reference to the publication which contains the article or work entered.

Dewey, in his Simplified Library School Rules, p.6, defines it as an "added entry for a distinct part of a work or collection, which may be either a part or the whole of a volume or volumes with or without a separate title page".

An analytical entry describes the part of a work catalogued, while an added entry, under subject or editor, etc., covers, the whole of a work. Therefore, an analytical entry is more specific than a regular added entry.

It should contain a reference to the work, from which the portion analysed is taken.The reference is written in curves, commencing with the word '*In*', heading of main entry, title, date of publication and lastly inclusive pages covered by the analytic. It should be indicated on the main entry like other added entries.

Three kinds of analytical entries can be made (author, title and subject). It is not necessary that all the three analytical entries should be made for every work selected for analytical treatment. One or all may be made for the portion analysed, depending on its need and usefulness to the reader. By making analytical entries, all the subjects, authors and titles of the part analysed are brought to the notice of the readers, which otherwise would have remained undisclosed to the users of the catalogue by the usual main and added entries. The smaller the resources of a library, the greater is the need and importance of these analytical entries. When individual books or treatise are not in the collection, the analytical entries serve to fill in the gaps in the book collection.

Analytical entries under author or title may be made for distinct parts of works or collections, whether with or without a seperate title page. But the making of analytical entries for subjects of parts of a work is equally essential.

When to make an author analytic? An author analytic is to be made (1) when part of a book is written by some person other than the author of the main part of the book, and (2) when two or more works of an author are published together with no indication of the second and subsequent works on the first title page. In both the cases, the included part or work, would not be brought to the reader's notice, if no analytic entry is made for its author; e.g. if you find Goldsmith's *Vicar of Wakefield* and Johnson's *Rasselas* in one book, make an author analytic for Johnson, as none could expect to find Johnson under the entry for Goldsmith; e.g. Dicken's *David Copperfield* and *A Tale of Two Cities,* in one book, requires analytic entry for the author of *A Tale of Two Cities*, as the reader cannot get at *A Tale of Two Cities*, when looking under *David Copperfield.*

*Main entry for a work requiring author analytic for the part*

**Winchell A.N.**

The Microscopic characters of artificial inorganic solid substances or artificial minerals; with a chapter on the Universal stage by R.C. Emmons; 2nd ed. N.Y., Wiley, 1931.

403p., 23cm.

1. Mineralogy. 2. Crystallography. (anal.)
I. Emmons, R.C.(anal.).II. title. III. title: The Universal stage. (anal.).

*Author analytic for a book containing part by a person other than the author of the main work.*

**Emmons, R.C.**

The Universal stage. (*In* Winchell, A.N.The Microscopic

characters of artificial inorganic solid substances or artificial minerals; 2nd ed. N.Y., Wiley, 1831, p. 126-150).

*Main entry for a book containing two or more works of the same author with title analytic for his subsequent works indicated.*

**Marcel, Gabriel**

A Man of God; Ariadne; The Funeral pyre; three plays with a preface on the drama of the soul in exile. Secker and Warburg, 1952.

282p.,19cm.

A Man of God; tr. by Marjorie Gabain.Ariadne and The Funeral pyre; tr. by Rosalind Haywood.

I. title. II. title : Ariadne (anal.). III. title : The Funeral pyre (anal.).

*Title analytic for a book containing two or more works of the same author*

Ariadne. 1952.
**Marcel, Gabriel**
(*In his* 'A Man of God.' Secker and Warburg, 1952, p. 115-224).

*Main entry for a book requiring author analytic for the part by the author of the first work*

**Mauriac, Francois**
The Desert of love (La Desert be I'Amour); tr. by Gerard Hopkins. Lond., Eyre and Spottiswoode, 1949. 279p., 19 1/2 cm.

*Includes his* "The Enemy"; (Le Mal); tr. by Gerard Hopkins. 1949. p. 165-279.
I. Hopkins, Gerard,tr. II. Mauriac Francois (anal.) III. title: The Enemy. IV. title.

*Author analytic for the part by the author of the work*

**Mauriac, Francois**

The Enemy. (*In his* The Desert of love. Lond., Eyre and Spottiswoode, 1949., p. 165-279).

Author analytics are not required for (1) an author's collected works with a general title, e.g. Complete works of William Shakespeare; Plays of George Bernard Shaw; (2) for collections of stories from periodicals, when published in a book form under a collective title; e.g. Short stories from the Mordern Review, and (3) for the part of a book whose title may fall under the same alphabet as the main title. In all such cases, contents should be given on the main entry cards. Genuine joint author works should not be considered for analytical treatment.

Title analytical entries are generally made for all works which are component parts of a large work. Fiction and drama usually need title analytics.

*Title analytical entry for part of a work*

The Funeral pyre. 1962.

Marcel, Gabriel.

(*In his* 'A Man of God.' Secker and Warburg, 1952, p. 225-282).

Subject analytics are made for parts of books, in which the subject dealt with is other than the subject of the book as a whole. When no separate book is avaliable in the library on the subject of the part, the subject analytics are most essential.

*Subject analytic entry*

**Crystallography**

**Emmons, R.C.**

The Universal stage. (*In* Winchell. A.N. The Microscopic characters of artificial inorganic solid substances or artificial minerals; 2nd ed. N.Y., Wiley, 1931, p. 126-150).

A-ACR 156 deals with analytical entries. The procedure for making analytical entries for (1) parts with separate title pages and separate paging, (2) parts with separate title pages and continuous paging, (3) parts without special title pages for (a) monographs and (b) for serials, and (4) parts of analysed parts which have been stated. These different types are based on physical characteristics present in the publication, while earlier in paragraph five, three kinds of analytical entries for (1) author, (2) title, and (3) subject have been suggested. Under each one of these three chief types of analytical entries, the physical features used as the basis of division in the A-ACR can be present.

## REFERENCE

1. **A.L.A. Cataloging Rules** 2nd ed. 1949 p. 229.

## 31

# SERIES NOTE AND SERIES ENTRY

A 'series' is defined as (1) "A number of separate works usually related to one another, in subject or otherwise, issued in succession, normally by the same publisher and in uniform style, with a collective title which generally appears at the head of the title page, on the half title or on the cover, (2) each of two or more volumes of essays, lectures or articles or other writings, similar in character and issued in sequence, e.g. Dickinson's Best Books of the decade first, second; (3) a separately numbered sequence of volumes, within a series or serial"[1] e.g. Prefaces to Shakespeare by Granville Barker, I series, II series, etc.

"A series note is a note stating the name of a series, to which a book belongs. The series note ordinarily follows the collation."[2]

"A series entry is an entry usually brief, of the several works in the library, which belong to a series under the name of that series as heading"[3]

If a book is one of the volumes of an important series, the series note should be given in curves, one centimeter after the last item of collation.

**Hammett, L.P.**

Introduction to the study of physical chemistry. N.Y., Mc-Graw Hill, 1952.

xii. 427p., tables, diagrs. bibliog., 24cm. (International chemical series).

If the publisher has assigned a number to each volume of the series, the number of the volume is given after a comma, at the end of the series note.

**Manley Gordon.**
Climate and the British scene. Lond. Collins, 1952. xviii, 314p., 56pl., (32 col.), maps, tables, diagrs., 22 1/2cm. (New naturalist series, 22).

Usually in handwritten and typewritten cards, reference to 'half title on cover', etc. is omitted. The series note is given on the main entry and subject entry only and omitted on the rest of the added entries.

Giving a series note on the main entry, does not imply that a series entry is to be made.

A series should be entered under its title, unless it is universally known under the name of the editor or publisher, with an added entry or reference under the editor; and a list of all the works in the library is to be given under the series heading, with the author's name, brief title, and date of publication of each item. The contents are to be arranged numerically, if the publisher has assigned a number for each volume under the series or alphabetically by the names of authors or by subjects if such an arrangement is most useful, as in the case of biography.

*Numerical arrangement of the works*

**New Naturalist series**

| | | |
|---|---|---|
| 599.09 42<br>M43 | 21 Matthews, L.H.<br>1952 | British mammals. |
| 551.5<br>M27 | 22 Manley, Gordon.<br>scence 1952. | Climate and the British |
| 595734: | 23 Harris, J.R.<br>1952. | An angler's Entomology. |

*Alphabetical arrangement of volumes*

**International library of psychology, philosophy and scientific method series**

| | |
|---|---|
| 104<br>B86 | Broad, C.D. Ethics and history of philosophy.<br>1952 |
| 192<br>F91 | Fritiz, C.A. Jr Bertrand Russell's construction of<br>the external world. 1952. |
| 121.1<br>H17 | Hall, E.W. What is value. 1952. |
| 137<br>R62 | Roback, A.A. Psychology of character. |

*Arrangement of volumes by subjects in which all the works are by one author and the order of the volume number in the series is overlooked in the arrangement.*

| | **Men of courage series by L.E. Walter** | |
|---|---|---|
| 910.4<br>C77W | 2 Cook | 1952 |
| 910.4<br>D16W | 5 Dampier. | 1952 |
| 919.8<br>F83W | 6 Franklin | 1952 |
| 916<br>L78W | 1 Livingstone. | 1952 |

*Arrangement of volumes by subjects in alphabetiical order*

| | **Leading figures in Jewish history series.** | |
|---|---|---|
| 922.96<br>A15M | Abrabanel by Melinek. | 1952 |
| 922.96<br>M22S | Maimonides by J.W. Slotki. | 1952. |
| 922.96<br>M53S | Mendelssohn By M. Simon. | 1952 |
| 922.96<br>R220 | Rashi by A. Owen | 1952 |

The arragement suggested in A.A. Code is very well adopted in a catalogue which uses the unit printed cards for each volume of the series. But in a catalogue in which handwritten or typewritten cards are used, the usual method is to give as many titles of a series, as a card can accomodate. When once the card is filled up no further additions, which may require entry in-between the items already entered, are possible. Leaving liberal space in-between two titles may solve the problem to a certain extent. But the best procedure seems to be to provide a separate series entry card for each work of the series, though it may mean more cards and added cost.

In very rare cases, a series is better known by the name of the editor of the series, e.g. English men of letters; ed. by John Morley. It is suggested by a few cataloguers that the series entry may be made under the name of the editor of the series, with a reference from the series.

The objection to this practice is that the editor is more liable to vary than the title, in which case a new entry or reference from the succeeding editors will be necessary. Perhaps the subsequent editors may not be so well- known as the previous editor under whose name the entry is made for the series. A better method will be to refer from the name of the editor of a series, to the series heading which should contain the editor's name at the end. If all the works belonging to a series happen to be the writings of a single author and if he himself is the editor of the series also, the series entry may be made under his name with the name of the series as title.

**Walter L.E.ed.**

| | Men of courage series | |
|---|---|---|
| 916<br>L78W | v.1 avid Livingstone. | 1952 |
| 910.4<br>C77W | v.2. Capton Cook. | 1952 |
| 910.4<br>D16W | v.5 William Dampier. | 1952 |

The series entry has no call number, which each volume entered under the series, must contain its call number, author's name, brief title, imprint date and number of volumes, if more than one. The function attached to a series entry is to enable a person consulting it to know all the works in a library of the series and their location on the shelves.

A-ACR 114 has two sections (A) and (B-G). The section (A) contains general rules applicable to almost all types of series found among modern publications. Special mention is made in a (3) for series statements of official ;publications, which preferably should be under the from used in official citations e.g.

[.Ssc. 4(II) 1968 (VI)] for the Supreme Court Reports, 1968, June.

[FRI. 14.246] for Indian Forests Bulletin (New Series) No. 246 Entomology revision of the Indian species of the genus *Microcerotermes silvestri, (Isoptera: Termitidae Amitermitinae).*

Section (B-G) provide guidance for making series statements of works in several volumes, series title in two forms, series title combined with monograph title. These types of series of infrequent occurrence but more complex than those explained earler in this chapter. Section

(G) directs the making of series statement for the same publication issued under two different series, one after another in parenthesis being separated by a semicolon.

REFERENCES

1. DW & A.L.A. Cataloguing rules for author and title entries, 1949 p 233.
2. A Code; English ed 1935, p.xx.

## 32

# CONTENTS, NOTES AND ANNOTATION

The contents of books are furnished on the entries, specially the main entry, when they contain (1) several works by the same author, (2) works by several authors, (3) works on several subjects and (4) a single work on a number of distinct subjects. Contents are necessary to be given when the collective title does not cleary indicate the works included in the book.

The designation of the volumes or parts is to be in the language of the book, e.g. volume (v) band (bd) etc.

The order of contents on the cards is to be in the order on the table of contents, but they may be arranged alphabetically be names or subjects if such an order is more helpful to the reader.

Two styles of giving the contents are in practice, (1) paragraph and (2) column. The first one is usually adopted as no loss of space in cards in involved. If the second style is followed. it results in greater facility to the reader but occupies more space on cards and sometimes extends over second and third card. The name of the author follows the title of his work.

*Contents for several works by the same author in volumes, in paragraph arrangement*

**Mayer, Adolf**

The Collected papers; ed. by E.E. Winters. Baltimore, Johns Hopkins Pr., 1950.

4v., front, illus, 23 1/2 cm.

*Contents:* v.1: Neurology-v.2: Psychiatry. v.3: Medical teaching-v.4 :Mental hygiene.

*Contents for several works by the same author in column arrangement*

**Mayer, Adolf**

The Collected papers; ed. by E.E. Winters, Baltimore, Johns Hopkins Pr., 1950.

4v. front., illus., 23 1/2 cm.

*Contents:-*

v.1: Neurology.

v.2: Psychiatry.

v.3: Medical teaching.

v.4: Mental hygiene.

*Contents for works by several authors contained in a book*

**Society for cultural relations with the U.S.S.R.** *Medical section*

British doctors in Russia. Lond., Lewis, 1952. 25p., illus., pl., tables, 22 cm.

*Contents:* Preventive medicine and health education by Ian Gilliland – General medical services, by Horace Joules.- Maternity and children's services by Marry Barber. – Note on the bacteriological services, by Mary Barber.

*Contents for work on several subjects*

**Bewely, Marius**

The Complex fate: Hawthorne, Henry James and some other American writers; into and two interpolations by F.R.Leavis. Lond., Chatto and Windus, 1952.

xvi, 248p., 20 1/2 cm.

*Contents :* Hawthorne and Henry James – Some aspects of modern: American poetry:– The Poetry of Wallace Stevens – Kenneth Burke as literary critic.

*Contents for single work on distinct subjects*

**Place, Robin**

Britain before history Lond., Rockliff, 1951. vii, 292p., illus., map, plan, facsims., diagrs., 22 1/2 cm.

*Contents:* 1 : No man's land.—2: An important family.—3: Shapers of stone.—4: The first farmers.—5: Men of bronze.—6: Masters of iron.—7: Colony of Rome.—8: The last stand.—9: Saxon and Stwidy.

*Notes.* The purpose of notes in a catalogue entry, is (1) to provide additional information, largely bibliographical, not contained in the title, imprint or collation, and (2) to explain the title or to correct any misapprehension to which it might lead, e.g. Sugar candy, "Stories for children, as sweet as sugar candy. It is conventional to give notes in English, except quotations from foreign sources and that it should cover bibliographies, authorities, etc., pseudonyms and anonyms, sequels, variations in title, editors and translators, editions, various places, publishers or dates, reprints, langauage of the text, source of the book, if first published serially no more published, imperfections in copy, bound with something else. These notes should not be confused with series note. These notes are made by the cataloguer, who uses his discretion, to use simple and concise terms in rendering the book, more intelligible to the reader. The normal limit set is thirty words but may be less or slightly more in a few cases. Notes are given on the line below the collation in a paragraph from, e.g. Title page wanting; Binder's title adopted, Two title pages, one in German and the other in Sankrit, etc.

*Bibliographical*

**Electricity undertaking of the world, 1952-53 the**
"Electrical Journal" red book; 62nd ed. Lond., Benn, 1952. 601p., 22/12 cm.
Previously published as "The Electrician" red book.

*Explanatory*

**Walmsley, Leo**
Invisible cargo. Lond., Joseph, 1952.
302. front, pl., 21 cm.
Includes an account of a voyage in a tanker from Britain to Venezuela and back. Maps on end papers.

*Annotation* in catalogue entries was a regular feature of the printed catalogues. As card gradually displaced the printed page catalogues, and open access to shelves became more popular, the practice of giving annotations became limited.

Dr. E.A. Savage, defines annotation as the "the term applied to all processes of describing the leading features and ideas of books in a succinct manner, whether be analysis or criticism or both together". W.C. Berwick Sayers in his *First steps in annotation in cataloguing;* 2nd ed. 1932 definest it as "as descriptive extension of the title page of a book in which the qualification of the author and the scope, purpose and place of the book are indicated".

Of the two definitions, the definition of Sayers is accepted for adoption. The bibliographical part of the annotation is included in the notes, on the main entry while the literary part, giving evidence of the author's authority on the subject or an explanation of the title or subject or the viewpoint of the author is given in the annotation. Sometimes, annotations look like literary appreciations and evaluation. The function of the catalogue is, not to inffluence the reader's choice of a particular book, but to lay before the user facts and figures and allow him full liberty of choice. Therefore, annotations of an evaluative type are not in keeping with the principles and traditions of the library catalogue.

Old and rare books, maps and incunabula, and other special material require annotation in their entries, as their titles and contents are not easily intelligible.

The cataloguer should guard against the faults of giving in the annotation valueless information like large edition, rewritten, etc., and he should keep off the functions of literary critic or reviewer.

A-ACR 145 directs the making of *notes* in a catalogue entry explains the purpose in (A) and describes the forms in (B) and the order in (C) which may be followed. It also contains instructions on giving the contents, but remains silent on the making of annotations. As already maintained annotation and notes are to be distinguished for the purpose served by each. There is general acceptance among cataloguers of the distinction between the two and Mr. P.J. Quigg in his Theory of Cataloguing; 2nd ed. 1968 defines annotation as a note on the intellectual content of a book, which is quite-reasonable and in line with our approach to it.

## REFERENCE

1. Manual of descriptive annotation for library catalogues 1906.

# 33

# REFERENCES

A reference is a direction from one heading to another. The beginner in a cataloguing needs to clearly understand that the entry of a book which is a record of the book is different from the references made, which refer across, one form of name to another or from one subject to another. A reference holds good for all books entered under similar headings once a reference is made, it is useless to repeat it when books of the same subject or by same author are catalogued subsequently. Therefore, the authority list which should indicate the references already made, should be maintained and kept up-to-date.

"The subject authority list will obviously resemble a general list in its principal features. It will show under each heading.:

1. the coordinate related headings found in the catalogue to which *"see also"* references have been made;
2. the less comprehensive, subordinate headings to which *"see also"* references have been made;
3. the broader, more comprehensive headings from which *"see also"* references have been made to the given headings;
4. the coordinate related headings from which such *"see also"* references have been made;
5. the synonymous terms, and, in general, terms equivalent to the given heading, from which *"see"* references have been made directing the reader to the chosen heading;
6. scope notes defining the heading and distinguishing it from other headings, in those instances where one or two or more meanings of the term has been chosen for its use as a heading, or where a distinction must be drawn between the given heading and others closely related to it."[1]

References are of two kinds (1) general and (2) specific. A reference is general when it indicates a group or class and furnishes an individual heading as an example, *e.g.* **History** *see also* under the names of individual countries with subhead *'History'*as **India***History;* Europe *History. History* of a subject, see under name of subject, with subhead *History,* as **Chemistry***History.* A reference is specific, if it mentions the particular heading, to which the reference is made, *e.g.***Medicine,** *see also* **Therapeutics; Political economy,** *see,* **Economics. Both kinds of references may be either** *'see'* or*'see also'.* The purpose of these references is to provide connecting links between synonymous terms and related terms, used as headings in a dictonary catalogue. They should direct the reader exactly to the heading under which he will find the entry or information required. Therefore references should be made when they prove helpfful in saving the time of the user of the catalogue. Without these references the related entries remain scattered under different alphabets and the lay reader fails to get a comprehensive knowledge of the material available in the library on a subject.

References should be freely made from alternative forms to the forms of heading chosen. It implies only *'see'* references. But *'see also'* references are more necessary in a dictionary catalogue.

A *'see'* reference is a reference from a term or name under which a reader might look for information but which the cataloguer does not use as a heading, to the term or name chosen for entry. These *'see'* references are generally made in the case of synonymous and opposite terms and various of names of a single author, *e.g.*

**Moral philosophy,** *see*
**Ethics.**
**Psychology, Religious,** *see*
**Religious psychology**
**Doubt,** *see*
**Belief and doubt.**
**Clemens, S.L.** *see*
**Twain, Mark,** *pseud.*
**Cross,** *Mrs.* **Mary Ann Evans,** *see*
**Eliot, George,** *pseud.*
**St. Albans, Francis** Bacon, *Viscount, see*
**Bacon, Francis,** *Viscount St. Albans*

A *'see also'* reference is a reference from a term or name to another already use in the catalogue. In effect *'see also'* reference are ordinarily made from general to specific headings, from one coordinate heading to another. Occasionally they may be made from a specific heading to a more general one, when the subjects dealt with are overlapping.

*General to specific*
  **Zoology,** *see also*
**Birds**
**Domestic animals**
**Insects**
**Mammals**
*Related headings*
  **Civil Rights** *see also*
**Liberty**
  **Civics** *see also*
**Political ethics**

The conventional symbol*x* = *see* and *xx* = *see also* is used in the text for the sake of brevity but on the catalouge card the terms *'see'* and *'see also'* are preferable as the users may not readily understand the meaning of x and xx.

In addition to these two conventional types of references *'see'* and *'see also'*, the need to provide a more adequate directionto the users of the catalogue arises. This is known as as an *Explanatory reference'.*

**Dictionaries**

The language-dictionaries will be found entered under name of language with subheading 'Dictionaries'. In case of bilingual dictionaries, the name of the language in which the meanings are given is given after the term *'dictionaries'*, e.g.
English languange. *Dictionaries*
French language. *Dictionaries. English*

The subject-dictionaries will be found entered under the name of the specific subject, used as subject heading with *Dictionaries* as subheading, *e.g.*
Physics. *Dictionaries*

Explanatory references also direct different categories of works of same person responsible for them; *e.g.*

**Radhakrishnan,** *President of India*

Under this heading private communications, public speeches and collection that include both private and official communications are entered.

Official acts of the President, address to parliament, proclamations, etc. will be found entered under the heading **India.** *President,* 1962-67 *(Radhakrishnan)*

When it will be helpful to make a *'see'* or *'see also'* reference to the title of a work, which is not anonymous, provide it in the form of an author-title reference in which the title is given following the heading under which it would be entered, e.g.:

**Creigton, Donald G.**
A History of Canada.
*see* his Dominion of the North: a history of Canada

**Chapman, Charles E.**
Colonial Hispanic America
*see also* his Republican Hispanic America.

Although A-ACR 120-126 limit the application of the rules for making reference entries for authors and titles only, it is equally important to extend and apply the principles to subject references as well. The student of cataloguing will find it helpful, if directions are available for subjects as well at one stretch. With this object in view, examples of subject references are also given in this chapter.

A note of caution seems desirable regarding the limit and number of references to be provided in a catalogue. The references will no doubt result in a syndetic catalogue, but too many of them made without imagination are likely to be irritating to the user who is apt to conclude that the headings adopted for entry are unreal and unnatural and to compensate for this deficiency the references are provided. This impression on the references should never be allowed to be formed. Therefore, the cataloguers should base their judgement on the real need and inevitability of the references and the only way to limit these references to a reasonable level is the choice of accurate and natural headings for authors, personal or corporate titles, and subjects, in accordance with the fundamental rules in the catalogue codes and list of subject headings.

## 120. Basic Rule

This is statement of general principles on the need and function of reference entries in a catalogue that the users of the catalogue are helped to get at the desired information or the heading of the entry of the bibliographical unit as directly and quickly as possible by the provision of directions to look at a heading used in the catalogue, instead of one known to them to contain the information. As this direction will hold good, for authors, titles and subjects in equal measure, the making of references entries in general would be governed by this rule.

A-ACR 121-126, provide detailed instructions, with numerous example under each and may profitably be looked into by cataloguers whenever the need is felt.

REFERENCE

1. L.C. Subject headings: **a practical guide** by D.J. Haykin, 1951, p. 92.

34

# DISPLAY OF ENTRIES

## DISPLAY OF ENTRIES ARRANGED FOR (1) A DICTIONARY CARD CATALOGUE

332.43 COINAGE, INTERNATIONAL
L97 Lutz, F.A.
International monetary mechanisms, the Keynes and White proposals, Princetion, Univ., 1943.

615.37 CONTAGION AND CONTAGIOUS DISEASES
Z78 Zinsser, Hans and others
Immunity principles and application in medicine and public health. N.Y., Macmillan, 1944.

332.43 CURRENCY-QUESTION
L97 Lutz, F.A.
International monetary mechanisms, the keynes and White proposals, Princeton, Univ., 1943.

159.96336 DREAMS
S79 Stekel, Wilhelm
.1 The Interpretation of dreams, N.Y., Liveright
.2 Pub. Corp., 1943.
2v.

615.37 Enders, J.F.
Z78 Zinsser, Hans and others
Immunity principles and application in medicine and public health. N.Y., Macmillan, 1944.

615.37 Fothergill, L.D.
Z78 Zinsser, Hans and others
Immunity principles and application in medicine and public health N.Y., Macmillan, 1944.

299.23 FREEMASONS, RITUALS
S76 Springett, B.H.
Secret sects of Syria and the Lebanon. Allen and Unwin, 1922.

332.43 GOLD
L97 Lutz, F.A.
International monetary mechanisms, the keynes and White proposals. Princeton, Univ., 1943.

615.37 IMMUNITY
Z78 Zinsser, Hans and others
Immunity principles and application in medicine and public health, N.Y., Macmillan, 1944.

615.37 Immunity principles and application in medicine and
Z78 public health, 1944.
Zinsser, Hans and others.

332.43 International monetary mechanisms, the keynes and
L97 White proposals, 1943.
Lutz, F.A.

159.96338 The Interpretation of dreams, 1943. 2v.
S79 Stekel, Wilhelm

332.43 Lutz, F.A.
L97 International monetary mechanisms, the keynes and white proposals, Princeton, Univ., 1943.
1. Money. 2. Coinage, International. 3. Currency question. 4. Gold. 1. Princeton University. International Finance Section. II. title.

332.43 MONEY
L97 Lutz, F.A.
International monetary mechanisms, the keynes and white proposals. Princeton, /Univ., 1943.

159.96338 Paul, Cedar
S79 Stekel, Wilhelm.
The Interpretation of dreams. N.Y., Liveright
.1 Pub Corp., 1943.
.2 2v

159.96338 Paul, Eden
S79 Stekel, Wilhelm
The Interpretation of dreams. N.Y., Liveright
.1 Pub. Corp., 1943
.2 2v.

332.43 Princeton University. International Finance Section.
L97 Lutz, F.A.
International monetary mechanisms, the keynes and white proposals. Princeton, Univ., 1943.

159.96338 PSYCHOANALYSIS
S79 Stekel, Wilhelm
The Interpretation of dreams, N.Y., Liveright
.1 Pub Corp., 1943
.2 2v.

199.23 Secret sects of Syria and the Labanon, 1922.
S76 Springett, B.H.

299.23 SECRET SOCIETIES. RITUALS
S76 Springett, B.H.
Secret sects of Syria and the Lebanon, 1922. Allen and Unwin, 1922.

615.37 SERUM THERAPY
Z78 Zinsser, Hans and others
Immunity principles and application in medicine and public health. N.Y., Macmillan, 1944.

299.23 Springett, B.H.
S79 Secret sects of Syria and the Lebanon, a consideration of their origin, creeds and religious ceremonies, and their connection with and influence upon modern free-masonry. Allen and Unwin, 1922.
1. Syria. Religion 2. Syria. Rites and ceremonies 3. Freedmasons Rituals. 4. Secret societies. Rituals. 1. Title

159.96338 Stekel, Wilhelm
S79 The Interpretation of dreams, new developments and
.1 technique; tr. by Eden Paul and Ceder Paul, N.Y., Liveright
.2 Pub. Corp; 1943.
2v.
1. Dreams 2. Psychoanalysis 1. Paul Eden, tr. II. Paul, Ceder tr. III. title

299.23 SYRIA RELIGION
S76 Springett, B.H.
Secret sects of Syria and the Labanon. Allen and Unwin, 1922.

299.23 SYRIA, RITES AND CEREMONIES
S76 Springett, B.H.
Secret sects of Syria and the Lebanon. Allen and Unwin, 1922.

615.37 Zinsser, Hans and others
Z78 Immunity principles and application in medicine and public health by Hans Zinsser, J.F. Enders and L.D. Fothergill. N.Y., Macmillan, 1944.
1. Immunity 2. Contagion and Contagious diseases 3. Serum therapy 1. Enders, J.F. jt. auth. II. Fothergill, L.D. jt. auth. III. title

## DISPLAY OF ENTRIES ARRANGED FOR (2) A CLASSIFIED CATALOGUE
### (a) MAIN ENTRIES

159.96338 Stekel, Wilhelm
S79 The interpretation of dreams, new developments and
.1 technique; tr. by Eden Paul and Cedar Paul. N.Y.,
.2 Liveright Pub Corp., 1943.
2v.

159.9642 Stekel, Wilhelm
The Interpretation of dreams, new development and techniques; tr. by Eden Paul and Cedar Paul., N.Y., Liveright Pub. Corp., 1943
2v.

Book at 159.963 38
S79.1
.2

299.23 Springett. B.H.
S76 Secret sects of Syria and the Lebanon: a consideration of their origin, creeds and religious ceremonies, and their connection with and influence upon modern freemasonry. Allen and Unwin, 1922.

332.42 Lutz, F.A.
International monetary mechanisms, the Keynes and White proposals. Princeton, Univ., 1943.
Book at 332.43
L97

332.43 Lutz, F.A.
L97 International monetary mechanisms, the Keynes and White proposals. Princeton, Univ., 1943.

366.109569 Springett, B.H.
Secret sects of Syria and the Lebanon. Allen and Unwin, 1922.
Book at 299.23
S76

332.5 Lutz, F.A.
International monetary mechanisms, the Keynes and White proposals. Princeton, University 1943.
Book at 332.43
L97

366.109569 Springett, B.H.
Secret Sects of Syria and the Lebanon. Allen and Unwin, 1922.
Book at 299.23
S76

394.409569 Springett, B.H.
Secret sects of Syria and the Lebanon. Allen and Unwin, 1922.
Book at 299.23
S76

614.4 Zinsser, Hans and others
Immunity principles and application in medicine and public health by Hans Zinsser, J.F. Enders and L.D. Fothergill, N.Y., Macmillan, 1944.
Book at 615.37
Z78

615.37 Zinsser, Hans and others
Z78 Immunity principles and application in medicine and public health by Hans Zinsser, J.F. Enders and L.D. Fothergill, N.Y., Macmillan, 1944

(b) ALPHABETICAL INDEX ENTRIES

| | |
|---|---|
| Coinage | 332.4 |
| Contagious diseases (Public health) | 614.4 |

| | |
|---|---|
| Currency | 332.5 |
| Diseases, Contagious (Public health) | 614.4 |
| Dreams : Interpretation | 159.96338 |
| Enders. J.F. Zinsser, Hans and | 615.37 |
| others, Immunity | Z78 |
| Principles and application in medicine and public health, 1944 | |
| Fothergill, L.D. Zinsser, Hans and | 615.37 |
| others. Immunity | Z78 |
| principles and application in medicine and public health, 1944. | |
| Freemasonry | 366.1 |
| Gold Standard | 332.42 |
| Immunology | 615.37 |
| Immunity principles and application in | 615.37 |
| medicine and public health, by Hans | Z78 |
| Zinsser and others, 1944. | |
| International monetary mechanism, | 332.43 |
| by F.A. Lutz, 1943. | L97 |
| Interpretation of dreams, by | 159.96338 |
| Wilhelm Stekel, 1943. | S79 |
| Lutz, F.A. International monetary | 332.43 |
| mechanism, 1943. | L97 |
| Money | 332.4 |
| Paul, Cedar. Stekel Wilhelm, | 159.96338 |
| Interpretation of dreams | S79 |
| Paul, Eden, Stekel Wilhelm, | 159.96338 |
| Interpretation of dreams | L49 |
| Princeton University—International | 332.43 |
| Finance section Lutz, F.A. International | L79 |
| monetary mechanism | |
| Psychoanalysis | 159.9642 |
| Public health : Contagious and infectious diseases | 614.4 |
| Religion diseases | 299.23 |
| Religion, Syrian | 299.23 |
| Secret sects of Syria and the Lebanon, | 299.23 |
| by B.H. Springett. 1922. | S76 |
| Springett, B.H. Secret sects of Syria | 299.23 |
| Secret Societies | 366 |
| Serum therapy | 615.37 |
| Springett, B.H. Secret sects of Syria | 299.23 |
| and the Lebanon | S76 |
| Stekel Wilhem. Interpretation of dreams | 159.96338 |
| | S79 |
| Syria. Religion | 299.23 |
| Zinsser, Hans and others, Immunity | 615.37 |
| principles and application in medicine | Z78 |
| and public health | |

# APPENDIX I

## SELECT AIDS AND GUIDES FOR THE CATALOGUER

The tools of a cataloguer connected with his daily work should be fully familiar to him. He should have a complete mastery over their use. The catalogue codes, the classification schedules and the list of subject headings are primary tools of his profession. The date of publication given may not hold good now; in such cases the latest publication and date should be adopted.

**Primary:**

1. Cataloguing Codes
2. Cataloguing manuals and textbooks
3. Classification schedules
4. Classification manuals and codes
5. List of Subject Headings
6. Filing rules

But the cataloguer needs many more secondary aids and guides in his performance. We may call them *"Cataloguers' working library"*.

This handy collection will contain the following types of books for his ready reference without which adequate standards in cataloguing quality cannot be maintained.

**Secondary:**

1. Cumulative Book Indexes
2. Standard catalogues of libraries

3. National bibliographies
4. Bibliograpies Best books
5. Subject bibliographies and source books and Dictionaries of subjects.
6. Language dictionaries
7. Standard encyclopedias
8. Biographical dictionaries.

**Primary Group**

*Cataloguing Codes*


1. A.L.A. Catalogue rules, Author and title entires; American ed. A.L.A. Pub. Board, 1908.
2. A.L.A. Cataloguing rules for Author and title entries; 2nd ed. Chicago, A.L.A., 1949.
3. CCR Code of Cataloguing Rules: Author and title entry, A.L.A., 1960.
4. Anglo-American Cataloguing Rules. British text. Lond., Library Association, 1967.
5. Anglo American Cataloguing Rules 2, 1978.
6. Anglo American Cataloguing Rules; 2nd ed. 1988 Revision.
7. Cutter, C.A. Rules for dictionary catalogue; 4th ed. Washington, Govt. Pr. Office, 1904 (Reprinted by the Library Association, London).
8. *National usages for the entry of names of persons.* A survey by A.H. Chaplin. Provisional ed. London, ICCP, c/o N.C.L., 1963.
9. Library of Congress Rules of descriptive cataloguing (adopted by the A.L.A) Wash., Govt. Pr. Office, 1949.
10. Columbia University School of Library Service Sample catalogue cards: 2nd ed N.Y., 1950.


*II Cataloguing manuals and textbooks*


1. Akers, S.G. Simple library cataloguing; 4th ed. Chicago, A.L.A., 1954.
2. Douglas, R.H. Handbook of card forms for use in Cataloguing Chicago, Willcox and Follett, 1948.
3. Mann, Margaret. Intro to Cataloguing and the classification of books, 2nd ed: Chicago, A.L.A., 1943.
4. Jolley, L. Principles of Cataloguing Lond., Lockwood, 1961.

5. Gorman, Michael. A Study of the Rules for Entry and Heading in the Anglo-American Cataloguing Rules, Lond., Library Assoc., 1967.

*III. Classification schedules*

1. Dewey, Melvil. Decimal classification and relative index; ed. Lake Placid Club, Forest Press Inc.
2. British Standards Institutions. U.D.C. abridges English ed. 3rd ed. rev. Lond., B.S.I., 1961.
3. Ranganathan, S.R. Colon Classification.

*IV. Classification Manuals and Codes*

1. Johnson M.F. Manual of cataloguing and classification for small schools.
2. Mann, Margaret, Intro to cataloguing and classification of books; 2nd ed. Chicago, A.L.A., 1943.
3. Phillips, Howard. A Priemer of Book, classification; 4th ed. Lond., Association of Assistant Librarians 1955.
4. Sayers, W.C.B. An intro. to Library classification, theoretical, historical and practical with readings, exercises, and examination papers; 9th ed. Lond., Grafton 1954.
5. Ibid. Manual of classification for librarians and bibliographers; 2nd ed. Lond., Grafton, 1944.
6. Merrill, W.S. Code for classifiers; 2nd ed. Chicago, A.L.A., 1939.
7. S.R. Ranganathan Prolegomena to Library Classification; 2nd ed. L.A., 1958.
8. J. Mills. A modern outline of library classsification Lond., Chapman and Hall, 1960.

*V. List of Subject Headings*

1. Cutter C.A. Choice of subject headings in his Rules for a Dictionary catalogue, (p. 66-82, 111-128).
2. Sears, M.E. List of subject headings for small libraries; 8th ed. N.Y., Wilson, 1949.
3. Pettee, Julia, Subject headings: the history and theory of the

alphabetic subject approach to books, N.Y. Wilson, 1946.
4. A.L.A. List of subject headings.
5. Library of Congress List of subject headings; Wash.
6. Haykin, D.J. Subject Headings: a practical guide, Wash. D.C. Govt. Printing Office, 1951.

*VI. Filing rules*

1. A.L.A. Rules for filing catalogue cards., Chicago A.L.A. 1980.
2. BLAISE: Filing rules Lond., British Library, 1980.
3. Library of Congress: Filing rules. Washington, L.C. 1980.

**Secondary Group**

*I. Cumulative Book Indexes*

1. Cummulative Book Index; world list of books in the English language, N.Y. Wilson, 1928-date.
2. British Books in Print : Reference, catalogue of current literature. Lond., Whitaker, 1969.-

*II. Standard Catalogues of Libraries*

1. Standard catalogue for public libraries : anannotated list of 12,300 titles with a full analytical index; comp. by D.E. Cook and D.H. West, N.Y. Wilson, 1950.
2. British Museum. Author catalogue with subject index.
3. Library of Congress. Catalogues.
4. India Office library. Catalogues.

*III National Bibliographies*

1. British National Bibliography a subject list of the new British books. Lond. Council of British National Bibliography, 1950-date. (British Library)
2. Indian National Bibliography, 1958—Calcutta, National Library.

*IV. Bibliographies Best Books, etc.*

1. A.L.A. Catalogue. 1926, Chicago, A.L.A.
2. Ibid.-Supplements.
3. Sonnenschein, William. The Best books; 3rd ed. Lond., Routledge, 1910-1935 6v.
4. World List of Scientific Periodicals; 4th edition. 3v Butterworth.
5. Viswanathan C.G., A Book on Books P.P.P. 1988.

*V. Subject Bibliographies and Source Books*

1. Baldwin, J.M.Dictionary of Philosophy and Psychology N.Y. Macmillan, 1902-1911 3v.
2. Hastings James Encyclopedia of Religion and Ethics, Edinburgh, Clark 1918-1926. 13v.
3. Seligman, E.R.A. Encyclopedia of Social Sciences, N.Y. Macmillan, 17v. and supplement, 1979.
4. Bodmer, Frederick. The Loom of language, a guide to foreign language, for the home student; ;ed. by Lancellot Hogben. Lond., Allen and Unwin, 1946.
5. Thomson, J.A. Outline of Science. Lond., Newnes, n.d. 2v.
6. Hawkins, R.R. ed. Scientific, medical, and technical books; 2nd ed. Washington, National Academy of Sciences.
7. Scientific encyclopedia, N.Y.Van Nostrand, 1968.
8. Harper's encyclopedia of art. N.Y., Harper, 1937 2v.
9. Esdaile, Arundell. Sources of literature. Camnbridge University Press, 1929.
   Cambridge Bibliography of English Literature. Cambridge University Press. 1940.
10. Cambridge ancient history. Cambridge University Press, 1923-39. 12v.
    Cambridge medical history. Cambridge University Press, 1911-36. 8v.
    Cambridge modern history. Cambridge University Press, 1902-26 13v. and Atlas.
    Cambridge history of India
11. Wright, J.K. and Platt E.D. Aids to georgraphical research; 2nd ed. N.Y., Columbia University Press, 1947.

*VI. Language Dictionaries, including anonyms and pseudonyms*

1. The shorter Oxford English dictionary. Oxford, University Press, 1933. 2v.
2. Cassell's French-English, English-French dictionary London Cassell, 1928.
3. Cassell's German-English, English-German dictionary Lond., Cassell, 1939.
4. Apte, V.S. The student's Sanskrit-English dictionary. Bombay Gopal Narayan, 1922.
5. Monier-Williams, Monier. A Sanskrit-English dictionary; 2nd ed. Oxford, Clarendon Press, 1899.
6. Bhargava's standard illustrated dictionary of the English language (Anglo-Hindi edition); compiled by R.C. Pathak Banaras Bhargava Bhushan Press, 1951.
7. Students' practical dictionary containing Hindi words with Hindi and English meanings. Allahabad, Ram Narain Lal.
8. Halkett, S. and Laing J. Dictionary of anonyma and pseudonyma, London, Oliver, 1934. 7v.
9. Patridge Eric. 'Slang today and yesterday'. Lond. Routledge, 1933.
10. Patridge Eric. A Dictionary of abbreviations. Lond. Allen and Unwin, 1943.;
11. Reaney P.H. Dictionary of British Surnames. Routledge. 1958.
12. Hadyn's Dictionary of Dates and Universal Information. N.Y., Dover, 1969.

*VII. Standard Encyclopedias*

1. The encyclcopedia Britannica, first published in 1765 is now issued under the title : The New Encylopedia Britannica; 15th ed., 1974, 32v., Also it is known as Britannica Three, as it is divided into 3 parts: (1) Propaedia (outline of knowledge) one volume; (2) Macropaedia, 19v., and (3) Micropaedia, 10v., and Index 2v.
2. Encyclopedia Americanna. American Corporation 1980, 30v.
3. The New Columbia Encyclopedia; 3rd ed. New York and London, Columbia University Press, 1975.
4. Everyman's Encyclopedia; 6th ed. London, Dent, 1978. 12v.

*VIII. Biographical Dictionaries*

1 Who's who (annual) Lond., Black, 1849 – date.
2. Who was Who. 1897 date., Lond. Black.
3. Dictionary of National biography. Lond., Oxford University Pr., 1908-1950. 22. + 5 Supply.v.
4. Dictionary of American Biography Lond., Oxford University Pr., 1928-44. 20v. and index and Supplement.
5. Kunitz, S.J. and Haycraft, Howard Twentieth Century Authors. N.Y. Wilson.
6. Who's who of Indian writers, New Delhi, Sahitya Academy.

The brief list of books furnished to serve the cataloguer as his primary and secondary tools, does not pretend to be exhaustive but only selective and comprehensive. These references will not help a cataloguer who does not know how to use them and with what results. It is expected that his education and training would have brought him close to these books. Every author, title and subject when treated brings in newer knowledge to the cataloguer. The opportunity to move in the world of books and make them readily available to the world of readers is thesupreme right and glory of cataloguers.

# APPENDIX II

## DEFINITIONS OF TERMS COMMONLY USED IN CATALOGUING

Access Point. A name, term, code, etc., under which a bibliographic record may be searched and identified. *see also* Heading.

Added Entry. A Secondary Entry, *i.e.*, Any entry other than the main entry. *Cf.* Main entry. There may be added entries for editor, translator, title, subjects, series, etc. Some cataloguers would restrict the use of the term "added entry" to any entry other than the main entry and subject entries, using "secondary entry" as a group term to include all entries other than the main entry. Others would make the opposide choice, using "added entry" as the group term to include secondary entry and subject entry.

Alphabetic Subject Index. An Index under specific subjects arranged alphabetically, as an independent periodical index, an index to an author or a classed list of books or articles, an index to a classification scheme, or an index to a classed catalogue.

Alphabetical Subject Catalogue. A catalogue limited to subject entries and the necessary references, alphabetically arranged.

Alphabetico-Classed Catalogue. A catalogue with entries under broad subjects alphabetically arranged and subdivided by topics in alphabetical order.

Alternative Title. The second part of title proper that consists of two parts, each of which is title; the parts are joined by the word *or* its equivalant in another language.

Analytical Entry. The entry of some part of a work or of some article contained in a collection (volume of essays, serial, etc.) including a reference to the publication which contains the article or work entered.

In special libraries it may be an entry for a significant paragraph, section, etc., or for a single statement or figure.

Anglo-American Code (of Cataloguing). A term used for the rules of author and added entry compiled originally by committees of the American Library Association and the (British) Library Association and in the main, representing the common practice of American and British libraries.

Annotation. 1. A note that describes, explains, or evaluates; especially, such a note added to an entry in a bibliography, reading list, or catalogue. Sometimes called Book Note. 2. The process of making such notes.

Anonymous Classic. A work of unknown, doubtful, or supposedly supernatural authorship, which has appeared in the course of time in many editions, versions, and translations, and which is designated in the catalogue by a fixed form of name, *i.e.* the most commonly used, most distinctive or first recorded title.

Author 1. The writer of a book, as distinguished from the translator, editor, etc. 2. In the broader sense, the maker of the book or the person or body immediately responsible for its existence. Thus, a person who collects and puts together the writings of several authors (compiler or editor) may be said to be the author of a collection. A corporate body may be considered the author of publications issued in its name or by its authority.

Author entry. Catalogue entry under the name of the author or the heading which, under the rules for author entries, corresponds to it.

Author Notation. *See* Book number.

Author Number. *See* Book number.

Author-Title Added Entry. *See* Name-title added entry.

Book Number. A symbol, usually consisting of a combination of letters and figures, which serves to identify a given book, among others bearing the same class number and, at the same time, to place books bearing the same class number in the desired order on the shelves, by author, title, edition, and the like. When used to arrange books alphabetically by author it is called "author number" or "author notation."

Card Catalogue. A catalogue made up of cards, each usually bearing a single entry. The card catalogue is to be distinguished from the printed catalogue, in book form, and the sheaf catalogue, which consists of sheets brought together in portfolios.

Catalogue. A list of books, maps, etc., arranged according to some definite plan. As distinguished from a bibliography it is a list which records, describes, and indexes the resources of a collection, a library or a group of libraries.

In a special library it may include entries for material outside the library and for various types of material, *e.g.* entries for abstracts of periodical articles and pamphlets, and entries under subject for research in progress and for organizations and individuals who are authoritative sources of information on specific subjects.

Cataloguer. A librarian who determines the forms of entry and prepares the bibliographical descriptions for a catalogue, and in many libraries, classifies the books and assigns subject headings.

Class Number. A symbol applied to a book indicating the class to which it belongs in the classification system used by the library. Together with the book number it forms the call number by which the location of the book on shelf is indicated.

Classed Catalogue. A catalogue arranged by subject according to a systematic scheme of classification. Also called "class catalogue", "classified subject catalogue", "systematic catalogue" and "catalogue raisonne".

Classification. 1. A systematic scheme for the arrangement of books and other material according to subject or form. 2. The assigning of books to their proper places in a system of classification. 3. In archives administration, the arrangement in logical order of the series or files within a record group or of the record groups within an archival collection.

Classified Subject Catalogue. *See* Classed catalogue.

Closed Entry. An entry with complete bibliographical information covering all parts of a given work, *viz.* a complete set.

Collaborator. One who works with one or more associates to produce a work; all may make the same kind of contribution, as in the case of shared reponsibility (cf. 21.6) or they may make different kinds of contributions, as in the case of collaboration between an artist and a writer (cf. 21.24). *See also* Joint author, Mixed responsibility, Shared responsibility.

Collation. That part of the catalogue entry which describes the work as a material object, enumerating its volume, pages, size, etc., and the type and character of its illustrations.

Collection. If by one author : three or more independent works or parts of works published together. If by more than one author : two or more independent works or parts of works published together and not written for the occasion or for the publication in hand.

Collective title. A title proper that is an inclusive title for an item containing several works. *See also* Uniform title 2.

Compiler. One who produces a work by collecting and putting together written or printed matter from the works of various authors. Also, one who chooses and combines into one work selection or quotations from one author.

Composite Work. A treatise on a single subject produced through the collaboration of two or more authors, the contribution of each forming a distinct section or part of the complete work.

Conventional Title. A title by which a work is commonly known but which differs from the title under which it was published. It is used as a filing medium to bring all editions of the work together in the catalogue.

Corporate Body. A group of individuals associated together as an organized unit, *e.g.* a government, a government department, a society, an institution, a convention, a committee, a corporation, and identified by a particular name which acts as an entity.

Corporate Name. The name of a corporate body as distinguished from the name of a person.

Curves. Curved marks ( ) enclosing inserted explanatory or qualifying words or phrases, or setting of some items in a catalogue entry, such as series note. To be distinguished from brackets [ ]. Also called Parentheses and Round Brackets.

Dictonary Catalogue. A catalogue, usually on cards, in which all the entries (author title, subject, series, etc., and their related references are arranged together in one general alphabet. The sub-arrangement frequently varies from the strictly alphabetical.

Direct and specific Heading. *See* Specific and direct heading.

Direct Subdivision. Subdivision of subject headings by name of province, country, city or other locality without intermediate subdivision by name of country or state.

[2]Dissertation, Academic. An essay called thesis presented by a candidate in partial fulfilment of the requirements for a degree.

Duplicate Entry. Entry of the subject matter under two distinct aspects of it, *e.g.* U.S. *Foreign relations. Gt. Brit.* and Gt. Brit. *Foreign relations. U.S. Cf.* Multiple entry.

Edition. 1. All the impressions of a work printed at any time or times from one setting of type, including those printed from stereotype or electrotype plates from that setting (provided however, that there is no substantial change in or addition to the text, or no change in make up, format, or character of the resulting book). A facsimile reproduction constitutes a different edition. 2. One of the successive forms in which a library text is issued either by the author or by a subsequent editor. 3. One of the various printings of a newspaper for the same day, an issue published less often, as a weekly edition, or a special issue devoted to a particular subject, as a weekly edition, or a special issue devoted to a particular subject, as an anniversary number. 4. In edition binding all of the copies of a book or other publication produced and issued in uniform style. *Cf.* Textbook Edition, Trade Edition.

Editor. One who prepares for publication a work or collection of works or articles not his own. The editorial labour may be limited to the preparation of the matter for the printer, or it may include supervision of the printing, revision (restitution) or elucidation of the text, and the edition of introduction, notes, and other critical matter.

7 Entry. A record of a book in a catalogue or list.

Entry Word. The word by which an entry is arranged in a catalogue or a bibliography, usually the first word of the heading. Also called "filing word".

File. (n) 1. A collection of cards, papers, or other material arranged systematically for reference or preservation. 2. A cabinet, case, or other device for keeping in order cards, papers, or other material. (v) To arrange cards, papers, or other material systematically.

Filing Word. *See* Entry word.

Form Entry. An entry in a catalogue which lists books according to (1) the form in which their subject material is organized as periodicals, dictionaries, or (2) their literary form as poetry, drama.

Form Heading. A heading used for a form entry in a catalogue, *e.g.* Encyclopedias and dictionaries, Periodicals, Short stories. Sometimes known as "form subject heading". *Cf.* Charles A. Cutter. Rules for a Dictionary Catalogue. 3rd ed; (1891), p. 13.

Form Subdivision. A division of a subject heading based on form or arrangement of subject matter in books, as for dictionaries or periodicals.

Form Subject Heading. *See* Form heading.

8 General Cross Reference. *See* General reference.

General (Secondary) Reference. A blanket reference in a catalogue to the kind of heading under which one may expect to find entries for material on certain subjects or entries for particular kinds of names. Also called "general cross reference" and "information entry".

Guide-Card. A card having a projecting, labelled edge or tab inserted in a file to indicate arrangements and to aid in locating material in the file.

9 Heading. In cataloguing the word name or phrase at the head of an entry to indicate some special aspect of the book (authorship, subject, content, series, title, etc.) and thereby to bring together in the catalogue associated and allied material.

Imprint 1. The place and date of publication and the name of the publisher or the printer (or sometimes both); ordinarily printed at the foot of the title page. Originally the term applied only to the printer's imprint which consisted of his name and place of business. Later the term was extended to include the name of the publisher and the place and date of publication. The printer's name with or without address is now more often printed inconspicuously on the verso of the title leaf or at the foot of the last printed page of the final signature. 2. The statement giving such information in a bibliographical description of a printed work. 3. A book or other publication that has been printed. The term is often used for a book printed in a particular country or place as "early American imprint".

Index. 1. A list of topics, names, etc., treated in a book or a group of books, with references to pages where they occur. 2. A card list in a library of references to material on a special topic, subject, etc. 3. A guide to material arranged by a different scheme from that used for the material itself, *e.g.*, a list in a special library by trade name of material filed by name of company. 4. In a special library, a list of special sources of information not in the library. 5. The character ☞ an old style reference mark, used to point to material. Also known as a Hand, a Fist or an Index Finger. 6. A shortened form for the index Librorum Prohibitorum.

Indirect Subdivision. Subdivision of subject headings by name of country or state with further subdivision by name of province, country, city, or other locality.

Information Entry. *See* General reference.

International Standard Book Number (ISBN). *See* Standard number.

International Standard Serial Number (ISSN). *See* Standard number.

10 Joint Author. A person who collaborates with one or more associates to produce a work in which the contribution of each is not separable from that of the others.

Language Subdivision. A subdivision of a subject heading according to language, *e.g.* English language. *Dictionaries, French* for a dictionary of English words giving their French equivalents.

Library Technology. Evolving and introducing machinery to perform library processes, formerly done by manual systems.

Local Subdivision. Subdivision by the name of the geographic area to which the subject matter is limited.

Machine Readable Data File (MRDF). A body of information coded by methods that require the use of a machine (typically but not always a computer) for processing. Examples include files stored on magnetic tape, punched cards, aperture cards, disc packs, etc.

Main Card. *See* Main entry.

Main Entry. A full catalogue entry, usually the author entry, giving all the information necessary to the complete identification of a work. In a card catalogue this entry bears also the tracing of all the other headings under which the work in question is entered in the catalogue. The main entry, used as a master card, may bear, in addition, the tracing of related references and a record of other pertinent official data concerning the work.

Meta-Books. All non-book reading material, and sources of information in audio visual form, e.g. pictures, microforms, video tapes, cassettes, discs, sound recordings, etc.

Mixed Authorship. *See* Mixed responsibility.

Mixed Responsibility. A work of mixed responsibility is one in which different persons or bodies contribute to its intellectual or artistic content by performing different kinds of activities (adapting or illustrating a work written by another person). *See also* Shared responsibility.

Monograph. A non-serial item, i.e., that is complete in one part or complete, or intended to be completed, in a finite number of separate parts.

Multiple Entry. Entry of the same subject under several headings, each representing a different approach. *Cf.* Duplicate entry.

Name Catalogue. a catalogue arranged alphabetically by names of person and places, whether used as authors or subjects.

Name-Title Added Entry. An added entry consisting of the name of a person or corporate body and the title of an item.

Open Entry. A catalogue entry which provides for the addition of information concerning a work of which the library does not have a complete set, or about which complete information is lacking.

Period Subdivision. A subdivision of a subject heading which shows the period treated or during which the work appeared. Also called "time subdivision" and "chronological subdivision".

Periodical. A publication with a distinctive title intended to appear in successive (usually unbound) numbers of parts at stated or regular intervals and, as a rule, for indefinite time. Each part generally contains articles by several contributors.

Personal Author. The person chiefly responsible for the creation of the intellectual or artistic content of a work (*See* 21.IAI for a gloss on this definition).

Phonorecord. *See* Sound recording.

Predominant Name. The name or form of a person or corporate body that appears most frequently (i) in the person's works or works issued by the corporate body; or (ii) in reference sources, in that order of preference.

Preliminaries. The title page or title pages of an item, together with the verso of each title page, any pages preceding the title page (s), and the cover.

Proceses Slip. A card or slip, sometimes a printed form, which accompanies a book through the catalogue department, acquiring on its way all the information and directions necessary for cataloguing fully. Also called Catalogue Card Copy. Catalogue Slip, Cataloguer's Slip, Cataloguing Process Slip, Copy Slip, Guide Slip, Routine Slip, Work Slip.

11 Qualified Heading. A heading followed by a qualifying term which is usually enclosed in parentheses, *e.g.* Bankruptcy (Cannon law). Bankruptcy (International law), Dumping (Commercial policy). Escape (Ethics), Escape (Law), Composition (Law), Composition (Art), Composition (Music).

Reference. A direction from one heading to another. *Cf.* Subject reference.

Related Body. A corporate body that has a relation to another body other than that of hierarchical subordination, e.g., one that is founded but not controlled by another body; one that only receives financial support from another body; one that provides financial and or other types of assistance to another body, such as "friends" groups; one whose membership have also membership in or an association with another body, such as employees' associations and alumni associations.

Relative Index. An index to a classification system in which all relationships and aspects of the subject are brought together under each index entry.

Romanization. Conversion of names or text not written in the roman alphabet to roman alphabet form.

Secondary Entry. *See* Added entry.

"See also" Reference. A reference to a less comprehensive or otherwise related term; the indication, in a list of subject heading, of such a reference.

"See " Reference. A reference from a term or name under which no books are entered to that used in place of it; an indication, in a list of subject headings, of such a reference, that is, of the term or terms, synonymous with, or equivalent to, the given heading, to which a *"see" references is to be made.*

Serial. A publication in any medium issued in successive parts bearing numerical or chronological designations, and intended to be continued indefinitely. Serials include periodicals; newspapers; annuals (reports yearbooks, etc); the journals, memoirs, proceedings, transactions, etc., of societies; and numbered monographic series, *See also* Series I.

Series. 1. A group of separate items related to one another by the fact that each item bears, in addition to its own title proper, a collective title applying to the group as a whole. The individual items may or may not be numbered. 2. Each of two or more volumes of essays, lectures, articles, or other writings, similar in character and issued in sequence, e.g. English men of letters series or, Peeps in many lands series. 3. A separately numbered sequence of volumes within a series or serial, e.g., Royal Society Transactions, series A; series B; etc.

Shared Authorship. *See* Shared responsibility.

Shared Responsibility. Collaboration between two or more persons or bodies performing the same kind of activity in the creation of the content of an item. The contribution of each may form a separate and distinct part of item or the contribution of each may not be separable from that of the others. *See also* Joint author, Mixed responsibility.

Shelf List. A record of the books in the library arranged in the order in which they stand on the shelf, that is, in the order of their class and book numbers.

Sound Recording. A record on which sound vibrations have been registered by mechanical or electrical means so that the sound may be reproduced.

Specific and Direct Heading. A heading for a specific entry which expresses the topic directly, that is, one which is not preceded by the broad subject or class heading which includes it.

Specific Entry. Entry of a book under a heading which expresses its special subject or topic as distinguished from the class or broad subject which includes that special subject or topic.

Specific Heading. A heading which is not broader than the subject matter covered by it.

Standard Number. The International Standard Number (ISN) *e.g.* International Standard Book Number (ISBN), International Standard Serial Number (ISSN) or any other internationally agreed upon standard number, that uniquely identifies an item.

Subject Catalogue. A catalogue consisting of subject entries only.

Subject Entry. An entry in a catalogue or a bibliography under a heading which indicates the subject.

Subject Heading. a word or a group of words indicating a subject under which all material dealing with the same theme is entered in catalogue or a bibliography, or is arranged in a file.

Subject Reference. A reference from one subject heading to another. Also called "subject cross reference". *Cf.* *"See"* reference, *"See also"* reference.

Subject Subdivision. The method of entering the subject heading by indicating the form of the subject matter, the place to which it is limited or the part, element, or phase of the subject treated.

Syndetic. Having entries connected by cross references; said of a catalogue.

Systematic Catalogue. *See* Classed catalogue.

Time Subdivision. *See* Period subdivision.

Title Entry. The record of a work in a catalogue or a bibliography under the title, generally beginning with the first word not an article. In a card catalogue a title may be a main entry or an added entry.

Title Page. A page at the beginning of a book or work, bearing its full title and usually, though not necessarily, the author's (editor's etc.) name and the imprint. The leaf bearing the title page is commonly called the "title page", although properly it is the "title leaf".

Tracing. In a card catalogue the record on the main entry card of all the additional headings under which the work is represented in the catalogue. Also the record on a main entry card or an authority card of all the related references made. The tracing may be on the face or the back of the card, or on an accompanying card.

Uniform Title. 1. The particular title by which a work that has appeared under varying titles is to be identified for cataloguing purposes. 2. A conventional collective title used to collocate publications of an author, composer or corporate body containing several works or extracts, etc. from several works in a particular literary or musical form.

Unit Card. A basic catalogue card, in the form of a main entry, which when duplicated may be used as a unit for all other entries for that work in the catalogue by the addition of the appropriate heading. Library of Congress printed cards are the most commonly used unit cards.

REFERENCES

1. Based on: 1. A.L.A. Glossary of library terms, 1943.
   2. L.C. Subject headings: a practical guide, 1951.
   3. A-ACR 2 Glossary (Appendix D) 1978.
   4. A-ACR2 1988 Revision, Glossary (Appendix D) 1988.
2. For a "large paper edition" (called also "large paper copy") the pages are usually though not always, reimposed.

# APPENDIX III

## CATALOGUING EXAMINATION SELECT QUESTIONS

A range of questions covering more or less the whole field of cataloguing is suggested, in order that the students of cataloguing can write the answers and attain sufficient practice before attempting the questions in the examination. The answers may extend from three to five pages of examination script books.

1. What are the chief objectives of a library catalogue?
   What important steps are necessary to be followed in achieving these aims?
2. Describe the component parts of a catalogue entry, and explain their functions and the purpose served by each one of them.
3. What are the various kinds of entries in an alphabetical dictionary catalogue? What significant features distinguish the *Main* from the *Secondary* entries?
4. State the important factors that will govern the policy and construction of the catalogue to be provided for (1) a city public library of medium size, or (2) a University library serving the faculties of Science and Technology, or (3) a special library like the library of the Imperial Chemical Industries or Inner Temple.
5. Draft a set of instructions, which you wish to be followed in cataloguing (1) Lending, (2) Reference, and (3) Children's books in a public library.
6. What are the chief varieties of catalogues commonly found in modern libraries? Describe the characteristics and values of any one of them.
7. Do you consider or not that a dictionary catalogue is more

complex, and less effective in serving the readers than a classified catalogue? Prove your case with appropriate examples of entries.

8. The classified catalogue is said to be not only logical but more economical than any form of alphabetical catalogues. Substantiate this view by making the essential entries for a classified catalogue for the book 'Science, Liberty and Peace' by Aldous Huxley.
9. Define the term *'Author'* of a literary work and state with examples all possible forms of authors.
10. What is the importance of a title page of a book in cataloguing the book? What treatment will you recommend in cataloguing (1) a book whose title page is wanting in it, (2) a book with two title pages in two different languages, and (3) a book in more than one volume, each having its own title Page and imprint.
11. State the reasons for determining the choice of the part and style of name of an author before adopting it as the author heading. Furnish an example of an author heading entered under (1) Surname followed by two or three forenames, (2) forenames, (3) compound surname, (4) prefixed surname, and (5) personal name.
12. What are reference entries? Why are they necessary to be made and state their kinds with examples.
13. Discuss the problem of cataloguing translated works when information on the author and title of the original works is not contained in the translation.
14. What are the distinguishing features of Indian and other oriental names of writers from that of Western (Christian) writers? Give simple directions for the entry of oriental writers, with examples.
15. Discuss the problem of treatment of (1) Pseudonymous authors, and (2) Anonymous writers and state the directions provided for entering them in Cutter, A-ACR and Vatican Codes.
16. State the chief differential characteristics between corporate authors and personal authors and justify the directions in the A-ACR for entering them in the catalogue.
17. What points of similarity exist between a society and an institution as the author of its own publications and state the extent to which a common set of rules have been provided for cataloguing

them in A-ACR 2.

18. State the circumstances in which the main entries for works should be made under their titles. Give examples of such types of books.
19. Write a critical exposition of the theory of subject headings in the dictionary catalogue based on Cutter's rules and point out the chief factors tending to their continuation.
20. Do you agree with the view that alphabetical subject catalogues have proved a hopeless failure and so must be totally discarded from modern cataloguing practice and be replaced by classified catalogues? Give examples in support of your views.
21. What measures will you adopt in securing consistency and uniformity in terminology, style, and fullness of subject headings chosen for books?
22. What are analytical entries in cataloguing? State their kinds and the need for making them with appropriate examples.
23. What is series entry? It is really necessary to provide series entries in library catalogues? If so, demonstrate the patterns of series entry you will make.
24. Define annotation in a catalogue entry? How do you distinguish it from notes? State the extent to which they are necessary in modern library catalogues.
25. Discuss the chief problems in cataloguing serial publication. State the alternatives you purpose to simplify procedures in cataloguing them.
26. Describe the modern methods of displaying the library catalogues and state their relative merits.
27. What are the chief factors involved in cost accounting of cataloguing procedures? Give a formula, providing data for cataloguing a book of fiction and non-fiction.
28. Describe the essential features of a catalogue, with instructions for its proper maintenance.
29. Prepare a brief set of instructions to the public in the use of (i) a dictionary catalogue and (ii) a classified catalogue and state how you will supplement them by personal guidance to the readers.
30. Describe the lay out of a printed catalogue and the supplementary lists of additions issued periodically and explain its advantages or otherwise over other forms of catalogues.
31. Does cataloguing non-book material pose any problems? If so,

mention the special treatment you will adopt in dealing with (i) manuscripts, (ii) phonorecords, (iii) maps, and (iv) musical compositions.

32. Describe a plan of centralised cataloguing suited to a district library service, with mobile libraries and branch libraries.
33. Define a union catalogue and outline a method for its compilation suited to your state? State the advantages resulting from its compilation.
34. Write a historical and critical account of the Anglo-American Cataloguing Rules, 1967 and indicate the current trends towards the formulation of a Universal code of Cataloguing practice.
35. Give a short accout of Panizzi's Rules and state the extent of their influence on Cutter's, Jewett's and the A.A. Code of 1967.
36. Evaluate the importance of Lubetzky's 'Critique' towards a simplified and pragmatic code of cataloguing practice, specially in the treatment of corporate authors.
37. State the relation existing between classification and cataloguing, and point out the extent to which close classification and open access in libraries tend to reduce the dependence of the reader in his use of the library catalogue.
38. What device will you adopt in economising labour and cost in the cataloguing department of a large city library system with several branch libraries.
39. If you are appointed librarian of a newly established city library charged with the provision of Reference, Lending, Junior, Commercial, and Technical library services to a population of 1,00.000 how would you begin to organize the work of its cataloguing department? Work out its annual expenditure.
40. 'Librarianship minus proficiency in cataloguing and classification ceases to be a profession'. Comment on this statement.
41. 'Effort, time, and funds spent on cataloguing and classification is considered disproportionate to the resulting achievement.' If you concede, suggest an alternative agency as a substitute, which will prove satisfactory and more economical.
42. Give a brief survey of the codes of cataloguing from 1908 to 1978, with special reference to A-ACR 1 and A-ACR 2.
43. Justify the need and necessity for producing A-ACR 2, close on the heels of A-ACR 1. State the significant reasons in support of your view.

44. How far computerization of cataloguing processes will help solve several problems confronted like cost, time, and effectiveness of catalogues in library services.
45. Assessment of manpower for cataloguing work, after the introduction of automation in library administration involves a number of problems, like recruitment of suitable staff, investment of initial funds, and proper planning, etc. Comment on them.
46. Briefly state the significant changes, amendments, deletions in the rules of A-ACR 2, 1988 revision.
47. Draft a set of rules for the guidance of users of computerised catalogue.

# APPENDIX IV

## IMPLICATIONS OF THE ADOPTION OF A-ACR 2

Richard Coward, Director General, Bibliographic Services Division, British Library, announced "with considerable regret" that the Library of Congress would not adopt the second version of the Anglo-American cataloguing Rules in its entirety. Instead, it proposed to continue, on a more limited scale, the policy of super-imposition, which had been a familiar and awkward feature of the Library of Congress Cataloguing since 1967. This procedure was justified, that substantial reduction in the percentage of headings requiring change in their own Catalogues and, by definition, in the catalogues across North America, could be effected.The Library of Congress would use certain *tolerable headings*, where these already exist. A new concept in cataloguing, that of *tolerable headings*, has been invented. "It is super-imposition MARC II."

But the British Library would adopt A-ACR 2 fully as already decided in 1976, A-ACR 2 has the virtue of providing long term benefits of a catalogue, based on a single, consistent set of principles.The adoption of this code would be effective from 1981.

It was felt that the new code, though late as a professional tool, was somewhat premature in the context of technological development in the field of library procedures and functions. "If data bases already had dynamic on-line authority files and were linked in an on-line net work, a new code could be introduced as though the system was but one library. All the other files would have to be upgraded towards A-ACR2 in much the same way as the UK MARC file. The impact of this on local systems would depend very much on the percentage of records that had to be changed in the central data base and in local catalogues."

The American librarians remarkable for their approach to library issues in a more pragmatic way than in a rigid system tied manner, with a view to cut down the already costly process of cataloguing and indexing, have waived the significant advantages cosequential to following fully and faithfully A-ACR 2, in favour of *'tolerable headings'* principle which would cut down appreciably the complexity and huge cost that might be involved in a total and complete changeover to A-ACR 2 style of headings in the Library of Congress and in the vast collections of University, other national, and public libraries of U.S.A. Ever since the 1908 code, the Americans, through A-ACR 1967 , had stuck to this insular but pragmatic approach.Perhaps the reluctant attitude of major national,special and research libraries to resort to major changes of headings in catalogues according to A-ACR 2 might have influenced this decision. So long as access points in the catalogues and information files could easily be located, there seems little justification for the changeover from the existing to the new style of headings. This caution is not only sensible, but very much needed and realised by libraries in developing countries, where library resources are quite limited and more often inadequate. Both classification and cataloguing are two such library operations where the new technique of *'tolerable headings'* and 'relocation of class numbers' would be applied and found satisfactory. In this context the relevance of the genius of C.A. Cutter in inventing the 'Syndetic' feature in catalogues and in indexes to schedules of classification should be understood and applied.

But, a new library, commencing the work of classification and cataloguing should always adopt the latest available schemes of classification and codes of cataloguing, as the accessibility of information or document would be quick, easy and consistent.

**Justification of Changes:PREM 436-38**

Any change in cataloguing, both major and minor, should be justified on two counts:

(i) it could produce better catalogue entries, and

(ii) it could be less costly than the existing practice.

On the basis of only the second benefit to the library, a decision on a change over to the new code would not be possible, and should not be recommended, for the simple reason that library techniques, of which classification and cataloguing are constantly undergoing research leading to new forms, heading style, and class relationships. When a change in one occurs, it will inevitably need introduction of suitable changes in the other. This could not be overlooked.

Turning to the reader or user, who refers library catalogues with a view to gain quick accessibility to the bibliographic information required or location of a document/book on the shelf, it is generally accepted that he is least inquisitive or even concerned about the code of cataloguing adopted by a library in the preparation of catalogues, because his main concern is not how the catalogue is compiled,but how much effective are the entries in a catalogue in obtaining the relevant information in the minimum possible time. But it would be irritating to users, if on account of changes adopted if they have to look for a given author at more than one place and under different styles of heading. This may even result in bypassing a catalogue by users, for whom it is to a large extent, provided for in libraries, and thus might not justify large sums of money set apart for the maintenance of this tool.

Even very large libraries,like national libraries,e.g. the British Library "cannot afford a complete recataloguing operation" on account of cost and time involved. John Joliffe has estimated that "recataloguing of all the 4 1/2 m. works in the British Library's General Catalogue of Printed Books would take 630 man years and cost rather over £ 7m. at today's prices".

A-ACR2 rightly envisages that not all libraries would need the detailed bibliographic description specified in the catalogue entries. It, therefore, has also provided for short catalogue entries. The three levels of description, the short, the more detailed (short standard), and the full standard,containing,"all elements set out in the following rules that are applicable to the item being described".

As A-ACR2 has been published just ten years after A-ACR1 libraries which changed over to A-ACR1 in 1968 might hesitate to change in 1969 by adopting A-ACR2 for cataloguing operations. The Anglo-American Code 1908 and the A-ACR 1967, had allowed a period of 60 years in between them. Library growth and cataloguing research at international level during this long gap perhaps, justified, and necessitated the change to A-ACR2 on the part of several large libraries.

Library technology, computer applications and automation of certain operations has gained momentum since 1960, together with the commercial and private data bases organised and functioning successfully in developed countries and it has decidedly influenced the system of maintaining the catalogues and their operations. It may be due to restricted finances for library expenditure and the thrust of information industry in capturing the mind of workers in research and development fields, and highly sophisticated manufacturing industries. Probably the Library of Congress appears to be farsighted by going in for '*tolerable headings*' and also thinking in the direction of discounting the conventional Library of Congress catalogue. Not only the other libraries of the United States and Canada, but also several outside North America would feel the impact and MARC records would be used more extensively and online information would vastly develop.

It should not be overlooked that small libraries in less economically advanced countries would still need to continue individual cataloguing operations in their libraries. A-ACR2 would still find favour and prove flexible enough to suit both very large and very small collections.

The Library of Congress has all along been a model directing agency, and a pace-setter for a large number of public and government libraries in regard to library cataloguing and some other procedures. The impending closing of "The Library of Congress Card Catalog" and the rush of technology in libraries mean difficult choices for every library concerning the form of its catalogue-book form, microform, on-line, and various combinations of the above, in relation to the technology, economics and the near-term prospects for the major choices.

## Varied Views and Insights on Displacement of the Traditional Card Catalogue in Favour of Automated Cataloguing

A comparatively younger generation of librarians, who have been exposed to the computer's performance for quick retrieval of data, and the consequential reactions of users are quite forceful and vociferous by expressing that the large wooden trays designed for filing catalogue cards and maintaining the card catalogue, occupying large floor space, in a vantage position of the library convenient to the users, since Cutter's time or probably earlier, are doomed. The traditional card catalogue, in their opinion is a dinosaur in the new age of burgeoning information. Automation is the only answer to the information explosion. The project of automating a library's Catalogue is bound to be exciting and challenging to library administrators and professional personnel; but it may suddenly land them in the midst of unexpected difficulties and be frustrating.

In a collection of essays by different writers setting forth, each his individual experience and comments, on one or more facets of providing an automated catalogue, under a title "Requiem for the Card Catalogue" edited by Daniel Gore, Joseph Kimbrough, and Peter Spyers-Duran, London, Aldwych Press, April, 1979, significant issues on the management of automated cataloguing are discussed, including the most interesting aspect-the user response and economic feasibility.

# INDEX

*(Numbers after entries refer to pages: italicised entries indicate titles of works; 'x' see reference and 'xx' see also reference)*


Academic disputations, 344
*Adigranth* (Sikh sacred book), 313
Alphabetisation, Letter by Letter, 184
  Word by word, 184
*A.L.A. Catalog*, 1926, 17
A L A Cataloguing rules, 1908, 24-26, 50
*A L A List of Subject Headings*, 16, 129
*Anglo-American Cataloguing Rules*, 1967, 21, 30-32
*A A C R 2 1988 revision*, 36, 308
A A C R 2 1978, 30-35, 163, 230, 315, 437-439
*A A Code, 1908*, 240, 261, 402, 439
Annotation, 405
Anonymous works, 299, 303
*Aranyakas*, 312
Authors, Attributed, 211, 322, 323
  Corporate, 250, 250-254, 258
  Personal, 210, 250-252
  Principal, 214
  Uncertain, 212
  Unknown, 209, 212, 289
Authorship, Shared, 213
*Avesta*, 313

B

*Bible*, 308
Bibliographies, National, 417
  Subject, 418
Bibliotheque Nationale de Paris, 9
Bishiop, W.W. 42
Bishops, 242
BLAISE Line, 15, 99, 110, 150
Bodleian Catalogues, 605, 620
*Brahmanas*, 312
British Library, 14, 15, 437, 439
  Bibliographical services Division, 151
  Research and Development Dept. 194
British Museum, 1, 2, 7, 9, 12, 13, 15, 16, 19, 20, 23, 147, 162, 163
British National Bibliography, 20, 58, 59, 99, 128, 147
BASIC, 110

C

Call number, 201
Callimachus, 2, 3
Carlyle, Thomas, 15
Carnegie Endowment, 42
Catalogue(s)
  Alphabetic Author, 113, 114
  Classed, 113, 118, 119, 123
  Subject, 46, 116
  Automation, 93, 137
  Cards, 84, 89, 91, 137, 187, 201
  Filing, 138
  Codes, 119
    Revision, 21, 59, 61, 62
  Dictionary, 127, 128, 162, 184, 251 252
  Functions of, 2, 8
  History of, 145
  Name, 114
  Physical forms of, 84, 105
  Planning, 45
  Printed page, 83-86, 92
  Title, 115
Cataloguer, Aids and guides, 414
  Education and training of, 140
  Tools and equipment, 134
  Cataloguing,
    Automated, 440

Analysis, 140
Centralised, 117, 148
Cooperation, 148
Cost of, 7, 135
Examination questions, 432 - 436
Evaluation, 144
Routine, 136
Selective, 143
Simplified, 143
Staff, 133, 135
Subject, 53, 57, 58, 125
Classification, 2, 125, 127, 384
*Classified catalogue code*, 42
Collation, 206
Collison, R.L. 163
Colon Classification, 198
Colvin, L.C. 253
Commentator, 222, 223
C O B O L, 110
Computer, 106
Applications in Library Science, 108
Computerisation of cataloguing processes, 149
C O M Catalogues, 95, 100, 101, 111, 112
Computer literacy levels, 100
Computer storage, 2
Constitutions, 262, 263, 353
Corporate bodies, 64
Contents, 405
Corporate bodies, 64
Corporate names, 41
Council on Library Resources, U.S. 32, 35
Crestadoro, 21
Cutter, C.A. 19, 21-23, 128, 129, 184, 231, 252, 385, 390
*Rules for a Dictionary Catalogue*, 21, 22, 50, 190-194

D

Dewey Decimal Classification, 46, 197
Dewey, John, 23
Dictionaries, Biographical, 420
Documents, 196, 199
Dunkin, Paul S., 25
*Dziatzko rules*. 251

E

*Eclectic, card catalogue rules*, 23
Ecole de medicine, Paris, 5
Editor, Main entry under, 215
Encyclopaedias, 419
Entry(ies)
added, 316, 347, 392
analytical, 395, 396
author, 114
choice of, 29, 50, 217
closed, 80
main, 3, 121, 160
noble men, 230
open, 80
series, 400
specific, 384
subject, 382
surname, 126, 130, 373
Event and Country, choice of, 385

F

Filing, 184
rules, 417
Films, 161, 179
Form of Heading, 29
Frarey, C.J. 130

G

German cataloguing practice, 24
Gladstone, William, 15
Gorman, Michael, 30, 34, 35
Gramaphone records, 161, 177
Guide cards, 139, 166
Gull, C.D. 54, 94
Guppy, Henry, 163

H

Hansen, J.C.M. 42

Headings
  Author, 228
  Direct or Indirect, 282
  Formation of, 388
  Persons, 228, 368
  Subject, 125, 127, 129, 383, 384
Hindu Sacred Works, 211

I

Imprint, 206
Incunabula, 161, 162
Indic names, 243, 246
Information sources of, 10
International cataloguing Code, 60
I.C.C.P., Paris, 1961. 19, 24, 27, 61
I.F.L.A. 35, 60
I.S.B.D.(G), 32, 151

J

Jast, L.S 24, 49
Jewett, Charles C. 21

K

K.W.O.C. 105
Koran, 313

L

Lewes, Peter R. 30
Leyden University Catalogue, 1595-1741, 9
Libraries, Medieval, 4
  , Monastic, 5
Library administration, 2, 7
  , Cooperation, 33, 160
Library of Congress, 2, 17, 18, 25, 26, 59, 231, 437
  Author catalog, 84
  National Union Catalog, 85, 86, 98
  Subject catalog, 84
  Subject headings, 129
Library technology, 95, 439
Liturgical works, 300, 367
London library, 15
  Catalogue, 7
Lubetzky, Seymour, 19, 25, 27, 30, 252

M

Maps, 161, 165
M A R C, 1, 2, 14, 95-98, 102, 135, 150, 437
MARC Database, U.K. 99
Manuscripts, 161, 168, 171-174
Married women writers, 238, 240
Microprocessor, 106
Multiple authorship, 65
Music, 161, 175, 178, 339, 340

N

Name(s)
  Biblical characters, 234
  Change of, 370
  Choice of, 370
  Compound surnames, 237
  Corporate, 389
  English form, 233
  Geographic, 284, 378
  Personal, 67, 228, 359
  Popes, 389
  Roman alphabet, 232, 372
National Library, Calcutta, 250
Nobility, under title, 377

O

On line catalogues, 102, 110
Open access, 7
Open entry, x Entry, Open
O. C. L. C. 100, 110
Osborn, A. D. 24

P

Panizzi, 10, 19, 22
Person and country, choice of, 384
Phrase entry, under, 38
Pinakes, 2, 4
Place names, 90
Popes, 241
Praeses, 223

Printed book catalogues, 119
Prints and pictures, 161, 165
P A S C A L, 110
*Prussian Code*, 251, 252
*Prussian Instructions*, 22, 23
Pseudonyms, 37, 230, 231, 370

Q

Quigg, P.G. 408
Quoran, x Koran

R

Ranganathan, S.R., 42, 127, 198
References, 379, 409
  x See, 118, 410
  xx See also, 128, 261, 410
Romanization, 279
Royalty, 241

S

Sacred Scriptures, 308
  Non, Christian, 309
Saints, 241
Savage, E.A., 408
*Sears' List of Subject Headings*, 129
Serials, 218-220
Series, Added entry, 347
  Note, 206, 400
Sharp, Henry A., 26, 27
Shera, J.H., 199
Stephen, Leslie, 16
Subject approach, 125
Subject Index to a classified catalogue, 128
Subjects overlapping, 386
Sumerian Clay Tablet, 2
Sumner Spalding, 27, 30
Surnames, Compound, 237, 375
  Hyphenated, 237
  Prefixes, seperately written, 238, 376
  Prefixex, 239
Syndetic catalogue, 128

T

Talmud, 310
Title as main entry, 66, 318, 329
Title entry, 144
Translations, 336
Translator, 225
Treaties, International, 268
*Tripithika*, 316

U

Uniform Heading, choice of, 63
Uniform titles, 299, 378
  Different, 381
Union Catalogue, 153-156
*Upanishads*, 312
Uniterm, 131
U.D.C., 197, 198

V

*Vatican rules*, 42
*Vedas*, 311

W

Winkler, Paul, 30, 35
Work measurement in P.L., 140